Yankee

BY JOHN W. ROWELL

THE UNIVERSITY OF TENNESSEE PRESS

KNOXVILLE

Artillerymen

THROUGH THE CIVIL WAR

WITH ELI LILLY'S

INDIANA BATTERY

Library of Congress Cataloging in Publication Data

Rowell, John W
    Yankee artillerymen.

        Bibliography: p.
        Includes index.
            1. United States—History—Civil War, 1861–1865—
    Regimental histories—18th Indiana Light Artillery
    Battery.   2.   United States.   Army.   18th Indiana
    Light Artillery Battery.   I.   Title.
    E506.818th.R68   973.7'41   75–5918
    ISBN 0–87049–171–7

Preface

The real authors of *Yankee Artillerymen* were the seventeen soldiers of
Eli Lilly's Eighteenth Indiana Light Artillery Battery whose journals,
letters, and other documents, most of them written when the events occurred, were available for this book. These sources were supplemented
with officers' reports and correspondence from *The War of the Rebellion: A Compilation of the Official Records of the Union and Confederate Armies*, contemporary newspaper accounts, and manuscripts
pertaining to the battery activities but written by others. As a result,
the history describes the events when they were observed and recorded,
while postwar accounts and publications were used principally to clar-
ify events, provide technical detail, and to relate the battery activities
to those of the army.

In addition to the unusual quantity of manuscripts, the writing was
of exceptional quality because the most prolific writers had attended
Wabash College or Indiana Asbury University, and were better observers and writers than the usual Civil War soldier.

The most frequently quoted source is the 360-page journal of Bugler Henry Campbell which included newspaper clippings and maps
in addition to Campbell's writing. Henry was an excellent observer
and writer of events, people, and places, and possibly was encouraged
to keep the record by Captain Lilly who "treated me more like a
brother than as a common soldier." Several letters that Henry wrote to

his mother, published in *The Soldier of Indiana in the War for the Union,* four postwar papers describing specific events, and a scrapbook containing newspaper articles relating to the war also were available for this study. The Campbell journal and scrapbook are in the Wabash College Archives, and other manuscripts are in the Indiana Division, Indiana State Library.

The next most quoted individual is Sergeant John Henry Rippetoe. In ninety-six letters written to his wife, Mary, John expressed his opinions of duty, religion, Negroes, politics, slavery, and other subjects in addition to describing his activities and those of the battery. He referred to his opinions seriously, but wrote lightly, sometimes humorously, about his experiences. In addition to John's letters, some letters that Mary and his father wrote to him also are quoted. John Rippetoe's letters were available because Ernest R. Davidson had typed all portions of military and family interest and had donated these excerpts to the Vigo County Historical Society.

William H. Anderson maintained a journal from his enlistment until his death in December 1862—a document that provides human interest details for the period when the recruits of the battery were being turned into soldiers, including some significant episodes not mentioned by Henry Campbell or John Rippetoe. The Anderson journal was available because Miss Eleanore Cammack, retired archivist of the Archives of DePauw University and Indiana Methodism, saw it in a "junk shop," bought it, and donated it to the archives.

The wartime papers of Eli Lilly, preserved in the Archives of Eli Lilly and Company and in the Archives Division, Indiana State Library, include his reports, letters to Governor Oliver P. Morton, official documents, and postwar speeches and correspondence pertaining to the battery. Also some items written by Lilly appeared in various Indiana newspapers.

Sergeant William O. Crouse wrote a journal after the war which is little more than a summary of the battery's history and contains few personal observations, but he wrote an article immediately after the war that was published in *The Soldier of Indiana* and, as secretary of the postwar Eighteenth Battery Association, corresponded with other veterans about wartime experiences. Crouse's journal is in the Indiana Historical Society Library and his postwar correspondence is in the Archives of Eli Lilly and Company.

Other available wartime writing of men of the battery included: seven letters by James C. Dodd; two letters and a report in the *Official Records* by William Benson Rippetoe; a petition and a report in the *Official Records* by Martin J. Miller; a history of the battery in verse by William J. Rinewalt; reports of First Sergeant Robert W. Lane; official correspondence of Charles D. Watson; single letters written by William J. Wolfe, James Emory Rippetoe, and Jason Lee Rippetoe; and a letter by Sidney Speed that was published in *The Soldier of Indiana*. Postwar letters of some of these men and of Joseph Addison Scott, and several newspaper articles by Moses Milton Beck contained information about the battery. The locations of the manuscripts quoted are shown in the footnotes.

Diaries and letters of soldiers in regiments that served with Lilly's battery also were reviewed for information pertinent to the battery history. Most of these were in the Indiana Historical Society Library, but the most frequently quoted of these related manuscripts is the diary of William M. Winkler, Fourth Indiana Cavalry, located in the Bartholomew County Public Library.

Generally punctuation and spelling were used as they appeared in the original documents. Exceptions are Henry Campbell's use of quotation marks in designating military units and his employment of dashes instead of more normal punctuation to provide thought breaks. For example, instead of 4" Indiana, as he wrote it (to indicate 4th Indiana), the simpler 4 Indiana now appears on the printed pages, thus avoiding possible confusion with regular quotation marks within the text. And whereas Henry sprinkled his diary liberally with both dashes and spaces for punctuation, the breaks now appear as exaggerated spaces only. Spaces are used similarly in a few other quotations. Also, the typewritten copies of the John Rippetoe letters had a note by Ernest R. Davidson that he was responsible for some spelling errors in transcription but mentioned that the original letters contained too few commas and no periods. Since the original letters were not available to observe actual punctuation, I followed the style of the typewritten copies but corrected spelling where typographical errors appeared probable.

Descriptive rolls, muster-in and muster-out rolls, clothing books, and other official documents were located in the National Archives and in the Archives Division, Indiana State Library. For a few men, the information in these records is incomplete, but available information is summarized in the appendixes.

Officers and noncommissioned officers in Appendixes A, B, and D are listed by seniority and rank in the same order in which they appear on the manuscript company rolls and as published in *Indiana in the War of the Rebellion: Official Report of W. H. H. Terrell, Adjutant General.* Although this method duplicates the names of some men, the organization as the war progressed is more apparent. Unfortunately, the information on a number of men is incomplete. Henry Campbell's journal indicates that the battery's rolls and clothing book were not properly made up until October 1863, when a paymaster refused to pay the men until they brought the records up to date. Consequently, personal information is not included on many men who had died or were discharged before this date.

The wealth of original material tells a story of war as seen by participants engaged in the great adventure of their lives, and they describe the hard marching, battles, foraging expeditions, sickness, camp life, and death, all part of the "soldiering" experience. The reader will find a great diversity among the men. There were heroes—Sidney Speed, John Runey, and William Winkler—and cowards, such as Isaac McCoy, who was "so awful afraid of being killed that he came very near dying." While most men enlisted for patriotic reasons and served through the war because they thought that it was their duty to do so, a few deserted as soon as they were paid their bounty money.

Most men drank whenever they had the opportunity, and Captain Lilly said that he lived on whiskey, quinine, and tobacco while in the service; but the Rippetoe brothers were temperance men who kept the pledges they had signed while children. There were the strong who went through the war without reported illness while a large number became sick—some recovered, some died, others were discharged, and still others spent a large part of their terms in hospitals. There also were incompetents among the officers whereas other men rose out of the ranks to become respected leaders.

The battery was recruited by Eli Lilly during the summer of 1862 with the intent that it would become "the crack battery of Indiana," and recruiting stations in the college towns of Crawfordsville and Greencastle enlisted many students of Wabash College and Indiana Asbury University. The battery first gained fame as a part of Colonel John T. Wilder's mounted infantry brigade during General William S. Rosecrans' Tullahoma campaign. The battery next shelled the Confederate stronghold of Chattanooga "opposed to the whole of [Confederate General Braxton] Bragg's army" and supported only by Wilder's brigade. They played a vital role in the Battle of Chickamauga, helping to stop the initial Confederate flanking movement and finally, along with Wilder's brigade, remaining the only organized and undefeated troops on the Federal right.

In the fall of 1863, the battery was transferred to the First Cavalry Division, Army of the Cumberland, and with this division they fought a bitter winter campaign in East Tennessee, played an active part in General William T. Sherman's Atlanta Campaign during 1864, and were a part of General James H. Wilson's powerful mounted force that swept through Alabama and western Georgia during the spring of 1865. During its service, the battery marched some 6,000 miles and traveled another 1,000 miles by rail.

They possibly were "the crack battery of Indiana." At least they were distinctive and were allowed, by special order, to use an extra team for their guns and caissons. For a while, they were the only ten-gun battery in the Department of the Cumberland, but for most of the war, they had the regulation six cannons. They joined the First Cavalry Division at a time when the Union cavalry was beginning to surpass the Confederates for hard riding, stout fighting, and skill; and with the aid of the Eighteenth Battery, this cavalry force became capable of attacking and driving infantry from their earthworks, an unexpected and previously unthinkable enterprise for cavalry.

My interest in Lilly's battery began while writing *Yankee Cavalrymen*. The Ninth Pennsylvania Cavalry, the subject of that book, and the Eighteenth Indiana Battery served in the same division for a time; and I located and referred to the Campbell, Rippetoe, and Crouse materials in writing *Yankee Cavalrymen*. The quantity and quality of information available about Lilly's battery made this unit an obvious subject for a second book.

JOHN W. ROWELL

Columbus, Indiana
February, 1975

Acknowledgments

Mrs. Leona Alig, manuscript librarian, Indiana Historical Society Library; Mrs. Mary Margaret Allard, Beck-Bookman Library, Holton, Kansas; Miss Eleanore Cammack, retired archivist, Archives of DePauw University and Indiana Methodism; Mrs. Dorothy J. Clark, Vigo County Historical Society; Mr. Ernest R. Davidson, Lynnwood, Washington; Mrs. Helen Davidson, archivist, Eli Lilly and Company; Judge Addison M. Dowling, Indianapolis; Miss Caroline Dunn, retired librarian, Indiana Historical Society Library; Mr. Robert S. Harvey, college archivist, Wabash College; Mr. Hubert H. Hawkins, Indiana Historical Society; James C. Hazlett, M.D., Wheeling, West Virginia; Mrs. Lillian Beck Holton, Manhattan, Kansas; Mr. Eli Lilly; Mr. Arthur G. Marshall, Maryville, Tennessee; Mr. Gene E. McCormick, corporate historian, Eli Lilly and Company; Mrs. Elizabeth R. Merrill, Vigo County Public Library; Mr. David J. Olson, former archivist, Archives of DePauw University and Indiana Methodism; Mrs. M. G. Rippeteau, Evanston, Illinois; Mr. John L. Selch, archives assistant, Archives Division, Indiana State Library; Mr. R. D. Shaffner, Phoenix Steel Corporation; Mrs. Louise Scott Stumbo, Topeka, Kansas; Mr. Donald E. Thompson, librarian, Lilly Library, Wabash College; Mr. Edward E. Tinney, chief historian, Chickamauga and Chattanooga National Military Park; Mrs. Charlotte Zeutenhorst, Tumwater, Washington.

Also, the staffs of the Bartholomew County Public Library; Manuscript and Photoduplication Divisions of the Library of Congress; Indiana Division, Indiana State Library; Indiana University Library; Montgomery County Public Library; Military Records, Pension Records, and Photographic Records Divisions of the National Archives.

And Lilly Endowment, Inc., for supporting the publication of this book.

Contents

Contents

Illustrations

Map of the Battle of Mossy Creek, by Henry Campbell
Map of the Fortifications at Vining's Bridge, by Henry Campbell
Esprit engraving of Lilly's battery

MAPS

Yankee Artillerymen

Captain Lilly and His Men

left home forever   never expecting to live through the hardship I shall have to endure   bid everybody farewell with a stout heart.

Seventeen-year-old Henry Campbell had good reasons to view his chances for survival pessimistically when he enlisted in Captain Eli Lilly's Eighteenth Indiana Light Artillery Battery during July 1862. The war then was in its second year; and being an intelligent, well-educated boy, Henry had read the dispatches and news from the war theaters in the Crawfordsville and Indianapolis papers and personally knew about local soldiers who had been killed and wounded or had died of sickness. Both the Crawfordsville *Journal* and *Weekly Review* devoted most of their first and second pages to war news, including telegraphic dispatches from the war theaters, except for a few weeks in the summer and two weeks in the winter when the county fair and lists of delinquent taxpayers dominated the front pages.

Henry's father, John P. Campbell, a native of Virginia, was a prosperous dry goods merchant in Crawfordsville and a trustee of Wabash College; and his mother, Mary Collett Campbell, was a member of a family that included respected leaders of the state in the fields of finance, agriculture, politics, and science. Henry, the oldest of the children of John and Mary, had been born July 2, 1845, in Vermillion County.

Henry had attended private schools and the preparatory department of Wabash College and, as a result, was better educated and more literate than most Civil War soldiers. But having worked in his father's store when not in school, he gave his occupation as "clerk" instead of "student" on his enlistment papers.

Crawfordsville was said to have been more military-minded than most cities in the state, and this attitude probably influenced Henry. The captains of two companies that were recruited during 1861 in Crawfordsville and Montgomery County had been promoted to high rank, and this well-publicized fact served to keep enthusiasm high. By 1862, one of these men, Lewis Wallace,[1] had become a major general commanding one of General Grant's divisions in the Fort Donelson and Shiloh campaigns, and the other, Mahlon D. Manson, had become a brigadier general.[2]

Henry Campbell was nearly denied his chance to serve. When the recruits were examined by the army doctor, Henry wrote, "All passed but myself   refused on account of my age   too young   thought I was gone sure but Captain Lilly told the Dr. that I was intended for his bugler and that 'it is essential to the interests of the service' &ct that I be retained   which was finaly done." Being only five feet, five inches tall, of a slight build, and still childlike in appearance, Henry could not easily pass for an eighteen-year-old.[3]

Henry was one of the fortunate soldiers who regularly received letters from home, many containing five dollars, and often he received packages with clothing and food. Others did not fare so well and another soldier of the battery wrote of a third, "Truman Shanks wants to know if his folks are all dead. I reckon he would like for them to write to him."[4] Correspondence with Truman would have required an amanuensis because he was one of three known illiterates in the company.[5]

1 General Lew Wallace, a Crawfordsville lawyer, later the author of *Ben-Hur* and other novels.

2 Manson was a Crawfordsville druggist and Mexican War veteran. H. W. Beckwith, *History of Montgomery County* (Chicago: H. H. Hill and N. Iddings, 1881), pp. 31–43.

3 National Archives, "Descriptive Book of the 18th Battery, Indiana Light Artillery" [hereafter cited as "Descriptive Book"]; Catherine Merrill, *The Soldier of Indiana in the War for the Union*, 2 vols. (Indianapolis: Merrill and Company, 1866–69), II, 187.

4 Vigo County Historical Society, John H. Rippetoe to Mary Rippetoe, Dec. 14, 1862.

5 Indiana State Library, Archives Division, 18th Indiana Battery "Clothing

The recruitment of the Eighteenth Indiana Battery was one small response to President Lincoln's call of July 2, 1862, for 300,000 volunteers to serve for three years and to reinforce those left of the 714,000 men who had responded to the call for troops in 1861. Governor Oliver P. Morton appointed Eli Lilly to recruit, organize, and lead the Eighteenth Light Artillery, one of nine field artillery batteries to be furnished by Indiana.

According to Henry Campbell, Captain Lilly "was an exceeding young man for so important a position, as the command of a battery in those days was more complex and important than a regiment. His youthful and slender appearance were decidedly against him, the men of the battery thought, as they gathered at Camp Morton .... But the first day of service dispelled all doubts as to the ability and qualifications of the youthful captain."[6]

Lilly's qualities of leadership may have come from a combination of heredity and environment. His ancestors have been traced to thirteenth-century Swedish bourgeois but, after the 1400s, the family lived in France. Eli's grandfather, Eli, emigrated to Maryland with his father when a small boy and became a businessman and landowner, operating some Baltimore taverns. He was Catholic, like all earlier Lillys, but he married Corilla Frost, known as a "shouting" Methodist, and all ten children of the marriage were raised in the mother's religion. Temperance was an important tenet of Corilla's faith, and this doctrine caused Eli to sell the taverns, after which he bought a plantation and became a slave owner. By the 1840s, abolitionism became another tenet of the faith of Corilla and the children; and when old Eli died in 1847, Gustavus, the oldest son, gave freedom to the slave that he received as part of his inheritance.

The younger Eli was the oldest of the eleven children of this Gustavus and Elizabeth Kirby Lilly, having been born in Baltimore on July 8, 1838. The following year, the family moved to Kentucky, residing in Lexington and later in Gallatin County, until 1852 when Gustavus

---

Book." Shanks was one who made his X. The record is incomplete since it does not have signatures of men who left the battery before Nov. 1863.

6 Jacob Piatt Dunn, ed., *History of Greater Indianapolis*, 2 vols. (Chicago: The Lewis Publishing Company, 1910), II, 689-93.

moved to Greencastle, Indiana, so his children could receive the excellent Methodist education offered by Indiana Asbury University.[7]

In Greencastle, as in other places he had lived, Gustavus Lilly was a carpenter and builder and a leader in the Methodist church, being especially active in the establishment and direction of sabbath schools. He retained strong abolitionist and temperance sentiments along with his other religious beliefs.[8]

The move to Greencastle was fortunate for young Eli since his education had been interrupted because of the frequent earlier moves of the family. In Greencastle he attended the preparatory department of Indiana Asbury University but left school in 1855 to become clerk to Henry Lawrence, a chemist and pharmacist in Lafayette.

His earliest military association began in Lafayette when a militia unit called the Lafayette Guards was organized in 1858 with Eli Lilly as second sergeant.[9] By this time he had progressed from clerk to pharmacist and the next year worked temporarily for wholesale druggists in Lafayette and Indianapolis. During the spring of 1860, he returned to Greencastle, opened his own drug store, and married Emily Lemon December 6, 1860.[10]

Young Eli remained a Methodist but possessed less abolitionist and temperance fervor than his father and grandmother. He voted for John C. Breckinridge, the Southern Democratic candidate, in 1860[11] and later remarked that he lived on whiskey, quinine, and tobacco while in the service.

During the wave of patriotism that swept the North following the fall of Fort Sumter in April 1861, Eli enlisted in a local company known as the Asbury Guards and was elected orderly (first) sergeant of the unit. The Asbury Guards went to Indianapolis on April 23, but by the time they arrived, Indiana's quota of six regiments for Federal service

7 Josiah K. Lilly, Sr., "The Name Lilly," *The Lilly Review*, Nos. 4–8 (Apr.-Aug. 1942).

8 Putnam *Republican Banner*, Aug. 11, 1870.

9 Lafayette *Daily Journal*, June 11, 1858.

10 Indianapolis *Journal*, June 7, 1898.

11 Archives of Eli Lilly and Company [hereafter cited as Lilly Archives], Thomas Aye to John Henry, Nov. 4, 1861.

had been filled. These regiments had been enlisted and mustered for only a three-month term; but Governor Morton, correctly believing that the government would soon need more soldiers, decided to organize and retain six additional regiments in state service.

A misunderstanding concerning the Asbury Guards took place in Indianapolis. According to a news account, the Asbury Guards ". . . had the alternative presented to them . . . of enlisting for three years or not at all, as they understood it. Choosing the latter expedient, most of the members of the 'Guards' returned to this place [Greencastle], on Thursday evening [May 1]." The men thought that they could be retained for three years, even if the war ended in three months, which most people thought was a more likely length of time needed to subdue the rebellion.[12]

Lilly and a number of other men stayed home when thirty-one of the Asbury Guards returned to camp on May 11. Accepting recruits for the men who had dropped out, the company was taken into the Sixteenth Regiment as Company K for a one-year term, to serve only in Indiana.[13]

Early in July 1861, President Lincoln issued a call for 500,000 three-year volunteers, and realizing that the war would last longer than originally expected, Lilly helped to recruit a new company in Greencastle known as the Putnam Rifles, which was accepted as Company E of the Twenty-first Indiana Infantry, with Lilly commissioned second lieutenant.[14]

Immediately after its organization in late July, the Twenty-first was shipped to Baltimore and was stationed at Fort Murray. Here Eli became frustrated and bored with infantry service, one reason being that he became fascinated watching the coast artillery practice. Some time later, on a visit to Fort McHenry, he watched a field artillery battery during maneuvers and this viewing led to his resolve to have an artil-

12 Putnam *Republican Banner*, Apr. 25, May 2, and May 9, 1861.
13 *Ibid.*, May 16, May 30, 1861; W. H. H. Terrell, *Indiana in the War of the Rebellion: Official Report of W. H. H. Terrell, Adjutant General*, 8 vols. (Indianapolis: Douglass & Conner, 1869), II, 135–36; IV, 320–22.
14 Lilly Archives, original commission.

7

lery company of his own.[15] He also desired to return to Indiana because a son, Josiah Kirby, was born on November 18.

Lilly resigned his commission on December 9, 1861,[16] returned to Indiana, and asked Governor Morton for an appointment as an artillery officer. Since no batteries were being organized at the time, Lilly had to wait. "Meanwhile," he wrote, "I studied artillery practice. I recited my lessons and learned the theory of maneuvers."[17] Governor Morton must have been very favorably impressed by the young six-footer because when artillery companies were authorized in July 1862, Lilly was given a chance to organize the first of nine new Indiana batteries.

Samuel Hartman, Joseph Addison Scott, Moses Milton Beck, Daniel W. Crosby, and William Benson Rippetoe [18] were appointed recruiting officers and established recruiting stations in Crawfordsville, Bainbridge, Greencastle, and Sandford. Posters that called for "Men with stout hands and willing hearts who will fight manfully for our just and holy cause" were printed and displayed. Each recruit was offered a $100 Federal government bounty and a $2.00 premium. The posters said that the battery was to be equipped with six, ten-pounder Parrott guns "as it is designed to make this the crack battery of Indiana." The men called for were: "1 captain, 2 First Lieutenants, 2 Second Lieutenants, 1 First Sergeant, 1 Quartermaster Sergeant, 6 Sergeants, 12 Corporals, 2 Buglers, 2 Blacksmiths, 2 Wagon Makers, 2 Harness Makers, 1 Wagoner, 122 Privates: Total 156 men."[19]

Lilly succeeded in recruiting all men required within one month after his appointment, an impressive accomplishment since the Union cause had reached a low point during the summer of 1862. In contrast, events of winter and spring had raised hopes that the war would be short. Indiana soldiers had helped win impressive victories at Mill Springs, Fort Donelson, and Shiloh that had shattered the Confederate

15 Lilly Archives, Eli Lilly, "Speech to Veterans of 18th Battery and 9th Cavalry," at G. A. R. Encampment, Indianapolis, Sept. 6, 1893.

16 Lilly Archives, Special Order No. 233, Maj. Gen. John A. Dix Headquarters; Eli Lilly, "Speech to Veterans."

17 Lilly Archives, Eli Lilly, "Speech to Veterans."

18 Scott, Beck, and Rippetoe were veterans of Company K, 16th Indiana Infantry. Terrell, IV, 320–22.

19 Lilly Archives, Recruiting Poster.

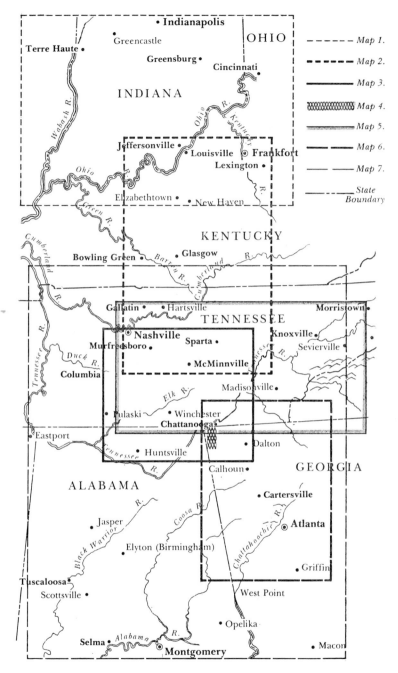

Legend:
- ------- Map 1.
- ▬ ▬ ▬ Map 2.
- ———— Map 3.
- ∭∭∭∭ Map 4.
- ▬▬▬ Map 5.
- ———— Map 6.
- —— —— Map 7.
- —··—··— State Boundary

GENERAL INDEX MAP
OF TERRITORY TRAVELED BY LILLY'S BATTERY

defense line in the west, and Union armies had occupied most of Middle and West Tennessee. Admiral David G. Farragut had run his fleet past the forts defending the mouth of the Mississippi, and a Federal army occupied New Orleans. In the east, the Army of the Potomac, the largest, best equipped, and best trained of all the Union armies had been moved to the Virginia Peninsula, and the capture of Richmond appeared imminent. Events looked so hopeful that the government stopped recruiting in the spring.[20]

By July, these bright hopes had faded. The Union armies had stalled in Tennessee, while the opposing Confederate armies were becoming sufficiently strong to threaten the Federal armies and capable of marching to the Ohio River. During July, Colonel John Hunt Morgan, with his Rebel cavalry, raided through Kentucky virtually unopposed. In the east, Confederate General Thomas "Stonewall" Jackson outmaneuvered and beat three Union armies in the Shenandoah Valley; and after moving to the environs of Richmond, the Army of the Potomac had been rolled back in the Seven Days' Battle, putting Washington itself in danger.

Unlike the enthusiastic 1861 volunteers, those of 1862 could, like Henry Campbell, measure their chances. Local papers had carried the names of both battle casualties and the larger number who had died from sickness, while hospitals for sick and convalescent soldiers had been established in a number of Indiana cities[21] and people could see the effects of war on strong men.

One of Lilly's volunteers saw "a man that had been in the Pitz Burg Landing fight [Shiloh]. He was shot through the face by a small bullet. The shot entered about midle ways his nose; and came out his rite ear, which deprived him of the sight of one of his eyes. It shatered one jaw bone. He layed under the doctor most ever since: and is now on his way home."[22]

20 Terrell, I, 348; Russell F. Weigley, *History of the United States Army* (New York: Macmillan, 1967), p. 206.

21 Terre Haute *Wabash Express Daily*, July 21, 1862; Emma Lou Thornbrough, *Indiana in the Civil War Era 1850–1880* (Indianapolis: Indiana Historical Bureau and Indiana Historical Society, 1965), pp. 171–75.

22 Archives of DePauw University and Indiana Methodism, William H. Anderson Journal.

The carnage of the Battle of Shiloh on April 6 and 7 still was a fresh memory because 1,277 Hoosier men were casualties of the fight. The army medical department had been unequipped to handle such large numbers of wounded, and the state government had to appeal to the citizens for donations of money and medical supplies to provide for the more than 1,000 Indianians wounded in the battle.[23] Men knew that if they were hurt or sick while in the service their chances of surviving were slim.

Still they volunteered in numbers that exceeded the state's quota because they realized, as a Hoosier expression of the day stated it, that the time had come for every man "to lift a pound."[24] The recognition that their own individual effort was needed was one incentive for enlistment, but events also played a role, with Morgan's raid in Kentucky during July being cited as an aid to recruiting in Indiana.[25] Also during the same month, a party of Kentucky guerrillas crossed the Ohio River, plundered the convalescent hospital in Newburgh and destroyed private property, causing a wave of anger throughout the southern counties.[26]

The convention of the Democratic party, referred to as the "Butternut Democracy" by the Republican press, further angered the loyal people of Indiana during July when the lengthy proceedings were reported in such detail by the newspapers that a story circulated that the proprietors of the Indianapolis *State Sentinel*, the Democratic organ, had asked to have the words "nigger" and "abolitionist" stereotyped.[27] With thousands of the most loyal voters in the army and unable to vote, the Democrats, dominated by the Copperheads,[28] won the legislature and most state offices in the fall election. Governor Morton then took personal control of the government and, ignoring the legislature, became a dictator running the state on borrowed money that was dis-

---

[23] Terrell, I, 41; Merrill, I, 383.
[24] Terrell, I, 17.
[25] Robert Emmett McDowell, *City of Conflict: Louisville in the Civil War 1861–1865* (Louisville: Louisville Civil War Round Table, 1962), pp. 73–74.
[26] Terre Haute *Wabash Express Daily*, July 21–25, 1862.
[27] *Ibid.*, July 31, 1862.
[28] The Copperheads were Southern sympathizers, numerous in Indiana, who obstructed the war effort and interfered with recruiting.

bursed through his office.[29] A soldier of Lilly's battery expressed his opinion, and probably that of most other soldiers, of the war obstructionists: " . . . of all the mean men on the face of the earth, an Indiana Copperhead traitor is the worst. I consider a southern man in arms an angel in comparison to a northern traitor." He said he tried to pray every day for his enemies "but it takes more grace to enable me to pray in my heart for a northern traitor than it does for all the human race besides."[30]

The Federal government's announcement that a draft would be instituted if quotas were not met on a voluntary basis also encouraged enlistments. The three-year volunteer received a $100 bounty for enlisting and, in most places, a bonus from the city or county.[31] One of Lilly's volunteers saw a possible benefit of the proposed draft—"I am in hopes that some of the southern sympathisers will be compelled to go and fight those that they have been offering their wishes for."[32]

For many, enlistment required some soul-searching because most of Indiana's population had Southern roots—their parents or grandparents had come from Southern states and they had near relatives south of the Ohio River. The feelings in the state before the war were so close to those in the South that an abolitionist orator described Indiana as "an outlying province of the empire of slavery."[33] For one reason or another, the men came forward and Indiana became one of the first states to exceed her assigned quota with voluntary enlistments.

Fifty-two of the recruits of Lilly's battery were from Crawfordsville and other Montgomery County towns. Forty-nine were from Putnam County, principally Greencastle and Bainbridge; twenty came from Vigo County; and the same number enlisted in Indianapolis. Eight were from Fountain and six from Madison County, while single enlistments were obtained in Hendricks and Shelby Counties.

Over half of the men, seventy-seven, had been born in Indiana,

---

29 Thornbrough, pp. 180–90.

30 Vigo County Historical Society, John H. Rippetoe to Mary J. Rippetoe, July 10, 1863.

31 Thornbrough, pp. 131–34, 137; Weigley, p. 207; Terre Haute *Wabash Express Daily*, July 26–30, 1862.

32 Anderson Journal.

33 Thornbrough, pp. 13–19.

twenty-six in other free states, fourteen in slave states, and seven in foreign countries—five Irishmen, one Englishman, and one Prussian. The birthplace of twenty-seven men was not shown on the descriptive roll.

Seventy-eight of the men gave their occupation as farmers. Twenty-seven other occupations were listed: blacksmith, bricklayer, brick-maker, butcher, carpenter, carriage maker, clerk, cooper, druggist, engineer, harness maker, horticulturist, mechanic, merchant, miller, nurseryman, painter, physician, saddler, shoemaker, silversmith, student, tanner, teacher, wagonmaker, watchmaker, and woolen factor. One man listed "none" for his occupation, and those of sixteen are not known.[34]

Of the 156 men who enlisted in the battery during 1862, only 77 were present when the company was mustered out of service in 1865.[35] Not until the summer of 1864 were replacements recruited for those who died, deserted, or were discharged.

Six Rippetoe men from Vigo County were among those to serve in Lilly's battery, five being the sons of Pleasant B. and Catherine Shewey Rippetoe, native Virginians, who settled about 1835 in Fayette Township, between the Wabash River and the Illinois line.[36] William Benson, aged twenty-one, their third oldest son, already has been mentioned as one of the recruiting officers of the battery. In April 1861, while a student at Indiana Asbury University, he had enlisted in the Asbury Guards, along with Eli Lilly.[37] William Benson, however, remained in the Guards when they became Company K of the Sixteenth Infantry, one of two regiments taken into Indiana state service for a one-year term.

Immediately after the disaster of Bull Run in July, the Federal government, needing any organized troops, accepted the Sixteenth for the

---

34 National Archives, "Descriptive Book."

35 Indiana State Library, Archives Division, "Muster-out Roll 18th Battery June 30, 1865."

36 National Archives, 1860 Census, Fayette Twp., Virgo County, Indiana. *Shewey* is also spelled *Shuey* and *Shoe* in various records.

37 Putnam *Republican Banner*, May 2, 1861. Moses M. Beck, Samuel H. Scott, and Jason Rippetoe, later members of the 18th Battery, also were members of the original Asbury Guards.

remainder of their one-year term. The regiment was shipped to Harpers Ferry, participated in the Shenandoah Valley campaigns of the next winter and spring, and was discharged in May 1862.[38] William Benson then aided Lilly in recruiting the Eighteenth Battery.

John Henry, the oldest Rippetoe son, enlisted in the battery when it was organized. He was more mature than most of the battery recruits, being twenty-five years old, married, a father, and a landowner, and also was well educated, having attended the scientific department of Indiana Asbury University. After leaving Asbury, he taught school while acquiring a farm, and in 1858, he married Mary Jane Malcom. They had a son, Peter, born November 1, 1860.[39]

When he left for the war, John complimented Mary on her business judgment but left their affairs in his father's hands without advising her. "... but what is the use of haveing the jugment without the power to execise that jugment," she wrote him, "if you had left the affare with me I think I could have been better fixed by this time. . . ." She said that, as a result of the arrangement, the wheat had not been threshed and that she had no money to buy winter clothes; that although she had saved it, she could not spend any of their money. She continued, "he [his father] never tells me a thing about what he is going to do with any thing . . . I am willing that any bargain you make shall stand but I am not willing to say that of him for I have not bin up there since you went away without haveing my feelings hurt . . . ."[40]

Arrangements were changed, and Mary competently handled the affairs at home for the remainder of the war. She paid off the debt on their farm with John helping by sending home nearly all of his military pay. He also offered advice frequently but was careful to tell Mary to use her judgment, generally adding that she knew best about the situation and values at home. She seems to have managed the business more competently than Pleasant, who without the help of his grown sons was in debt at the end of the war. ". . . we could have been out of

38 Terrell, II, 135–36.
39 H. W. Beckwith, *History of Vigo and Parke Counties* (Chicago: H. H. Hill & N. Iddings, 1880), p. 451; Ernest R. Davidson Collection, Mary J. Rippetoe to John H. Rippetoe, Nov. 1, 1862.
40 *Ibid.*, Oct. 26, 1862.

debt if you had all staid at home and made money off the war as the cowards of our country have done yet I am glad you all took the course you did in this war for when its history is written your names will live in honor while those cowardly sneaks . . . will go down in shame and everlasting disgrace."[41]

James Emory, the fourth oldest son at nineteen, also was one of the original recruits of the battery, and Leonidus Hamline, the next son, entered the battery for a three-year term in the spring of 1864. Then to the surprise of the other brothers, Jason, the second oldest brother, enlisted during the fall of 1864. Jason was another of the Asbury Guards who, like Lilly, dropped out before muster-in and then completed his education, graduating from Asbury in 1863. He was principal of Danville Academy when he enlisted in Lilly's battery.[42]

A cousin, David W. Rippetoe, was another of the original battery enlistees. In 1860, he appears to have been the principal support of his widowed mother in operating their farm. David joined the Asbury Guards when they were mustered into the Sixteenth Indiana and was a veteran with one year's service when he joined Lilly's battery.[43]

The Rippetoes were staunch and faithful Methodists having joined the local Pisgah church when small children. They regularly went to camp meetings and met many ministers of both Indiana and Illinois churches. John saw several of these men serving as chaplains during the war, one of whom was an uncle, John P. Shewey, chaplain of the One hundred twenty-third Illinois Infantry, and another was chaplain of the Ninety-eighth Illinois, "old brother [William] Cliffe who used to travel our circuit when we were quite small."

For the first year and one-half of the war, the Rippetoes observed their religion in private but in 1864, when other soldiers showed a renewed religious interest, the Rippetoes became the leaders and organizers of a society in the battery for the purpose of conducting religious

41 Ernest R. Davidson Collection, Pleasant Rippetoe to John H. Rippetoe, Mar. 3, 1865.

42 National Archives, "Descriptive Book"; Putnam *Republican Banner*, May 2, 1861; *Catalogues of Indiana Asbury University*, 1853–65.

43 National Archives, 1860 Census, Sugar Creek Twp., Vigo County, Ind.; Terrell, IV, 320–22.

services. They also were temperance men, having signed the pledge not to drink while small children.[44] Their characters were strong enough for them to keep these pledges even under the stress of war.

Once, when the battery had a two-hour layover in Shelbyville, Tennessee, the soldiers found many "rum shops" in operation. Henry Campbell commented, "Beer flowed freely all over town to judge from the apperance of the Batt as we left. Every man in the Co, *with the exception of the Rippetoes and Scott*[45] was in a tightly, slight condition." On the same occasion, John Rippetoe remarked, "Some of the boys found some whiskey and a good many of them got tolerably drunk and of course acted very foolish."

Like most other Northerners, Indianians did not enlist to free the slaves, and except for a small minority, the Hoosiers of the era were neither pro- nor anti-slavery. They were anti-Negro, being opposed to the mixing of the races and the state had "black laws" that excluded Negroes from settling in the state and prevented those already in from owning land, voting, and attending school.[46]

John expressed this anti-Negro sentiment while campaigning in the South: "you know that though I have always been opposed to the institution of slavery that I never was in favor of associating with them as my equals, and never expect to in this world." When the battery reached one of the poor sections of Kentucky that had few blacks he wrote, "I did not see very many negroes which was some relief for I am tired of seeing them, not that they do anything out of the way, but I do not believe they were intended to be mixed up with us as they are as a general thing in this state."

One soldier lost a little of his racial prejudice, or ignorance, shortly after the battery moved to Kentucky. "We have negro cooks in camp; and have our meals got up in the best of stile," he wrote. "I find that it is a very pleasant thing to eat after [a] negro cooks; still I used to think I would not like to eat after they had cooked the victuals."[47]

William O. Crouse of Tippecanoe County was different from the

---

44 Terre Haute *Tribune,* Mar. 8, 1911; Jan. 25, 1932.
45 Author's italics. Second reference probably is to Samuel H. Scott.
46 Thornbrough, pp. 13–19.
47 Anderson Journal, Sept. 10, 1862.

majority of the enlisted men because he was from a northern family. His father, Simeon, was a member of a well-established Philadelphia family who settled on a farm near Westpoint. William was born on the farm, July 28, 1840, was educated in the public schools of the county, and planned to enroll in Wabash College in 1862 but enlisted in Lilly's battery instead.[48]

Crouse was one of the battery writers. Unfortunately, his original diary was lost when a bullet struck it during the Battle of Chickamauga; three passbooks of his notes were lost when his horse drowned at Eastport, Mississippi; and his remaining notes were lost when another horse drowned in the Black Warrior River during the final campaign of the war. He reconstructed a journal after the war, however, from letters that he had written to his parents, and this journal has been preserved.[49]

Charles D. Watson certainly was another patriotically motivated recruit. "Dr. Watson joined the battery at the time of its organization, anxious only to serve his country, and depending on her to decide in what capacity he could be most useful," Captain Lilly and the other officers of the battery told Governor Morton in an attempt to break through army regulations to get Watson discharged and reappointed as assistant surgeon, assigned to the battery.[50] Watson, a physician in civilian life, was named quartermaster sergeant when the battery was organized.

In October, Watson passed an examination to practice given by the Board of Medical Examiners, State of Kentucky, and J. Frazier Head, medical director, Department of the Ohio, requested a discharge for Watson, "in order that he may have a contract as Physician to said battery in which capacity he is now acting." The request was denied because regulations did not provide for a discharge for such a purpose[51]

---

48 *Tippecanoe County, Indiana, Past and Present of,* 2 vols. (Indianapolis: B. F. Bowen & Co., 1909), II, 585–89; Lafayette *Journal and Courier,* July 8, 1926.
49 Lafayette *Journal and Courier,* July 8, 1926; Lilly Archives, William O. Crouse to Eli Lilly, the captain's grandson, Aug. 1923; Crouse to Joseph A. Scott, Sept. 17, 1919.
50 Indiana State Library, Archives Division, Eli Lilly and other officers to Oliver P. Morton, Nov. 5, 1862.
51 Indiana State Library, Archives Division, J. F. Head to A. A. G., Dept. of the Ohio, Oct. 7, 1862, and endorsement by C. W. Foster, A. A. G, Oct. 9, 1862.

but Watson finally was transferred on December 20, 1862, and promoted to assistant surgeon of the Fifty-fourth Indiana Infantry regiment.[52]

Robert Madden of Lockport, New York, visiting in Indiana when the battery was being recruited, decided that he wanted to be an artilleryman and joined. And Hosier Durbin "was one of those jolly, cheerful, never despondent boys who made more fun than a cage of of monkeys and did more to keep his comrades from giving down under the hardships of camp life than all the doctors and hospital stores to which we had access."[53]

Among these good men and true were some scoundrels. On August 20, Daniel W. Crosby, one of the recruiters of the battery, received permission to go to Greencastle with $600 that the soldiers were sending to their families.[54] The men never saw Crosby again, and the families did not receive their money. Probably Crosby was disappointed because he was not elected to be one of the battery's officers; a second lieutenant's pay was $45, while his pay as sergeant was only $17 a month.[55] He had enlisted sixteen men, but William Benson Rippetoe had recruited twenty and was named junior second lieutenant.[56] Captain Lilly offered a reward for information that would lead to Crosby's arrest and sent a detachment under Sergeant Martin J. Miller to Greencastle and to Crosby's parents' home in Ohio, but he was not found.[57]

Oliver B. Gorham reported sick and was left in Indianapolis when the battery moved south and, failing to rejoin the battery, he was listed as a deserter.[58] Later, he turned up in Tennessee and was arrested. After deserting from Lilly's battery, he had enlisted in the Forty-third Indiana and the Eighteenth Regulars, deserting both as soon as he had

52 National Archives, "Descriptive Book.'
53 Moses M. Beck, "A Second Visit to Chattanooga," Holton (Kan.) *Journal*, *ca.* 1899 (clipping in Henry Campbell Scrapbook, Wabash College Archives).
54 National Archives, "Descriptive Book"; Eli Lilly notice, Indianapolis *Journal*, Aug. 30, 1862.
55 Francis A. Lord, *They Fought for the Union* (New York: Bonanza Books, 1960), pp. 123–24.
56 Indiana State Library, Archives Division, Robert W. Lane certified lists of men recruited by Crosby and Rippetoe, Aug. 9, 1862.
57 Anderson Journal
58 National Archives, "Descriptive Book."

been paid his bounty money. He was caught, drummed through the brigade, and sentenced to serve out his term of enlistment in the Nashville military prison.[59]

Drumming-out was the usual punishment for desertion, and both Henry Campbell and John Rippetoe told of the drumming-out of "a hard looking fellow" of the Seventy-fifth Indiana. "His head was shaved and then branded on the right cheek with a red hot iron in the shape of the letter D." Then the brigade was assembled and the culprit marched through the lines "with eight bayonets after him." John Rippetoe wrote, " . . . He was a bad looking spectacle after his head was shaved, how bad I should hate to be in his place. He can never do any good where he is known but the laws must be enforced . . . what would life be worth to a man disgraced this way . . . ."

Sometimes bounty-jumpers did not get so far. At Camp Morton on August 6, 1862, William H. Anderson wrote, "There was a man shot today trying to desert; he drawed his pay an then attemted to leave and they pursued him, and comanded him to stop and he would not do it; and they prest him too close and he shot one of the guards in the brest and the guard returned the fire which had affect on his head; they think he will not live but for a few hours."

William Anderson was an introvert who had difficulty adjusting to army life both mentally and physically, and his happiest moments were those when he was away from camp in a nearby grove reading or writing or practicing bugle calls by himself. A student from Indiana Asbury University, he was disappointed that the other soldiers showed little interest in intellectual discussions and seemed to prefer trivial and obscene subjects. Ezra Lloyd, a classmate, was the only soldier who talked with Anderson about subjects that interested him.

Appointed first bugler, Anderson practiced regularly on his calls but admitted that he had trouble remembering them. He became sick a few days after becoming a soldier and, at Camp Morton, he wrote, " . . . we had to walk downtown and back which is two miles & a half; and the boys walked tolarbly fast which maid the walk more laborious,

---

[59] John H. Rippetoe to Mary J. Rippetoe, June 21, 1863. Regulars were United States Army troops, as distinguished from state volunteers.

and caused me to sweat heartly which I was afraid would impare my health more than ever."

Some others were unable to adapt to army life, and when Isaac Mc-Coy was discharged, John Rippetoe wrote, "He was the poorest soldier that I ever did see, he was so awful afraid that he would be killed that he came very near dying, now this is not a joke but the facts of the case." On July 12, 1862, Henry Campbell answered the call and was enrolled by Samuel Hartman, and on July 20, Hartman took a group of his recruits—Henry Campbell, James Binford, Fred Sperry, Martin J. Miller, John Albert Crawford, Augustus E. Newell, Charles Butcher, James M. Johnson, John Perry Shepherd, and William Scott—to Eli Lilly's temporary headquarters at the drugstore in Greencastle. The next day, the men went on to Indianapolis, drew tents, and encamped at Camp Morton, on the north edge of the city.[60] Campbell reported, "Joined in the evening by detachments from all parts of the country Battery filling up rapidly more tents and more recruits daily."

Newspapers reported the arrival in Indianapolis: "The 18th battery, Capt. Lilly, marched into Camp Morton on Thursday evening last, July 24, ninety men strong, all of whom are fine able-bodied men, who will make splendid soldiers. Capt. Lilly left for Greencastle and Montgomery County on Saturday, to bring up a number who are already recruited, and to enlist a few more to complete the battery, which will be completed one month from date of Capt. Lilly's commission which was issued July 8th."[61]

William Anderson found Camp Morton to be the opposite of the quiet of the college campus and wrote, " . . . every nois that can be heard anyplace may be recognized here today for the camp furnishes a variety and the naborhood around: Some hallowing; other singing; others talking and using profane language as loud as they can as if they want to let everyone her them sware that it is something dignifyed."

On August 8, the recruits had their physical examination, Ander-

---

[60] Camp Morton was bounded by present 19th Street, Talbott Ave., 22d Street, and Central Ave. Hattie Lou Winslow and Joseph R. H. Moore, *Camp Morton 1861–65: Indianapolis Prison Camp* (Indianapolis: Indiana Historical Society, 1940), p. 237.

[61] Terre Haute *Wabash Express Daily*, July 29, 1862.

son reporting that they were examined "by an old doctor that looked as ferce as an eagle." All recruits passed "but eight, who was to small or disabled to much to enter as a batery-man." The doctor may have had his doubts about a few of the others because William Black and James V. Carter were blind in one eye, Samuel B. Agnew had false teeth, John B. Bishop was hard of hearing, and four men were forty-five years old.[62] Probably there were more who were under eighteen and falsified their ages. Sidney Speed, a student at Wabash College, was one who had just turned sixteen when he enlisted. Another was William E. Starr, described as "a sickly, spindling youth of sixteen."[63]

At Camp Morton the men began to learn about soldier life: "Tryed another new idea or task that a soldier has to do," Anderson wrote, "that is to wash his own cloths which goes very awkward with me . . . the boys have great times washing; but spend but little time irning." He also commented, "I often look at boys that never done any thing in the cooking line and notis them staggering around among the pots and pans . . . and I have often saw the mother in camp watching her son, and [others] of the boys cooking; and looking at them with a longing look, as if she thought that I never raised you to be a cook."

As was customary in Indiana companies, the men elected their officers. Henry Campbell gave the results of the election held at Camp Morton: "Eli Lilly Capt. Saml Hartman, Sen. 1 Lt. A. D. [Joseph A.] Scott of Bainbridge Jun 1 Lt. [Moses] Milton Beck Sen 2d of the same place and Wm. Rippetoe Jun 2d." The election was so certified by Robert W. Lane, orderly sergeant,[64] and the men were furloughed for one week following this event.

The election was in keeping with the attitudes toward democracy of the day letting the men think that they had some control over who would lead them and also giving the appearance of a democratic procedure to the citizens. Actually, the recruits generally understood that the men who had done the recruiting were those who were to be elected,

---

62 National Archives, "Descriptive Book."

63 Crawfordsville *Journal,* July 13, 1923; Beck, "Second Visit."

64 Indiana State Library, Archives Division, Robert W. Lane certification of election of officers, Aug. 7, 1862.

and Governor Morton reserved the right to disregard the vote and to appoint some other officer in the place of the elected man.[65]

By August 17, John Rippetoe was voicing a common soldier complaint: "We have not drilled yet and we get very tired laying around all day with nothing to do but cook and eat but I reckon we will have drilling enough to do in a few days." They also had inspection, and Lieutenant Rippetoe told them that everything was in order except a pan or two were not as clean as they should be. John said, "but the boys will not let this be again for we will take the lead in cleanliness if there is leading done in that direction and we are the most civil and sober mess in camp and as brave as any."

Henry Campbell's mess may not have fared as well on inspection because "All of mess No. 1 (ours) drownded out last night   haven't learned the art of ditching our tents yet."

The soldiers ate well while at Camp Morton because they were near enough to home that visitors brought in delicacies, and William Anderson described a typical dinner menu: "We had rostenears and boild and baked chicken and cake; and rice; and corn bread."

On August 20, the men moved from Camp Morton, and John Rippetoe reported, " . . . it was a little like marching I reckon for we carried our knapsacks on our backs and tramped 2½ miles and it was a very warm day, but it was nothing but fun to walk that distance." He said that the new camp was in a much prettier place and "right in the sunshine which suits my notion of a healthy place." The new camp was on the commons west of town, between the city and White River and south of the city hospital.[66]

Probably it was well that the men moved their bivouac some distance from Camp Morton because, in addition to being a reception center for new recruits, it was a prisoner of war camp at the time. With so many men and limited sanitary facilities, Camp Morton was becoming an unhealthy spot.[67]

[65] Terrell, I, 85–88.

[66] Indianapolis *Journal*, Aug. 29, 1862.

[67] Winslow and Moore, pp. 293–301; Indianapolis *State Sentinel*, Feb. 24, Aug. 20, Sept. 3, 1862. The first prisoners, captured at Fort Donelson, arrived at Camp Morton on Feb. 22. The last prisoners were shipped out Aug. 29, and Camp Morton

The recruits were not there long enough to become soldiers. While marching, men frequently dropped from the ranks, and William Anderson observed, " . . . the boys is very deficient in corage in making a march for they want to stop as soon as they get a little tired." Also without weapons or horses, they could not learn field artillery drill and maneuvers, but before leaving Indianapolis, they did learn that soldiers were not free to come and go as they desired. Anderson reported, " . . . there were some been kept diging stumps all day for taking french furlows."

---

was renovated by Sept. 3. William Anderson's Journal reports the release of a group of prisoners who took the oath of allegiance and of a larger group who were shipped south under guard to be exchanged.

II

Arms, Organization, Equipment

*Our guns came today 3 in. rifled
Rodmans ... Marching orders were
received about 12 o'clock   6 o'clock
found Guns, Harness, and camp
equippage all loaded on the Jeffersonville cars and at dark we
bid adieu to Indianapolis, bound
for the seat of the war.*

Henry Campbell's Journal entry for September 1, 1862, tells how the battery was rushed off to the war without receiving any drill or training with their weapons and, because they did not yet have horses to pull the guns, the men manhandled the guns, limbers, and caissons onto the train. The battery was fortunate to receive six cannons, commonly called Rodman guns but officially named "The 3-inch Ordnance Rifle." The weapons had been received at the Indianapolis Armory on August 30, part of a shipment of twenty-four Rodmans, twelve Napoleons, and a quantity of Enfield rifles.[1]

The Rodman became the favorite weapon of the mounted artillery attached to cavalry brigades because of its accuracy, range, light weight, and maneuverability. The reputation of the Rodman for not bursting also endeared this gun to the cannoneers. The 10-pounder Parrott cannon, which the battery had expected to receive, also was a three-inch rifle used in similar light artillery service but was of a cast iron construction that occasionally burst, killing and injuring the gun crew.

The 3-inch Ordnance Rifle was unique, being manufactured of

[1] Indianapolis *State Sentinel,* Sept. 1, 1862. The Napoleon was a 12-pounder smoothbore cannon designed by Napoleon III and the most common field piece in the U. S. Army. Albert Manucy, *Artillery Through the Ages* (Washington, D.C.: U. S. Government Printing Office, 1962) p. 13.

wrought iron at the Phoenix Iron Company of Pennsylvania by a welding and rolling process invented by John Griffen, superintendent of the company. The ordnance department tested the Rodmans with a charge of six pounds of powder, compared to a two pound test charge for other cannon of similar caliber. During the war, the War Department purchased 965 of the guns which proved so sound that the Army converted 202 of them into breechloaders when it began to change artillery to this more modern method during the 1880's.[2]

The guns were called "Rodmans" because they were similar in shape to large iron cannon used in siege and coast defense service that were cast by a method developed by a Captain T. J. Rodman. Since this name was used by officers and soldiers alike to describe the 3-inch Ordnance Rifle, the two names are used interchangeably in the text.

Rifled cannon were still a new development in artillery during the Civil War,[3] and at the outbreak of hostilities, the U.S. field artillery was equipped almost entirely with smoothbore guns. These generally were cast of bronze and were classified by the weight of the projectile— 6-pounder and 12-pounder being the most common sizes. The smoothbores generally were ineffective beyond 1,500 yards, while the 3-inch rifles had a range of from 3,000 to 3,500 yards with the 12-degree elevation that the carriages permitted; and by digging a hole for the trail, a trick quickly learned by the artillerymen, the range could be increased to 5,000 or 6,000 yards. The rifles used shells and other elongated projectiles weighing 9.60 pounds which maintained velocity, had greater impact, and more accuracy than the spherical projectiles used by the smoothbore guns. A charge of 1 pound of powder was used.[4]

The Rodman guns weighed about 820 pounds, lighter than the 6-pounder smoothbore and the 10-pounder Parrott, and were mounted on the standard 6-pounder carriage. Like all guns of the era, they were

2 James C. Hazlett, "The 3-inch Ordnance Rifle," *Civil War Times Illustrated* VII, No. 8 (Dec. 1968), pp. 30–36; Indianapolis *State Sentinel*, Sept. 1, 1862. The weapons also were named Griffen guns, after the inventor.

3 Manucy, p. 14. The first rifled cannon were developed in Italy and Germany during the late 1840s. Crawfordsville *Weekly Review*, Apr. 6, 1861, described the effectiveness of 80 rifled cannons at the siege of Gaeta, Italy, during the winter of 1860–61.

4 Hazlett, pp. 30–36; Francis A. Lord, *They Fought for the Union* (New York: Bonanza Books, 1960), pp. 78–79, 156.

muzzleloaders and were aimed with a "nubbin" front sight and a pendulum hausse at the breech.[5]

With reference to the accuracy of the guns, Henry Campbell told about target practice in November: "The target was ¾ mile distant and consisted of an old wheat sack hung in a fence corner. The practice was excellent, two center shots, one from each gun under charge of Corpls. [Francis] Evans and [William O.] Crouse." A few days later he reported another practice session: "They fired down the river at a white Sycamore tree, distant 2 miles   the firing was splendid   the gun corporals seem to understand their business without any drilling whatever. None of the shells hit the tree   that wasn't expected, but some very close indications were made near it. Corps [Nelson] Corey and Evans put a shell through a stump in the river ½ mile distant at the first shot."

A Confederate artilleryman also attested to the accuracy of the Rodman guns: "The Yankee three-inch rifle was a dead shot at any distance under a mile. They could hit the head of a flour barrel more often than miss, unless the gunner got rattled." He told how three shells hit one gun of their battery and destroyed it when a Federal battery fired the projectiles through an embrasure only one foot in width from one-half mile away.[6]

With each gun, the field artillery had two limbers and one caisson. Each limber had an ammunition chest mounted with seats for three of the gun crew, while the caisson carried two additional ammunition chests and a spare wheel. When enroute, the gun's trail was hitched to the rear of one limber and the combination was pulled by six horses. This was followed by the second limber and caisson, also hauled by six horses.[7] Lilly's battery was unusual in using eight horses for each

[5] Hazlett, pp. 30–36; Fairfax Downey, *Storming of the Gateway: Chattanooga 1863* (New York: David McKay Co., Inc., 1960), p. 49; Francis A. Lord, *Civil War Collector's Encyclopedia* (New York: Castle Books 1963) pp. 38–39. A pendulum hausse utilized a plumb line and scale to allow the gunner to correct his aim when the trunnions were not horizontal, as when the carriage was on uneven ground.

[6] Hazlett, p. 30.

[7] Henry Richard Huebner, *Civil War Artillery Manual* (Indianapolis: Indiana Civil War Centennial Commission and Indiana Historical Society, 1962), n.p.; Jack Coggins, *Arms and Equipment of the Civil War* (New York: Doubleday, 1962), pp. 68–69.

combination while serving as a unit of Wilder's mounted infantry brigade.[8]

In firing formation, the gun limber was placed behind the gun with its pole six yards behind the cannon's trail. The guns of a battery were spaced fourteen yards from each other with the second limber and caisson placed in a reserve position in the rear. This was parade ground formation, and the guns were placed in the most advantageous positions during combat in rough and wooded country.[9]

John Rippetoe explained the artillery organization to Mary: "A battery consists of six guns . . . A section consists of two guns and a detachment of one gun, each detachment has 16 men . . . They are called right, left, and center sections, the right rank first, the left second, the center third, but I believe that our section if it does rank as third is about the best of any of them, at least the captain will always risk us before he will the first section. The second section is a splendid section. One reason for all the differences is our officers. The Lieutenant who commands the first is a very poor concern, the lieutenants commanding the other sections are good men and good officers."

As John mentioned, each detachment was made up of sixteen men under the command of a mounted sergeant. Rippetoe described his duties as one of these officers: "My place is in command of the men that manage one gun and [I] have the duty to see that they do their duty. My detachment consists of two corporals, seven cannoniers, and six drivers and it is my place to give them the orders of the lieutenants."

Three of the lieutenants had command of the sections, transmitting their orders through the sergeants, and the fourth lieutenant had command of the line of caissons. Each detachment had a gun corporal who gave all executive orders to the cannoneers and also was responsible for aiming the piece with the second corporal serving as chief of caisson, in charge of the ammunition.

The cannoneers were numbered one through seven, and each had his specific duty while the gun was in action. A command to "change posts" indicates that the duties sometimes revolved and each man had

<hr />

[8] Lilly Archives, Special Order No. 166, Army of the Cumberland, June 18, 1863.

[9] Huebner; Coggins, pp. 69–71.

to understand and be proficient in all tasks. Number one sponged the gun barrel and rammed the charge and number two received the charge from number five, powder cartridge in right hand and shot in left,[10] and loaded these into the gun muzzle.

While the gun was being loaded, number three covered the vent hole with a thumb stall to prevent a draft of air that could explode the charge if a spark remained from the previous firing, and after the piece was loaded, he pierced the powder cartridge by inserting the priming wire through the vent. Number four's task was to insert the lanyard into the ring of a friction primer,[11] to drop the primer tube into the vent at the command "ready," and to pull the lanyard, firing the gun. At the command "load," number five ran to the ammunition chest, received the cartridge and projectile from number six or seven, who shared the task of preparing and issuing the ammunition under the supervision of the chief of caisson, and carried them to number two.

Each man had his assigned position when the battery was enroute, with the sergeant riding to the left of the lead horses of the gun. The gun corporal and two men rode in seats on the limber of the gun, three privates on the limber of the caisson, and the chief of caisson and two men on the chest of the caisson.[12] On rough roads the cannoneers marched beside the gun because the unsprung vehicles bounced fearfully and men could be seriously injured by falling under the wheels.

The near, or left-hand, horses were saddled and ridden by the drivers. During battle, horses were unhitched and taken to some nearby sheltered location to protect them, especially from enemy sharpshooters.

In addition to the gun crews, the battery had two buglers, whose position was near the captain; two blacksmiths; a saddler; a harness maker; and two wagonmakers. The battery had one wagoner who drove the wagon in which the tents, supplies, rations, spare equip-

---

10 John Batchelor and Ian Hogg, *Artillery* (New York: Scribners, 1972), p. 9. The powder cartridge was a bag containing the powder charge and it had a wooden center pin to hold it rigid to facilitate loading.

11 Manucy, pp. 26–27. A friction primer was a tube filled with powder and had a compound at the top that would ignite with friction through which a roughened wire was pulled by the lanyard.

12 Huebner; Coggins, pp. 70–71.

ment, and other baggage were carried and the blacksmiths had a traveling forge, another wheeled vehicle.[13]

Artillery manuals prescribed specific procedures and methods for each man and all of his actions so far as the handling and firing of the gun were fully described. Of course, the men had little understanding of these duties and procedures when they left Indianapolis on September 1.

Lilly's battery was accompanied to Kentucky by a drillmaster, Major W. W. Frybarger, U.S.A., who had just arrived in Indianapolis following his appointment by General in Chief Henry W. Halleck to superintend the raising, equipping, and drilling of Indiana batteries.[14]

The men quickly became proficient in drill and maneuvers, and during March 1863, Henry Campbell wrote, "Yesterday we drilled in the presence of Gen. Thomas who remarked that it was more like an artillery drill than anything he had seen yet."[15]

Artillery commissioned officers and sergeants were armed with sabers, and the men were issued revolvers; but even with these weapons, batteries were vulnerable to sudden attacks by infantry or dismounted cavalry and to attrition from sharpshooters. Thus they depended upon supporting riflemen for protection during battles.[16]

Field artillerymen wore cavalry uniforms except that the yellow cavalry trim was replaced with scarlet and crossed cannon insignia were used instead of the crossed saber emblems. The uniform consisted of a single-breasted, dark-blue jacket with stand-up collar, light-blue trousers, and cavalry boots. For winter wear, overcoats were issued and, for protection from rain, the soldiers were supplied with ponchos of rubberized cloth. Head cover sometimes was the regulation black felt artillery hat and, at other times, the peaked forage cap.[17]

After campaigning one winter with and one without an overcoat, John Rippetoe formed a strong opinion about this item. He told Mary,

13 National Archives, "Descriptive Book"; Coggins, p. 68.

14 Indianapolis *State Sentinel*, Aug. 29, 1862; Terre Haute *Wabash Express Daily*, Sept. 3, 1862.

15 Major General George H. Thomas, commanding the XIV Corps, Army of the Cumberland.

16 Downey, p. 55; Lord, *They Fought for the Union*, pp. 77, 81.

17 Lord, *They Fought for the Union*, p. 77; Lord, *Encyclopedia*, pp. 290–310.

"I have received your good letter written Christmas [1864] in which you gave me fits for not drawing an overcoat. Well all I have got to say is that to me an army overcoat is more trouble than it is worth in rainy weather. A rubber Poncho will keep me dry and does not tire me to death to carry it and in cold weather they do not do such a powerful sight of good in keeping one warm for they are split so far up the back that they let the cold in on the rear, and do but little good on the shoulders."

At the time Lilly's battery received its guns, soldiers were desperately needed in Louisville and all Indiana troops that had been organized were rushed to Kentucky. By August 21, thirteen new Indiana regiments numbering 14,000 recruits were in that state.[18] The veteran soldiers were with the Army of the Ohio, commanded by Major General Don Carlos Buell, that was in Middle Tennessee opposing General Braxton Bragg's Confederate Army of Tennessee, headquartered in Chattanooga.

The Indiana recruits had been rushed to Kentucky when Confederate Major General E. Kirby Smith's 20,000-man army invaded the state from Knoxville.[19] Smith's immediate target was Lexington and the Bluegrass area from which he could threaten both Louisville and Cincinnati. Smith's march was the first movement of a joint operation by which General Bragg expected to capture Louisville and occupy Kentucky. By the time Smith reached Lexington, Bragg's army was approaching the Kentucky line east of Bowling Green, having moved past Buell's army. Bragg's army approaching Louisville from the south and Smith's from the east became the most serious military effort of the war to take Kentucky out of the Union.

On August 30, Brigadier General Mahlon D. Manson marched out of Richmond, Kentucky, contrary to his orders, with 7,000 green Indiana and Ohio troops to fight Smith's veterans. The Union force was quickly routed, with only 800 escaping to Lexington.[20] After the rout

18 Indianapolis *Journal*, Aug. 21, 1862.

19 E. Kirby Smith commanded the Confederate district of East Tennessee. Crawfordsville *Weekly Review*, Sept. 6, 1862, reported that Smith's force numbered only 10,000 to 12,000 men.

20 U. S. War Department, *The War of the Rebellion: A Compilation of the Official Records of the Union and Confederate Armies*, 128 vols. (Washington, D.C.:

had begun, Major General William Nelson²¹ arrived on the field, rallied some of the soldiers for a brief stand, was wounded and surrounded, but managed to escape.²² After the battle, Major General Horatio G. Wright ordered all Union soldiers in Lexington to retreat to Louisville and declared martial law in Louisville, Cincinnati, and Covington because of the threat to those cities.²³

He also telegraphed Governor Morton and Governor Richard Yates of Illinois, "When and how fast can regiments and batteries be forwarded from your State? Let them all go to Louisville as fast as transportation to that place is available."²⁴ During the following weeks, Indianapolis papers reported regiments from other parts of the state and from Illinois and Wisconsin passing through the city on their way by rail to Louisville.

Thus as soon as they received their weapons, Governor Morton ordered Lilly's battery to the war theater. Their train arrived in Jeffersonville at 9:00 A.M. on September 2, the cars were unloaded, and the men went into camp one-half mile east of town.

Government Printing Office, 1880–1901) [hereafter cited as *O.R.*] Ser. 1, XVI, pt. 1, 885; Henry M. Cist, *The Army of the Cumberland* (New York: Scribners, 1898), pp. 52–55.

21 Nelson commanded the Army of Kentucky and had field command of the defense of the state.

22 Indianapolis *Journal*, Sept. 9, 1862, criticized Nelson's "barbarity," reporting that he cut some men; fired his pistol at others; and used profane, vulgar, and abusive epitaphs when rallying the troops.

23 *O.R.* Ser. 1, XVI, pt. 1, 907; Terre Haute *Wabash Express Daily*, Sept. 3, 1862. Wright commanded the Department of the Ohio, outranking General Nelson.

24 *O.R.* Ser. 1, XVI, pt. 2, 459.

III

Kentucky 1862

drew our horses from Louisville
Bragg expected accross the river
great consternation in Louisville
Battery ordered to the South side
of the river.   Horses had to be
hitched up in harness that had
never been put together before,—
by inexperienced hands.   every-
thing in confusion   guns sent
down to the ferry one at a time. All
across by 12 oclock   camped East
of the city at the Fairgrounds
Completely dusted out by the
cavalry passing us   retreating
from Lexington.

On September 3, Henry Campbell described the confusion among the untrained artillerymen when moving to their battle station on the Shelbyville road along which a Federal column from Lexington was retreating, pursued by the Confederate cavalry. All signs indicated that Kirby Smith's Rebel army was marching toward Louisville, defended only by recruits as green as Lilly's men.

William Anderson elaborated on the difficulties in crossing to Louisville, " . . . we hitched up and started over the river and the horses maid some big starts to absent themselves from the old cannon wagons but they found it some trouble. Wen we got down to the river and the horses saw the old ferry bote; and heard the noiz it maid it caused considerable fright to some of them and they wer not for going towards such an object."

When the men were told to go out and buy their breakfasts on the morning after reaching their new camp, William Anderson "and some more went over the rode to an old rich planters and called for our breakfast; and the negroes got up us one that was rite." Rations had not been brought from Indiana, and the men had to forage and learned that "The peaches wer mostly ripe and we went in on them." Anderson continued, "There was a sweet potato patch close and we tried how we could cook sweet potatoes; and irish potatoes went the same way."

On the same morning, the Confederate cavalry reached Shelbyville, about twenty-five miles east of Louisville, where they had a sharp skirmish with the Ninth Pennsylvania Cavalry, which delayed them and gained sufficient time to allow the retreating Union foot soldiers to reach Louisville.[1] The Federal command expected the enemy to be on the heels of the column and prepared to defend the city.

While drilling on September 6, the artillerymen heard firing to the south and John Rippetoe wrote, " . . . news came that the rebels were coming and we put into camp and filled our haversacks with provisions and our canteens with water and then waited orders to march out to meet them." The orders were not issued because General Smith had settled down in the Bluegrass Region to replenish supplies and to await the appearance of General Bragg's larger Rebel army before moving toward Louisville. Smith did feint toward Cincinnati, causing some Union troops to be diverted from Louisville.

The distant firing, caused by the appearance of some Confederate cavalry, frightened the civilians living near the fairgrounds. "Some of the citizens thought that there was going to be a batle and they scedadeled from their houses to the city for the purpose of getting out of dainger," Anderson reported. The citizens' property was endangered whether there was or was not a battle because the empty houses aroused the curiosity of the soldiers.

Avoiding the guards around their camp, a few of Lilly's men entered a nearby house one night, and by accident, found the trap door to a well-stocked wine cellar. They carried all the bottles they could back to camp and, of course, gave their battery-mates directions. Most men made several trips to the cellar.

When Henry Campbell went to awaken Captain Lilly the following morning, he "found the capts tent full of long dark looking bottles, Jugs, demijohns, etc. each man, that was on the raid last night, thinking that he ought to make the Capt a present had left him a mark of their esteem in the shape of Sundry bottles of Wine, Brandies, &c. until his tent was litteraly full   some not content with this display of their regard had filled buckets with whisky and placed them inside along with the remainder of the plunder. Capt Lilly Knew nothing of this

[1] John W. Rowell, *Yankee Cavalrymen: through the Civil War with the Ninth Pennsylvania Cavalry* (Knoxville: Univ. of Tennessee Press, 1971), pp. 75–79.

until his eyes discovered it the next morning. Camp full of Wine, Brandies, and whiskies of the very finest quality. everybody drunk. a wagon load of it was collected and returned the next day. but still every hollow log and stump was full of it."

Captain Lilly called the other officers and sent for the sergeant of the guard, who was found doubled up between two bales of hay "completely oblivious to any cares or duties, "and mustered only about ten men fit for duty. Lilly reported the incident to brigade headquarters and the battery was placed under arrest with guards posted around the camp. The owner of the house returned the next day, accepted Captain Lilly's apologies in good humor, and even thanked the men for not damaging the house and the furnishings.[2]

Perhaps this incident convinced Lilly that he would have to discipline his men severely if he was to have "the crack battery of Indiana" as advertised in the recruiting posters. He came down hard and began to drill his soldiers during the forenoons and afternoons. William Anderson reported that a usual incident of this training was "for the capton to scold us and to drill us like so many wild men . . . . The officers comes in off of drill most every day mad as thunder, for they get so much abuse that they can not take it without getting mad."

When someone stole the captain's freshly boiled ham, he made the entire First Section march in a circle for several hours, each man carrying several fence rails. However, he never learned the identity of the thief.[3]

Lilly's newness to field command of a battery and his hard discipline were reflected in the attitudes of the men, with William Anderson writing, " . . . the capton is not much acquainted with his duty." And, in comparison to other officers appointed to similar responsibilities, Lilly was young and inexperienced. Samuel J. Harris, for example, who was made captain of the Nineteenth Indiana Battery, had spent four years in the U. S. Army horse artillery, including the Mexican War,

---

[2] Indiana State Library, Indiana Division, Henry Campbell, "A Spirited Raid." Campbell may have exaggerated the incident and the numbers involved since Anderson's journal and Rippetoe's letters do not mention the event.

[3] Lilly Archives, Sidney Speed to Eli Lilly, the captain's grandson, July 6, 1918, identified Marion Barr as the culprit.

and nine months in command of the Seventh Indiana Battery during the Civil War.[4]

On October 2, Sergeant Martin J. Miller wrote a petition to Governor Morton that forty-six men of the battery signed requesting that Lilly be removed from command. The paper stated these reasons: that he was incompetent—too young, that he encouraged stealing, that he hurled insults at the noncommissioned officers, that he had no knowledge of how to keep horses, that he had deprived the men of their "writes" as Americans, and that they all had suffered abuses and insults which "we cannot and shall not suffer any longer."[5]

Governor Morton appears to have ignored the petition, but Captain Lilly did not. The next day he "raised peticular thunder; reduced the non commishined officers to the ranks, and we all had to shed off our soldier armes; and every thing that uncle sam had furnished us but our clothes." Anderson, whose name was third on the list, was reduced from first bugler to "powdermonky" and he wrote, "the sargents all submited to their fates with the highest polity. I must acknowledge that I was very ancious for the thing to go."

The following day drill went poorly under new sergeants and corporals, and, as time went on, Lilly restored some of the men to their earlier rank. As Anderson wrote, the reduced men were "some of the best boys in the company." Martin Miller, the instigator, eventually moved through the ranks to become first lieutenant. The Rippetoes were not involved with the petition and escaped the captain's retribution, and Henry Campbell became first bugler as a result of Anderson's demotion.

The incident made the captain even more severe in disciplining the men and William J. Wolfe tried to get out, asking his half brother, an officer in the Twelfth Indiana Infantry, to see if William could get a lieutenancy in one of the companies of his regiment, or any other " . . . any thing to get me from under the command of the tyrannical captain who I am under now."[6]

4 Terrell, III, 435.

5 Indiana State Library, Archives Division, Martin J. Miller and others to Oliver P. Morton, Oct. 2, 1862.

6 Indiana Historical Society Library, William J. Wolfe to John Q. A. Blackwell, Oct. 9, 1862.

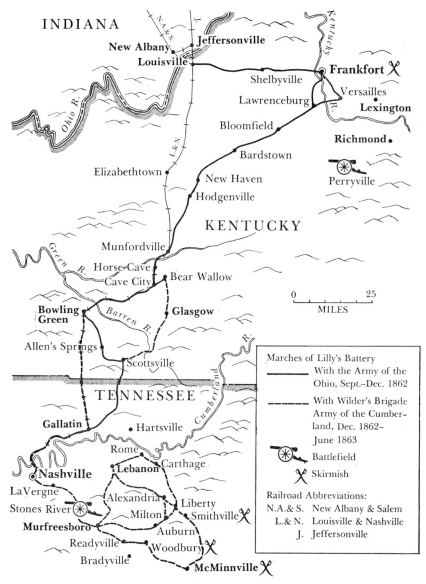

INDIANA

New Albany
Louisville
Jeffersonville

Shelbyville
Frankfort ✂

Lawrenceburg
Versailles
Lexington

Bloomfield

Richmond •

Bardstown

Elizabethtown
New Haven
Perryville ⊛

Hodgenville

KENTUCKY

Munfordville

Horse Cave
Bear Wallow

Cave City

Bowling
Green
Glasgow

Allen's Springs

Scottsville

TENNESSEE

Gallatin
Hartsville

Rome

Nashville
Lebanon
Carthage

LaVergne
Alexandria
Liberty

Stones River ⊛
Milton
Smithville ✂

Murfreesboro
Auburn

Readyville
Woodbury ✂

Bradyville

McMinnville ✂

Ohio R.
Green R.
Barren R.
Cumberland R.

0   25
MILES

Marches of Lilly's Battery

————— With the Army of the
Ohio, Sept.–Dec. 1862

— — — With Wilder's Brigade
Army of the Cumber-
land, Dec. 1862–
June 1863

⊛ Battlefield

✂ Skirmish

Railroad Abbreviations:
N.A. & S. New Albany & Salem
L. & N.   Louisville & Nashville
J.   Jeffersonville

Map 2.
MARCHES OF LILLY'S BATTERY, SEPTEMBER 1862—JUNE 1863

37

General Bragg's Confederate army, 28,000 strong, had marched out of Chattanooga on August 28. Major General Don Carlos Buell could not be sure whether Kentucky or Nashville was the target of this army, and he consolidated his Union Army of the Ohio around Nashville and did not start north until Bragg's army had crossed the Kentucky line south of Glasgow on September 5. As a result, when the veteran Federal army did begin to march, Bragg's army was several days' marches nearer to Louisville than was Buell's.

With the approach of Bragg's army, consternation and activity increased in Louisville with green troops, many just organized and unarmed, coming into the city from Indiana and Illinois. General William Nelson, partially recovered from the wound received at the fight at Richmond, took command and energetically prepared to defend the city by organizing the new soldiers into an army, calling up the home guard, and putting slaves to work building fortifications. Nelson was a driver, and seven forts, connected with rifle pits, were constructed on the outskirts of the city.[7]

To raise the morale of the citizens, Nelson held a grand review of his army on September 16. The route, at least for Lilly's battery, went from Brigadier General William R. Terrill's headquarters at the two-mile house and down Broadway, giving the soldiers a chance to see the city and its citizens. "I did not like the apperance of the city at all," William Anderson reported, "The inhabitants was very ornery; and the buildings was most as trifeling lookin as the people ... The inhabitance that maid their apperance was Irish; duch; and french, and some Americans. I did not believe their patriocism was very reliable; although there was a great nois maid over us: but it was mostly by the children. we were waited on by the people to water plentifuly; and some times a few cakes or apples or peaches."

The day was extremely hot and sultry and the artillerymen were exhausted after the march, although they had ridden the route. Anderson did not understand how the infantry had completed the march since the soldiers were nearly all recruits. Several dropped dead in the ranks, and many more passed out and were carried back to their camps. The officers drove some men back into the ranks and veteran cavalry-

7 McDowell, pp. 83–87.

man William Thomas of the Ninth Pennsylvania remarked that he saw Brigadier General James S. Jackson "strike one poor fellow with His sabre."[8]

This was a cruel march and harsh treatment for new soldiers. These were western men who sometimes threatened that martinets who were unreasonably cruel might be killed in the next battle,[9] and perhaps it was only a coincidence that the three principal officers involved in the grand review were killed during the next three weeks. Generals Jackson and Terrill were killed at the Battle of Perryville on October 8 during the confusion resulting from the rout of their troops, and General Nelson was shot by Brigadier General Jefferson C. Davis on September 29 after Nelson had, in Davis's opinion, abused and insulted him.[10] William Anderson recorded that Nelson's death "was not morned by the soldiers; but rather rejoiced . . . that all the soldiers is imbitered against him from the fact that he treated his men bad at the richman [Richmond, Ky.] fight."

On September 20, Henry Campbell wrote, "Moved out the Bardstown pike 12 miles. camped on a hill   roads dusty and Hot. Found a Pocket book containing $103.00 in postage stamps.   Toll gate keeper said it belonged to a sergeant in the 9 Penn cavalry."

William Anderson wrote that the battery had poor accommodations at their new camp: "we had some trouble in getting water at the springs; for we had to go in squads of six men with a corperal; and a writen pass from the Cernal; or of the capton of the batry before we could get water. I was arested for the first time in the army . . . . We were all arrested; for we had not heard of the order yet; and we were marched up to head quarters and releaced. The only thing that payed was; that I got to see General Woodruff [11] at his quarters."

On September 22, the battery moved back to their old camp, marching ahead of the infantry "on acct of the dust choaking the horses."

---

8 Rowell, p. 81.

9 Robert Hale Strong, *A Yankee Private's Civil War*, ed. by Ashley Halsey (Chicago: Henry Regnery Co., 1961), pp. 84–85; Bell Irvin Wiley, *The Life of Billy Yank* (Indianapolis: Bobbs-Merrill, 1952), p. 199.

10 McDowell, pp. 91–94, 99–101. Davis, a protégé of Governor Morton, was not tried in either a military or civil court for the murder of Nelson.

11 Col. W. E. Woodruff, commandant at Louisville during July 1862.

On the twenty-fourth, the battery moved into Louisville "behind the fortifications in the south part of the city near Broadway," and Henry Campbell reported, "Louisville completely deserted   business houses all closed   women and children all ordered across the river to night by 12 oclock.   Gen Nelson expects an attack before daylight."

William Anderson thought the battery was "situated to have some effect if we are called to try our powers; but I am afraid that we will not have the pleasure of geting to fight for if Brag hears of our force; and determination I think that he will come to a halt, and probably turn the other way." The Federal command, ordering the evacuation of women and children, had a less optimistic opinion of the abilities of their army of recruits.

An attack did not come that night and the threat to Louisville evaporated when General Bragg's Confederate army halted at Bardstown and Buell's Union army continued marching on the Elizabethtown pike to the west. On September 24, cavalry scouts from Louisville met the advance elements of Buell's column[12] and, by September 27, the Army of the Ohio was in Louisville.

On September 26, Lilly's battery marched through the streets until 10 P.M. when they halted, tied their horses to a fence, spread tarpaulins on the stone pavement, and, according to Campbell, "slept soundly for the remainder of the night." Anderson did not agree: "I would lay down and roll over part of the time; and then I would set up part of the time to rest my back that fellt like that I was an old patient to the rheumatism . . . . "

The next morning the battery moved two miles from town and camped "on the Banks of the Ohio." Henry Campbell commented, "We have marched over 100 miles since we have been in Ky and have never been out of sight of the Blind Asylum Steeple."[13]

The arrival of the Army of the Ohio ended the anxiety in Louisville, and General Buell now gained the initiative in the campaign. He, not Bragg, would determine the next move but his first task was

12 Rowell, p. 82.

13 McDowell, p. 206. The Blind Asylum on the Shelbyville road later was converted into a military hospital.

to reorganize his army, incorporating the new soldiers with the veterans who had marched from Nashville.

In the new organization, the Eighteenth Indiana Battery was attached to Brigadier General Ebenezer Dumont's Twelfth Division, an independent command (not attached to a corps), consisting of four infantry brigades, part of the Fourth Indiana Cavalry, the Thirteenth Indiana Battery, and the Chicago Board of Trade Battery, in addition to Lilly's battery.

While Buell was reorganizing his army, General Bragg postponed military activity and devoted his efforts to political actions, issuing proclamations inviting the Northwestern states to make peace, establishing a Confederate government in Kentucky, and instituting a draft in the state. He would not be allowed enough time in Kentucky for any of these activities to become effective.

As a diversion to start his campaign, General Buell sent Brigadier General Joshua Sill's division, followed by Dumont's division, toward Frankfort to make Bragg believe that the Federal army was moving toward that city. While this force was holding Bragg's attention, Buell marched with 58,000 men toward Bardstown, where the principal part of Bragg's army was positioned, a campaign that ultimately led to the Battle of Perryville on October 8 and a retreat by the Confederate army from Kentucky.

On October 3, Henry Campbell reported, "Moved out on the Shelbyville Road about 4 P.M. march until daylight   rested until the infantry caught up and then moved to Shelbyville   Staid here two days   drank water out of a cattle pond." The battery began the march at the rear of the column and Anderson wrote, "We marched tolarbly fast. The infantry begin to give out the first three or four miles; and from that time the rode was lined with fellows that had give out to the place where we camped which was about fifteen miles."

At Shelbyville, William Anderson reported, "The country has been very nice. A great many of the farmers are rich; and living in all the luxury of life. You talk to them about the war and they will say that they are in favor of the union but they can not stand lincoln that he does not do his duty about the negro; that they can not stand his proclamation;[14] that they want him and Jeff Davis hung on the same tree. They are as good secesh[15] as ever there was. They will have a union flag out but I expect there was another kind out when Kerby Smith was up hear last week."

This was Anderson's first observation of an army on the march and he reported, "The boys will get over into gardens and anyplace to get things to eat. They will come in with a hog; and with a lot of poltry; and honey; and hams, and evry [thing] that they can find. I do not know what the army would do with the rations that they draw; if it was not for the produce that they get along the road; and at the same time seem not to have half enough to eat."

At noon on October 4, the Confederates inaugurated a governor in Frankfort, but his term was short. At 3 P.M. the Rebels began to evacuate the capital of the State, taking the new governor with them and, by October 6, only cavalry remained in the town.[16]

On the same day, Henry Campbell wrote, "Started for Frankfort the capitol of the State   splendid pike   reached the Kentucky river about 10 oclock at night.   rebels in force at the Bridge. Battery ordered to the front at a gallop   whiped up and *out run* a Co of cavalry that was trying to get to the Bridge   After an exciting race of one mile the 1st Sec [Section] arrived at the end of the bridge, unlimbered, and went into position, but could not open on the rebels as our cavalry were fighting in this end of it. Rebels had taken up the plank in the middle for a small distance which prevented our cavalry from charging. Bullets whized past thick. one cavalryman was killed and one wounded close to the Battery."

"Soon as the enemy discovered our Batt. in position, they disappeared in a hurry.   the floor was soon laid and we were over into the town in short order   Rebs had all left for parts unknown   leaving their sick and wounded behind." John Rippetoe identified the Confederates as "700 of Scott's rebel cavalry,"[17] and he also wrote that "there were some killed and wounded on both sides . . . not over 7 or 8

---

14 The preliminary Emancipation Proclamation issued Sept. 22, 1862.
15 "Secesh" was slang for secessionist.
16 *O.R.* Ser. 1, XVI, pt. 1, 1020.
17 Col. John S. Scott, First Louisiana Cavalry.

apiece. I saw one of our wounded last night, one poor fellow was hit 4 or 5 times and has since died, it looks like barbarous work for men to be killing each other, but I did not feel afraid."

Private James C. Dodd missed the skirmish at the bridge, being one of the walking sick that Dr. Watson had been ordered to bring from Louisville.[18] "I do not feel like riting to day for I just got here night befor last at twelve Oclock after marching 53 miles," he wrote. "I came up with the forage wagons from Louisville and they were heavy loaded so I had to walk and run about half the way which made me So Sore and tired that I cant hardly walk to day . . . ." About his health, Dodd said, "I am well but not very stout yet."[19] Anderson and others who became sick on the march rode to Frankfort in the supply wagon.

After Frankfort was occupied, Sill's division marched south to rejoin Buell's principal army, leaving Dumont's force to garrison the city.[20] The battery sections were placed in positions to cover the railroad and wagon bridges and the road from Lexington.

Sill's and Dumont's march to Frankfort had convinced Bragg that the principal Union army was following, and he held a large part of his army north of Harrodsburg, causing much of the Confederate army to miss the Battle of Perryville on October 8. As it was, the Rebels nearly won the battle, and the Federal officers expected that the fight would resume the next morning, but Bragg withdrew during the night and began to retreat from Kentucky. This ended the most serious threat to Union control of Kentucky, and the Confederates never again were able to muster enough strength to attempt another invasion, although their cavalry frequently raided in the state.

With the enemy withdrawing from Kentucky, the soldiers had leisure to sightsee in Frankfort. William Anderson found Frankfort "one of the most picturesque places that I ever saw. I could not get satisfyed looking at the river; and at the town. the high clifts was an entire new sight to me."

Henry Campbell thought, "Frankfort is a peculiar little town for the capitol of the state, situated on the south bank of the Ky. river sur-

[18] William J. Wolfe to John Q. A. Blackwell, Oct. 9, 1862.
[19] Lilly Archives, James C. Dodd to Rueben and Mary Hinkel, Oct. 12, 1862.
[20] *O.R.* Ser. 1, XVI, pt. 2, 601.

rounded on all sides by high hills and abrupt bluffs. the town is about the size of Crawfordsville built on a level place along the bank of the river. The only attraction about the place, aside from its being the capitol of Ky. is its beautiful Cemetry, situated on a high bluff over hanging the Ky. River, on the west side of town, with a beautiful view of the little green valley lying to the South west   the railroad winding its serpentine way along the foot of the rocky cliffs . . . ."

William Anderson and John Rippetoe also were impressed by the monuments in the cemetery. Rippetoe wrote, "the military monument of the Kentucky soldiers who have fallen in battle is a very nice structure, also the monument over Daniel Boone is very interesting . . . ,"[21] and Anderson wrote a detailed description of these and other monuments in the cemetery.

At Frankfort, the artillerymen had daily target practice and William Anderson wrote, "The cannons shoot tolarbly well. they shot them about half a mile. They hit a door in about half a dozen shots."

On October 11, Anderson went foraging with a party that marched along the railroad until "We came across two negroes; and they took us to whare we could get old corne out of the crib all ready shucked." He commented, "The negroes tells us more about the rebles than we can find out any other way. They are more truthful than many of the white people that talk so much. I have all the confidence in some of the negroes. I have watched them and they tell the tail the same way every time." On October 12, James Dodd reported, "we have caught several spies that was coming through our camps we taken too from our camp yesterday evening and we left them I dont no wat they will do with them."[22]

After harassing Brigadier General George Morgan's Federal division during its retreat from Cumberland Gap to the Ohio River, Colonel John Hunt Morgan's Confederate cavalry rejoined Bragg's army near Harrodsburg on October 10. For a week his force retreated with the army, serving as rear guard but, because the retreating army had

---

21 The monument to Kentucky's dead of the Indian Wars, the War of 1812, and the Mexican War and the Daniel Boone monument remain attractions of the Frankfort cemetery.

22 Lilly Archives, James C. Dodd to Rueben and Mary Hinkel, Oct. 12, 1862.

cleared the line of march of all provisions, Morgan convinced Kirby Smith that he, Morgan, and his men would reach Middle Tennessee in better condition if he took another route. He received permission to circle around Buell's army and began to march on October 17 with about 1800 men.[23]

On October 23, word reached General Dumont in Frankfort that Morgan's force had passed through Versailles, about half way between Frankfort and Lexington, headed for Lawrenceburg, twelve miles south of Frankfort. That night, Dumont tried to catch Morgan by sending a small force of infantry and a section of Lilly's battery directly to Lawrenceburg while another section of the battery and three infantry regiments marched to Versailles. Morgan camped that night at Shyrock's Ferry, four miles from Lawrenceburg, with two regiments west of the Kentucky River and one camped on the east bank.[24]

John Rippetoe accompanied the smaller force that left Frankfort at 10:00 P.M. and marched to Lawrenceburg. Upon arriving there, they were told that Morgan had passed through four hours earlier, so the column returned to camp without searching for the Rebel force.

The other column, according to Henry Campbell, reached Versailles at 3:00 A.M. and laid over until daylight "refreshing ourselves with a little coffee   made out of a mud hole." Then they marched toward Lawrenceburg and "At the ford of the Ky. river we overtook the rear guard of the rebels and fired into them, causing them to abandon their wagons and leave on their horses   trotting right away from our Infantry   after a fruitless chase we returned to Frankfort firmly believing it useless to attempt to catch Cavalry with Infantry."

Colonel Basil Duke, who commanded the Second Kentucky Cavalry of Morgan's brigade, the unit encamped east of the river, wrote that the strategy of the Union force was poorly conceived because the shelling commenced before the Federal infantry was in a position close to the Rebel camp. He wrote, "It was a generous act of the officer [General Dumont], who came in our rear, to shell us, and it saved us a vast deal of trouble, if nothing worse. He had not even disturbed our pick-

23 Basil W. Duke, *A History of Morgan's Cavalry* (Bloomington: Indiana Univ. Press, 1960), pp. 268–83.
24 *Ibid.*, p. 287.

ets, but turning off the road, planted his guns on the high cliff that overlooks the ferry on that side, and sent us an intimation that we had better leave."[25] Possibly, General Dumont thought that discretion was the better part of valor. His soldiers were all recruits as green as the One hundred fifth Illinois which had been organized only six weeks and had received arms only two weeks before this action.[26] Better to scare Morgan off with some artillery fire than to challenge his veteran troopers with a force of untrained soldiers.

Mary Rippetoe, for one, was pleased with the result of the event. "I am glad you was disappointed in your race with Morgan," she wrote, "and hope that will be the way all the time altho I want reblion put down but I think as long as you are not in any engagement you are in not so much danger."[27]

After Bragg's retreat from Kentucky, the Federal army marched back to Nashville, and General Buell was replaced as its commander by Major General William S. Rosecrans, who changed the name to "The Army of the Cumberland." On October 26, "Entire Div. left Frankfort this morning   destination unknown   weather cold snow on the ground." A march of 150 miles in ten days went through Lawrenceburg, Bloomfield, Bardstown, New Haven, Hodgenville, Bacon Creek, Munfordville, and Horse Cave to Bowling Green. In addition to the larger towns, the battery passed through what John Rippetoe called "string towns consisting of one or two houses: the towns of this state are rather eccentric for they are nearly all strung out having but one street."

William Anderson described the appearance of the Bardstown area: "I never saw farms so spoiled so in my life. The fences is mostly burned along the road by soldiers marching through all the wood they get is fence rails. Brags army had marched through a few weaks before we came along. I saw many houses that they had toren down; and ruined forever, some of the very best of fraime and brick houses."

Near Hodgenville, "We passed the place where it is said that Aber-

25 *Ibid.*

26 Strong, pp. 5–9.

27 Ernest R. Davidson Collection, Mary J. Rippetoe to John H. Rippetoe, Oct. 26, 1862.

ham Lincoln was borned the house has been toren down; but the well still remains; and a heap of the rubbish of the house." Anderson also found that the ridges at the old Lincoln farm "was the greatest place for fruit I most ever saw."

On November 11 the battery began a march from Bowling Green toward Scottsville through "a very hilly country covered with Chestnut trees" but over bad roads that rains had made nearly impassable. They camped at Allen Springs in a meadow full of tall dry grass, which caught fire from the camp fires. "The guards that are usually stationed over the horses must have been asleep as no alarm was given until an old log stable situated near at hand was almost consumed," wrote Henry Campbell. "I had placed my horse in this stable along with Capt. Lillys and Just waked up in time to save the Capts horse. mine was burned to death   nothing left but the halter rings   Capts horse was unfit for use was obliged to give him to a citizen. his back was burned raw."

About the citizens of Scottsville, John Rippetoe wrote, "The most noticeable fashion of the ladies was their white sunbonnets, but as I do not notice the ladies much I do not recollect how they dressed otherwise, but the men wore the customary butternut pants and coats with stripped vests and they seem to be rather ignorant and as a man said the other day a for God saken set of people." At this time, John Rippetoe had his own horse, not a government issue, and asked Mary, "Now what would you think if I would buy Flingo. I have been riding him for the last two days and Benson says I may ride him from this on. He says he will sell him to me but to no one else and if I should ride him through the remainder of this war and we should both come out safe I think that I shall ride him home. Benson offers to let me ride him and if he should be lost he will bear the loss and if not he will sell him to me at the close of the war."

Mary apparently told him not to buy the horse because, on March 22, 1863, he wrote, "Benson's horse is dead, he took sick this morning and died in the evening. I thought it a Providential affair that you would not consent for me to buy him last fall."

Sickness among the men increased with the coming of cold, wet, winter weather. Twenty-three men died from sickness during the first year of the battery's service and another nineteen were discharged, apparently for poor health during the same period. Two others were transferred to other commands, and six were listed as deserters. Thus the battery was reduced one-third in strength before they began to campaign actively.[28]

Before leaving Frankfort, John Rippetoe told Mary that her brother, John R. Malcom, was sick and, with understandable concern, Mary asked John for all the particulars, requesting that he write " . . . and let us know whether the railroad is clere from Louisville to Frankfort and if a person can get there in safety . . . and if you are not gone and do go away try and have him sent to someplace that we can get to him . . . and whether he is taken good care of . . . or if you can do get him a furlough to come home and stay until he gets able for servis again . . . ."[29] John, of course, did not receive this letter until he was in Bowling Green and then advised Mary that John Malcom was in the hospital in Louisville.

By mid-November five men left at Indianapolis, New Albany, Frankfort, and Bowling Green had died with the first being Simpson Howard, who died of typhoid fever in Indianapolis on September 2. When news of this death reached the battery the entire company was shocked and took a proper democratic action to express their feelings and regret.

On September 11, a meeting of the entire company was called, with Albert Allen presiding and Lieutenant Scott serving as secretary. A motion by Captain Lilly was approved appointing a resolutions committee composed of Lieutenant Beck, Martin J. Miller, Dr. Watson, John D. Johnson, and David Rippetoe. The resolutions adopted: first, " . . . calls for him a name among the heroes of the land who have martyred themselves in the cause of freedom" although Simpson had served for only a few weeks; second, " . . . with friends of the deceased, we greatly sympathize in their bereavement;" and third, that the resolutions be sent to Greencastle, Crawfordsville, and Indianapolis papers.[30]

28 National Archives, "Descriptive Book."
29 Ernest R. Davidson Collection, Mary J. Rippetoe to John H. Rippetoe, Nov. 1, 1862.
30 Crawfordsville *Journal*, Oct. 16, 1862.

On November 22, Henry Campbell reported, "Drill with four guns. not sufficient men able for duty to man the entire battery. Bad weather has caused a great deal of sickness." A few days later he continued, "Two cases of measles broke out in the battery. Hope I won't get them." On December 2, he and William Anderson reported that there were thirty-four men on the sick list, and John Rippetoe wrote on November 30 that brother Benson had the mumps, one of several cases, and that there were incidents of camp diarrhea.

On December 14, John Rippetoe wrote, "John Davis died yesterday at 6 o'clock, he has been sick more than a week with the fever. I feel sorry for his poor wife and little ones, no husband comes to cheer her any more, no father to their poor children." He also reported a number of cases of measles—William Art, Thomas Evinger, Albert Scott, and Tilghman Edmiston "of our boys"—and that "[Isaac] McCoy and [Francis] Cummins I believe are a little homesick."

Henry Campbell reported on December 8 that John Perry Shepherd and Theodore Lyons were very sick, and ten days later, Shepherd's father arrived in camp to take John home. On January 3, Campbell wrote that three more men had died, including William Anderson on December 28. Although Campbell attributed Anderson's death to homesickness, William's mother wrote that he "caught a heep of cold and then took the yellow jaundice and then had a light atact of the tipoyd fever and got better of that and then ericipelis and that took him in a few days."[31]

On February 5, Campbell sat with George Grey, who was very sick; and when he died two days later, Henry wrote, "Whos turn next?" He was not in good health during this period, writing that he had a severe fever, and on February 21 "Went over to the camp of the 14 Ohio and bought 2 bottles of Wine and one of whiskey of their sutler costing $4. Was recommended by our surgeon to get a supply of these as I have been unwell for some time."

James C. Dodd wrote, "... was not very sick but can't gain any Strength I have rheumatism ever few days so that I can't hardly navi-

---

[31] Indiana Historical Society Library, Elizabeth Anderson to John and Eliza Boggs, Jan. 26, 1863. The father brought the body home and buried William at "our meeting house . . . in site of home."

gate." By February 8, "It [a letter] found me about well and stout as I was but it is a late thing Ruben I have had a hard time of it for about five months . . . ." But by autumn, Dodd was "well and healthy as a buck. geting fat once more."[32]

In his letter of March 22, John Rippetoe wrote, " . . . one of our neighborhood boys, James Reese was taken sick last Wednesday a week and last Thursday morning he died of typhoid pneumonia and as his constitution was not very strong it took him directly. I was with him when he died. He was not conscious during the part of the night I was with him which was from one till morning. He died about daylight. He seemed to be suffering very much all night till a little while before he died. This is the first person I ever saw die, it made me feel solemn."

When First Sergeant Robert Lane became so sick on an expedition to Lebanon, Tennessee, that he had to be left at a house, Henry Campbell wrote, " . . . a country Dr. that lives near here promises to attend him. But it don't make much difference, because if disease don't kill him, the bushwhackers will, we never expect to see him again." The sergeant died on April 11, 1863, "and was buried near the house, and no one to mourn over his death and no friend to even mark the place of his grave."

With so many men dead, sick, and discharged, the battery depended on men detailed from the infantry regiments to help man the guns, and the artillerymen were responsible for such men. John Rippetoe was interrupted while writing a letter to Mary: " . . . I was called on to take our section to bury a soldier. He was a man detailed out of seventy fifth Indiana regiment into the battery, he had some kind of lung disease."[33]

Although the company records do not always state the causes of the deaths in the battery, they do show that men died of typhoid fever, smallpox, chronic diarrhea, pneumonia, consumption, and "disease." Also they do not indicate the reasons for most discharges.

On November 15, the men cleared a dense thicket from a hill near

[32] Lilly Archives, James C. Dodd to Rueben and Mary Hinkel, Jan. 16, Feb. 8, Oct. 13, 1863.
[33] National Archives, "Descriptive Book" identifies the soldier as Thomas F. Montgomery.

Scottsville, Kentucky, and "made a very comfortable camp." The next day, Lieutenant Moses Beck arrived from Bowling Green with the wagon train "bringing 25 new horses for the battery, besides ammunition, clothing, and Stoves for our tents. quite a comfort for the damp weather, for it has been raining for the last three days constantly, keeping us in quarters pretty close." Four days later, Campbell reported, "Dick Gains our Sutler Just got in with a large load of goods."

"Boys have been at work between showers packing the new ammunition, which we got in place of that we had condemned," Henry Campbell recorded on November 21. "This new lot is the 'Hotchkiss' Shell. half percussion and half fuze has the reputation of being the best shell in use. The leaden band that fills the rifles of the gun are in the middle of the shell, instead of the rear end, as on the former."[34] That afternoon they drilled, using blank cartridges and fought a sham battle with the Seventy-first Indiana Infantry, firing 125 rounds.

On November 25, the battery received marching orders "to our intense delight . . . for the boys are all heartily tired of the hills and knobs of this benighted state." They marched on the Gallatin Pike, and when they passed a monument marking the Tennessee line, "The boys gave three cheers as it hove in sight." The road took them down a valley "so extremely narrow here, that the sun dont rise until 10 o'clock and sets about 4 P.M." and they "Crossed some streams of water to day that were the clearest I ever seen. the bottoms in some places were eight feet deep and looked as if you could touch them with your hand." The next day the battery camped south of Gallatin, a place that Campbell thought was "Like Bowling green it is one vast hospital for sick soldiers." He also remarked that the town "is now deserted by every body that used to live here."

[34] Coggins, pp. 78–81. The Hotchkiss shell was made in two pieces so that, upon firing, the explosion forced the base forward expanding a lead band into the grooves of the gun barrel. The ragged edge of lead remaining when the shell left the gun caused a tremendous scream, noted for its effect on morale. The ammunition condemned was probably the Parrott or Reed shell that had a cup of soft metal at the base which expanded into the rifling. The percussion shell was activated by a detonator that screwed into the nose and exploded the shell upon impact. The fuse shell used a metallic fuse that was cut to the desired length to explode the shell above or near the target. The fuse was lit by the flash of the gun discharge.

William Anderson made the trip in the hospital wagon. He wrote, "I have almost come to the conclusion that this war is going to destroy my health." This was about the last he wrote in his journal, and as previously told, he died on December 28.

The battery now was a part of Brigadier General William T. Ward's division and on December 7, Campbell reported, "Courier came in a few moments ago with the report that Moore's Brig. of our Div. had been surprised this morning and the entire brigade captured. They were posted about 15 miles from here at a place called Hartsville. The rebels under Morgan crossed the river early this morning and attacked our troops from the rear about daylight completely surprising and routing them. Most of the 2d Ind. cav. Cut their way out. 13 Ind Batt lost all their guns." Northern papers headlined the event "The Hartsville Disgrace."[35]

On December 10, Lilly's battery moved near to the fort on the east side of the railroad, which Henry Campbell reported was "a very substantial structure built in the shape of a Star with a gun in each point has just been finished."

On December 16, the battery received a change in their assignment of divisions that would have a profound influence on their future activity and morale. They were assigned to the Second Brigade of Brigadier General John J. Reynolds's Fifth Division, XIV Corps, Army of the Cumberland,[36] which became famous as "Wilder's Lightning Brigade" during the next year.

---

35 Crawfordsville *Journal*, Dec. 18, 1862, reported that the battery captured was two guns of the 5th Michigan.

36 *O.R.* Ser. 1, XX, pt. 2, 305.

IV

Wilder's Brigade

*The 17 Ind Col Wilder com'd
Joined our Brigade today   Col
Wilder assuming command of the
Brigade out ranking Col Miller.[1]
The 17 is an old well tried regiment
and we gladly welcome them to our
Brigade.*

December 24, 1862, was a more important day than Henry Campbell realized when he wrote this entry in his journal. The aggressiveness and intelligence of Colonel John T. Wilder and the pride and enthusiasm of the men of the Seventeenth Indiana, which quickly infected the other regiments, made this brigade the swiftest, most powerful, and best known force of its size in the Army of the Cumberland during 1863.

John T. Wilder was one of the imaginative and aggressive civilians who became army officers during the war. A native of the Catskill Mountains of New York, he had moved west in 1849 at the age of nineteen; and in his first job as a combination draftsman, patternmaker, and millwright at Ridgeway's Foundry in Columbus, Ohio, he did so well that, after a few years, he was offered half interest in the firm. He declined the offer, moving to Greensburg, Indiana, in 1857 to establish his own foundry, which grew to an establishment of one hundred employees by 1861.[2]

He was a recognized hydraulic-engineering authority, erecting mills throughout the Old Northwest and Upper South, and was called upon as a witness and umpire throughout the country in lawsuits concerning this specialty.

1 Abram O. Miller, colonel of the 72d Indiana.
2 Samuel C. Williams, *General John T. Wilder* (Bloomington: Indiana Univ. Press, 1936), pp. 1–6.

When war fever struck in 1861, Wilder cast two wrought iron cannons in his foundry and organized an artillery company, but because the state then required infantry, the unit, with Wilder as captain, became a part of the Seventeenth Indiana Infantry. The regiment was sent to West Virginia on July 1, 1861, and participated in the early campaigns in that region. Because his leadership qualities quickly became apparent, Wilder was promoted to lieutenant colonel, jumping over the rank of major.

At the expiration of their three-month enlistment, the Seventeenth came home, re-enlisted for a three-year term with Wilder as colonel, and were assigned to the Army of the Ohio, headquartered in Louisville. At this time, Wilder's original company was detached, organized into an artillery battery designated the "First Independent Battery," and later "Wilder's Battery," and returned to West Virginia.[3]

During the Confederate invasion of Kentucky in 1862, Wilder attracted national attention when, with a force of 3,500 recruits of whom only 1,200 were armed, he held up General Bragg's army for three days at Munfordville with a little fighting and a good deal of bluff before surrendering the post.[4]

Wilder's intelligence, imagination, mechanical knowledge, and topographical intuition were revealed in the activities of his brigade. As shall be seen, his initiative resulted in the mounting of the brigade, the first mounted infantry force in the Army of the Cumberland; and his mechanical understanding led to obtaining the best arms available for his men. His soldiers believed he had an intuitive sense of topography since he always seemed to know his way out of a tight spot. Actually, "It was his habit to interview the natives very closely and before he started anywhere he knew where he was going and where he could get out, if necessary."[5]

Wilder's brigade originally was made up of the Seventeenth, Seventy-second, and Seventy-fifth Indiana and the Ninety-eighth Illinois Infantry Regiments, in addition to the Eighteenth Indiana Bat-

---

3 *Ibid.*; Terrell, III, 448.

4 Williams, pp. 7–8; Indianapolis *State Sentinel*, Aug. 26, 1862.

5 W. H. H. Benefiel, *History of Wilder's Lightning Brigade* (Pendleton, Ind.: The Times Print, *ca.* 1913), p. 11; Williams, p. 13.

tery.[6] A few months later, when the brigade was being converted into a mounted force, the men of the Seventy-fifth decided that they preferred to remain foot soldiers, and their place was taken by the One hundred twenty-third Illinois Regiment.[7]

After the Seventeenth arrived on December 24, the battery moved their tents onto a hill near this regiment's camp. The next day, Henry Campbell reported, "Some of the boys had about half their things stolen last night the consequences of camping near an old Regt. they swear they will get even with them before long." He also noted that "17 Boys have a splendid String band with them they serenaded Capt Lilly last night."

On December 26, Reynolds's division, including Wilder's brigade, broke camp at Gallatin and marched fifteen miles toward Scottsville, Kentucky, because John Hunt Morgan again was raiding in Kentucky. Rain began to fall at 10:00 A.M. and continued during the next day, causing Henry Campbell to comment, "Raining The most disagreeable thing in the world to a soldier is marching in the rain. he don't mind sleeping in it, but to be continually dripping knapsack blanket rations and everything else wet. growing heavier and heavier every moment is the very worst of misfortunes." At 5:00 P.M. on December 27, the brigade went into camp at Scottsville with "everything soaked."

John Rippetoe also commented about the rain, " . . . I tell you it poured down certain, it ran down one of my legs and nearly filled my boot but Providence favored us in the evening by letting the rain stop and we pitched our tents at Scottsville for the night and burned a good many rails drying our clothes so the next morning we were ready for the march with a clear day and dry clothes . . . ."

At 2:00 P.M. on December 28, the brigade reached and forded the Barren River and camped nearby. The next day they marched to Glasgow, where they remained until December 31, when the brigade moved toward Munfordville, camping that night at Bear Wallow.

By this time, Morgan was on his way back to Tennessee after raid-

---

6 *O.R.* Ser. 1, XX, pt. 1, 179. Col. Milton S. Robinson commanded the 75th Indiana, and Col. John J. Funkhouser commanded the 98th Illinois.

7 Benefiel, *Wilder's Brigade*, p. 6; *O.R.* Ser. 1, XXIII, pt. 1, 412. Col. James Monroe commanded the 123d Illinois.

ing to within eighteen miles of Louisville, and on January 1, his scouts reported the presence of Reynolds's division, which he attempted to ride around. When Union pickets saw some of his men, Wilder's brigade marched after them, but, as might be expected, the foot soldiers were unable to come close to the cavalrymen. In desperation, Wilder attempted to mount men of the Seventeenth Indiana on mules from the wagon train; but these animals, never having been ridden, objected, and the attempt was a fiasco. Wilder retained the idea of mounting his men, however, with important future results.[8]

On New Year's Day, Henry Campbell reported, "Plenty of 'Apple Jack' in the country   nearly every house has a small distillery connected with it. Boys all Jolly   as a general thing all about half drunk."

While Wilder's brigade was chasing Morgan, the major Battle of Stones River was fought during the three days of December 31, 1862, through January 2, 1863, just north of Murfreesboro by the Union Army of the Cumberland and the Confederate Army of Tennessee. The result of the battle was generally considered to have been a draw, even though Henry Campbell heard, "All of our army has achieved a glorious victory at Murfreesboro. completely whiped Braggs army." After the battle Bragg withdrew to a new defense line centered at Tullahoma on the Plateau of the Barrens, forty miles southeast of Murfreesboro, leaving the field to the Federal soldiers.

Orders for Reynolds's division to march to Nashville arrived on January 2, and Lilly's battery marched six miles into Cave City the following day. Campbell wrote, "Commenced loading our Battery on the cars last night about 12 o'clock. Guns and Caissons and wagons were crowded together on platform cars, while the horses and mules were placed in box cars, takes 12 cars to hold our Battery. hurried every thing as rapidly as possible and got everything ready to go by 9 o'clock A.M. Rained all the time we were loading and continued until we arrived at Bowling green. Train started as soon as we were ready . . . . Rode on top of a boxcar going through one of the tunnels and liked to have suffocated from the smoke   staid most of the way on the Engine . . . . Arrived at Nashville Just after dark. began raining again as soon as

[8] Glenn W. Sunderland, *Lightning at Hoover's Gap: Wilder's Brigade in the Civil War* (New York: Thomas Yoseloff, 1969), pp. 21–23.

we got in. Unloaded the battery on a large platform built upon a level with the cars—in two hours time we got everything off and hitched up

moved thro the city to the south side and camped at the foot of Fort Negley   throughly drenched."

On January 5, the division marched south as a guard for the longest wagon train the men had ever seen, over 1,000 wagons hauling rations for the Army of the Cumberland. At LaVergne, Campbell reported passing a train of 250 ambulances filled with wounded, and he saw "hundreds of our wagons burned by Wheelers Cav. during the Battle."[9] The battery encamped for the night seven miles from Murfreesboro, but the wagon train moved on to get rations to the troops at the front. Rain continued all night, and Campbell "slept on two fence rails over a mud hole."

In the Battle of Stones River the North had suffered 13,249 casualties and the South 10,266.[10] When they marched through a part of the battlefield on January 6, Lilly's men could see the carnage, and John Rippetoe wrote, " . . . the graves are tolerably thick, we saw some rebels burying their comrades under guard. they were throwing the dirt on some while there were three lying in the mud where they had been thrown out of the wagon in which they had been brought. it seems hard to be treated in such a manner after one is dead but I suppose it was the best that could be done under the circumstances. there were said to be a great many poor secesh lying out in the woods unburied but were being hunted up and put away as fast as possible." Henry Campbell said, "Every house in town [Murfreesboro] has been converted into a hospital   over 5000 rebel wounded in town beside our own."

James C. Dodd also described the battlefield: "Last camped by a brick house that had been Shatered to peces by the Canon balls the trees were torn to peces too just as there had been a big storm passed threw & the horses lay Scatered over the fields by the hundreds but the little ridges that were freshly thrown up and a Small board Sot up at one end Seemed to be more plentyer than anything else I could see.

[9] Stanley F. Horn, *The Army of Tennessee* (Indianapolis: Bobbs-Merrill, 1941), p. 198. Maj. Gen. Joseph Wheeler, commanding the cavalry corps, Army of Tennessee, rode completely around the Union army, destroying 300 wagons and $1 million worth of army stores.

[10] Downey, p. 58.

they was in every direction Seemed as though they were baried where they was killed & the Rebels a great many of them was baried in cornfields just laid in a furrow and a little dirt thrown on them some of there hands and feet sticking out."[11]

On January 8, Campbell reported, "Boys went out foraging and gobbled some hogs. plenty of fresh meat now." Three days later, Henry rode over the battlefield with Lieutenant Hartman and observed, "Large trees nearly one foot in diameter were completely torn in two by the shell and lay in thick profusion all through the woods." He also reported, "No water near us fit to drink, had to take our horses through Murfreesboro to Stone river for water. That we get for ourselves scarcely fit for hogs."

The weather turned so cold on the night of January 15 that the soldiers "Had all the horses out exercising to keep them from freezing we have no shelter nor blankets for them and they are obliged to stand out in the open air." Snow also fell, and the next afternoon "Boys all turned out in the field in the rear of our quarters and had a rabbit hunt caught four."

At dusk on January 23, the entire brigade left camp and marched on the Bradyville pike; "moved light," wrote Henry Campbell, "taking one days rations and leaving our caissons." They stopped for an hour at 4:00 A.M., made coffee, and then resumed their march toward Woodbury, twenty miles east of Murfreesboro; "began raining and continued all day a cold disagreeable rain. making the roads very bad, worst we ever had the misfortune to travel over," Campbell wrote. That night they camped on a hill four miles from Woodbury and "Made tents out of the Tarpaulins and slept on wet grass mud knee deep." Returning toward Murfreesboro the next day, Campbell wrote, "Gobbled two good horses on the road hid among the ceader thickets."

John Rippetoe was unable to see that the march accomplished anything important; "the object of the expedition," he wrote, "was to act with some other troops that had gone by another road in the capture of a rebel camp of some 1200 or 1500 men. We were to attack the rebels

11 Lilly Archives, James C. Dodd to Reuben and Mary Hinkel, Jan. 16, 1863.

in the rear but they did not wait till we got to the place and had a fight with the rebels when the latter took to their heels and were gone when we got there; if those who were to cooperate with us had used a little stradegy and instead of pushing them when they had found out that we were not in the rear and had fallen back till they knew we were there and then pushed on them again we might have taken them all prisoners with very little loss of life . . . ."

Like all soldiers, Henry Campbell became expert with thread and needle. "Have turned taylor for the last day or two. been lining the cape of my coat with rubber so that on unbuttoning it off the collar and turning it wrong side out it becomes water proof." On January 27, he mentioned that Captain Lilly and the Second Section had gone to Nashville as a guard for a wagon train.

On February 1, Captain Lilly returned bringing two mountain howitzers for the battery. "They are about 2 feet long and of a 12 lb. bore," Henry Campbell wrote, "mounted like a field piece only on a smaller scale." The mountain howitzers were smoothbore brass cannon with a bore of 4.62 inches, the same as the 12-pounder Napoleon, but with a tube only 32.9 inches long. A one-half pound charge of powder could throw an 8.90-pound projectile 900 yards with 5-degree elevation. Weighing only 220 pounds and mounted on a 120-pound carriage, they were light enough that two horses or mules could haul them and keep up with the cavalry. Ammunition was carried in boxes that were attached to pack saddles.[12] The guns also were light enough that they could be disassembled and carried on mules when campaigning in inaccessible areas.[13]

Confederate cavalry officer Basil Duke thought "that no gun is so well adapted in all respects to the wants of cavalry, as these little guns." He wrote that they could travel any kind of road, over ravines, up hills, through thickets, almost anywhere a horseman could go; and without attracting attention, they could be moved very close to the enemy and advanced by hand as the battle line moved. They were accurate up to

[12] Lord, *They Fought for the Union*, pp. 49–51, 156; Coggins, p. 75.
[13] Indiana Historical Society Library, William O. Crouse, "Journal of W. O. Crouse"; Coggins, p. 75.

800 yards with shells and could fire canister from 200 to 300 yards as effectively as a 12-pounder, ranges usually adequate in cavalry skirmishes.[14]

The next day, Campbell wrote, "Boys at work fixing amunition for the 'Jackass Battery' as the howitzers are called. Taking the 12 lbs. Napoleon charge and cutting it down to ½ the amt of powder."

Faced by a superior cavalry force commanded by Joseph H. Wheeler, Nathan Bedford Forrest, and John Hunt Morgan, General Rosecrans tried in vain to get the government to authorize the raising of additional cavalry regiments. As late as May 10, he reported having only 6,356 cavalrymen mounted and could count on fewer than 5,000 on duty and fit for service at any time and he estimated that the Confederates facing him could field 6,000 or 8,000 more cavalry. He could not guard his long supply line, running from Murfreesboro to Louisville, could not adequately protect the Union people in the areas supposedly occupied by the Federal army, and could not obtain sufficient forage unless he had more mounted men. Although he was not allowed to recruit cavalry, he did receive approval during January to mount 5,000 infantry, but did not receive authorization to purchase horses.[15]

Colonel Wilder proposed to General Rosecrans that he be allowed to mount his brigade by impressing horses from the Rebel citizens in the surrounding country, a suggestion that Rosecrans enthusiastically accepted. On February 3, Reynolds's division began a sweep of the country to capture horses because "Gen Rozencrans intends to make our brigade a mounted one and has given orders for Col. Wilder to 'press in' all the horses he can find in the country."[16] The mountain howitzers under the command of Lieutenant Rippetoe were a part of the expedition that marched through Auburn, Liberty, Alexandria, and Lebanon to the east and north of Murfreesboro. They returned to Murfreesboro

---

[14] Duke, p. 179; Lord, *They Fought for the Union*, p. 157. Canister shot was a tin can loaded with musket balls. On firing, the can disintegrated, turning the cannon into a giant shotgun, especially effective at short ranges.

[15] A. H. Guernsey and H. M. Alden, *Harper's Pictorial History of the Civil War*, 2 vols. (Chicago: The Puritan Press, 1894), II, 526.

[16] *O.R.* Ser. 1, XXIII, pt. 1, 74. Rosecrans gave Reynolds oral orders for the expedition and followed with Special Order 44, Feb. 16, 1863.

on February 7, after capturing 43 of the enemy, 300 horses and mules, and 50 beef cattle at a cost of five men missing.[17]

During the march, the soldiers entered the plantations of Rebel citizens, driving off horses, mules, and cattle and then loading corn from the cribs into wagons. The quartermasters gave receipts for the stock and grain that read, "to be paid for at the close of the war, on proof of loyalty," which were not very satisfying to the plantation owners.[18]

The mounting of the brigade required a change from infantry to cavalry uniforms from which the men removed the distinctive yellow markings so they would not be mistaken for cavalrymen, who were not highly respected by the foot soldiers. Since they would use the horses for transportation but would fight dismounted as infantry, they were not issued sabers, but Wilder equipped each man with a hatchet with a two-foot handle—a weapon in combat and a tool in camp and the unit was temporarily known as "The Hatchet Brigade."[19] The soldiers also had to learn cavalry regulations for bivouac and the care of animals, a task in which Henry Campbell assisted: 'The bugler of the 17 Ind. was over to day to get some calls, as they have one or two Cos. mounted. Wrote him 'Stable,' 'Water,' 'Feed,' and 'Boots and Saddles'—thats all they need at present."

The soldiers adopted some of their leader's aggressiveness by building their own wagons from wrecks found along the road, shoeing their own horses, and when possible, securing coal for their forges themselves, not content to requisition and await action by the quartermaster department. Probably no other group had as many distinguishing characteristics as Wilder's brigade.[20]

After the first expedition, the men spent a few days in camp. On February 10, Henry Campbell wrote, "Some cuss stole my bran new horse blanket off my horse last night. Some body has to lose one to night." The next day, Campbell helped Captain Lilly build a wood

17 *Ibid.*, 42.
18 John Fitch, *Annals of the Army of the Cumberland* (Philadelphia: J. B. Lippincott, 1864), p. 631.
19 Williams, p. 13.
20 *Ibid.*

floor in his tent and then he and James Binford built bunks in their tent, an improvement since they had been sleeping on the ground until then.

On February 15, Campbell reported that four Crawfordsville visitors were in the camp: Zack Mahorning, who had ridden in with the sutler; Dr. M. Herndon, who came to take James Binford home because of illness but failed to get a discharge for him; Harry Morgan; and George Hough, sutler of the First Kentucky Infantry. "Looks something like home to night to see four familiar faces sitting around the camp fire and chatting about folks and matters at home."

On the sixteenth he reported, "Was introduced to Gen. Cruft[21] to day" and, on the twentieth, he received his pay amounting to $60.65, from which he paid the sutler $16.35 that he owed, and sent $25.00 home. John Rippetoe sent home "all I can possibly spare and if I should keep my health I will not need much."

Rippetoe wrote that the battery celebrated Washington's birthday "by firing thirty four guns one for each state. some of the states think that they are out of the union, but we do not intend that to be the case long if we can help it." He also reported that the war situation looked favorable: "There are men who are leaving their homes here in Tennessee and other southern states in the western department, who wander among the hills and mountains to avoid being pressed into the southern army, a great many come into the union camps. There is a regiment forming at this place of Tennesseans which now numbers over four hundred and they are daily coming in . . . ."

On March 3, Henry Campbell reported, "Had two more Mtn. Howitzers added to our Batt making 4 in all. These with our 6 Rodmans makes us a 10 gun Battery the only one in the Department." Because Lilly did not have enough men to work the extra guns, Colonel Wilder wrote to Governor Morton requesting that Wilder's battery be sent to him.[22] This company, originally recruited by Wilder in 1861, had just been reorganized in Indianapolis after being captured and exchanged. Upon reorganization they were renamed "Wilder's Battery"; but in-

21 Brig. Gen. Charles Cruft, a Terre Haute lawyer and alumnus of Wabash College.
22 Indiana State Library, Archives Division, John T. Wilder to Oliver P. Morton, Mar. 8, 1863.

stead of being assigned to Wilder, they were sent to the Department of the Ohio and participated in Major General Ambrose Burnside's Knoxville campaign.[23]

On March 3 a part of the battery left with the brigade for Readyville on the road to Woodbury, and since John Rippetoe's Rodman gun was not taken along, "I went with the little brass guns which are drawn by mules so I was more at liberty than common and had more time to look around."

The expedition camped at Readyville during the night of March 3, and the next day part of the Seventeenth Indiana made a charge into Woodbury, driving a force of Rebels out of the town and capturing the rear guard of 150 men. After the Yankees left, the Rebels moved back into Woodbury, and the Union force made plans to capture them.

On March 6, John Rippetoe wrote, "We went to Woodbury to drive the Rebels from that place and I tell you we had the roughest roads you ever saw. We left the pike and went right over the mountains to take them in the rear, another party being sent to the left to meet us in the rear, while the third party took the pike to the town, but our trap was laid in vain, some scroundrel of a rebel warned them and they left before we got there, so there was another fight spoiled." During the night of March 7, the force rendezvoused at Readyville and, the next day, returned to Murfreesboro. According to Rippetoe, the Seventeenth Indiana and the battery traveled a roundabout way, covering thirty miles, and were in the saddle for twelve hours.

Wilder advised Governor Morton of the success of this expedition and of the plans for the brigade, telling him that the Seventeenth Indiana were all mounted and the Ninety-eight Illinois were then getting their horses. "We take Evry Horse from the Rebels, and a busy time we have. So far, it has Not Cost the Government one dollar to Mount My Men, or to forage the Horses   if I can Get My Brigade in such a shape as I wish, the Guerrillas Will Not hover around this army so closely. I am to have Six Hundred Pack Mules attached to the Brigade, and a small pontoon train, to use as Batteaus for rivers, or as a Bridge for streams."[24]

23 Terrell, III, 448–49.
24 John T. Wilder to Oliver P. Morton, Mar. 8, 1863.

On March 9, Henry Campbell reported, "Captain Lilly left for Nashville this Evening to meet his wife who is coming down to stay with us a while." The captain and Mrs. Lilly arrived in camp two days later and were quartered in "old Mrs. Bivins house" that had been used exclusively by Colonel Wilder, but he gave up part of the house to the Lillys. Wilder had encouraged Lilly to invite his wife because he was hoping that Mrs. Wilder would visit him and thought that Mrs. Lilly's presence might help his wife decide in favor of the trip.

The day after Mrs. Lilly's arrival, Henry Campbell visited Nashville with Lieutenant Hartman to requisition horses. "Had a very pleasant trip   drew 20 horses   sent them through by the pike under charge of one of the Sergts. Returned with Ltd. Hartman on the cars this morning [March 15]. Seen Harry Dunlap at the City he is a Capt. in the 2d. Ind. Cav." On March 18 camp was moved closer to Colonel Wilder's headquarters, and Henry Campbell commented, "Our camp is much better situated than formerly   although it is in very close proximity to the soldiers grave yard that every day receives a dozen new inmates."

On March 22, John Rippetoe wrote to Mary that John Malcom, her brother, had been discharged and was on his way home. Rippetoe was going to have Malcom carry oral messages to her but "my feelings overcame me so I could not tell him what I wanted to tell you . . . I am still trying to do what is right and by the grace of God I intend to be religious. In the next place I am satisfied that I am doing my duty at present by trying to serve my country as a soldier battling for the old flag for which very many patriots in other years have bled and died. I also wanted John to tell you that I would like very much to see you and little Peter but I could not for when I commenced talking about home I broke down; the thought of home overcame me so I could not talk." He also reported that he had been out foraging and told the results of a fight that Colonel A. S. Hall's First Brigade of the division had with Wheeler and Morgan.[25]

Hall had marched from Murfreesboro on March 18 with 1,828 men looking for Rebels who had been demonstrating in Wilson County. The Confederate force under Joseph Wheeler and John Hunt Morgan

---

[25] Hall commanded the 1st Brigade, 5th Division, XIV Corps.

were reported to number 4,000 and were looking for a fight with the smaller Yankee force, but Hall picked his ground well, Vaught's Hill near the town of Milton, about fifteen miles northeast of Murfreesboro, on what was called the Las Casas pike. The Rebels were confident of defeating this smaller force, but Hall's position was strong and his men were willing to stand. After the Yankees had repulsed several attacks, the fight became an artillery duel. Hall, not knowing how badly he had hurt the enemy, expected another attack, but the Confederates retired late in the day, leaving about four hundred killed and wounded, whereas the Union losses were only seven killed and thirty-three wounded.[26] This action created a good feeling throughout the Army of the Cumberland and especially among the men in Wilder's brigade, who were so closely associated with Hall's. Henry Campbell reported that one hundred of the Confederate wounded were brought into Murfreesboro.

On March 23, Campbell told of the decision that was to make Wilder's brigade the most powerful fighting force of its size in the army:

> The 17th Ind. our most enterprising Regt. had all intended buying themselves the Henry 16 shot rifle[27] and paying for them out of their wages ... Gen. [Colonel] Wilder admiring the zeal manifested by this Regiment, to make themselves the most effective command in the service   has Just Closed a contract with Mr. Spencer   the inventor of the celebrated "Spencer 7 shooting rifle"   to furnish our entire Brigade with them at the expense of each man.

Christopher M. Spencer had patented a repeating rifle in 1860 that had a magazine in the stock into which a metal tube with seven bullets could be inserted. The soldier could preload a number of tubes and was able to fire fifteen rounds a minute compared to one or two rounds that an ordinary soldier could fire with the standard muzzle-loading musket used throughout the war by the infantry. The Spencer was a .52 caliber rifle that used a copper, rim-fire cartridge, at a time when most weapons used percussion caps. The rifle had a range of 2,000 yards and could penetrate 13 inches of pine at 50 yards.[28]

[26] "Battle of Vaught's Hill," Cincinnati *Gazette*, Mar. 24, 1863.
[27] "News from Murfreesboro," Cincinnati *Gazette*, Mar. 11, 1863.
[28] Spencer Wilson, "How Soldiers Rated Carbines," *Civil War Times Illustrated* V, No. 2 (May 1966), pp. 40–44; Lord, *They Fought for the Union*, p. 164.

Spencer had demonstrated the effectiveness of the rifle to the army ordnance department, but this group, under Brigadier General James W. Ripley, "combated all new ideas in the fabrication of firearms, artillery, and projectiles." They did not authorize the purchase of the weapon because they claimed the soldiers with such a gun would waste ammunition. A more legitimate concern was the difficulty of maintaining large supplies of ammunition at the front with a transportation system dependent on wagons.[29]

The ordnance department did not become interested in the Spencer rifle until after President Lincoln had received a personal demonstration by the inventor during which the President fired the gun at a target. According to John Hay, Lincoln's secretary, the new weapon "was a wonder, firing seven shots, readily and deliberately, in less than half a minute."[30] The President overcame Ripley's objections, and 10,000 Spencer rifles were ordered in early 1863.[31] When delivery was delayed and the ordnance department appeared to be on the verge of cancelling the order, Spencer began visiting the field armies to gain their support. Thus he came to Murfreesboro and demonstrated the rifle to General Rosecrans, General Thomas, General Reynolds, Colonel Wilder, and Captain Lilly.[32]

Wilder and his men were so impressed with the weapon that Wilder received an enthusiastic approval when he proposed that each man buy one of the repeaters out of his pay. Wilder then contacted his bankers in Greensburg and arranged to borrow the money to buy the rifles needed to arm the entire brigade at a price of $35 each. The soldiers signed notes, which Wilder cosigned, but before the men began actual payment, the government agreed to pay for the rifles and the notes were cancelled.[33] Wilder's foresight was rewarded because the repeaters for his brigade arrived before the start of the next major campaign, whereas 2,000 Spencers consigned to Rosecrans by the ordnance department

29 Lord, *They Fought for the Union*, p. 154; Weigley, p. 224.

30 Carl Sandburg, *Abraham Lincoln: The War Years*, 4 vols. (New York: Harcourt, 1939), II, 241.

31 Robert V. Bruce, *Lincoln and the Tools of War* (Indianapolis: Bobbs-Merrill, 1956), pp. 252–56.

32 Benefiel, *Wilder's Brigade*, pp. 4–5.

33 Williams, p. 14; W. H. H. Benefiel, *The Seventeenth Indiana Regiment: A History from its Organization to the End of the War* (n.p., ca. 1910).

arrived during the campaign and were issued to the Ninety-second Illinois and the Thirty-ninth Indiana that were being converted into mounted infantry regiments.

Wilder's men were not allowed to sit idly until their new weapons arrived, and on April 1, began a broad sweep through the area east of Nashville and Murfreesboro. The units making the raid were mounted men of the Seventeenth, Seventy-second, and Ninety-eighth regiments, four Rodman guns and the four mountain howitzers of Lilly's battery, the unmounted Seventy-fifth Indiana, all from Wilder's brigade, and the One hundred first Indiana and One hundred twenty-third Illinois of Hall's brigade. The expedition moved from camp at 2:00 P.M., marched through Murfreesboro, and on the Lebanon pike toward a pontoon bridge across the North Fork of Stones River.[34] Along the way, Henry Campbell "Seen a Cotton Gin in operation. Worked for the U. S. by willing contrabands."[35]

At 6:00 A.M. on April 2, the foot soldiers and the Rodman guns of the battery, all commanded by Colonel Monroe, took the pike for Lebanon, while the mounted force, under Wilder, with the four mountain howitzers, took the Las Casas road to the east and then the Cainsville road to the north bringing them into the rear of Lebanon. The two columns met in the square at Lebanon at 3 P.M. but failed to capture any Rebels except a few loiterers.[36] The battery, according to Henry Campbell, camped in the yard of the "Cumberland Institute, a College erected for the education of the ministers for the Cumberland Presbyterian Church." He also remarked that the citizens of Lebanon were very aristocratic, and that the town was "a regular hot bed of secesh."

The next morning, while visiting downtown stores, "A few things stuck to my fingers." The soldiers particularly appropriated medicine from a drugstore for use in their hospital "which at present is rather

[34] *O.R.* Ser. 1, XXIII, pt. 1, 200–203.

[35] Negroes were popularly referred to as "contrabands" after Maj. Gen. Ben Butler, in discussing the legal question of whether slaves held in his camp should be returned to their owners, wrote, "The Negro must now be regarded as contraband, since every able-bodied hand, not absolutely required on the plantations, is impressed by the enemy into the military service as a laborer on the fortification." Sandburg, I, 278–79.

[36] *O.R.* Ser. 1, XXIII, pt. 2, 200–203.

poorly stocked." Their shopping was interrupted: ". . . we had quite a scare   Rebels were reported advancing on us.—Our battery was un-hitched and the boys scattered all over town, but in five minutes time we had everything hitched up and ready for action. The infantry was quickly formed in line of battle and everybody eagerly expecting to see the enemy appear from the woods opposit camp but it proved to be a company of our men returning from a scout."

At 3:00 P.M. the expedition marched again, this time toward Rome on the Cumberland River east of Lebanon. After traveling six miles, the battery camped on a large farm, and while feeding their horses with hay from a barn, the artillerymen "discovered a lot of nice hams hid away under the straw, which we very quickly appropriated for our use."

During the march to Rome on April 4, they passed a "Sugar and tobaco manufactory," and the contents, including 5,000 cigars, were confiscated and distributed among the men. The column reached Rome at 10:00 A.M. and there was joined by the mounted force and mountain howitzers.

A small force of guerillas attacked a Seventy-second Indiana picket post and captured two men who, Colonel Wilder reported, " . . . were inhumanly butchered by their captors the next day, near Lebanon."[37] The two men had been tied to a tree, shot three times, and then cut loose; but one of the men, John Vance, although hurt badly, feigned death until the bushwhackers had left. He crawled eight miles and met a detachment of Union soldiers who took him into Murfreesboro.[38]

Campbell wrote that Rome "is quite a small dilapidated town on the south bank of the Cumberland. The best part of the town was burnt by our gunboats last year when they shelled the place." On April 5, the column marched east of Rome to Carthage, the head of navigation on the Cumberland River, and Henry told his mother, " . . . we have been marching over classical ground   journeying from Lebanon to Rome, and from Rome to Carthage."[39]

The column divided again on April 6, the infantry force marching south on the turnpike to Alexandria while the mounted men and the

37 *Ibid.*
38 Merrill, II, 203.
39 *Ibid.*, 201.

Second Section of Lilly's battery took a route called the Sandcastle road that John Rippetoe described as "the roughest, hilliest, worst institution to be called a road that we ever had the misfortune to travel over."

They "passed the residence of Col. Stokes brother   a rank Rebel. The Col.[40] who was along with us told the boys to help themselves, that his brother was a rebel and no better than any other rebels." After leaving this place, the column crossed into a little valley that the war had not visited and the men found "chickens, turkeys, and other good things" in abundance.

That evening, Henry Campbell went over to a house near camp to see if he could talk himself into a good supper. "Found quite a good looking girl, dressed in 'home spun', superintending the baking of a hoe cake," he wrote; "... I turned the conversation to herself   remarking that I had travelled over a great deal of the South but had failed to see a good looking girl until now. 'Pshaw,' says she, 'yer poking fun at me.' " Henry assured her that he was in earnest and that she was the prettiest girl in Tennessee. She told him that if he really thought so, "you just oughter seen me before I had the di-a-ree." The conversation was interrupted by a loud laugh from outside the door. Captain Lilly had followed his bugler out of curiosity and told the story around camp. Henry did not get his supper there because, in his embarrassment at being discovered, he "immediately vamosed."

The column marched at six o'clock the next morning. Campbell wrote, "One man of our battery was captured this morning. He straggled off from the road, and a little afterward we heard two shots fired. That was the last we ever saw of him."[41]

Soon the force began marching "over the roughest limestone rocks imaginable—5 miles out dumped down a steep hill into a very beautiful valley. at the bottom of the hill is the residence of Col. Stokes. his wife and two daughters are living there in spite of the threats of the bushwhackers to kill them and burn the house over their heads." Just

[40] William B. Stokes, colonel of the 5th Tennessee Cavalry, was greatly feared by the Rebels in the area because of his knowledge of them and the country. Merrill, II, 202.

[41] *Ibid*; National Archives, "Descriptive Book." The soldier probably was Alexander Day, listed as a deserter on Apr. 9.

beyond this place, the advance guard encountered Confederate cavalry, "and the column started up at a gallop which we continued for about 1 mile and then formed a line of Battle accross the creek facing Snow Hill where the rebels retreated to."

The Rebels were Brigadier General John A. Wharton's brigade of Wheeler's cavalry. Colonel Wilder tried to trap them by sending the Seventeenth to get in the rear while the battery, supported by the Seventy-second and Ninety-eighth, crossed "the creek on a bridge and went into position on a slight hill near a grave yard." The Confederates retreated, however, before the Seventeenth could get into position, so only the rear guard of thirty-nine men was captured. Campbell wrote that the Rebel position was a very strong one, and he thought "it was our Battery that scared them as it was in plain sight from the gap."

After making sure the enemy had fled, the column marched on to the Liberty turnpike where they rejoined the foot column, and on April 8, Colonel Wilder reported, "Having our hands full of animals, prisoners, and negroes, it was deemed best to return to Murfreesboro . . . ." He had with him 400 horses and mules, 194 Negroes, and 88 prisoners[42] while the artillerymen had "captured a good cow . . . we now have fresh milk for our coffee."

On April 20, Reynold's entire division, with eight guns of the battery and Colonel Eli Long's cavalry brigade, marched for Readyville and McMinnville, taking twelve days' rations. In the evening, the battery camped at Cripple Creek near Readyville, and Henry Campbell wrote, "Took my horse 'Pet' down and washed her off until she was white as snow."

Reveille was sounded at three o'clock the next morning, and the column marched toward McMinnville, where John Hunt Morgan's Rebel cavalry brigade was bivouacked. The infantry took the direct road, while part of the cavalry brigade, the mounted men of Wilder's brigade, and the battery went a roundabout way to come into the rear, reaching the east side of the town at 5:00 P.M. Here the Seventeenth Indiana scouts captured a picket post "and then with out loss of time, formed with the 4 Regular Cav. and led a saber Charge through town. John Morgans force scattered in every direction without waiting to

42 *O.R.* Ser. 1, XXIII, pt. 2, 200–203.

see what was the matter. The scouts came very near capturing Morgan himself. he escaped by the fleetness of his horse. The 4 Reg. Captured Dick McCann, the celabrated bushwhacker."

Sidney Speed wrote that the only reason Morgan escaped was that the officer in command of the advance would not allow the men to go ahead of him in the pursuit, but after missing Morgan, the soldiers ignored the officer and chased and caught up to McCann, who refused to surrender until the troopers knocked him off his horse. McCann, however, escaped during the night.[43] Meanwhile, Long's main force struck the railroad, destroyed the telegraph and bridges, captured a train with seventy-five Confederate soldiers, and recaptured a company of Federals who were P.O.W.'s.[44]

Wilder's brigade in McMinnville destroyed the depot, bridges, 600 blankets, 30,000 pounds of bacon, 200 bales of cotton, a cotton factory, two mills, the courthouse, the homes of some leading Rebels, and some small amounts of sugar, rice, and whiskey. In all, they captured 130 men and held Mrs. John Morgan in custody for a short time.[45] Campbell wrote, "Camped for the night on a hill north of town with our guns pointing over the town. Boys discovered some whiskey down among some of the houses and are having a lively time around their bivouac fires."

At 9:00 A.M. on April 22, the mounted force left McMinnville and reached Smithville about 7:00 P.M., having marched north thirty-five miles over very bad roads. The next day they marched to Alexandria by way of Snow Hill and Liberty. The infantry meanwhile marched over the more direct road from McMinnville. The mounted force remained in camp at Alexandria on April 24 where "Boys captured a large quantity of hams in a house near camp belonging to a rebel Bushwhacker." Sidney Speed identified the guerrilla as a man who had helped to kill two soldiers on the previous expedition and reported that the troopers burned his house.

On April 25 one section of Rodman guns and the mountain howitzers marched with the Ninety-eighth Illinois to Lebanon. "Scouts

43 *Ibid.*, 272; Merrill, II, 204.
44 "News for Murfreesboro," Cincinnati *Gazette*, Apr. 24, 1863.
45 *Ibid.*

fired the house of the Rebel Col. Allison which was burnt to the ground when we passed," wrote Henry Campbell. He noted that several Union families lived in Lebanon and reported that the supply train from Murfreesboro arrived in Alexandria with five days' rations. The next day, General Reynolds and the infantry rejoined the mounted force in Lebanon.

Captain Lilly accompanied two companies of the Seventeenth to Gallatin to visit General Ward, and he returned about dark "with 2 Jugs of 'Robinson Co.' compliments of General Ward." Meanwhile Henry Campbell and others went into Alexandria to obtain forage for the horses and "procured it of an old Jew who beged hard to have us leave it   the boys ransacked his house finding a 'Henry' repeting pistol and a Shot gun which we appropriated for our own use."

Sidney Speed and two of his battery mates mounted mules and "went out about three miles to a Rebel settlement, where they refused to take Lincoln money, so we bought there hams, turkies and chickens with *fac simile* Confederate notes. I laid out thirty dollars in hams at thirty-five cents a pound and with five dollars bought two turkies and four chickens."[46]

The expedition returned to their camp at Murfreesboro the next day after capturing 200 prisoners and 678 horses and mules. During the 11-day expedition, the brigade marched over 50 miles a day, and General Rosecrans said "we beat everything he has known of."[47]

On May 2, camp was moved two miles from town on the Manchester pike "near the boiling spring," which Henry Campbell thought was a much better location than the old one "so close to a grave yard that had we staid there much longer we should have been dug under to make room for graves   the day we left they were digging one in front of my tent door." He described the spring: "The spring that boils up out of the ground like an artesian well furnishes us with plenty of clear cold water." Here the artillerymen turned in their large Sibley tents and drew two-man dog tents. "The boys like them very well," Campbell reported.

On June 2, "Capt. Lilly treated the boys to a barrel of ale this even-

46 Merrill, II, 204.
47 *O.R.* Ser. 1, XXIII, pt. 2, 200–203; Sunderland, pp. 32–33.

ing which with the Sanitary Stores[48] we were fortunate enough to get the other day gives us quite a bill of fare and no doubt suprises our stomachs considerably." The same day Lieutenant William Benson Rippetoe described camp activity: "We are not very busy now, as everything is about ready to advance or stay here as the case may be. I drill a Howitzer battery once or twice a day, as I see fit. Read a little occasionaly in a greek testament read my Bible regularly every day. Write home to my girl, and my friends generally, just when I feel like it, Study the intricacies of chess, go to Murfreesboro whenever I have business and some times when I haven't. Read the papers and what books please me, study mathematics a little when I feel like it . . . the rest of my time [is given] to the laudable exercises of talking, eating, sleeping, and fighting flies alternately, interposed with an occasional horse trade for the battery, in which I and all the boys try to get the best horse, from our trading neighbors."

He continued, "In a consultation by the commanding generals night before last it was determined to move yesterday by daylight, but the order was countermanded before it was published to the army. I have got so I don't care how soon they move us, for its believed generally that we can whip our Friend Bragg very decently and we'd like to do it."[49]

By this time, the Spencer rifles for the brigade had arrived, and the men soon were given an opportunity to see what the new weapons would do. On June 4, Wilder's brigade marched to Liberty, and the battery had a casualty when "Corpl. Cassiday fell off his caisson coming down a hill and was badly hurt by the wheel running over him." Upon reaching Liberty, Campbell reported, "Run about 500 Rebels [of Wharton's brigade] out of the place scattering them in all directions through the woods Captured about 20 all well dressed in new uniforms. Destroyed their camp."

On June 5, part of the brigade and a section of the battery commanded by Lieutenant Beck marched to Smithville and had an en-

[48] From the Indiana Sanitary Commission, organized in 1862 to receive donations and to provide special provisions to soldiers in the field and in hospitals. Terrell, I, 314–20.

[49] Ernest R. Davidson Collection, William Benson Rippetoe to Mary J. Rippetoe, June 2, 1863.

gagement with Wharton's brigade. John Rippetoe wrote, "We got a chance to fire our guns at last. The two guns fired 6 rounds apiece, one of our shells killed one man and wounded another and killed three horses, that was a pretty effective shot but it was a mere accident that it did as much mischief as it did, for we were not shooting at any that we could see, but were shelling the woods where they were . . . . The gun of which I have charge was the first one of our battery to fire after the rebels, the boys of our section are pretty proud of being the first to have a chance at the rebels, the ones belonging to our gun seem to feel a little larger than the other detachments."[50]

On June 19 the battery again moved their camp to a location "across the road into the woods near old Mrs. Bivins house to the great annoyance of the old Lady." Then on the twenty-first they moved to a place on the bank of Stones River, five miles east of Murfreesboro on the Lebanon pike which Henry Campbell reported was made into one of the most cheerful camps they had ever established with the tents and horse lines in the shade and the new dog tents arranged "in the highest style of Art."

They had little time to enjoy their new camp because orders arrived for the battery to be ready to march with all equipment at 4:00 A.M. on June 24. This was the start of the campaign that would make Wilder's the most famous brigade in the Army of the Cumberland and give Lilly's battery a share of the glory.

[50] For another account of this expedition, see James Austin Connolly, "Major Connolly's Letters to His Wife." *Transactions of the Illinois State Historical Society* No. 35 (1928), pp. 257–60.

V

Lightning at Hoover's Gap

Since I wrote you last, I have seen the elephant and he was mad and although the balls fell for a little while around me like hail and wounded one of my detachment severely in the side, I by the providence of God escaped unhurt ... our brigade was all that was engaged in the little fight which was at beech grove in a gap of the mountains east of Murfreesboro.

John Rippetoe briefly told Mary about the Battle of Hoover's Gap in which Wilder's brigade surprised a superior force of Confederates and opened the road for the Army of the Cumberland to flank the Confederate Army of Tennessee, forcing its retreat to Chattanooga. "Seeing the elephant" was the soldier expression of the day for viewing the wonder, a battle, that they had enlisted to see, in the same way that seeing the elephant was the reason for going to the circus.

Major General William S. Rosecrans had planned a campaign that he hoped would bring on a decisive battle in Tennessee and which ultimately succeeded in driving Braxton Bragg's Army of Tennessee out of the state. General in Chief Henry W. Halleck had been prodding Rosecrans to move all spring, but Rosecrans had delayed because his cavalry seemed too weak, which the command in Washington interpreted to be an excuse for not campaigning. At the start of the campaign, the Army of the Cumberland numbered approximately 60,000 men and the Army of Tennessee about 46,000.[1]

Rosecrans' initial strategy was to feint with his cavalry toward the strong point of Shelbyville, the western anchor of Bragg's line, where 18,000 of the Confederate army were posted behind five miles of earthworks. Then his infantry was to force their way through gaps in the

[1] Guernsey and Alden, II, 525–29.

mountains southeast of Murfreesboro, which were held by 12,000 Rebels. A successful campaign through the mountains could cut off the Confederate line of retreat along the Nashville and Chattanooga Railroad and force Bragg to fight a major battle in Tennessee. Rosecrans did not expect to take the gaps without hard fighting and heavy casualties when the cavalry corps started the campaign with the feint toward Shelbyville on June 23.[2]

Lilly's battery had just become settled comfortably in their new camp when orders arrived for them to march at 4:00 A.M. on June 24 with all equipment. Henry Campbell sounded reveille at 2:00 A.M., and the men had packed up and were on the road by four. They passed through Murfreesboro, accompanying the other units of Wilder's brigade, and marched out the Manchester turnpike; but after passing the last Federal picket posts, the column was halted for an hour while a pioneer detachment repaired a bridge.[3] At eight o'clock, rain that would be nearly continuous for the next seventeen days began to fall, turning the roads into quagmires and making the campaign especially arduous for both men and animals.[4]

On the Manchester pike, Wilder's brigade was in the lead of Major General George H. Thomas's XIV Corps. Major General Thomas Crittenden's XXI Corps was marching toward Bradyville on the McMinnville road, while Major General Alexander McCook's XX Corps headed toward Liberty Gap and Shelbyville. Wilder's men believed that they were in excellent condition to begin a campaign since each regiment had more than 500 men present for duty.[5]

When Wilder was six miles out of Murfreesboro, the remainder of Thomas's corps began to march. At 10:00 A.M., when nine miles from town, the advance of Wilder's brigade reached the Confederate picket posts at the entrance of Hoover's Gap and Wilder sent twenty-five scouts into the advance, followed by five companies of the Seventy-second Indiana commanded by Lieutenant Colonel Samuel C. Kirkpatrick. This small force quickly drove the Confederate cavalry pickets

---

2 *Ibid.*, 529–30; O.R. Ser. 1, XXIII, pt. 1, 547.

3 The pioneers were men detailed from the regiments to repair roads, bridges, and railroads; i.e., they filled the function of civil engineers.

4 O.R. Ser. 1, XXIII, pt. 1, 538.

5 Benefiel, *Wilder's Brigade*, p. 7.

from their posts toward the main fortifications of the gap five miles beyond, and the main body of the Confederate Third Kentucky Cavalry came forward to meet the Yankees on the approaches to the gap.

These graybacks tried to make a stand on a cedar covered hill but two companies assaulted the position without hesitating and drove the Johnnies toward the fortifications in the gap. Wilder ordered Kirkpatrick to keep moving, take possession of the gap, and if possible, to keep the Rebels from occupying the fortifications. The advance followed the retreating Confederate horsemen so closely that they were unable to get into positions in the breastworks.[6]

Henry Campbell reported the capture of the signal station at the entrance to the gap, which had been deserted so suddenly when the Yankees appeared that instruments and other equipment had been left. The action continued: "Moved up the gap about one mile to a small creek[7] without any opposition. Here we could distinctly hear the long roll of the rebel drummers   we had taken them completely by surprise. The Scouts dashed across the creek over into the rebel camp, captured and brought away seven wagons loaded with corn.   all this right under their very noses."[8] In the race through the gap, some of the artillery horses gave out, and men of the battery and the brigade had to manhandle the guns through the mud.

The rapid advance through the gap took the Confederates so completely by surprise that Brigadier General Bushrod Johnson's[9] first knowledge of the attack came at 1:00 P.M. from two boys who were muddied from hard riding. They soon were followed by wounded cavalrymen and the adjutant of the Third Kentucky Cavalry, who reported that the assaulting force was cavalry. Apparently, the Confederates were not too concerned about their ability to drive the "cavalry" from the gap because Brigadier General William B. Bate did not receive orders until 2:00 P.M. to march with his brigade, followed by

6 *O.R.* Ser. 1, XXIII, pt. 1, 454, 457.
7 McBride's Creek, which flows into Garrison Fork of Duck River.
8 Also see *O.R.* Ser. 1, XXIII, pt. 1, 457–61.
9 The gap was defended by two brigades of A. P. Stewart's division, W. J. Hardee's corps, under Brig. Gens. William C. Bate and Bushrod Johnson. Bate's brigade included five infantry regiments, a sharpshooter detachment, and two light batteries. Johnson's brigade had four infantry regiments and a battery of four Napoleon guns.

Johnson's force, from his camp at Fairfield, two miles down Garrison Fork, to Beechgrove. Upon reaching the field, Johnson observed that the Federals were already in complete control of the gap.[10]

Upon hearing the long roll of the Confederate drummers assembling the Rebel force, Wilder pushed the remainder of his command through the gap and took position on the hills to the south. He ordered the two advanced companies of the Seventy-second to return to the main body, which they did after they had plundered a store taking "hats and a great many other things."[11]

The Seventy-second was posted on a hill on the right of the road with two of Lilly's howitzers, and four Rodman guns were placed on a second hill facing Fairfield, also on the right side of the road but behind the howitzers. These units were supported by the One hundred twenty-third Illinois and part of the Seventeenth Indiana. Most of the Ninety-eighth Illinois was held in reserve on a high hill in the rear, but two companies of this regiment were to the left of the road. Four companies of the Seventeenth were positioned on the extreme right of the line on a low hill.[12]

The Confederate infantry came up to the Federal pickets at 3:00 P.M. and deployed opposite the Federal position. Two Rebel batteries on the Confederate right, about 1,200 yards distant from Lilly's position, opened the affair, catching the mountain howitzers in a cross fire that killed two gunners and the mules of one gun.[13] Campbell said one shell passed through the bodies of both mules and cut the driver's legs off, and another shell that passed overhead fell into the reserves posted along the road, killing John R. Eddy, chaplain of the Seventy-second Indiana.

Captain Lilly replied with his Rodman guns, dismounting one of the Confederate pieces and forcing the Rebels to change position several times. Lilly reported that the enemy battery was hidden in timber, and Campbell wrote that the Yankee gunners fired at the gun flashes

10 *O.R.* Ser. 1, XXIII, pt. 1, 601–14.

11 Indiana Historical Society Library, John M. Barnard to his wife, Margaret, July 2, 1863.

12 *O.R.* Ser. 1, XXIII, pt. 1, 457–61; Lilly Archives, Eli Lilly reports July 7 and 16, 1863.

13 Lilly Archives, Eli Lilly reports July 7 and 16, 1863.

Map 3.
MARCHES OF LILLY'S BATTERY,
JUNE–NOVEMBER 1863

and smoke of the enemy guns. William R. Rennels, a private of the One hundred twenty-third Illinois, wrote that he was standing near the first of Lilly's guns to fire, and when Captain Lilly and the cannoneers did not see where the shell landed because of the smoke, he told Lilly, "About ten feet to the right of the gun." Lilly said, "I will try them again," and the next shell hit the muzzle of the Rebel gun, raising a cloud of smoke as high as the trees.[14] After about ten rounds, one Yankee gun had a shell to wedge and explode[15] in it and had to be removed from the field, and the Third Section was brought up from the reserve to replace it. Campbell commented, "This was our first fight but the Boys were all cool   no excitement   the gun corporals sighted each gun and dropped the shells thick and fast around the rebel battery."

While the artillery duel continued, Bate concentrated his brigade to attack the position of the Seventeenth Indiana on the Federal right, and Wilder reacted by sending the remainder of the Seventeenth to the threatened position. The attack by four regiments of Rebels reached the bottom of the hill and began to charge up the slope, with the men "cheering wildly" before the Seventeenth opened fire.

Here, both sides discovered the effectiveness of the Spencer repeating rifles as the Indianians poured a rapid fire into the advancing line while Lilly's battery was enfilading the line with double charges of canister. This stopped the attack some fifty feet from the Union line. After falling back and reorganizing, the Confederates moved farther toward the flank and again attacked, but Wilder sent the Ninety-eighth to the Seventeenth's assistance and they met the Rebels near the crest of the hill with a "murderous fire" from their seven-shooters. The Johnnies broke in disorder and fled down the hill.[16]

While this action was going on, two regiments of Johnson's brigade attempted to capture Lilly's battery, but three companies of the One hundred twenty-third Illinois had moved into a ravine seventy-five yards in front of the battery. Lieutenant Joseph Scott also had his guns

14 Lilly Archives, William R. Rennels to Eli Lilly, Jan. 25, 1895.
15 Lilly Archives, Eli Lilly report July 16, 1863. The explosion did not damage the gun.
16 *O.R.* Ser. 1, XXIII, pt. 1, 457–61.

loaded with double-shotted canister, and when the Confederates approached the ravine, Scott "let them have it." At the same time, the One hundred twenty-third rose up and "poured a continuous volley into their already thinned ranks," and "Colonel Miller of the Seventy-second Indiana opened an enfilading fire which caused them to fall to the ground to escape the tornado of death."[17] Lilly's guns fired canister at the retreating soldiers, who were crawling away on hands and knees. Lilly wrote, "Their loss must have been considerable at this point from the number they were seen to drag off by the arms."[18]

According to Henry Campbell, "The rebel battery kept belching forth a perfect shower of shot and shell . . . but had done us no damage, every one of their shots going above us or striking the ground in our front and glancing over our heads." The reason for the enemy shells missing the mark was that Lilly's guns were posted behind the brow of the hill so that only the muzzles were visible. The shells fell mostly among the reserve force and horses, forcing them to move behind a large hill. Some shells also fell among the infantry, and John M. Barnard of the Seventy-second wrote, "Had to lay flat on thay ground nearly all thay time as we were right in range of their cannon . . . there was several shells struck within a few feet of where I was."[19]

After this, the Confederates positioned guns on the right and left, and along with the guns remaining in the front, caught Lilly's battery in a three-way cross fire. Lilly's guns finally silenced the artillery in their front, and as the firing of the other batteries was very wild, the battery suffered no losses. Henry Campbell's assignment was to stand on a rise next to the guns and, whenever he saw the flash of an enemy gun, to shout, "Down," and the men at the guns would fall flat to avoid the pieces of shell. Campbell wrote, "The Activity of the boys in lying down and Jumping up again when they could hear a shot whizzing over them and the overshooting of their shells (Rebel) is what we owe our escape to." Sometimes, Lilly's guns fired at sharpshooters along the creek instead of at the enemy artillery. Campbell said the sharpshooters were

---

[17] *Ibid.*; Connolly, p. 267.
[18] Lilly Archives, Eli Lilly report July 16, 1863.
[19] John M. Barnard to his wife, Margaret, July, 2, 1863.

more annoying than the artillery shells, and that they wounded a driver of the battery through the knee.[20]

After these attacks, General Reynolds's adjutant arrived on the field with an order for the brigade to retire. Wilder refused to obey, saying he could maintain his position until Thomas's corps, then six miles in the rear, could come up. The adjutant threatened to put Wilder under arrest, but Wilder told him that he (Wilder) would take full responsibility for the consequences. The adjutant rode back to Reynolds to report.[21]

The Rebels made one last attack with five regiments on the Federal right, but it was easily broken up by the rapid fire of the Spencer rifles in the hands of fewer than 700 men of the Seventeenth and Ninety-eighth. The Confederates then fell back and resumed cannonading in competition with Lilly's battery, without much damage done by either side.[22]

Shortly after 4:00 P.M., General Reynolds arrived with two infantry brigades, which were placed on both sides of the road to elongate the line. The Nineteenth Indiana Battery also arrived, and by double-teaming, got one gun on the top of the highest hill in the area.[23] This gun, along with percussion shell from Lilly's battery, which exploded among the Rebel guns, caused the Confederates to retire about dark. The lead brigade of Brigadier General Lovell Rousseau's division also came up about nightfall along with the Twenty-first Indiana Battery[24] which relieved Lilly's battery. During the night more of the XIV Corps arrived and Wilder's brigade was removed from the line. In addition to the loss of one man, five horses of Lilly's battery had been wounded —one totally disabled. The battery had fired 350 rounds in the action.[25]

Henry Campbell had two narrow escapes after the arrival of Captain Samuel J. Harris's Nineteenth Indiana Battery. Carrying an order to Harris, Campbell was riding up the hill on which the Nineteenth was posted when "a shell whizzed past me just missing the back of my

---

20 National Archives, "Descriptive Book." The driver was James Bigham, a detail from the 72d Indiana. His leg was amputated, and he died the next day.
21 Sunderland, p. 42.
22 *O.R.* Ser. 1, XXIII, pt. 1, 457–61.
23 Lilly Archives, Eli Lilly report July 7, 1863.
24 *Ibid.*; Cincinnati *Gazette*, June 29, 1863; *O.R.* Ser. 1, XXIII, pt. 1, 454–61.
25 Lilly Archives, Eli Lilly report July 16, 1863.

horse and passing within two feet of me." Riding his white horse all day, he was a conspicuous target for the sharpshooters and "Once, as I was walking and leading her up the high conical hill, . . . they came very near to killing us both."

With the arrival of the infantry column, Generals Rosecrans, Thomas, and Reynolds came up, and General Thomas told Wilder that his action probably had saved one thousand men. In the fight, the brigade lost sixty men killed and wounded.[26] The enemy casualties were less certainly known; reports varied from two hundred to five hundred.[27] The soldiers credited the Spencer rifles with the victory, and they were justified. Based on the fire power, General Bate thought the Confederates were outnumbered five to one.[28]

The victory at Hoover's Gap opened the way for Thomas's corps to move on toward Tullahoma and Manchester, flanking Bragg's position and causing the Confederate army to retreat. "Thus the first and most critical step of the campaign was won by Wilder's soldiership," commented the Cincinnati *Gazette*.[29]

When they were relieved after marching and fighting for more than twelve hours, Lilly's men camped for the night in a barnyard, out of range of the enemy artillery. "Fed our tired horses from the supply train," wrote Henry Campbell. "The boys made coffee and then lay down in the mud and rain sleeping as soundly as if they were in their camp at Murfreesboro. I found an empty hog trough and slept in that." He spread his blanket in the bottom, covered the trough with his rubber blanket, and claimed that he had the only dry bed in the brigade.

On June 25, Lilly's guns were positioned on the right of the conical hill but had little action until late in the forenoon, when the Confederates emplaced two guns opposite the Federal right. Lieutenant Scott's section silenced these after a few rounds. The Union now had an overwhelming superiority in numbers with four divisions on the field[30]

[26] *O.R.* Ser. 1, XXIII, pt. 1, 457–61.

[27] *Ibid.*, 610, 614. Bate and Johnson reported 222 casualties. Guernsey and Alden, II, 530, reported that Confederate losses were 500.

[28] *O.R.* Ser. 1, XXIII, pt. 1, 611–14.

[29] Cincinnati *Gazette*, June 29, 1863.

[30] Reynolds's, Rousseau's, Negley's and Brannan's divisions of the XIV Corps. *O.R.* Ser. 1, XXIII, pt. 1, 454–57.

instead of the single brigade that had defended the position the day before.

In the evening, the Confederate batteries moved into a position to cover the road and began to duel with Lilly's, Cyrus O. Loomis's First Michigan, and Harris's Nineteenth Indiana batteries. Campbell reported the Union guns "rained shot and shell in on them like hail. They got out in a few moments. They evidently opened fire to cover their retreat for on the next morning nothing was left but Cavalry."

At 2:00 P.M. on June 26, the battery rejoined the brigade, marching up Garrison Fork and over a chain of hills that separated it from McBride's Creek. This move flanked the Confederate cavalry, forcing them to fall back before Reynolds's infantry. Wilder's brigade then moved up McBride's Creek to a tableland, where they found the Union infantry marching along the pike, meeting no resistance.[31]

On the march, Henry Campbell rode over to the position occupied by the Confederate batteries during the fight and found several horses that had been killed by the shellfire. He wrote, "The trees under which their Bat. was placed all cut to peices   our shells going entirely through some that were 2 ft. thick . . . Rained all day   roads terrible   every body wet, tired, and hungry." That night the battery camped "in an old muddy orchard: within five miles of Manchester."

During the night the infantry caught up to Wilder's brigade, and the next morning the column moved toward Manchester. They had now reached a tableland called "the Barrens," which Henry Campbell described as "an elevated plateau of waste land bordering the Cumberland mountains, about 50 miles in width, and extending all along the range of mountains. This plateau, or shelf of the mountains is almost as level and flat as a floor, sandy unproductive soil, producing nothing but 'Jack Oaks.'   very thinly settled and then only in spots where an oasis occurs.   where the inhabitants are of the lowest order of whites, and eak out a miserable existance from the sandy, barren soil upon which they live."

On June 27, Wilder's brigade swept into Manchester, located on the McMinnville Railroad, before the Rebels were aware of their approach and captured forty prisoners, including four officers. Four companies

31 *Ibid.*, 457–61.

of the Seventeenth Indiana and the brigade's pioneers moved on and destroyed the trestle bridge on the McMinnville Railroad, four miles from Tullahoma.[32]

On the morning of June 28, Wilder's brigade began a campaign to get into the rear of Tullahoma, which had been Bragg's headquarters, to destroy enemy communications and to interfere with the Confederate retreat. He was ordered "to strike quick and heavy blows."[33] Wilder took two of the mountain howitzers with his force, leaving the remainder of the battery to march with the infantry.

The brigade marched to Hillsboro and then toward Decherd on the Nashville and Chattanooga Railroad south of Tullahoma but found that they could neither ford nor swim the swollen Elk River because the current washed the horses downstream. Consequently, the force marched to Pelham, farther east, crossing streams "that swam our smallest horses" and required that the howitzer ammunition be carried across on the men's shoulders. The Rebels were planning to destroy the bridge at Pelham, but a dash by Wilder's scouts saved the bridge and captured two prisoners and seventy-eight mules.

Leaving Pelham, the brigade forded the South Fork of the Elk after a mill was dismantled to make rafts on which the howitzers were floated across. Then they marched to Decherd, where they attacked a stockade on the railroad, using canister to drive its eighty defenders away. During the night, Wilder's men tore up track, blew up a trestle on the railroad, and destroyed commissary stores and telegraph instruments at the depot.

Wilder heard that six Confederate regiments were about to attack his force and the brigade left Decherd, skirmishing until night, when they camped without fires. Next they marched up Cumberland Mountain past University Place[34] and destroyed track of the Tracy City railroad. By this time, Nathan Bedford Forrest's Confederate cavalry was on Wilder's tail, and so Wilder took the road toward Chattanooga, and after a heavy rain had obliterated the track, the brigade moved into woods where they waited until the Confederate cavalry had passed.

[32] *Ibid.*
[33] *Ibid.*, pt. 2, 474.
[34] Now the University of the South at Sewanee.

Then they marched back to Manchester, by way of Pelham, reaching Manchester and the Army of the Cumberland just ahead of Forrest and nine regiments of cavalry. For eleven days, the brigade had ridden and fought for twenty hours out of the twenty-four, all the time drenched by the rain. Most remarkable, not a single man was lost.[35]

On June 29, the battery and the infantry of Reynolds's division began to march on the Tullahoma road, "or rather under it," wrote Henry Campbell, "as the mud is hub deep   some places the wheels would sink until the guns would drag on the ground." He reported the roads were entirely covered with water, and that "All day long we passed wagon after wagon, mired down and upset   teamsters swearing   mules pulling their utmost and everybody mad. By constant prying   lifting and doubling teams, we managed to get the Battery 9 miles before dark. Don't think the transportation wagons will ever get through." The artillerymen had just unharnessed the weary horses when orders arrived to send two guns back to Manchester. "1st Sec. was detached and about 6 o'clock they began their weary way back over the road that they had all day been plodding over."

That night the soldiers could hear the train whistles in Tullahoma and knew the Rebels were either reinforcing or evacuating the place "as they seemed very busy all night." The Confederates were evacuating, and when the Second Kentucky and Twenty-ninth Indiana infantry marched into town at noon the next day, they found only the rear guard of Wheeler's cavalry, which they chased away.[36]

Lilly's battery struggled along "over almost impassable roads" to reach Tullahoma at 6:00 P.M., and from the appearance of the place, Henry Campbell thought the Rebels "must have been in considerable of a hurry to leave." Among other things, they left four heavy siege guns and "about 1500 good wall tents, all standing in their places." The Union soldiers slept in the tents that night and set fire to them the next day.[37]

Henry Campbell thought, "The town is a very small and dirty place   built on the only elevated piece of ground in the entire sur-

35 *O.R.* Ser. 1, XXIII, pt. 1, 457–61; Connolly, pp. 268–71.
36 "The Occupation of Tullahoma," Cincinnati *Gazette*, July 1, 1863.
37 Cincinnati *Gazette*, July 4, 1863.

rounding country." Others also were surprised at the appearance of the town. One newspaper reporter wrote, "I had fancied to myself a romantic little town amongst the mountains, and lo! a miserable village on a plain as flat as the desert of Sahara!"[38] Earlier, a Southern correspondent had written, "Sir, it [Tullahoma] is nondescript. A hell of a place the soldiers say . . . ."[39]

On July 2, the battery began a march on the Winchester road, over which the Confederates had retreated, and Henry Campbell observed, "roadside strewn with broken down and abanded wagons   indications of a hasty retreat. Their [Confederate] army wagons seem to consist of old wagons 'pressed' in from the farmers." The battery marched only six miles over "fearful bad roads   No bottom to them in these everlasting 'Jack Oak Barrens'."

The next day, the men and animals struggled along the Winchester road to the Elk River, where they camped because the bridge had been destroyed and the river was too swollen to ford. The need to spare the horses as much work as possible became obvious and the load was lightened "by throwing away every thing, but what was absolutely necessary to get along with. Only two camp kittles, 2 frying pans, and 2 buckets allowed to the detachment, those to be carried on the caisson.

one change of under clothing to each man and one blanket for two men. All the officers bunks were destroyed also the captains mess chest. Everything in the way of tent furniture, except the Company desk was consigned to the flames. Officers messes was consolidated into one with as few cooking utensils as could be conveniently gotten along with. In this manner our wagons and teams were lightened up considerably, as we had a great deal of baggage."

Campbell also reported the presence of General Rosecrans, who had come up to inspect the bridge over the Elk River. By the next morning, the river had gone down sufficiently to allow the battery to ford and they resumed their march toward Winchester. Campbell said the roads were worse than ever, and the only way they managed to move on was by corduroying the worst places with small trees. Morale improved

---

38 *Ibid.*

39 J. Cutler Andrews, *The South Reports the Civil War* (Princeton: Princeton Univ. Press, 1970), p. 339.

about noon when General Rosecrans rode down the line and told the soldiers about the Union victory at Gettysburg "which was received by the troops with prolonged cheers." About dark the battery encamped two miles from Winchester at a place called "Church cross roads," and from camp they could see "A dim blue out line visable in the distance . . . is the top of the Cumberland mountains. At last we are through the everlasting bottomless Barrens." That evening the battery fired a salute of thirty-five guns to celebrate the Fourth of July.

On July 5, morale was raised still higher when word of the capture of Vicksburg was received and a thirteen-gun salute was fired. On the sixth, the news of Gettysburg was confirmed and called for a thirty-five gun salute. Henry Campbell wrote, "The last two days has brought us glorious news, and raised the spirit of the army wonderfully. Some of the boys have even packed their knapsacks, expecting the war to be over in a week or two." James Dodd thought that he would be home by December if not sooner,[40] and James Emory Rippetoe wrote, "I look forward with pleasing anticipation to the time of our return home . . . . Judging from present appearances that time is near at hand . . . ."[41]

Campbell reported, "We are waiting for our wagon train to arrive with rations and feed. Our horses have nothing to eat but wheat straw." During the next week the battery marched to Normandy, on the railroad north of Tullahoma, where they rejoined Wilder's brigade, finding them "encamped in a very pleasant little valley." The brigade had been strengthened with the addition of the Ninety-second Illinois Mounted Infantry, another Spencer rifle equipped regiment, commanded by Colonel Smith D. Atkins.

July 27 was payday, and nearly $4,000 was sent home by the men of the battery on the allotment rolls. Campbell drew $52 and paid the sutler $12, and John Rippetoe kept only $10, sending the remainder home, since he had spent only $2.50 during the previous four months.

At Normandy, the soldiers found "plenty of vegetables, fruit, and forage . . . apples are ripe   also all kinds of garden vegetables, and Blackberries are in abundance." Campbell reported that he was ill with

---

40 Lilly Archives, James C. Dodd to Rueben and Mary Hinkel, July 27, 1863.

41 Ernest R. Davidson Collection, James Emory Rippetoe to Mary J. Rippetoe, Aug. 14, 1863.

chronic diarrhea, and that a number of other men were sick with the same. He was improving "thanks to the abundance of Blackberries," but two weeks later he went on a foraging expedition and rode forty or fifty miles in the hot sun "which made me very bilious and quite sick ever since   Am indulging in rations of Castor oil and quinine for a change."

On August 2, the brigade marched to Decherd, and the next day, Campbell reported, "Capt. placed Lt. Hartman in arrest and prefered charges against him for buying a Govt. Horse from one of the scouts." On August 11 the order dismissing Hartman was received, and "The Battery was drawn up in line and the order read before them." Henry Campbell continued, "He was dismissed more for his incompetancy as an officer than for the charge that was brought against him. Capt. Lilly's influence at Gen. Reynolds Hd. Qrs. was the cause of his dismissal by special order.[42] Our brigade has the authority to keep themselves supplied with horses from off the country.   consequently the officers speculate considerably in horses. Had Hartman been tried by a Court martial he would have been cleared, as the scout he purchased the horse of had his trial and was cleared."

The Tullahoma campaign was one of the most successful of the war, with the Army of the Cumberland maneuvering the Confederates out of Middle Tennessee and back to Chattanooga at a cost of fewer than 600 casualties.[43] For the first time the Federal cavalry was nearly equal in numbers to the Rebel cavalry because John Hunt Morgan had taken his brigade on his famous raid into Indiana and Ohio. John Rippetoe gave his opinion of the results of the raid when he wrote, "It is one of the best things to rouse the people. I expect that it is the last raid that will be made into the free states. The rebels seem to be in a rather poor fix not only here but throughout the entire south. They seem as if they did not know what to do, and there is a terrible reaction taking place."

[42] Indiana State Library, Archives Division, William S. Rosecrans General Field Order 218, Aug. 9, 1863, and General Order 253, same date.
[43] Guernsey and Alden, II, 531.

VI

Chattanooga

There was no thought of an attack. Bang! Bang! Then the bursting of a shell too close for comfort. Bang! Bang! Then the rattle of shell fragments on the roof. On the other side of the river the Yankees were upon us.[1]

Henry Watterson, editor of the Chattanooga *Rebel*,[2] expressed the surprise of the citizens of Chattanooga and of the Confederate military command when the first shells from Captain Eli Lilly's guns exploded on the edge of that town on Friday, August 21, 1863. So far as the civilians and the military knew, Rosecrans's Union army was west of Cumberland Mountain, bogged down in the mud.

At the time of the attack, the leading citizens and ranking officers were attending a church service celebrating Jefferson Davis's fast day. Watterson wrote that a Dr. B. M. Palmer of New Orleans was well into the long prayer of the Presbyterian service when the first shells burst, and that "The man of God gave no sign that anything unusual was happening. He did not hurry. He did not vary the tones of his voice. He kept on praying. There was no panic in the congregation, which did not budge . . . . That was the longest prayer I ever heard . . . ."

Henry Campbell confirmed the surprise, and although Watterson claimed that the people finally left the church "in the most orderly

1 Henry Watterson, *"Marse Henry": An Autobiography*, 2 vols. (New York: George R. Doran Co., 1919), II, 308–309. Watterson later became the nationally known publisher of the Louisville *Courier-Journal*.

2 James W. Livingood, "The Chattanooga *Rebel*" Publication No. 39 East Tennessee Historical Society, (1967), pp. 42–55. The *Rebel*, published in Chattanooga, had a large circulation in the Army of Tennessee.

manner," Campbell wrote, "they poured out like bees from a hive." He also reported that the guns opened fire "right in the face of the whole of Braggs army, and to the consternation and supprise of that great chief himself, who was enjoying himself in fancied security, when the shells of our guns awoke him to the truth that his bosted stronghold was no longer safe for his person as his hasty removal of Hd. Qrs. afterward testified."

Campbell did not overstate Bragg's surprise when Lilly's shells began to land. Bragg had felt so secure in Chattanooga that he had proposed taking most of his army to join General Joseph E. Johnston in Mississippi for a combined operation against General Grant's recently victorious army. About the situation at Chattanooga, he wrote, "I do not think the enemy can advance here in force for six weeks." Johnston did not think such a move would accomplish much as Grant already held Vicksburg, and Bragg remained at Chattanooga.[3]

Chattanooga was a more important place than its prewar population of 2,500 would indicate because it was the junction of railroads from Virginia, Georgia, Memphis, and Nashville. Thus its capture would cut the most direct routes by which armaments from the arsenals of Virginia and Georgia moved to the Confederate western armies and by which food from the west reached the Army of Northern Virginia.

General Bragg had withdrawn the Army of Tennessee to Chattanooga, presenting the Federal army with an extremely difficult task if they hoped to capture the place. It was a natural fortress with the only approaches being through the mountains that surround it. Bragg believed that the Army of the Cumberland would attempt to use a northern route across Cumberland Mountain and constructed strong works on the south bank of the Tennessee River.

General Rosecrans took advantage of Bragg's belief of an attack from the north when he developed his plan to capture Chattanooga. He sent a small part of his army[4] on the routes over Cumberland Moun-

---

[3] Horn, *Army of Tennessee*, p. 239.

[4] National Park Service, *Chickamauga and Chattanooga Battlefields*, Historical Handbook No. 25 (Washington, D.C.: Government Printing Office, 1956; reprint, 1961), p. 8. Wilder's mounted infantry brigade, Hazen's and Wagner's infantry brigades, and Minty's cavalry brigade crossed Cumberland Mountain. *O.R.* Ser. 1, XXX, pt. 1, 445. During this campaign, Wilder's brigade was composed of the 72d

tain, Sequatchie Valley, and Walden's Ridge, the direction from which Bragg expected the army to come. This force was led by Wilder's brigade, and it demonstrated so aggressively that Bragg remained convinced that the attack would come from that direction.

Meanwhile, Rosecrans was placing most of the Army of the Cumberland on the Tennessee River below Chattanooga with the intention of crossing Raccoon and Lookout mountains southwest of the town. He had repaired the Nashville and Chattanooga Railroad to Stevenson, Alabama, and had accumulated sufficient supplies for the campaign by the end of August. These supplies were needed because the army could not hope to obtain adequate forage in the mountainous country through which it would march. Rosecrans hoped that the demonstration north of town would hold Bragg in Chattanooga until the Federal army could get astride the railroad from Atlanta, south of Chattanooga and besiege Bragg there.[5] The soldiers had confidence in the strategy, so far as they understood it, and James Dodd wrote, " . . . we are aiming to go to Chattanooga on the Tennisea River & dont think we will have to fight any there it will be another Tullahoma Spree I think, but I may be mistaken about that . . . ."[6]

On August 16 the Army of the Cumberland began the campaign. Lilly's battery, accompanying Wilder's brigade, left camp at 1:00 P.M. with ten days' rations of hardtack and forage, and after marching nine miles, began to ascend Cumberland Mountain in a heavy rainstorm. They found the road "extremely steep, slippery, and winding" and near the top of the mountain they encountered dense fog. As they continued to climb the rain ceased, and on reaching the top, they were on dry land above the cloud and the rain.

"Below us, lay one of the grandest sights I ever witnessed," wrote Henry Campbell. "We were above the cloud of rain where the sun was shining brightly,   making hundreds of rainbows on the sides of the mountain beneath us   occasionally the cloud would brake away and let us catch a glimps of a most beautiful landscape underneath all

Indiana, Col. A. O. Miller; 17th Indiana, Lt. Col. Harry Jordan; 92d Illinois, Col. Smith D. Atkins; 98th Illinois, Col. J. J. Funkhouser; 123d Illinois, Col. James M. Monroe; and 18th Indiana Battery.

5 Guernsey and Alden, II, 537.

6 Lilly Archives, James C. Dodd to Mary Hinkel, July 27, 1863.

gleaming like silver as the sunlight shone on the rain. Towards evening it broke away and afforded such a landscape that no pen could describe. Went into camp on the edge of the mountains at a place called University Springs. a spring of pure water right *on top of the mtn.*   The State of Tenn. intended to start a college here before the war." From camp, the men enjoyed the views to the west, but the site had drawbacks: "Rattle snakes are thick but nobody bitten."

On August 17 the battery marched to Tracy City through country that Campbell described as " . . . exceeding flat, sandy soil, producing nothing but Jack oaks   almost destitute of water and very thinly settled." He wrote that Tracy City consisted of three houses and a depot, and that "The largest coal mine in Tenn. was in opperation here before the war. a branch rail road has been built here expressly for the coal."[7]

On the eighteenth the column marched in a generally northeast direction through thick blackjack oak woods, and in the afternoon, "we passed through a forest of large Pine trees   the first I ever seen growing wild." At 3:00 P.M., Wilder's brigade passed Brigadier General George D. Wagner's brigade of the XIV Corps with the infantry moving to the side of the road to allow the mounted force to pass. In camp by a small stream that night, "the rattle snakes were so thick that we were obliged to sleep up on the Ammunition chests."

At noon on August 19 the column reached the edge of the mountain. The road on the descent proved to be bad, forcing the battery to halt frequently to repair it so that they could move the guns. Two hours were used in going down the steep side of Cumberland Mountain into Sequatchie Valley. The valley was entered at a place called Therman's Crossroad, a few miles south of Dunlap.

Coming into the valley, scouts of the Seventy-second Indiana surprised and captured fourteen Rebel soldiers and freed five Union men they were about to hang.[8] The brigade marched six miles north and

---

[7] Gilbert E. Govan and James W. Livingood, *The Chattanooga Country 1540–1962* (Chapel Hill: Univ. of North Carolina Press, 1963), p. 352. The mine and railroad development was the original property of the Tennessee Coal, Iron, and Rail Road Company which later became the largest iron and steel producer in the South and, in 1907, a division of United States Steel Corporation.

[8] *O.R.* Ser. 1, XXX, pt. 1, 445.

encamped near Dunlap. Henry Campbell observed that the inhabitants of the valley raised livestock for a living. "Corn crops splended," he wrote; "enjoyed a grand feast on green corn   with ripe peaches for dessert   served up in genuine Cream   quite a relief from hard tack."

At 6:00 A.M. on August 20 the battery marched through Dunlap, leaving behind all baggage, including knapsacks and tents. The men were allowed to take only the clothes they had on their backs. Campbell, assisted by "Claybrun," a Negro, was in charge of headquarters' food, which was transported on a pack mule. "He ["Claybrun"] leads the mule & does all the work," wrote Campbell.

After marching two miles north, where they passed Brigadier General Charles Cruft's infantry brigade, Wilder's column forded the Sequatchie River and began the ascent of Walden Ridge, passing Brigadier General William B. Hazen's infantry brigade on top of the ridge. Henry Campbell observed that the ridge was twelve miles wide with the same characteristics as the top of Cumberland Mountain. About 4:00 P.M. they descended into North Chickamauga Valley, where scouts captured eleven Confederate soldiers "who were exceedingly astonished to find the yankee cavalry so far from home" and released three Union men they were holding.

That night the battery camped at Poe's Tavern, fifteen miles from Chattanooga on the bank of North Chickamauga Creek, which Henry Campbell described as "one of the cleanest streams I ever seen. the bottom is covered with very large round rocks and looks as if you could easily touch them with your hand when in reality the water is ten or twelve feet deep." But the valley "furnished nothing for our horses but rye straw. This valley aint to be compared with Sequatchie   in regard to fertility or beauty."

At 6:00 A.M. on August 21 the march was resumed, when the first section of the battery under Lieutenant Joseph A. Scott accompanied the Ninety-second and Ninety-eighth Illinois to Harrison's landing on the river above Chattanooga. Campbell commented, "This force was sent up there to prevent the rebels from crossing the river and getting in our rear   as they done with Buell last year."

The remainder of Wilder's brigade and Lilly's battery moved down the valley toward Chattanooga, and along the way, "numbers of Union people came down from the mountain sides, all dressed in their sunday clothes to watch us as we moved by. These people had been hiding in the mtns dodging the conscript officers for two years and their greeting that 'we'uns' mighty glad to see 'youens'   told more in the expression of their faces than their words conveyed."

At noon, this column reached the foot of Stringers Ridge, a range of sharp, pointed hills from 200 to 450 feet high running parallel to the Tennessee River and separated from it by a level bottom about one-half mile wide and distant about one mile from Chattanooga.[9]

Scouts rode across the ridge and down to the bank of the river, where they captured forty Confederate soldiers who were attempting to cross the river in a horse ferryboat, "Taking them right out from under the guns of the forts across the river," according to Henry Campbell. "This was the first knowledge the rebels had of our approach. Took them so much by supprise, that the forts did not open out on them until they were safely back out of range." The charge by the scouts came within fifty yards of capturing the horse ferry and did seize four empty wagons and the mules of an artillery battery in addition to the soldiers.[10]

When the enemy guns did start firing, the Second Section, under Lieutenant Rippetoe, was ordered to take position about 100 yards from the road on the highest of the hills and directly opposite one of the Confederate forts.

Henry Campbell and Captain Lilly described the Confederate defenses across the river. Downstream, to the Union right, on Cameron Hill was a fort with two James rifles located about 300 feet above the river. Just below this hill and 150 feet high was another hill with a large fort having embrasures for nine guns that bore on Stringers Ridge and the ferry crossing. Just below this, along the river was a water battery of three guns.

Near this battery and upstream was a large distillery pierced for muskets, and at the end of the main street of Chattanooga, commanding the ferry crossing, was an earthwork into which two field guns were

[9] Lilly Archives, Eli Lilly report Sept. 1, 1863, and accompanying map.
[10] *O.R.* Ser. 1, XXX, pt. 3, 122–23.

placed after the action started. At the edge of town, on a stone bluff ninety feet above the river, was a fort with ten embrasures, back of which were two smaller works to defend against attacks from the northeast. These were all the Confederate forts that were visible from Lilly's position.[11] The Confederates also had a pontoon bridge along the levee, ready to swing across the river.

Two steamboats, the "Dunbar" and "Paint Rock," were tied at the levee when the Second Section went into position at 10:30 A.M. and the gunners made these boats their first targets. Very quickly both were riddled with shot and the "Paint Rock" sank in about one hour. An attempt had been made to get steam up on "Paint Rock," but the shells from Lilly's guns forced the crew to leave the boat.[12]

The first shots at the boats were those that surprised Henry Watterson and the church congregation, and Henry Campbell wrote, "As soon as the boom of our first gun resounded and reverberated in the astonished ears of the Rebels in their boasted stronghold, they commenced running in every direction in the wildest confusion, Soldiers to their posts, and what few citizens that were in the place broke from the churches and rushed to places of safety in the forts."

The Confederates first answered Lilly's guns with a shot from a 15-pounder James rifle emplaced on Cameron Hill, but the shell did not quite reach the battery and landed on the hillside below. A shell from one of Lilly's pieces dismounted this gun. Then three or four guns in the fort below Cameron Hill commenced firing, but these did not have sufficient range to reach the position. Campbell gave the distance as 4,000 yards and claimed, "We could put the shots right through their embrasures every time with only 4½ deg. elevation."

While the Second Section was firing on the forts downstream from the ferry crossing, the Third Section was brought up and began firing on the upstream forts. About noon all of the enemy guns replied briskly, but finding their shells would not reach the position, soon slacked off. The Yankee Rodman guns at this range consistently exploded their shells inside the Confederate forts.[13]

11 Lilly Archives, Eli Lilly report Sept. 1, 1863, and accompanying map.
12 *O.R.* Ser. 1, XXX, pt. 3, 123, 135–36.
13 Lilly Archives, Eli Lilly report Sept. 1, 1863.

Campbell noted that the streets of the town were deserted but, "Now and then some lone and forlorn individual would skurry across the street from one house to another with his head down like a school boy dodging a snow ball." One citizen, in a show of bravado, began to drive up and down the levee in a buggy, but as soon as the artillerymen appreciated the challenge, one of the corporals trained a gun and exploded a shell directly over him and "He immediately turned and went up the street in 2.40 style."

By 4:00 P.M. most of the firing had ceased; only number six gun was firing, trying to sink the horse ferry, and most men of the battery were lying down resting or sleeping. Henry Campbell was sitting in front of number five gun watching the effect of six's firing through the captain's glasses and reported:

No. 6 had just fired their gun and at the same instant exactly that the report of our gun rang out through the air and while every ones attention was engrossed in watching the shot strike The rebels fired a shot from a 32 lb James Rifle that they had been mounting during the time they were silent   in the large fort direct in our front. The shell whizzed over my head   under the axle of No. 5, striking the ground near the trail Just at the spot where Corp. [Abram S.] McCorkle was lying asleep, cutting his leg entirely off below the knee   ricocheting, struck the right lead horse of the limber square in the breast   passed entirely through him endways, striking the next horse just above the chest passing clear through   hitting the next horse in the throat, splitting his back bone from one end to the other, making its exit above the tail. the wheel horse in the rear of this horse escaped by having his head down close to the ground eating grass but unfortunately his mate   the near wheel horse had his head around in the rear of the off swing horse and the shell struck him in the side of the head Just below the ears carrying his brains entirely out. then passed over the Caisson struck a tree and fell to the ground. The horses were killed so suddenly that their mates never moved. The harnes of the lead horse was driven clear through his body. McCorkle was carried in a blanket to an Ambulance and sent back to Poes Tavern . . . . Just as the shot came over we read orders to limber up and move down in the valley to find a camping place for the night. Had this order come 5 minutes sooner, it would have saved us 1 man and 4 horses.

Wilder reported, "Lilly did fine shooting. Deserters report three men killed and eleven wounded as the result of our first day's shelling."[14] During the action, the two sections of the battery expended 263 shells,

14 *O.R.* Ser. 1, XXX, pt. 3, 135–36.

and to replace these, Wilder requested Brigadier General James A. Garfield, Rosecrans's chief of staff, to send 200 rounds of percussion shell, 200 rounds of Hotchkiss fuse shell, and 1,000 friction primers to Tracy City.[15]

On August 22 the battery remained in camp, except that the Third Section went forward at 5:30 P.M. to shell the 32-pounder gun that had fired the fatal shot on the previous day. They fired twenty rounds, and the large cannon replied four or five times without coming close to Lilly's guns. The men became convinced that the fatal shot of the previous day was a chance shot and that the Rebel gunners could not approach such accuracy again, but Captain Lilly did not rely on continued inaccuracy. He wrote, "Their thirty-two's being *rather* uncomfortable metal, I constructed works . . . by digging in from the rear of the crests which are very narrow, which made excellent cover for my guns and caissons."[16] Wilder learned later that the 32-pounder burst during the action on August 22.[17]

The soldiers enjoyed their camp "in an exceedingly beautiful spot. Abounds in the best of roasting ears, sweet potatoes, peaches, and everything that pertains to make a soldiers mouth water." The next day the pack-mule train, under the charge of Sergeant James Binford, returned to Dunlap for supplies of sugar and coffee; "the country furnishes the remainder of the subsistence."

Also on the twenty-third, Henry Campbell accompanied Captain Lilly into North Chickamauga Valley to visit the First Section, which had gone into camp after their service at Harrison's Landing. The section had reached the landing two days before, opened fire on the fort covering the crossing, dismounted the only gun in the fort before it could be fired, and killed and wounded twelve men.[18]

On August 24, Captain Lilly, accompanied by Henry Campbell, went back to Poe's Tavern to see Corporal McCorkle and reported that McCorkle "looked very bad. didn't think he would live long." Upon their return to the main camp, they found that Sergeant Binford had returned from Dunlap "with a mule load of Shugar and Coffee and

15 *Ibid.*, 122–23
16 Lilly Archives, Eli Lilly report Sept. 1, 1863.
17 *O.R.* Ser. 1, XXX, pt. 3, 366.
18 *Ibid.*, 152.

with a keg of whiskey strapped on top." Lieutenant Rippetoe now was absent because he had taken two caissons back to Dunlap for a supply of ammunition. Deserters came into camp and told Wilder that the Confederates were evacuating Chattanooga.

The next day, Campbell and some of the other men climbed the mountain in back of the camp, "a very hard and fatiguing climb of one hour. the last 100 ft. up a perpendicular cliff of solid limestone, we arrived at the top, 2000 ft. above our camp and was richly paid for our toil by the magnificent and beautiful view that lay spread out before us." From this spot, they could see the mountains of North Carolina, Georgia, and Alabama, and they remained on the mountain until almost dark. On their return to camp, they found that Lieutenant Rippetoe had brought back 400 rounds of ammunition.

On August 26 and 27, the men constructed the works mentioned by Captain Lilly, digging the holes large enough and deep enough so the guns could be emplaced in them with just the muzzles showing. When this work was finished during the morning of the twenty-seventh, the guns were placed in position and began firing into Chattanooga. "Most of the shot were directed at the depot," wrote Henry Campbell, "our shells exploding all around it. the distance is 2½ miles requiring 35 deg. elevation to reach it   looks about the size of a hat from our position. Corpl [Nelson H.] Corey finaly succeeded in hitting the building. we could see the brick fly with our glasses."[19] After this, "Put several shots through the Crutchfield house,[20] Chattanooga Rebel office, and several other prominent houses. Caused a considerable scattering in that part of town among the citizens who supposed they were far out of our range."

On August 28, Campbell and Binford went foraging. They followed a cow path over the mountain and "into one of the finest little Coves I ever seen. Abounding in Peaches, Apples, Potatoes, Milk and Butter. We feasted on peaches cut up in a big bowl of cream. Bought all the

---

[19] They learned later that the shell exploded in the clerk's office, killing and wounding several people.

[20] Govan and Livingood, pp. 153, 175. The Crutchfield House, owned by brother William, an outspoken Unionist, and Thomas Crutchfield, a Confederate sympathizer, was the principal hotel in Chattanooga and served as Bragg's headquarters.

fruit and vegetables we could carry and returned to camp." A part of Campbell's duties was to keep Captain Lilly's table supplied.

The next day part of Wagner's brigade with a section of the Tenth Indiana Battery reached Wilder's camp behind Stringer's Ridge and the Tenth's guns went into Lilly's redoubts on Stringer's Ridge to try their gunnery but " . . . didn't make as good shots as we did. Rebs only replied twice," Henry Campbell commented.

While the artillery was causing confusion in the city, Wilder's brigade was convincing General Bragg that an attempt to storm Chattanooga from the north was in the offing, and that the activity downstream was merely a diversion. During the days, Wilder made sudden appearances in force opposite the upstream fords, and two regiments marched as far as Sale Creek, forty miles above Chattanooga. At night he sent details to build fires over large areas, making the Rebels believe that large forces were camping just across the river, and had men saw wood and throw the end pieces into the creeks to give the appearance of boatbuilding. He convinced the Confederates that 10,000 men were north of the river and kept two Confederate divisions above Chattanooga to prevent a river crossing while the three corps of the Federal army assembled and crossed the Tennessee downstream at Shellmound, Bridgeport, and Caperton's Ferry.[21]

On August 30, William Crutchfield, co-owner of Crutchfield House, the principal hotel of Chattanooga, swam the river and stayed with Colonel Wilder. He told Wilder that Bragg was being reinforced by 10,000 men from General Johnston's army in Mississippi.[22]

The sector opposite Chattanooga was quiet August 31 through September 2, possibly because ammunition was in short supply. Lieutenant Beck started for Tracy City on August 30, returning with 400 rounds on September 2, and the next day, Lieutenant Rippetoe took temporary command of the First Section at Poe's Tavern so that Lieutenant Scott could go forward and "See the Elephant."

On September 4, Campbell busied himself building a log house, covering the roof with a tarpaulin, and finishing a twenty-page letter

21 Lilly Archives, John T. Wilder, "Address to Reunion of 18th Battery and 9th Cavalry" at G. A. R. encampment, Sept. 6, 1893; Benefiel, *Wilder's Brigade*, p. 17; *O.R.* Ser. 1, XXX, pt. 3, 152, 164

22 *O.R.* Ser. 1, XXX, pt. 3, 253.

to his parents. On September 5, the First Section came up from Poe's Tavern and shelled the Rebel pontoon bridge, which had been repaired the previous night and appeared ready to be swung across the river, a prelude to an attack.

"Last night about 11 oclock we were aroused out of our sleep by the report of a volley from what we supposed was the picket," Henry Campbell wrote on September 6, "and immediately afterward we heard that the rebels were across the river and advancing up the valley on us. Battery was harnessed and hitched in a moment, tents struck, wagons loaded and started up the mtn. in a great hurry. Everything was gotten out of the way as if the entire rebel army was on this side of the river. Batt. and troops moved down the road towards the cross roads, and one Sec. went down to the river, but no enemy could be discovered anywheres. All returned to camp about 2 oclock. The alarum was caused by one of the 17th boys hanging his cartridge box on a log, that had a camp fire built against it. during the night the fire got up to the box and heated the copper cartridges, and they shot off like a small volley of musketry."

On September 6, Lieutenant Beck's Third Section and a section of the Tenth Indiana Battery took the positions on Stringer's Ridge and "kept up a steady fire all afternoon. Rebels replied several times from their 32 lb gun." During the morning of September 8, heavy cannonading was heard at Friar's Island, eight miles above Chattanooga, and Lilly's entire battery went into action, firing several shots into the Confederate forts but receiving no reply. One gun was sent to the river opposite Lookout Mountain and fired on the rifle pits there, but there was no reply.

The guns were moved closer to town, and Scott's section shelled the forts from the opposite bank, drawing no reply except from sharpshooters on the levee. The sharpshooters prevented the Federals from securing boats along the river, so they could not cross.

On September 9, Campbell wrote, "To day the Union troops entered the boasted stronghold of the West without the loss of a man." During the morning the Second Section took position across the river from Lookout Mountain and shelled the Confederate works, driving out Rebel skirmishers and assisting the advance of the Ninety-second

Illinois, which had crossed the river at Battle Creek, that drove the Johnnies from the foot of the mountain. By 9:30 A.M., the advance guard of the Ninety-second was in Chattanooga, and at 10:00 A.M. the regiment's colors were flown from atop the Crutchfield House.[23] Soon afterward, Captain Lilly and Colonel Milton Barnes of the Ninety-seventh Ohio Infantry crossed the river and hoisted a flag on the largest fort.

Henry Campbell thought, "The town has a dirty, dreary appearance, almost deserted by the citizens   very few nice houses and all old ones. The 'Chattanooga Rebel' was printed in the vault of the Chattanooga Bank to keep out of the way of our shells."[24] He reported that a great many of the houses had holes from the shelling, "depot and Crutchfield house in particular."

The men of Wilder's brigade and Lilly's battery were proud of what they had done, and Henry Campbell wrote, "Our Brigade had the honor of first opening out on Chattanooga. also the first to enter it. Our Battery fired the first and last gun at the town   fired over 600 rounds altogther . . . . We were here from the 21 Aug. till today with Wilder's Brigade and Wagners for our support nearly three weeks opposed to the whole of Braggs Army." After elements of Crittenden's XXI Corps came into Chattanooga, the Ninety-second Illinois rode up the south bank of the Tennessee River and rejoined the balance of Wilder's brigade that had forded the river at Friar's Island.

Because the Union retained possession of Chattanooga for the rest of the war, its occupation was one of the most decisive events. In addition to breaking the most convenient routes for moving armaments and food between the sections of the Confederacy, Chattanooga provided a base for supporting the occupation of East Tennessee and for the later invasion of Georgia.

23 *Ibid.*, pt. 1, 453–55.
24 Livingood, "Chattanooga *Rebel*," pp. 50–51. The power press and equipment of the *Rebel* had been shipped to Marietta, Georgia, shortly after the shelling of the town commenced. The paper continued publication with an old hand press located in the bank rooms next to the vault.

VII

Chickamauga

*Began fording the Tennessee at 9
Oclock at a point just below Friers
island .... Entire Brigade—transportation and all, go safely over
by 2 P.M.*

As indicated by Henry Campbell on September 10, the soldiers did not
tarry in captured Chattanooga but immediately began the next major
campaign of the war. Wilder's brigade marched toward Ringgold,
Georgia, forming the left flank of the Army of the Cumberland. The
right flank was forty miles away at Alpine, Georgia.

General Rosecrans thought the Confederate army was demoralized
and retreating toward Atlanta. Bragg had left Perryville and Stones
River when his army had appeared capable of fighting and had evacuated his Tullahoma position when the Union armies broke through
the gaps in the mountains. There was no reason to suppose that he
would do anything different after losing the citadel of Chattanooga.
Deserters also informed Rosecrans that the Army of Tennessee was in
full retreat.

If Bragg was retreating, there appeared little danger for the Army
of the Cumberland, even though the three corps were separated by
forty miles of mountainous terrain. Crittenden's XXI Corps was marching through Rossville, in pursuit of Bragg's army while Thomas's XIV
Corps was in McLemore's Cove between Lookout and Pigeon mountains some twenty miles to the south, and McCook's XX Corps was
twenty miles beyond at Alpine with the First Cavalry Division scouting
toward LaFayette and Rome.

Bragg, however, intended to fight and had retreated only as far as

LaFayette. He had been reinforced by Major General Simon Buckner's corps of 8,000 men from Knoxville and two divisions from the Army of Mississippi commanded by Major Generals John C. Breckinridge and William H. T. Walker. Lieutenant General James Longstreet's corps also was in transit from the Army of Northern Virginia. With these reinforcements, Bragg would have a numerical superiority over the Army of the Cumberland, an unusual advantage for a Confederate commander.[1] To maintain the illusion that he was retreating, however, Bragg sent soldiers as deserters into the Union lines to advise Rosecrans that the Confederate army was in flight.[2]

Bragg planned to use his full strength to defeat the widely separated Union army in detail, and on the same day that Wilder's brigade crossed the Tennessee, Bragg ordered an attack on the advance division of Thomas's corps in McLemore's Cove. The officers assigned hesitated and sent recommendations back to headquarters, and during the delay, the Federal commanders saw the danger and withdrew to the foot of Lookout Mountain. Two days later, Bragg ordered an attack by Polk's corps on an isolated division of Crittenden's corps at Lee and Gordon's Mill on West Chickamauga Creek; but Lieutenant General Leonidas Polk procrastinated, and so Bragg lost two opportunities in three days.[3]

By this time, Rosecrans began to learn the truth about the situation and gave orders for his divided forces to concentrate, but before Rosecrans ordered the consolidation of his army, Wilder's and Lilly's men learned that some of the enemy were not running. On September 10, Wilder's brigade marched twelve miles and camped at Taylor's Gap with four companies of the Seventy-second Indiana scouting to Ringgold; but finding no Confederates in town, they returned to camp.[4]

On the march, Henry Campbell observed, "Face of the country is altogether different from what it is on the other side of the Tennessee,

---

1 National Park Service, p. 24. At the battle, the Confederates had a total strength of 66,326 men; the Union, 58, 222.

2 Glenn Tucker, *Chickamauga: Bloody Battle of the West* (Indianapolis: Bobbs-Merrill, 1961), pp. 23–30.

3 *Ibid.*, pp. 60–71; Thomas Lawrence Connelly, *Autumn of Glory: The Army of Tennessee 1862–1865* (Baton Rouge: Louisiana State Univ. Press, 1971), pp. 186–89.

4 *O.R.* Ser. 1, XXX, pt. 1, 446, 449.

being very level, fertil soil and large corn crops on all sides. Plantations are in better condition, generally having nice large houses on each one, surrounded by the negro quarters   it looks like a small town."

Before the brigade began marching toward Ringgold at 8:00 A.M. on September 11, the soldiers had some amusement: "Scouts that were out last night captured a rebel mail. Had the fun of reading the letters from the rebel soldiers to their family and friends." The mail had been captured at Tyner's Station by scouts of the One hundred twenty-third Illinois. Wilder was not amused by the letters because, from them, he determined that Bragg was being reinforced with troops from Virginia and Mississippi, and he sent his evidence to Rosecrans.[5]

At 1:00 P.M. the Ninety-second Illinois with two of Lilly's mountain howitzers, one mile in the advance of the brigade, encountered John S. Scott's brigade of Confederate cavalry in line along the edge of some woods, about one mile from Ringgold. The Ninety-second dismounted and engaged the enemy in a lively skirmish, until the Third Section of the battery was placed in position near the railroad and "shelled the rebels out of the woods." They fell back through Ringgold after losing thirteen men killed and wounded, while the Ninety-second had two wounded in the skirmish.

Wilder had sent the Seventeenth Indiana to get behind the Rebel force; but before they reached their position, the advance units of Brigadier General H. P. Van Cleve's division of Crittenden's corps came into town from the west, and the Johnnies left before they were trapped. By not knowing of the other's approach, Wilder and Van Cleve missed an opportunity to capture the entire Rebel brigade.[6]

Marching from Ringgold toward Dalton, the men saw several covered railroad bridges on fire, set by the retreating Confederates, and also were shelled while fording East Chickamauga Creek, but no one was hit. In the advance, skirmishers slowly drove the Confederates back toward Tunnel Hill until they found Scott's cavalry, reinforced by Frank C. Armstrong's brigade, posted across the road in a narrow valley about three miles from Ringgold, with artillery positioned on a hill in the center of the valley, from which they commanded the road.

[5] *Ibid.*, 450, 459; Benefiel, *Wilder's Brigade*, p. 13.
[6] *O.R.* Ser. 1, XXX, pt. 1, 446, 450, 454.

Wilder deployed the Seventeenth Indiana in front of the position and sent the One hundred twenty-third Illinois to the left and up a hill to flank the Confederate force. The First Section of the battery was emplaced on the left of the road, with the Seventy-second Indiana in support. These guns had just been positioned when the Confederate battery opened fire, starting an artillery duel that lasted for one-half hour. The other cannons were placed on the right and caught the Rebel battery in a cross fire, forcing it to withdraw. No one in Lilly's battery was hurt, although it was the target of the enemy fire, but one man of the Seventeenth Indiana was killed and two were wounded by an exploding shell. Prisoners said that a fragment of one of Lilly's shells wounded General Nathan Bedford Forrest, who was personally directing the Confederate operations.[7]

After the Rebels retreated, Wilder's brigade continued up the valley, skirmishing with the Confederate rear guard until dark, when they encamped near Tunnel Hill. The enemy were in a strong position at Buzzard Roost Pass, through which the road passed Rocky Face Ridge, and Henry Campbell wrote, "I suppose we are to attack in the morning   No camp fires allowed."

An enemy force was in the rear also, which the Ninety-second Illinois discovered when they received orders to report to General Reynolds at Rossville. After marching eight miles they ran into a strong Confederate force and were forced to make a hasty retreat to Ringgold.[8]

Instead of attacking on September 12, the brigade marched back to Ringgold in response to orders to join General Reynolds at LaFayette. They remained two hours at Ringgold until Van Cleve's wagon train had moved out and then marched down the Ringgold-LaFayette road. They did not anticipate any difficulty because the tone of the orders implied that Reynolds already was in LaFayette. The brigade's strength was reduced because the Ninety-second Illinois had left to establish a courier line on Lookout Mountain.

About four miles from Ringgold, the skirmishers met pickets of Brigadier General John Pegram's division of Forrest's cavalry, whom they drove slowly to Leet's tanyard, about ten miles south of Ringgold.

7 *Ibid.*, 446, 466.
8 *Ibid.*, 450, 453.

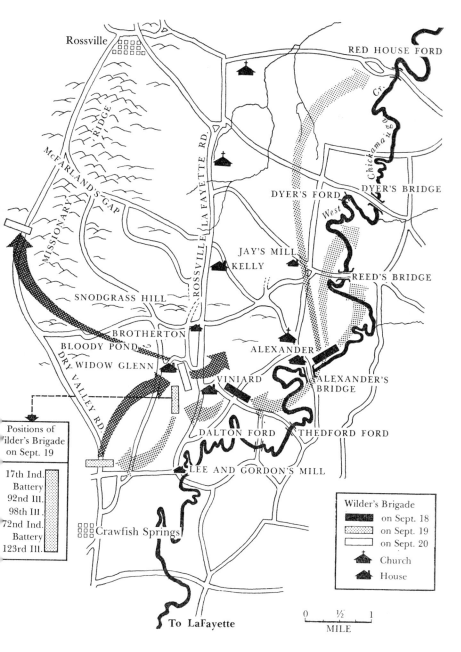

Rossville

RED HOUSE FORD

McFARLAND'S GAP

RIDGE

MISSIONARY RIDGE

ROSSVILLE LA FAYETTE RD.

Cr.

Chickamauga

DYER'S BRIDGE

DYER'S FORD

West

JAY'S MILL

KELLY

REED'S BRIDGE

SNODGRASS HILL

BROTHERTON

BLOODY POND

DRY VALLEY RD.

WIDOW GLENN

ALEXANDER

VINIARD

ALEXANDER'S BRIDGE

DALTON FORD

THEDFORD FORD

LEE AND GORDON'S MILL

Positions of Wilder's Brigade on Sept. 19

17th Ind. Battery
92nd Ill.
98th Ill.
72nd Ind. Battery
123rd Ill.

Crawfish Springs

Wilder's Brigade

on Sept. 18
on Sept. 19
on Sept. 20
Church
House

To LaFayette

| 0 | ½ | 1 |
MILE

Map 4.
MOVEMENTS AND POSITIONS OF WILDER'S BRIGADE AND LILLY'S BATTERY
DURING THE BATTLE OF CHICKAMAUGA,
SEPTEMBER 18–20, 1863

Just beyond the tanyard, the advance guard of the Seventy-second suddenly encountered Pegram's main force hidden in underbrush, "posted Indian fashion behind trees." One soldier told of the surprise: "... I thought I was about to go up that Spout ... I got almost on them before I knew it. We got in A rod of Some of them."[9] The men fought their way out of the ambush with their revolvers.

When Wilder attacked Pegram's position in front, Armstrong's brigade appeared on the left, and Colonel Miller sent four companies of the Seventy-second to meet this threat. These men charged up a ridge with a yell, and with their seven-shooters, drove the enemy down the ridge; but the effort cost seven dead and eight wounded. Meanwhile, Scott's brigade was discovered in the rear and the One hundred twenty-third was placed to hold them off while the Seventeenth and Ninety-eighth forced Pegram to retreat.

The battery could not help in this fight because the woods were so thick that the guns could not be loaded without clearing away the trees. After they were driven from the woods, the Confederates retreated toward LaFayette. The brigade lost six killed and eleven wounded in the action against Pegram, while Pegram had fifty killed and wounded in what he termed "an unequal conflict with the picked brigade of General Crittenden's corps."[10]

After pushing Pegram's division down the road toward LaFayette, Wilder learned that Brigadier General O. F. Strahl's Confederate infantry brigade of Polk's corps was at Pea Vine Church and across the road to Lee and Gordon's Mill, where Wood's division of Crittenden's Union corps was posted. Wilder's Brigade was virtually surrounded.[11]

In addition to Forrest's cavalry and Strahl's infantry, Campbell reported, "Way over the open fields to the left of us could be seen a long dark line of battle, guns glistening in the setting sun   everything ready to receive the charge of an entire corps instead of the little Brigade that was in front of them." John Rippetoe wrote, " ... there was a rebel corps on that road and our brigade was very nearly surrounded and it was supposed that they intended to wait till morning and then

9 Indiana Historical Society Library, John M. Barnard to his wife, Margaret, Sept. 16, 1863.
10 *O.R.* Ser. 1, XXX, pt. 2, 523–29.
11 *Ibid.*, pt. 1, 446–47, 450, 459, 466–67; pt. 2, 528–31.

take them [the brigade] prisoners, but Col. Wilder was a little too sharp for them . . . ."

The long line on the left was Polk's corps, which had been ordered to attack Brigadier General Thomas J. Wood's Union division at Lee and Gordon's Mill the next morning, but instead of attacking, Polk went into a defensive position and called for more men.[12] Perhaps Wilder had something to do with this because Polk said that cavalry reports made him believe that Crittenden and Wilder were concentrating on Pea Vine Creek to the east of him[13] and General Rosecrans acknowledged that Wilder's reconnaissance by Leet's tanyard to Gordon's Mill "unquestionably checked a very serious movement on Crittenden's corps, at a time when it would have been most dangerous to us."[14]

Upon discovering his serious situation, Wilder detailed men at dusk to build fires over a large area to make the enemy believe that his was a large force and to give the appearance that they were camping for the night. A line of battle was formed by the Seventy-second, Ninety-eighth, One hundred twenty-third, and Lilly's battery. The Seventeenth Indiana, meanwhile, began to search for a way out, pressing in all the old inhabitants to act as guides, threatening them with death if they failed to lead them out of the trap.

About 8:00 P.M., the Seventeenth's scouts found a way out to the north of Strahl's position. The brigade was formed in column and began to march; Henry Campbell wrote, " . . . accross the fields, over ditches, hollows, fences, stumps, and everything in the way of obstructions   finaly came to a small road, followed it a short distance and turned off in the woods, passed within 300 yds of the Rebel pickets that was posted on the road we turned off of. 17th stationed a man every short distance so the column would not loose the road, crossed and recrossed roads, followed cow paths &c and after marching about 8 miles we reached Crittenden's Corps with greatly releived minds. Got out of the situation without the loss of a man." The brigade reached Crittenden's lines about midnight.

12 Tucker, *Chickamauga*, p. 71.
13 Horn, p. 253; Connelly, pp. 186–89. Crittenden was concentrating his corps at Lee and Gordon's Mill, west of Wilder's position.
14 *O.R.* Ser. 1, XXX, pt. 1, p. 79.

Polk remained under orders to attack Crittenden in the morning. Only Wood's division had been at Lee and Gordon's Mill on the twelfth, but by morning Crittenden had assembled his previously divided XXI corps behind West Chickamauga Creek, and no longer could the parts of his corps be defeated in detail.[15]

On September 13, the Confederates made an attack on Crittenden's pickets, but after a brief exchange of shots they retired and then Wilder's brigade moved two miles to where they could see the strong forces of the Rebels. They skirmished in the advance, "but the Gen commanding dont want to bring on a general engagement," Campbell commented. A scout was sent toward Pea Vine Church and also observed strong enemy forces. That night the battery camped one mile south of Lee and Gordon's, and Campbell reported, "Things begin to look dark, the rebels are evidently receiving reinforcements or they wouldnt make a stand in such open country. All our officers have felt uneasy since we left Ringgold."

The next day, the brigade marched fifteen miles southwest to rejoin Reynolds's division at Pond Spring in McLemore's Cove. Here they found a quantity of old corn, and Campbell reported, "the first good feed they [the horses] have had since we crossed the Tennessee." The horses were in such bad condition because of the hard marching and their diet of green corn that "Capt Lilly put his horse in the teams yesterday, in place of one that gave out   riding an old plug. My horse is fortunately a small one and of a white color and cant be used in the teams or it would have went long ago." That night Henry Campbell slept on the floor of a schoolhouse "before a rousing big fire in the fire place. This is soldiering with more comfort than we have had for some time."

The battery remained at Pond Spring on September 15 and 16, and Henry Campbell moved from the captain's mess to that of the quartermaster, which was "presided over by 'Sam' a famous darkey cook." Henry had eaten in Captain Lilly's mess for over a year and "am very thankful for the kindness and interest he has shown me, ever since the organization of the Battery, by taking me into his mess when I was in-

15 Connelly, pp. 186–89. Crittenden's corps was composed of Wood's, Van Cleve's, and Palmer's divisions.

experienced in soldiering, treating me more like a brother than a common soldier."

While Wilder's brigade was resting at Pond Spring, General Rosecrans was consolidating the Army of the Cumberland. Thomas's XIV Corps had marched north to join Crittenden in the area of Crawfish Springs, and Davis's division of McCook's Corps had reached Pond Spring and tried to drive the Rebels through Catlett's Gap but "could not move them."

On September 17, Wilder's brigade moved north past Crawfish Springs and Lee and Gordon's Mill, taking position at Alexander's bridge, "a broken down bridge over Chickamaga Creek" three miles downstream from the mill and two miles east of the Rossville-LaFayette road. The First Section of the battery went into position at a log house, covering the bridge, and the other sections camped in the woods.

Near camp, the men found a potato patch and some, Campbell included, began to dig them. The provost marshall appeared, arrested all the men in the field, and ordered all to put their potatoes in one large sack; "a big Corpl of the 72d was ordered to tote the sack and all to follow him to Hd. Qrs.," Henry Campbell reported. As they marched along, the men dropped off whenever they saw their opportunity, and when the procession reached the headquarters picket posts only the corporal and one or two men remained. Here the provost marshall ordered them to wait while he went after a guard. Meanwhile, Campbell had told First Sergeant Martin Miller about the situation, and "He seeing the probability of our scanty dinner, marched boldly up to the Sack   just as if he had been ordered   shouldered and marched off with it. Picket post seeing the joke never said a word and when the Provost returned, he was so completely sold out that he made tracks with his guard as soon as possible."

Having failed to attack the Army of the Cumberland in detail in McLemore's Cove and at Lee and Gordon's Mill, General Bragg developed a new plan to defeat it. Believing that the Union left flank was at Lee and Gordon's, he planned to cross Chickamauga Creek at Alexander's and Reed's bridges downstream, interpose his army between Chattanooga and the Federal army, and drive it back into

McLemore's Cove where he might defeat and capture it. Since Bragg persisted in this strategy, the Battle of Chickamauga became a series of attempts by the Confederates to move around the Union left flank and countermoves by Rosecrans to prevent it.

Bragg's orders for September 18 called for Bushrod Johnson's division to cross at Reed's bridge, for W. H. T. Walker's corps and Forrest's cavalry corps to cross at Alexander's, and for Simon Buckner's corps to cross at Thedford Ford, farther upstream. Then all were to sweep south toward Lee and Gordon's.[16]

Wilder's brigade, however, had been posted at Alexander's bridge, and Colonel Robert H. G. Minty's cavalry brigade was near Pea Vine Creek, east of Reed's bridge, downstream from Alexander's and it was these two small bodies that frustrated Bragg's well-conceived plan. Although the Battle of Chickamauga is historically recorded as a two-day battle, for Wilder's brigade and Lilly's battery, it became a three-day fight.

At 7:30 A.M., Forrest's cavalry began skirmishing with Minty's men one mile east of Reed's bridge, but when long lines of Confederate infantry appeared, overlapping Minty's lines, he retreated toward Reed's bridge. Observing dust clouds farther north on the Dyer's Ford road, Minty called on Wilder for reinforcements. Wilder sent seven companies of the Seventy-second Indiana, the One hundred twenty-third Illinois, and a section of Lilly's battery. The One hundred twenty-third and the artillery went beyond Reed's bridge to guard Dyer's Ford while the Seventy-second detachment joined Minty's force.[17] This left only two regiments and two sections of the battery at Alexander's bridge.

The four guns of Lilly's battery were emplaced on a knoll 400 yards southwest of the bridge near the log house of the Alexander family, the Seventeenth Indiana was deployed in the woods on the left of the road, and the Ninety-eighth Illinois on the right. The planking of the bridge was removed, and a lunette was built commanding the road. A company of the Seventy-second Indiana was on picket duty east of the creek when the Confederates appeared; "the

---

16 Tucker, *Chickamauga*, p. 112.
17 *Ibid.*, pp. 112–14.

rebs came on us so sudden we hadent time to mount our horses," one of the pickets wrote, "but we concealed ourselves thay best we could and fought them till they shot all our horses but at last we was ordered to fall back and done so under a heavy shower of bullets. Lost mule blankets haversack canteen and every thing except my gun."[18] The pickets had skirmished with the advance of Walker's corps, then marching toward Alexander's bridge.

Their advance was stopped short of the bridge by canister and shells fired by Lilly's battery that ripped holes in the Confederate line of battle. Sergeant William O. Crouse has been credited with firing the first artillery shot of the Battle of Chickamauga,[19] but a section of the Chicago Board of Trade Battery, serving with Minty's cavalry, generally is believed to have opened the battle before any of Lilly's guns went into action.[20]

To counter Lilly's fire, General Forrest, who had personally joined Walker's column, had his chief of artillery, Captain John Watson, emplace two guns[21] which, Henry Campbell reported, fired only four rounds because "we made it too hot for them." The first shell fired by the Confederate battery, however, landed in front of one of Lilly's guns, ricocheted against the corner of the house, and bounced back among the cannoneers, the fuse still burning. Private Sidney Speed picked up the shell and threw it over the house before it exploded.[22] When the shell had come screaming in, Henry Campbell "with four or five of the boys doubled down behind a little bit of a sapling not big enough to stop a small bullitt. We all knew from the sound of it, that it would strike some place close by."

The Confederates charged the bridge twice but were repulsed both

[18] Indiana Historical Society Library, John M. Barnard to his wife, Margaret, Sept. 26, 1863.

[19] *Lafayette Journal and Courier*, July 8, 1926; Thornbrough, p. 155.

[20] Indiana Commissioners, *Indiana at Chickamauga: Report of Indiana Commissioners Chickamauga National Park* (Indianapolis: Sentinel Printing, 1901), p. 11.

[21] Tucker, *Chickamauga*, p. 114.

[22] *O.R.* Ser. 1, XXX, pt. 1, 466–67. In 1916, Joseph A. Scott initiated an attempt to obtain a Medal of Honor for Speed, and Eli Lilly, the captain's grandson, had his attorney contact the Indianapolis congressman. Speed wrote Lilly that he "didn't give two hoots for the medal," but he understood that he would receive an additional pension and was "willing to have the medal forced on me." Lilly Archives, correspondence, Dec. 26, 1916, to Jan. 27, 1917.

times by the seven shooters. In these attacks the Rebels lost 105 men while only one of Wilder's men was killed, causing General Walker to write, "I can only account for this disproportion from the efficiency of this new weapon [the Spencer rifle]."[23]

While the fighting at the bridge continued, the four guns of the battery moved back to a church at the intersection of the Jay's Mill road and that leading toward the Viniard house on the LaFayette-Rossville road. The men cleared away trees that would obstruct their fire and were in better position to protect a ford on the right of the position where the Confederates were assembling preparatory to crossing. The guns "opened out hot and made the shell fly through the woods, driving the rebels and greatly relieving the 17th who had time to strengthen their position." This firing stopped Brigadier General William B. Bate's division from crossing at Thedford's Ford, upstream from the bridge.[24]

Colonel James Monroe of the One Hundred twenty-third successfully guarded Dyer's and Dalton's fords below Reed's bridge. About 4:00 P.M., he sent a company and John Rippetoe's gun to Red House Ford on the Rossville-Ringgold road, where they were ambushed by Confederates already across the creek.[25] Rippetoe's account said, " . . . when we got there the enemy had crossed and we came very near being trapped and we had to get out of that in a hurry, we fell back to the main force . . . ." Walker also gained a foothold at Byrum's Ford between the two bridges forcing Minty to retire from Reed's bridge after pulling back the force at Dyer's Ford. He sent word to Wilder, who also began to retire toward the LaFayette-Rossville road.

The battery and Wilder's brigade retired just as the enemy were getting batteries into position, and had marched only one-half mile when the Rebel guns furiously shelled the just abandoned position. The retreat was made quickly but in good order, and one dismounted man wrote, "I had to run like the Devil to keep up."[26]

Wilder retired about three miles and took position east of the La-

23 Tucker, *Chickamauga*, p. 117; *O.R.* Ser. 1, XXX, pt. 2, 239-43.
24 *O.R.* Ser. 1, XXX, pt. 2, 383-87.
25 *Ibid.*, pt. 1, 459-60.
26 John M. Barnard to his wife, Margaret, Sept. 26, 1863.

Fayette road in the vicinity of the Viniard house. Here he was rejoined by the One hundred twenty-third and the Seventy-second, while Minty's cavalry dismounted to extend Wilder's line. These mounted troops were reinforced by the Forty-fifth and Eighty-sixth Indiana Infantry of Colonel George F. Dick's brigade of Van Cleve's division.[27]

Brigadier General Bushrod Johnson's Confederate division followed Wilder's line of retreat; but having already learned about the seven shooters, he advanced cautiously, giving Wilder time to establish a strong line with rail barricades. Finally, the Rebels began to feel the Union position and then launched an attack, "yelling furiously," but after a hard fight, Johnson's men were repulsed and moved back into the woods. Sporadic firing continued until well after dark.

The battle of the next two days overshadowed the events of September 18; but the resistance of Wilder and Minty at the bridges had prevented the turning of the Federal flank, and their evening fight, with the help of Dick's brigade, had kept the Confederates from crossing the road to Chattanooga. General Rosecrans wrote, "His [Wilder's] command merits the thanks of the country for his noble stand at the crossing of the Chickamauga."[28] At dark, Wilder's position was the left flank of the army. At 9:00 P.M., this force was relieved by Major General John M. Palmer's division of Crittenden's corps, and Wilder retired to a position across the LaFayette road on the edge of the woods west of the Viniard field.

The Confederate plan for moving around his flank now was clear to General Rosecrans, and he in turn began to extend his left. Beginning a march that lasted all night, Thomas's XIV Corps moved past Crittenden's corps, and by 8:00 A.M. on the nineteenth, two of Thomas's divisions had reached the vicinity of the Kelly house, well to the north of Wilder's position.

Henry Campbell reported that the night was "dreadfully cold   no fires allowed   no supper   no feed for our horses   the monotonous tramp, tramp of the passing troops, the rumbling of the artillery carriges and the ominous thoughts of the morrow   all combined rendered it a miserable night." The headquarters wagon with their

27 Indiana Commissioners, pp. 12–13.
28 *O.R.* Ser. 1, XXX, pt. 1, 79.

blankets had become lost during the retirement and did not reach the battery until midnight; "...we shivered it out until they arrived," Henry wrote. The next morning, the artillery horses had two ears of corn and the men breakfasted on sweet potatoes.

Wilder's men now found that they were at the right of the battle line, whereas they had been at the left the previous night, because Thomas's corps and most of Crittenden's had marched to their left and McCook's corps was moving up on their right.

The battle on September 19 began far to the left of the battery, gradually mounting in intensity as division after division entered the fray. Henry Campbell wrote, "The firing was very heavy exceeding anything I ever expected to hear. It was one continual roar. It gradually came rolling down the line, almost to our front." Although there were few good positions for artillery because of the thick woods, Henry counted twenty discharges in one minute[29] and added, "The roar is perfectly awful   nothing can be compared with it   if ten million peices of sheet iron were all shaken at once it wouldnt be a drop in the bucket."

Wilder's brigade was not engaged during the morning, being held in reserve on a small rise, some distance west of the Federal line. The position was in the edge of woods south of the Widow Glenn house, which was Rosecrans's headquarters and faced a corn field and a one-half-mile-wide gap in the Federal line, which then was east of the LaFayette road. The gap was between Van Cleve's division to the left and Davis's division on the right. Four of Lilly's guns were near the right of the open field in their front and two guns in the left corner, all sited in the edge of the woods. A ravine or depression, in which skirmishers were posted, crossed the field in their front about two-thirds of the way to the LaFayette road. The Ninety-second Illinois had rejoined Wilder, and thus the brigade was at full strength except that stragglers had stolen some of this regiment's horses while the men were in action at another part of the line.[30]

Lilly's battery did not become engaged until 2:30 P.M., when A. P. Stewart's Confederate division drove Van Cleve's men back across the

29 Merrill, II, 438.
30 *O.R.* Ser. 1, XXX, pt. 1, 455–57.

road near the Brotherton house. In front of Lilly's position, Bushrod Johnson's Confederate division began to cross the road to the left of Davis's division, but Wilder's men moved forward and drove this force back across the road while Lilly shelled the woods in support.

After Wilder's brigade had returned to their original position, the line was extended to the left and the four guns were moved in that direction, but Lieutenant Scott's two guns remained at the left corner of the field. During the move Andrew Johnson was shot through the lungs by a sharpshooter and died instantly.

At 4:00 P.M., Major General John B. Hood's Confederate division attacked Davis's division in an assault that drove it back to the west of the road and to Wilder's line. Lieutenant Scott's guns fired canister at the advancing line, and the four guns on the left fired obliquely into the Rebels. The Johnnies reached the ravine in front of the position, in which they took shelter from the firing of Wilder's seven shooters.

Captain Lilly understated the effect of his guns in this situation, with his report saying that his guns fired " . . . until they reached the ravine when they fell back in disorder except a few who laid down in the ravine and were captured." Henry Campbell wrote, "Capt. Lilly moved forward two guns on the left to a position where he could rake the ditch from end to end. opened out with thrible charges of canister down the ditch which compelled the rebels to retreat in confusion. The ditch was literally full of dead and wounded and proved to be a self made grave for hundreds of them."

Colonel Wilder agreed, reporting that Lilly fired 200 rounds of double-shotted canister at ranges of from 70 to 350 yards. Later he commented, "At this point it actually seemed a pity to kill men so. They fell in heaps, and I had it in my heart to order the firing to cease, to end the awful sight."[31]

This repulse of the Confederate drive gave Davis time to reorganize his division, and Wood's division made a timely arrival. These divisions and Wilder's brigade drove the Confederates back to their original position east of the road. Then Wilder moved back to his line behind Viniard's field, while Davis's division was moved to the left to fill the

31 *Ibid.*, 448; Benefiel, *Wilder's Brigade*, p. 16.

gap through which the Confederates had attacked earlier. Their place was taken by Major General Phillip H. Sheridan's division.

While his men were moving into position in front, General Sheridan rode up behind Wilder's brigade, his staff officers shouting, "Make way for Sheridan, make way for Sheridan." Wilder advised Sheridan of the heavy enemy forces in the woods across the road and told him that Davis's division had just been driven back, but Sheridan ignored the implication of Wilder's information and ordered an attack. His men charged into the woods across the road, but a counterattack drove them back toward Wilder's position; and when Sheridan's men and the general himself reached this line, some of Wilder's men shouted, "Make way for Sheridan, make way for Sheridan."[32]

The Rebels did not follow Sheridan's men, possibly because Lilly was "playing on him with deadly effect,"[33] and because these were the same men who had earlier encountered Lilly's fire and Wilder's repeating rifles. John Rippetoe wrote, "we were not much engaged as a brigade for the rebels, it seemed, tried to avoid us on account of being armed with seven shooters . . . it is reported that a rebel general when he found out that it was our brigade that he was fighting ordered his men to retreat at the doublequick."

John's opinion was relative only to the fighting done by some other units of the army, because the brigade and the battery had their share of action. During the various attacks, Lilly's battery used all of their canister, and Henry Campbell wrote, "boys would carry up cannister from the caisons by the arm full." Captain Lilly also carried canister to the guns on horseback, making himself a target for Rebel sharpshooters.

In addition to Andrew Johnson, casualties included David Lane, shot in the knee, and James Sommerville, stunned by a spent ball. According to Campbell, Sergeant William O. Crouse received a shot that passed through the rear of his saddle, his blanket, overcoat, and his portable writing desk and lodged in his coattail.

After dark both armies remained in the positions they occupied when the firing died down. Rations were issued, but "No fires allowed,"

---

[32] Benefiel, *Wilder's Brigade*, p. 53; Benjamin F. McGee, *History of the 72d Indiana Volunteer Infantry of the Mounted Lightning Brigade* (Lafayette: S. Vater & Co., 1882), p. 177.

[33] *O.R.* Ser. 1, XXX, pt. 1, 452.

wrote Campbell, "and consequently no supper except hard tack and raw bacon. Thankful to be alive to eat that." The horses were watered at a nearby pond, later named "Bloody Pond," but they received only cornstalks to eat. Campbell commented, "They have been standing in harness since Friday morning and are nearly worn out. Heavy, sporadic firing along the lines continued all night."

"A great many badly wounded men of both armies lay between the lines that are unable to get away or be moved on account of the rebels shooting at anything they see moving between the lines," reported Henry Campbell. "The cries and groans from these poor fellows is perfectly awful. they are more dreadful than the storm of bullets that showered on us all day. friend and foe lying side by side, the friends of each unable to assist, in the least." He told his mother, "It was the hardest part of the battle to lie within hearing, and not be able to assist them."[34]

Shortly after daylight on September 20, the lines on the Federal right were adjusted, and Wilder's brigade with Lilly's battery went into position southwest of the Glenn house. Captain Lilly said the location was the first ridge west of the Crawfish Springs–Chattanooga road, more commonly called the Dry Valley road. The brigade was faced south protecting the extreme right of the principal battle line, although Colonel Edward M. McCook's First Cavalry Division still was at Crawfish Springs holding off Wheeler's cavalry corps but was not connected with the main battle line.

Sheridan's division was nearest to Wilder, facing southeast, being refused from the main battle line along the LaFayette road. Next was Davis's division, then Wood's and Van Cleve's divisions, and then other units forming the center and left of the line, generally in the same positions as on the previous day. The Confederate line was in the woods east of the LaFayette-Rossville road.

Again the battle began on the extreme left, with General Bragg persisting in his plan of trying to turn the Union flank. His officers, however, delayed beginning the action, and Henry Campbell wrote, " . . . the battle seemed to be waiting until everything got a good ready." Once started, the action again moved toward the right. Oppo-

34 Merrill, II, 438.

site Wood's and Davis's divisions, Lieutenant General James Longstreet,[35] who had arrived on the field during the night, prepared an assault to be led by Johnson's and Major General T. C. Hindman's divisions. The attack, according to Colonel Wilder, was on a one-half mile front and was five lines deep.

At about 11:00 A.M., a command error pulled Wood's division out of the line, with Davis's division ordered to move to Wood's position and Sheridan ordered to march to the left in response to General Thomas's call for reinforcements. Longstreet's assault struck just after Wood had pulled out and while Davis's and Sheridan's divisions were in column, marching to the left. Johnson's men struck the hole in the line, and Hindman's division hit Davis's men, who had left their barricades and were on the march. This division broke and ran back across the Dry Valley road, while Sheridan's men caught the panic and also were routed by the charging Rebels.[36]

Meanwhile, Wilder had been ordered to clear Sheridan's front and had moved back to the ridge near the Widow Glenn house, where he could survey the situation, and saw that the Rebels were approaching the ridge. With the battery firing over a thin skirt of timber and into the open field beyond, the Seventeenth Indiana and One hundred twenty-third Illinois struck the Confederate flank, Brigadier General A. M. Manigault's brigade of Hindman's division, clearing the Rebels from the timber. Lilly then sent one section up to the right of the Glenn house and began to fire canister at the retreating enemy as Wilder's men drove them for one-half mile, and back beyond the LaFayette road. In the action, 220 Confederates were captured and the Ninety-eighth Illinois recaptured a battery at the Glenn house but lost Colonel Funkhouser, who was wounded severely.[37]

When the men of the Seventeenth and One hundred twenty-third returned to the main body, Wilder struck the rest of Hindman's division in the vicinity of the Bloody Pond, driving them northeast along the ridge, but this action ended quickly because the Confederates

35 Longstreet commanded the Confederate left wing on Sept. 20.

36 Tucker, *Chickamauga*, p. 298.

37 *O.R.* Ser. 1, XXX, pt. 1, 448, 457–58, 466–67; James Longstreet, *From Manassas to Appomattox: Memoirs of the Civil War in America* (Philadelphia: Lippincott, 1896), p. 449.

had been ordered to move north to assail Thomas's exposed flank. Wilder then sent a suggestion to Sheridan to bring up his division, but Sheridan advised Wilder that he was trying to collect his troops and recommended that Wilder "fall back to the Chattanooga Valley."[38]

Wilder did receive some reinforcements. When Sheridan had been ordered to move out of line, General McCook's aide, Major Gates Thruston, had been sent to Crawfish Springs to bring up the Thirty-ninth Indiana, another Spencer-carbine-equipped, mounted regiment. On reaching Crawfish Springs at sundown on the nineteenth, the Thirty-ninth had become good Samaritans when they gathered up canteens and carried 1,000, which they had filled at the springs, to soldiers in the field.

They now reached the field just at the time of Longstreet's attack and took position between Wilder's brigade and Sheridan's division. Charging up the ridge on which the Glenn house stood, they suddenly met Confederates at thirty paces charging in the opposite direction. Their Spencer rifles drove the enemy back.[39]

Thruston, with a small escort, took the 220 prisoners Wilder's men had captured directly across the fields to Thomas's position, showing that the Confederate lines were not solidly formed at the time, although Thruston admitted that the gray uniforms of the prisoners gave protection to the column.[40]

The actions by Wilder delayed the Confederates just long enough to allow General Thomas to extend his lines to the west to meet the attacks of Longstreet's victorious left wing. General Thomas personally told Wilder this the next day,[41] and after the war, General Longstreet told Wilder that the racket of the repeating rifles led him to believe that a corps was attacking his left flank, delaying his assault on Thomas's position.[42]

Wilder was ready to do more and decided to march directly across the fields to join General Thomas. He formed his men into a hollow

[38] *O.R.* Ser. 1, XXX, pt. 1, 448.
[39] *Ibid.*, 547–48.
[40] Tucker, *Chickamauga*, p. 298.
[41] *Ibid.*, pp. 318–19.
[42] R. J. Johnson and C. C. Buel, *Battles and Leaders of the Civil War*, 4 vols. (New York: Century Co., 1887–88), III, 663–64.

square, with the battery in the center, but the brigade had just started to march when a panic-stricken civilian came up to him.

The man was Charles A. Dana, assistant secretary of war, who had been sent to the Army of the Cumberland by Secretary of War Edwin M. Stanton to advise Stanton of Rosecrans's actions. Dana had become separated from the general when the Rebel assault neared headquarters at the Glenn house, forcing the general and staff to flee. Dana luckily found the only organized body of troops still in the field on the right.[43]

Dana told Wilder that the entire army had been routed, that Rosecrans was probably killed or captured, and "that it was a worse rout than Bull Run." He ordered Wilder to escort him to Chattanooga, but Wilder, observing that the sounds of battle on the left were continuing with the same intensity, knew that the largest part of the army was still intact. He could not convince Dana, however. He told Dana that his scouts could escort him to Chattanooga, which was finally agreed to, but Dana ordered Wilder to leave the field, so the direct march to Thomas was called off. Wilder thought he could have made the march successfully "with five lines of repeating rifles" but he reluctantly and slowly began to leave the field.[44]

The retirement was made in good order bringing along two recaptured guns of the Eleventh Indiana Battery and escorting wagon trains, ambulances, some recaptured ammunition wagons, and stragglers of Davis's, Sheridan's, and Van Cleve's commands who had been wandering in the woods, not knowing where to go.[45]

At 4:30 P.M., Wilder received new orders from General Thomas to form a line beginning east of the Dry Valley road and over the hills to Lookout Mountain to prevent Confederate cavalry from coming up in Thomas's rear and interfering with his retreat through McFarland's Gap. Soon the Union cavalry from Crawfish Springs reached the line and fell in with Wilder's men, strengthening the position. Lilly's battery encamped at the foot of Lookout Mountain five miles from Chattanooga.[46]

43 Williams, pp. 34–35; Tucker, *Chickamauga*, pp. 315–16.
44 *Ibid; O.R.* Ser. 1, XXX, pt. 1, 449.
45 *Ibid.*, 449–53; pt. 3, 751.
46 *Ibid.*, pt. 1, 16, 465–67; Tucker, *Chickamauga*, p. 318; Williams, pp. 33–34.

During the battle the battery had fired 778 rounds. Lilly reported his losses as two killed and eight wounded, six horses killed and one slightly wounded, and one mountain howitzer lost in action.

The howitzers had been detached from the battery and were placed in action by General Reynolds during the battle. The guns were manned by men detailed from the regiments, commanded by Sergeant Eli W. Anderson of the Seventy-second Indiana. When Anderson was severely wounded, Sergeant William B. Edwards of the Seventeenth Indiana took charge and successfully brought off three of the guns, although the supporting troops had run away during the Confederate breakthrough. About the two sergeants, Captain Lilly wrote, "Either of these men would do honor to the commission of the miserable shoulder strapped poltroons who allowed the support to run away in the hour of danger."[47]

During the night of September 20, the Federal left, serving under General Thomas, retreated through McFarland's Gap; established a new position at Rossville; and ultimately, withdrew to Chattanooga. On September 21, Lilly's battery crossed the Tennessee River, took position covering the ford at Friar's Island, and "camped on our old ground." Wilder's brigade again spread out along the north bank of the river, protecting the fords.[48]

Union losses in the battle were 16,600 and the Confederate casualties 17,800. Some of the more aggressive Rebel officers wanted to attack the Federals in Chattanooga, but General Bragg, stunned by his losses, decided on a siege. Although the Confederate positions did not surround the town, they controlled the railroad and the river and supplies could only reach the Army of the Cumberland by a long, difficult wagon road, vulnerable to cavalry, that ran from Bridgeport, Alabama, up the Sequatchie Valley, and across Walden Ridge. Thus the hold on Chattanooga was tenuous because only a trickle of military supplies and provisions could reach the soldiers, even if the trains were unmolested.

By September 26 the Union soldiers were settled along new defense lines, and Henry Campbell reported, "Rebels made their appearance

[47] *O.R.* Ser. 1, XXX, pt. 1, 466–67.
[48] Benefiel, *Wilder's Brigade*, p. 17; *O.R.* Ser. 1, XXX, pt. 3, 780.

on the other side of the river some came down to the bank and hallooed accross to the boys stationed in the redoubts. they aggreed not to shoot at one another and to permit horses to be wattered in the stream." Colonel Atkins also wrote, "All quiet along the river. Pickets opposite talking with my pickets and agreeing not to shoot."[49]

On September 30, the brigade marched to Sale Creek, forty miles upstream from Chattanooga, passing Poe's Tavern and Corporal McCorkle's grave; "boys built a rail pen over it," Henry Campbell wrote, "the only mark of respect we could show him."

General Thomas recommended that Colonel Wilder be promoted to brigadier general after the battle, and General Rosecrans also hoped that he would be advanced, adding that his command deserved the thanks of the country for their actions.[50] Unfortunately, on September 22, Wilder reported that he was too unwell for duty and turned the command of the brigade over to Colonel Abram O. Miller.[51] Three days later he was authorized to take a leave of absence and did not recover his health sufficiently to resume active command permanently, although he rejoined the brigade in late October.

49 *O.R.* Ser. 1, XXX, pt. 3, 879.
50 *O.R.* Ser. 1, XXX, pt. 1, 79.
51 *Ibid.*, pt. 3, 779.

VIII

Wheeler's Tennessee Raid

Wheeler's cavalry is reported to have crossed the river at Blythes ferry, 8,000 strong, and gone up over Waldron Ridge with the intention of getting in Sequatchie valley to cut off our wagon train and from there to strike north and make a desent on our railroad communications and in this manner to force us to evacuate Chattanooga by cutting off our supply of rations. Our orders are to intercept him in Sequatchie valley and destroy them if possible.

On October 1, Henry Campbell correctly stated the purpose of Major General Joseph Wheeler's cavalry raid into Tennessee. Wheeler's first objective was the destruction of the wagon trains hauling supplies from Bridgeport to the Army of the Cumberland beleaguered in Chattanooga. Then Wheeler would ride to Middle Tennessee and try to break up the Nashville and Chattanooga Railroad to disrupt the supply line and interrupt the movement of two corps, some 20,000 men commanded by Major General Joseph Hooker, that the Federal government had detached from the Army of the Potomac in Virginia and was sending to the relief of Chattanooga by rail.

Henry Campbell's estimate of Wheeler's numbers was somewhat high and most Union reports placed the raiding force at from 5,000 to 6,000 men.[1] Wheeler reported crossing the Tennessee River above Chattanooga on October 1 with most of the cavalry corps of the Army of Tennessee and three brigades of Forrest's cavalry[2] and expected to meet Brigadier Generals Phillip D. Roddey and Stephen D. Lee with their commands during the march.[3]

[1] *O.R.* Ser. 1, XXX, pt. 2, 685.

[2] *Ibid.*, 722–23. Wheeler's command consisted of two divisions of his cavalry corps under Brig. Gens. John A. Wharton and William T. Martin and three brigades of Forrest's cavalry commanded by Brig. Gen. H. L. Davidson.

[3] *Ibid.*, 644. Roddey commanded a brigade of Wheeler's cavalry, and Lee commanded all cavalry in Mississippi.

Wheeler's force "was neither well organized, well equipped, well armed nor well mounted," wrote Isaac W. Avery, colonel of the Fourth Georgia Cavalry. "A considerable portion were from the command of General Forrest, who were by no means well affected to Wheeler. The troopers, however, were all veterans, hardy, fearless fighters . . . We all felt a little out of sorts. The want of harmonious organization was a perceptible thing."[4]

When Wheeler crossed the river, the Union cavalry corps, commanded by Brigadier General Robert B. Mitchell, was dispersed along the Tennessee River above and below Chattanooga to patrol and guard the various crossings. Colonel Edward M. McCook's First Division was spread for forty-five miles downstream, and Brigadier General George Crook's Second Division was extended fifty miles above[5] with Wilder's brigade, now commanded by Colonel Abram O. Miller, posted at Sale Creek, forty miles above Chattanooga.

Wheeler reached the Sequatchie Valley on October 2, capturing thirty-two six-mule wagons which he destroyed, taking the mules with the command. Approaching Anderson's Cross Road, a few miles south of Dunlap, Wheeler divided his command; and while the main body, commanded by General Wharton, began to cross Cumberland Mountain, headed for McMinnville, a brigade from Wharton's and another from Martin's divisions under Generals Wheeler and Martin attacked a train of 800 Union army wagons in a column ten miles long containing ammunition, ordnance, quartermasters' and commissary stores moving across Walden Ridge. The Rebels drove away or captured the 600 guards, seized and burned over 500 wagons, and sabered or shot 1,500 mules.[6]

In addition to the military goods, " . . . there was a delicious quota of sutlers' wagons filled with good things to eat and wear. And the hungry and soiled Confederates went after the unwonted luxuries with a gusto born of long deprivation."[7] Officers and men indulged too

---

4 Isaac W. Avery, "Wheeler's Raid—Unwritten History of the War of the Rebellion," *Cincinnati Enquirer*, n.d. (clipping in Henry Campbell Scrapbook, Wabash College Archives).

5 *O.R.* Ser. 1, XXX, pt. 2, 675, 684.

6 *Ibid.*, 723; Avery.

7 Avery.

freely and efforts to assemble the command were ineffectual until Yankee cavalry was sighted at 4:00 P.M., when the Johnnies mounted and left, covered by a rear guard of 300 men.

Being nearest to the scene, the First Wisconsin and Second Indiana of McCook's division were the first Union troopers to arrive, reaching the train just as the last of Wheeler's men were leaving. The Yankees drove the rear guard away from the burning train, captured forty Confederate soldiers, recaptured a number of Union soldiers, and rescued some wagons and 800 mules. Riding past the burning wagons, they remarked, "the explosion of the ammunition was terrific,"[8] and, hearing the explosions from a distance, Lilly's men thought mountain howitzers were in action.

Lilly's battery and Wilder's brigade had started to march toward Walden Ridge from Sale Creek at 3:00 P.M. on October 1. Henry Campbell wrote, "Our horses were in such a bad condition that after selecting all of the best, we could only fit out 3 guns   the 1st Sec. and No. 4 detachment of the 2d Sec." One wagon and the forge also went on the expedition, and the remainder of the battery was left at Sale Creek under the command of Lieutenant Beck. Campbell reported that one-fourth of Wilder's brigade had to be left in camp because of unfit horses; and General Crook, under whose command the brigade served during the campaign, reported that his division was in poor condition since his horses were much jaded, "especially those of the Eighteenth Indiana Battery."[9] This, according to Henry Campbell, created problems on the march, " . . . horses pulling badly   constantly baulking   always the fault when teams are changed from one gun to another and placed under different drivers than those they are accustomed to."

Because of rain and the balky horses, the battery did not reach the foot of Walden Ridge until nearly dark and then found the ascending road very steep, slippery, and bad. "Horses stalded constantly," Campbell wrote, "doubled teams on the first gun and succeeded in getting it about half way to the top of the first assent, when it became so dark that we could go no further without danger of rolling gun, horses, and all down some of the ravines." They returned to the valley and encamped

[8] *O.R.* Ser. 1, XXX, pt. 2, 683.
[9] *Ibid.*, pt. 4, 49.

since the ascent was deemed impassable with balky horses, slippery road, hard rain, and pitch darkness. Wilder's mounted infantry did not cross either, to the disappointment of General Crook, who wanted to begin the pursuit of Wheeler early the next morning.[10]

On October 2 the battery marched down the valley two miles and tried a different road that also was steep and slippery. They were able to reach the top only because men for each gun were detailed from the brigade to drag them up. On top of the ridge about noon they joined General Crook's division.

The division crossed the top of the ridge and descended into Sequatchie Valley, reaching the floor about 5:00 P.M., where they halted for an hour to gather forage and while so occupied could hear the exploding ammunition of the wagon train ahead. Learning that Wheeler's main force had some fourteen hour's head start crossing Cumberland Mountain, Crook decided to take a short cut to make up time, choosing a trail called Robinson's Trace for a night march[11] and hoping to make contact with the Rebels that had destroyed the wagon train. McCook's division followed Crook's the next day after all his troopers had arrived from Bridgeport and Caperton's Ferry.

Campbell reported Robinson's Trace to be much worse than the road over Walden Ridge since it was covered with loose stones that caused the horses to stumble and slip so that they could pull very little. Twenty-five men for each gun and caisson were detailed from the brigade to manhandle the artillery up the mountain, and at one particularly difficult place, the horses themselves had to be pushed and dragged. The top of the mountain was reached at midnight—a two mile march that had required six hours. Campbell thought that if they had tried the climb in daylight when the men and animals could see the difficulties and dangers ahead, they would not have reached the top. They went into camp on top of the mountain with nothing for the fatigued horses to eat and resumed the march at daylight on October 3.

About 3:00 P.M., the advance of the column came upon the rear guard of Martin's force at a place just before the road began the de-

10 *Ibid.*, pt. 2, 684.
11 *Ibid.*, 685.

scent from Cumberland Mountain and drove these men down the slope slowly and cautiously for fear of an ambush. In Hill's Cove[12] at the foot, they found a brigade of Rebels posted behind rail barricades which the Union cavalry was unable to dislodge, and so Wilder's mounted infantry was dismounted and with their seven-shooters, quietly approached the Rebel lines until challenged by the Johnnies. "The next instant," wrote Colonel Avery, "a vivid sheet of continuous flame blazed and lit up the woods some thirty yards in front of us, while a rolling, unbroken, deafening volley invaded the quiet of the night with startling effect. The storm of noise and flash fairly took one's breath away. The thought that that hurricane of blinding sound represented a solid rush of death dealing bullets was terrifying."[13]

Colonel Avery reported that the firing was high and resulted in few casualties, but "Had the aim been low, our line would have been swept out of existance." In this action, Lilly's men were spectators since there was no suitable position to emplace artillery. When it became too dark to distinguish friend from foe, the Yankees ceased firing and, during the night, the Rebels slipped through the lines and escaped, leaving their dead on the field.

Camp that night was in an old corn field so full of stones that the soldiers had difficulty clearing a place to sleep; but Henry Campbell, after a search, found a soft spot in a brier patch and "slept as well as one could not having anything to eat all day. . . . Our poor horses had only what they could get off old corn stalks."

At 4:00 A.M. on October 4, the chase was resumed with the Federal force pursuing Wheeler's men toward McMinnville, passing some dead Rebels (Crook reported ten)[14] and arms and accoutrements scattered along the road. They also passed the Johnnies' camp of the previous night and found that the site was "strewn with pickle bottles, sardien cans   Cove Oyster cans &c the remainder of the sutler stores that they had captured when they destroyed the train in Sequtchie valley. The sight of these luxuries caused many a mouth to watter among our hungry boys."

12 Addison M. Dowling Collection, Joseph A. Scott, "Engagements in which the 18th Battery has participated," Mar. 26, 1864.

13 Avery.

14 *O.R.* Ser. 1, XXX, pt. 2, 685.

Henry Campbell remarked that the march to McMinnville was "through a beautiful and fertile country a rich spot which had not been visited by the ravages of war yet as the countless Chickens, Hams, sides of bacon, Bags of Sweet potatoes, &ct. hanging to the saddles of the men amply testify." The column halted for a short time about noon to feed the horses and to permit the men to dig potatoes, causing Campbell to comment that an advantage of being in the advance on a march was that they got all the choice forage.

The rest period was unusual on this march, and Henry Campbell said, "Our aim is to push the rebes hard and give them no time to do much harm and consequently we have no rest from the time we start in the morning until we reach camp at night and the poor worn down horses sometimes hardly have time to get a bite to sustain them thro the day."

Meanwhile, Wheeler's main body had reached McMinnville; and during the afternoon of October 3, Davidson's division, supported by Wharton, had accepted the surrender of the garrison, about six hundred men of the Fourth Tennessee Infantry. After occupying the town, Wheeler's men spent the night and the next day destroying government stores and a train of railroad cars.[15]

Wilder's brigade in the lead of the Union column reached McMinnville during the afternoon of October 4, skirmishing with and driving the Confederate rear guard through town along the Murfreesboro road. A short distance from town, the rear guard made a stand, but was dislodged by a charge of the Second Kentucky Cavalry. When Wilder's men came on the scene, they saw a number of Rebels who had been sabered.

The battery went through McMinnville at 3:00 P.M. "to the great relief of the union citizens who had been robbed and terrified by the Rebel cavalry." Henry Campbell said, "Wheelers men destroyed every store in the place carrying off the goods scattering Rations thro the streets our boys filled their haversacks as we trotted thro the town." Among the supplies destroyed by Wheeler were the overcoats and extra

---

15 *O.R.* Ser. 1, XXX, pt. 2, 723–24, 726–27.

blankets of the First Cavalry Division that had been stored for the summer in McMinnville.[16]

As soon as word had spread earlier that the Confederates were in the town, some prominent citizens from the country drove their wagons to town "for the purpose of getting all the extry coffee & sugar that the soldiers could not carry with them. How the tables were turned though," Henry Campbell wrote; "instead of getting the coveted supplies, we gobbled up their teams & put them in the Battery in place of our worn out horses." The artillerymen also loaded their transportation wagon with coffee and sugar from the wagons that were carrying it to the country.

West of town, the Seventeenth Indiana took the lead of the Union column and kept up a running fight for six miles, moving so fast that the battery had to gallop part of the time to keep up. The rapid advance drove the Confederate rear guard back onto the main body, which formed a line of battle along the edge of some woods, seven miles west of McMinnville.

Colonel Miller dismounted the Seventeenth and Seventy-second Indiana and positioned Lilly's battery in an orchard on the left of the road one-half mile from the Rebel line. While the infantrymen advanced across open fields, the battery fired thirty rounds into the edge of the woods, causing Colonel Miller to report, "Captain Lilly now opened on him with his artillery, at one time killing 1 man and 4 horses with one shot."[17] The Confederates retreated from the position, and Miller's men pursued for two miles when darkness ended the action. In spite of having to stop to fight, the brigade had marched thirty miles that day.

During the morning of October 5, Wheeler's advance reached the vicinity of Murfreesboro and made a demonstration with the apparent intention of capturing Murfreesboro and moving along the railroad to LaVergne, destroying track and equipment. The strength of the fort at Murfreesboro and the close pursuit by the Federals frustrated this plan, and Wheeler was able only to capture the stockade

16 *Ibid.*, 693.
17 *Ibid.*

and fifty-two guards at Stones River and to tear up three miles of track before being driven toward Shelbyville by Crook's advance.[18] Henry Campbell thought that Wheeler "did not like to risk the 100 lbrs. that were sticking through the embrasures [of the fort at Murfreesboro]."

The Yankees had resumed the chase at daylight following the direct road toward Mufreesboro through Woodbury to Readyville, which place they reached at 5:00 P.M. Here they turned off on a secluded road to the right that led into the Liberty pike with the purpose of interposing themselves between Wheeler and LaVergne and also to avoid a possible ambush. Campbell said the move was made in an attempt to reach Murfreesboro ahead of the Rebels, and that they then were only one hour behind.

The Federal column rode into Murfreesboro at dark and here the battery had the good fortune to meet Lieutenant Rippetoe who had been in Nashville procuring horses for the battery and had arrived in Murfreesboro with twenty excellent artillery horses when word of Wheeler's approach reached the town. Campbell wrote, "It was a lucky thing for us as our teams were so exhausted that they could not have made many more days of forced marches without rest." Also in Murfreesboro the men were issued three days' rations, which they did not begin to draw until morning "through the want of proper attention to duty on the part of the assistant quartermaster and commissary of subsistance."[19] In spite of the delay, the command marched twenty-six miles and camped within four miles of Shelbyville. Brigade scouts discovered the Rebel camp four miles beyond town on the Farmington road.

Wheeler's men had reached Shelbyville on October 6, and again his troops were uncontrolled, sacking and looting the town. Henry Campbell said that ten or twelve stores were completely destroyed.

At 7:00 A.M. on October 7, Lilly's battery passed through Shelbyville and Henry Campbell observed, "this is the only *union* town in Tenn. all the citizens out waving their handkerchiefs and cheering the column as it passed thro town." The column marched out on the

18 *Ibid.*, 686, 724.
19 *Ibid.*, 686.

Farmington road with Wilder's brigade leading in pursuit of the Johnnies. At Shelbyville, Chief of Cavalry Robert B. Mitchell and the First Cavalry Division caught up with Crook's division, and the First Division pursued a part of Wheeler's force on the Unionville road.[20]

Henry Campbell wrote, "Wheeler thought he would play it smart on the Yanks here   he made a strategic movement, expecting to out wit us and get in our rear   He moved about half way to Farmington on the direct pike, then cut across the country about 2 miles to a small road, on the north of the main road leading to Farmington, and running nearly parallel with it   this road leads into the pike leading to Shelbyville about 5 miles from town." The Rebels got to within one-half mile of the pike, following this route, expecting that the Federal column would be beyond this point on the road.

Colonel Avery disagreed with Campbell's assessment that Wheeler had a strategic movement in mind and wrote that Wheeler made "the error of the raid" by placing his troops in camp out of supporting distance with Davidson's division camped south of Duck River while Martin's and Wharton's divisions were north of the river.[21]

Learning about Davidson's troops north of the pike, Colonel Miller ordered his brigade across country until they encountered the Rebel pickets of Colonel John S. Scott's brigade. The Seventeenth Indiana and four companies of the Ninety-eighth Illinois made a mounted charge into the Confederate camp, but when the enemy responded, killing and wounding some men and horses, the Yankees dismounted and charged across the fields against a determined resistance, "but [the Rebels] soon fled, betaking themselves to their horses, when they were thrown into the utmost confusion, and completely routed, closely followed by the Seventeenth Indiana, who, while they [the Confederates] were mounting and passing through a narrow lane, closely massed, poured into them a most deadly and destructive fire." The Seventy-second Indiana also arrived on the scene, and Colonel Miller reported that Davidson's division left the field thorougly demoralized and "ev-

20 *Ibid.*, 688–89; Benefiel, *Wilder's Brigade*, p. 22.
21 Avery.

erywhere was strewn stolen goods, abandoned arms, and Government clothing."[22]

Henry Campbell wrote that entire companies were surrounded and captured when the advancing Yankees captured the horses of the Rebels on the firing line and these men, forced to flee on foot, threw away their guns and knapsacks. Campbell remarked, "The road & the fields on each side was literaly covered with dead & wounded rebels laying in every direction. you could hardly get through the road for the bodies."

The appearance of the Rebels angered the Yankee soldiers: ". . . nearly all of the dead, wounded & prisoners were clothed in *our uniforms* (captured at McMinnville) and store clothes taken from the stores in Shelbyville. These were stripped off by our boys as fast as they fell into our hands," Campbell wrote. "Gold waches   money   hats boots &cc were taken from them. Such was the feeling against them for their depredations against stores and private property, that even the dead and wounded were strip[p]ed if they wore any stolen clothes. Captured horses were loaded down with the fruits of the raid saddles were completely covered with bundles of Calico   Clothes, Boots & everything conceivable in the way of plunder."

Those Confederates who were made prisoners and stripped of Federal uniforms were fortunate because General Crook had ordered that no prisoners dressed in U. S. uniforms were to be taken, and a number who tried to surrender were killed.[23]

The rout was so complete that when Confederate Colonel George B. Hodge, who was bringing his brigade to the relief of Scott's brigade, met the routed force on the road, they were "crowded in frightful and horrible confusion, wild and frantic with panic, choking the entire road and bearing down upon me at racing speed."[24]

Now instead of the move to get in the rear of the Federal column, Wheeler was forced to retreat to Farmington with Martin's and Wharton's divisions to cover the rout of Davidson's men. He established a line of battle one mile from Farmington in a cedar thicket.

---

22 *O.R.* Ser. 1, XXX, pt. 2, 693–94.
23 Benefiel, *Wilder's Brigade*, p. 22.
24 *O.R.* Ser. 1, XXX, pt. 2, 727.

General Crook came up to this position with only Colonel Eli Long's cavalry brigade, the mounted infantry force, Lilly's battery, and Captain James H. Stokes's Chicago Board of Trade Battery, about 1500 men total against Martin's and Wharton's divisions and the remainder of Davidson's division.

A Confederate battery, posted in the cedar thicket, began firing canister and shell at the line of Union troopers less than 400 yards away, but when the Board of Trade Battery moved a gun into range, "They turned their fire from the infantry on to Captain Stokes' battery, mowing down his horses and men." Sighting his own cannon, Stokes fired three shots, one disabling a Confederate field piece, and another blowing up a caisson.[25]

At the same time, Wilder's brigade made a charge, broke through the Confederate line, and captured the three guns, some wagons, and men. Again Wheeler's men were routed, and Crook ordered Long's cavalry to pursue the Rebels; but as it was now nearly dark, the Federal command encamped at Farmington.

Crook believed that he would have captured Wheeler's entire force if Colonel Minty's brigade, still enroute from Murfreesboro, had been on the field. As it was, 86 dead and 137 wounded Confederates were counted at Farmington, and an unknown number of wounded were left in houses along the retreat route.[26] In the brigade's attack, Colonel Monroe of the One hundred twenty-third Illinois was killed, and the brigade casualties totaled nearly 100.[27] For the campaign, Colonel Miller commended Captain Lilly "for his energy in keeping up with the command at all times, and for the handsome manner in which he paid his respects to the enemy whenever called on."[28]

The next morning the Union scouts discovered that the Johnnies were retreating through Pulaski for the Tennessee River ford at Muscle Shoals, and although the Yankees pursued as fast as their jaded horses could carry them, they failed to catch up to Wheeler's main force but did skirmish frequently with the rear guard. Many more prisoners were picked up, and the Yankees found the route

25 *Ibid.*, 687–88.
26 *Ibid.*
27 *Ibid.*, 687–88, 694–95.
28 *Ibid.*, 695.

strewn with discarded plunder from the stores of McMinnville and Shelbyville.

General Crook placed Wheeler's total loss for the raid at 2,000 men, with one entire regiment, the Fourth Alabama, deserting and scattering in the mountains. General Mitchell thought Wheeler's loss was not less than 3,000 and reported, "My men are destitute of provisions and clothing; are much in need of horses and rest." But most important, the rapid, aggressive pursuit of Wheeler had prevented extensive damage to communications in Middle Tennessee and reinforcements and supplies continued to move, with only minor interruption, to the Chattanooga area.

The chase now took the battery "thro a series of extreamly beautiful valleys   covered with fine plantations, good corn fields, large residences & plenty of sweet potatoes, our main staff of life Just now every potatoe patch generaly has half a regt of Cavalry in it & the Battery boys aint far behind." The battery reached the Tennessee River at 5:00 P.M. on October 9 and went into camp about two and one-half miles from the river near Rogersville, Alabama, with headquarters in a log school house, "a very scarce article in Tenn."

At Murfreesboro, Lieutenant William Benson Rippetoe was waiting until it was safe to march to Sale Creek with his horses. He wrote, "I get so tired doing nothing scarcely here, that I got permission of Gen. Geary[29] to go out guerrilla hunting today. I didnt find any, but had the pleasure of doing something and being busy a little while. Yesterday while I was looking over the battle field, five 'Gray Backs' got after me, but I was lucky enough not to be caught. I was some what surprised to see them so near town as they were."

He also reported on the condition of Murfreesboro—"Tomorrow will be sunday, and I hope to be able to enjoy the privilege of attending church But the churches here seem to be forsaken. This place has been the 'hot-bed' of rebellion, and I believe has been given over to work out its own just destruction. What hasnt been destroyed by neglect and want of someone to take care of, the army has destroyed, and what the soldiers have left   the 'Rats' will destroy without doubt.

[29] Brig. Gen. John W. Geary, commanding 2d Division, XII Corps, Army of the Potomac.

The rats are being killed by the thousands daily, and yet seem to be as numerous as ever."[30]

On October 11, the battery began a march to Huntsville by a route that took them through what Henry Campbell described as "some of the finest country I ever seen in my life   large well furnished Plantations.   elegant residences,   plenty of negroes and everything arrainged as I fully expected to find all through the South from descriptions I had read . . . As we neared Huntsville the scenery was grand. Across a level plain dotted with elegant mansions lay the city in all the beauty of a setting Sun. the numerous Church Steeples glistening and shining like gold rendering their outline beautifully distinct against the dark blue background of the Pigeon Mtns."

Like other Yankees, Henry Campbell was deeply impressed with Huntsville: "The city contains many Elegant residences, the summer homes of wealthy planters   each seemed to vie with the other in building picturesque houses, all were of the most fanciful style of architecture and none like the other.   Streets paved with stone and lighted with Gas. Column moved through town without stopping, everything was closed up and except for the negroes that thronged the streets, and the white inhabitants peeping out of half closed windows, had the deserted appearance that southern towns present when a column of Yankee troops pass through."

That night the battery camped in the park of one of the mansions on the outskirts of town, but when the headquarters tent was drowned out in heavy rain, the officers moved into a house that was occupied by Colonel Wilder, who had returned from sick leave.

At dusk on October 12, the First Cavalry Division, marching from Huntsville to New Market, collided with Roddey's Confederate cavalry that had ridden into Tennessee in an attempt to join Wheeler but now was retreating toward the Tennessee River fords.[31] At 5:00 A.M. the next morning, Wilder's brigade accompanied by Lilly's and Stokes's batteries marched toward New Market.

The battery's first action occurred at a place called Buck's Tavern,

30 Ernest R. Davidson Collection, William Benson Rippetoe to Mary J. Rippetoe, Oct. 11, 1863.

31 *O.R.* Ser. 1, XXX, pt. 2, 677–78.

where the "boys stormed the place & carried off a BBl. of whiskey in their canteens   all very lively." As they approached New Market, the artillery was ordered to march to Decherd, Tennessee, but the brigade was ordered to return to Huntsville, leaving the two batteries without an escort "in a country notorious for bushwhackers."

Marching through mud that was "hub deep and horses playing out every mile," the artillery reached New Market and camped in a church yard. The enlisted men slept in the church, except for the cannoneers, who were posted as pickets "armed with pistols, revolvers, shotguns, & sabers."

Campbell's fears of guerrillas were justified, and on the march the next day, bushwhackers attacked the rear of the column, capturing Captain Lawson Kilborn of the Seventy-second Indiana, four men, and a wagon loaded with 4,000 rounds of Spencer rifle ammunition. The remainder of the column continued to struggle along the muddy roads and reached Decherd at 2:00 P.M. on October 15, where they were unable to obtain rations or horse feed. The men foraged through the country but found little in this area that had been stripped of provisions earlier. Here the soldiers first saw men from the Army of the Potomac who had arrived to aid in the relief of Chattanooga. The One hundred forty-fifth New York, "nearly all boys," were guarding the railroad at Decherd.

On October 16, Lilly's and Stokes's batteries with about fifty stragglers from Wilder's brigade, all under Captain Lilly's command, marched out of Decherd and through Winchester and Salem, over the same muddy roads, some parts entirely under water, that they had traversed two days before. They camped at Branchville, where Major Henry M. Carr of the Seventy-second Indiana and a battalion arrived to serve as an escort.

The next day the column marched to New Market, where they spent the night grinding corn in a mill, which improved rations since all the men had to eat for several days before this had been "parched corn and what little we could obtain off the country."

After marching five miles on October 18, Lilly received orders to encamp and await further orders. And so the force went one mile from the road to Bell Factory, a large woolen mill that Campbell remarked was owned by a Yankee from Connecticut named Faber and was a very substantial brick building, four stories high. The mill had a foundry and machine shop connected with it, but of more immediate importance to the soldiers was a large flour mill at the opposite end of the dam. The soldiers operated the mill all night and "ground out 3000 Lbs of flour & meal. more rations than we have had for a long time." The next day they rejoined the brigade and encamped at Brownsboro.

On October 20, the battery remained in camp having "the first days rest we have had since leaving Friers Island Sep 30. . . . twenty one days of constant marching   travelled over 600 miles   some days averaging 45 miles   only drew 5 days rations during the march . . . . Havent had a change of clothes for 25 days. part of the time havent had time to wash my face." The soldiers spent this rest day washing the gun carriages and cleaning harness.

On October 21, Captain Kilborn, who had been captured during the march to New Market, came into camp after escaping from the guerrillas. Henry Campbell reported, "While in the hands of the rebels he learned the whereabouts of the notorious bushwhacker Guirley [Frank Gurley] who killed Gen. McCook[32] last year. Informing Col. Wilder of the fact, he [Wilder] immediately sent him [Kilborn] in charge of a Squad of men to attempt his capture, which proved successful and Guirley is in safe hands."

Henry Campbell bought "a very fine violin" for $13 from Joel Woods, who had "captured" it near Huntsville. Campbell now was messing with First Sergeant Martin J. Miller, Quartermaster Sergeant John D. Johnson, and Wagonmaster and Company Clerk James Binford. "Sam" cooked for them and they thought he was "one of the best of his profession now following the army." Campbell described him as "a little, short, chunky darky, black as midnight with a continual grin on his sable countinance and a joke for everybody." The army also employed skilled Negroes in other occupations, and Campbell

---

[32] Brig. Gen. Robert G. McCook was shot by guerrillas near Salem (now Old Salem), Tenn., Aug. 6, 1862. For Kilborn's account of Gurley's capture, see McGee, pp. 213–19. On Dec. 2, 1863, Gurley was sentenced by a military court to be hanged for the murder of McCook, but President Lincoln did not sign the papers and he was ultimately released and paroled after the war. *O.R.* Ser. 2, VIII, 741–42; 817–21; 898.

"Had 'Tony' our Colored asst blacksmith shoe my mare all around and a very neat Job he did."

On November 6, First Sergeant Martin J. Miller[33] was promoted to second lieutenant, and the soldiers gave three cheers when it was announced, with Campbell predicting, "He will make a good officer." Three days later, the paymaster arrived with funds to pay off the command but advised that the company records were not acceptable. Henry Campbell commented, "Began work on the rolls this morning employing everyone that can write correctly in the Batt. have 6 to make out. Clothing Acct. has to be settled this time."

Henry apparently drew the assignment to make up the clothing accounts, "which has been kept on slips of paper thrown promiscuously in the Co. desk and in very bad condition to place on the rolls." He found that some of the men owed nearly $90 for clothing.

Meanwhile, at Sale Creek the remainder of the battery and the men of Wilder's brigade possibly were taking advantage of their dismounted state because Brigadier General James G. Spears, commanding the area, complained to headquarters that he was having to forage for and protect Wilder's convalescents. He was advised, "Wilder's troops must do all they can, and fight as well as work."[34]

James Dodd reported, " . . . we have been living on half rations . . . that is such as Uncle Sam gives us but we generally live better then than any other time for we forage the Country and get irish and sweet potatoes fresh pork Chickens bunkens apples and all such produce." In his letter he included exotic seeds for his mother. "They grow just like a grape and are as big as marbles, the name is muskdines." He cautioned her to plant them in sandy ground.[35]

John Rippetoe resumed an earlier occupation—"I have got to teaching school and I have one scholar and he is a colored man over thirty years of age   he asked me to hear his lessons twice a day when we are in camp.   he can spell in three syllables in McGuffey's spelling book and he can read a little in the first reader. Now it seems strange that a

---

33 Martin J. Miller had completed his sophomore year at Wabash College before enlisting in Lilly's battery. College catalogues show that his residence was Cologne, Prussia.

34 *O.R.* Ser. 1, XXX, pt. 4, 422–24.

35 Lilly Archives, James C. Dodd to Rueben and Mary Hinkel, Oct. 23, 1863.

man of his age should want to learn but he is very anxious to acquire an education."

He identified his student as "a very sturdy negro, he cooks for Benson and Beck and Scott." He said that Benson had been teaching him but that Benson and David Rippetoe had gone to Nashville for horses. John wrote, "he sometimes wants to know what will become of negroes after the war and I am very particular to inform him that I think they will be sent off to a colony by themselves and if he will try he may be very useful among those of his own color especially if he becomes religious . . . I give him to understand that the white race and negroes can never in my opinion be on an equality, that the training of each race in the past if nothing else, would keep them from it, and that I think that both would enjoy themselves more to be separated . . . ."

On October 25, John wrote that Benson and David Rippetoe had returned from Nashville and also told Mary, "There are a great many union people in this part of the country, out of one hundred and eighty seven votes, there was only twenty for secession, which is better than some places at home." He also wrote that the soldiers were glad to hear that the "Butternuts" were defeated in Ohio and Pennsylvania elections, and "also we hear that there is a majority for the union in our own state of Indiana which will greatly depress the rebels and is to us of more importance than a great victory would be, as it shows that there is still a majority at home who are the soldiers friends."

While part of the battery was resting at Sale Creek and the others were recuperating from their chase across Tennessee, command changes were made at the highest level. Major General U. S. Grant was given command of all western armies and moved to Chattanooga to try to break the siege and to drive Bragg's army away. Grant replaced Rosecrans as commander of the Army of the Cumberland with George H. Thomas.

Rippetoe expressed an opinion common among the soldiers: "We hated to give up Gen Rosecrans but probably it is for the best as we have some good and tried men with us yet of whom Gen Thomas is not the least but one of the bravest of the brave . . . one thing certain we have a great deal of confidence in him."

General Grant opened a water route to bring supplies into Chattanooga and then built up overwhelming strength. Major General Joseph Hooker, with two corps of the Army of the Potomac, had already reached the vicinity of Chattanooga while Grant's own Army of the Tennessee, now commanded by Major General William T. Sherman, was marching across Tennessee to join the Cumberland and Potomac boys. On November 12 and 13, Henry Campbell watched while two divisions of Sherman's force marched through Brownsboro.

The battery was united once again on November 15 when Lieutenant Beck's men arrived from Sale Creek. However, the battery was not in condition to resume active campaigning, since they could muster only four horses for each gun, and Albert Allen, who had been at Nashville, was able to get only seven horses—"our share of all that could be procured." After the Wheeler raid, the cavalry corps, as well as the artillery, were in desperate need of new, fresh mounts.

IX

With the Cavalry in
East Tennessee

*Received an order today very
unexpectedly to leave the Brigade
& report to Elliotts Cav. Div. without
delay.[1] never was there an order that
was obeyed with greater reluctance
than this. we are linked and bound
to the different Regts of Wilders
brigade by more than one tie having
fought side by side with them in
many a hard fight gaining the confidence and respect of all & having
an equal share in the celebrated
name it bears.*

The order to leave Wilder's brigade and to join the cavalry was received on November 17, and the men who had been detailed to the
battery from the various regiments were sent back to their units on the
same day. Henry Campbell wrote, "all wanted to stay with the Batt &
and we hated to leave them. some even felt so badly as to cry over it.
The Brigade all hate to have us leave."

John Rippetoe viewed the change of commands more philosophically—"We did not like the idea of leaving our old brigade, but it may
be that it will be for the best, indeed I believe that a kind Providence
will take care of us in every place that we may be put. It was pretty
hard to give up some detailed men .... The most of them wanted to
stay with the Battery and as they had been with us ten months we had
become attached to them."

All regiments of Wilder's brigade were assembled at 8:00 A.M. the
next morning and cheered when the artillerymen rode by on their way
out of camp. The men of the battery felt so sad about the move that
few words were exchanged on the twenty mile march that day during
which they were joined by an escort of twenty men of the Ninth Penn-

1 Indiana State Library, Archives Division, Special Field Order 278, Army of
the Cumberland, transferred Wilder's brigade from the XIV Corps to the Cavalry
Corps, and Special Order 130 assigned the 18th Battery to the First Cavalry
Division.

sylvania, one of the regiments of the First Cavalry Division, to which the battery was assigned.

Although the artillerymen were disheartened about their leaving Wilder's brigade, they were to find that their new division was one of the highly respected, veteran cavalry forces of the Army of the Cumberland. This was one of two cavalry divisions commanded by Brigadier General Washington Lafayette Elliott, chief of cavalry, Army of the Cumberland.[2]

The division was commanded by Colonel Edward M. McCook and was divided into two brigades. The First Brigade, under Colonel Archibald Campbell, was composed of the Ninth Pennsylvania, Second Michigan, and First East Tennessee Regiments; the Second Brigade, commanded by Colonel Oscar LaGrange, consisted of the Second and Fourth Indiana, First Wisconsin, and Seventh Kentucky.[3] The division had served as a unit in the Chattanooga campaign, the Battle of Chickamauga, and in the chase of Wheeler's cavalry.

Edward Moody McCook, under whom Lilly's battery was destined to serve for the remainder of the war, was another of the competent civilians who became an excellent military leader. Born in Steubenville, Ohio, in 1833, he was one of the famous "Fighting McCooks" that included four brothers, seven cousins, and his father, all of whom served in the Union army, and a brother in the navy.

At age sixteen, Edward left home to seek his fortune in the wilds of Minnesota Territory and, a few years later, joined the gold rush to even wilder Colorado, then a part of Kansas Territory. Here he became a lawyer and political leader, being elected his district's representative in the Kansas legislature.

Arriving in Washington a few days after the fall of Fort Sumter, McCook served in The Frontier Guard, a group of Kansans assigned to defend the White House,[4] and when the guard was disbanded after

[2] Allen Johnson and Dumas Malone, *Dictionary of American Biography*, 11 vols. (New York: Scribners, 1933), III, 100–101. Elliott, Rosecrans' choice for chief of cavalry, had attended Dickinson College and West Point, had served in the Mexican War, and in frontier duty prior to the Civil War. He had a distinguished war record established in the Army of the Tennessee and in the Army of the Potomac.

[3] *O.R.* Ser. 1, XXXI, pt. 3, 556.

[4] Library of Congress, Manuscript Division, "Records of the Frontier Guard."

THE 18TH IND. ARTILLERY

INDIANA BOYS ON EVERY FIELD!

THE UNION FOREVER!

LILLY'S HOOSIER BATTERY!

In This Great Emergency Our Government Wants Men!
Men with stout hands and willing hearts, men who will fight manfully for our just and holy cause.

Arouse

MEN OF INDIANA!

And respond nobly to this last call as you have done to others. Listen not to those who would keep you from going; they will approach you in a thousand ways; heed them not; they have oily tongues but are TRAITORS AT HEART.

The undersigned has been authorized by His Excellency O. P. MORTON, Governor of Indiana, to raise a Battery, to be known as the 18th Battery Indiana Artillery; headquarters, for the present, at Greencastle, to be organized as follows: 1 Captain, 2 First Lieutenants, 2 Second Lieutenants, 1 First Sergeant, 1 Quartermaster Sergeant, 6 Sergeants, 12 Corporals, 2 Buglers, 2 Blacksmiths, 2 Wagon Makers, 2 Harness Makers, 1 Wagoner, 122 Privates; Total, 156 men. The Battery will consist of

SIX, TEN POUNDER PARROTT GUNS!

AS IT IS DESIGNED TO MAKE THIS THE CRACK BATTERY OF INDIANA,

No man need apply for enrollment unless he is sound in every particular.
"A premium of $2,00 will be paid for each acceptable recruit. Every Volunteer who enlists for three years or during the war, shall receive his first month's pay in advance, upon mustering his company into the service of the United States, and shall in addition thereto receive $25,00 of the One Hundred Dollars Bounty, which shall be paid when the company is raised to the minimum number. (Gen'l Orders No. 49.) Each recruit receives $100,00 Bounty, and from $13,00 to $21,00 per month.

ELI LILLY,

July 9, 1862.   Headquarters at the Drug Store, S. E. Corner Public Square, Greencastle, Indiana.

. SCOTT of Bainbridge, late of the 16th Indiana, is fully authorized by me to recruit for the above Battery.   E. LILLY

Recruiting poster.

Above, Emily Lemon Lilly; *below*, Colonel (later Brevet Brigadier General) John T. Wilder.

Captain (later Colonel) Eli Lilly.

Left, Captain Moses M. Beck; *right,* Captain Joseph Addison Scott.

Bugler Henry Campbell.

Left, Corporal Sidney A. Speed; *right,* Sergeant Marion Barr.

The 3-inch Ordnance Rifle (Rodman gun) attended by officers of Battery A, Second U. S. Artillery.

Above, Crutchfield House, Chattanooga; *below,* ruins of Georgia Railroad roundhouse, Atlanta, 1864.

Above, Atlanta after Federal bombardment, 1864; *below,* Chattanooga from the north after Federal occupation.

1ST BRIGADE WILDER
4TH DIVISION. REYNOLDS
14TH CORPS. THOMAS

18TH IND. BATTERY

Eighteenth Indiana Battery Monument, Chickamauga Battlefield.

Colonel Eli Lilly revisits Eighteenth Battery position at Chickamauga Battlefield, November 1895.

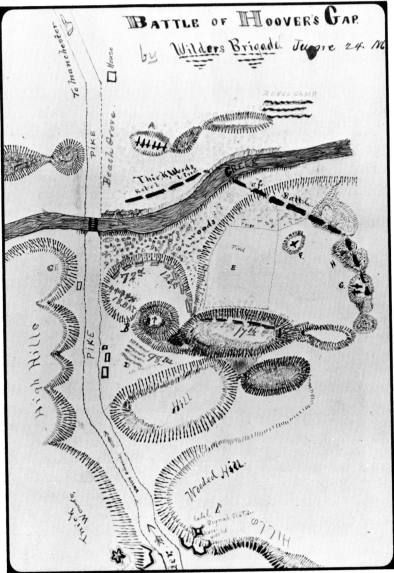

Map of the Battle of Hoover's Gap, by Henry Campbell, showing: *A*, Confederate six-gun battery; *B*, high conical hill; *C*, position of Nineteenth Indiana Battery; *D*, position of reserves and artillery horses; *E*, Confederate attack on Seventeenth Indiana; *F*, Confederate gun that was moved to *H* when the Rebels were forced to withdraw; *G*, two Confederate guns moved here from *A*, placing Lilly's battery in crossfire.

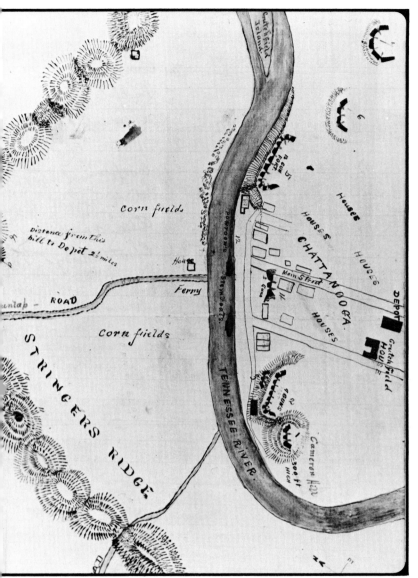

Map of Lilly's battery opposite Chattanooga, by Henry Campbell, showing: *1*, fort with two James rifles; *2*, fort with embrasures for ten guns; *3*, water battery with three guns; *4*, earthwork for two guns; *5*, fort on high bluff with twelve guns; *6* and *7*, forts defending against attacks from upstream; *8* and *9*, earthworks for guns constructed here and also at *10* and *11*, August 27, 1863; *10*, position of Third Section, August 21; *11*, position of Second Section, August 21; *12*, pontoon bridge.

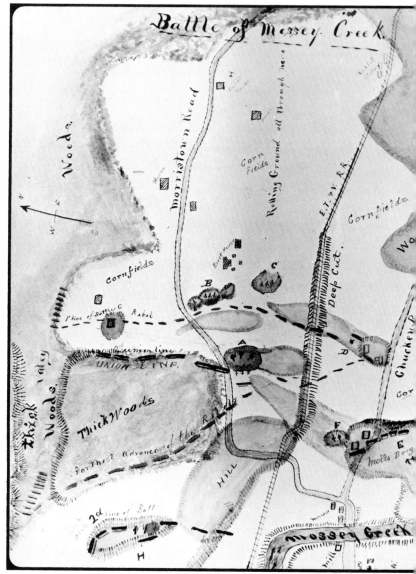

Map of the Battle of Mossy Creek, by Henry Campbell, showing: *A*, first position of Lilly's battery; *B*, Confederate four-gun battery; *C*, Confederate three-gun battery; *D*, Confederate left flank; *E*, Confederate attack on Union right flank repulsed; *F*, position of Fifth Illinois (Elgin) Battery; *G*, attack by the Second Michigan and the First East Tennessee; *H*, second position of Lilly's battery.

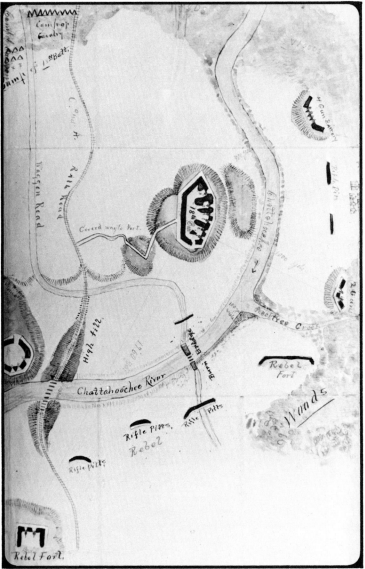

Map of the fortifications at Vining's Bridge, Georgia, July and August 1864, by Henry Campbell.

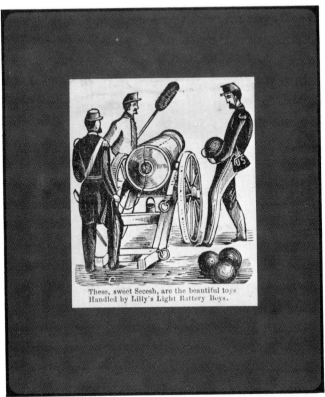

These, sweet Secesh, are the beautiful toys
Handled by Lilly's Light Battery Boys.

Engraving used on stationery and as a paste-on device by Lilly's battery, rendered in its actual size. James Dodd used it as a letterhead for his stationery, and Henry Campbell used it as a bookplate in his journal.

Northern troops came into Washington, McCook became a secret agent carrying dispatches through Maryland for General Winfield Scott, a dangerous mission because of the strong secessionist sentiments in parts of that state. As a reward, he was commissioned a lieutenant in the U. S. cavalry.

He assisted in recruiting and organizing the Second Indiana Cavalry in September 1861 and was appointed a major in that regiment. McCook rose rapidly to colonel, and in April 1863, he became commander of the Second Brigade, First Division Cavalry, Army of the Cumberland. When Chief of Cavalry David S. Stanley became ill during the Chickamauga campaign, Brigadier General Robert Mitchell took his place and McCook, still a colonel, was promoted to the command of the First Division.[5]

McCook could be tough. When guerrillas waylaid and murdered Union soldiers during the Chattanooga campaign, he ordered that all captured bushwackers be hanged and that all property be destroyed in areas where attacks took place.[6]

He did not achieve the fame of some of the more flamboyant, West Point trained cavalry division commanders, such as Hugh Judson Kilpatrick and George Custer, perhaps because his service was limited to the Western armies; but both General Grant and General Sherman came to consider him to be one of the most promising young cavalry leaders. Grant's respect continued after the war, and when president, he appointed McCook governor of Colorado Territory and later offered him the office of United States postmaster general; but McCook declined this appointment because of his growing business interests in Colorado.[7]

Captain Lilly was not with the battery at the time of the transfer and learned of the order on the evening of November 19, when Lieutenant Beck sent a telegram from Decherd to Nashville where Lilly was negotiating for fresh horses. On November 20, the battery rode out on the Shelbyville road from Winchester, passing a spa "boasting a billiard room, Bowling alley, dancing hall and all the accompaniments

[5] Johnson and Malone, VI, 602–603.
[6] *O.R.* Ser. 1, XXX, pt. 3, 106.
[7] Johnson and Malone, VI, 603.

of a Watering resort." That night they camped at Black Creek store with headquarters in a doctor's shop, and Henry Campbell slept among the "skulls and crossbones."

The following night the battery camped near Guy's Gap. John Rippetoe commented that his detail had marched 100 miles in five days, and that they had had only two days rest after their 130 mile march from Sale Creek. He wrote, " . . . we have been traveling a good deal in the last two weeks but that is what I like. I want only time to write to you and time to wash my clothes the rest of the time I want to be going till this rebellion is put down."

Upon reaching Shelbyville at noon on November 21, the men observed a vast change from the devastated town they had last seen when they had passed through during the campaign against Wheeler. Stores had been reopened along with a number of "rum shops," one of which Henry Campbell and Lieutenant Beck patronized, having a few Tom and Jerries "that tasted better than any thing I've had for a long while."

On November 22, the battery reached Murfreesboro, and Henry Campbell had a pleasant dinner for seventy-five cents at the Keystone Restaurant, commenting, "civilization is advancing southward, shurely." The following day he joined a detail of twenty-five men that were to go to Nashville to bring back the seventy-five horses that Captain Lilly had procured. The officers made their selection for the detail while the battery was in the town and Campbell observed, "the boys improved the opportunity, not often met with, to get all the Lager Beer they could hold."

The battery's need for horses must have been severe for them to obtain so many horses from the Nashville depot since General Elliott had directed his cavalry regiments "that all serviceable horses and mules be taken for the benefit of the United States, 'cash' vouchers to be given to parties known to be loyal, vouchers 'to be paid as the Government may direct' to those known to be disloyal or doubtful." When orders came to campaign, Elliott had rebuilt the First Division to a mounted strength of 2,500 men.[8]

At 2:00 P.M. the battery marched out of town toward Alexandria

8 *O.R.* Ser. 1, XXXI, pt. 1, 219, 379.

while the horse detail walked to the depot, but when the train failed to arrive, these men found lodgings in the town. Henry Campbell stayed at the Keystone where "the landlord has one of his rooms boxed off into staterooms each one containing a blanket & a board   which you are expected to occupy and ask no questions." But when he "Passed a very pleasant evening around the stove in the barroom talking over old times & drinking the landlords excellent beer," he concluded, "don't seem much like war   If we had such quarters as these every night I wouldnt mind Soldiering forever."

On November 25, when the trains began to operate again, the detail took "deck passage (on top of the train) " for Nashville, and upon arrival there, most of the men put up at the Zollicoffer Hotel; but Campbell stayed at the Sewanee House with Captain Lilly. On November 27 the detail collected "75 fine, large artillery horses . . . the best lot we ever had" and marched to Murfreesboro. Like the other soldiers, Campbell had three horses in his charge, riding one and leading the others. At LaVergne they passed a train of twenty-five cars "loaded with Rebels taken in the Battle of Chattanooga."[9]

The following day, the detail marched over muddy roads to Auburn. That night it snowed and the next day's cold march went through Liberty to Smithfield, where they learned that the battery was at Caney Fork, seven miles beyond. They rode on and arrived at Caney Fork about dark to find "the Batt & Cav Div all mixed up in a little valley making preparations to cross the river which at this point is very deep & swift, running between two high ranges of hills."

Elliott had marched with the First Division from Murfreesboro to Caney Fork in response to orders to "move what cavalry you have with you" to East Tennessee and the relief of Knoxville, then besieged by Lieutenant General James Longstreet's Confederate corps. Before the Battle of Chattanooga, General Bragg had sent Longstreet to Knoxville to try to drive Major General Ambrose Burnside's Army of the Ohio out of East Tennessee. On November 27, after the victory at Chattanooga, General Grant started a column of infantry under Major General William T. Sherman to march from Chattanooga to Burn-

---

[9] The Battle of Chattanooga, Nov. 23-25, 1863.

Map 5.

MARCHES OF LILLY'S BATTERY DURING EAS

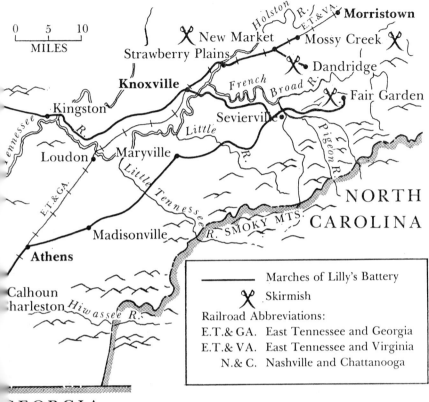

MILES
0 5 10

Morristown
New Market
Strawberry Plains
Mossy Creek
Dandridge
Knoxville
French Broad R.
Fair Garden
Kingston
Sevierville
Little R.
Loudon
Maryville
Pigeon R.
Little Tennessee R.
NORTH
CAROLINA
SMOKY MTS.
Madisonville
Athens
Calhoun
Charleston
Hiwassee R.
E.T.& GA.

Marches of Lilly's Battery
✗ Skirmish
Railroad Abbreviations:
E.T.& GA.   East Tennessee and Georgia
E.T.& VA.   East Tennessee and Virginia
N.& C.   Nashville and Chattanooga

GEORGIA

TENNESSEE CAMPAIGN, NOVEMBER 1863–APRIL 1864

side's relief and ordered Elliott to move to East Tennessee to provide cavalry support.[10]

Crossing the swift flood at Caney Fork in two dilapidated ferryboats, the only conveyances available, was both slow and hazardous, but Colonel Campbell's First Brigade reached the east bank without incident on November 29. While the Second Indiana was crossing on the thirtieth, however, the horses in one boatload became frightened and unmanageable, upsetting the boat and spilling men and horses into the torrent. Eight of the twelve troopers aboard drowned.[11] John Rippetoe wrote that a sergeant, who was able to swim, seized an oar and could easily have made the shore, but noticing a comrade who could not swim nearby, the sergeant gave up his oar to the soldier who then managed to struggle to shore. The sergeant drowned, and Rippetoe wrote that Colonel LaGrange said he would have given $1,000 to have saved that brave man.

On December 1, Lilly's battery was ferried across Caney Fork without accident, although Rippetoe called it, "a tolerably dangerous job." After going into camp, Henry Campbell visited the Indiana regiments and met Crawfordsville friends Captain James Willson, division quartermaster, John Schuler, Second Indiana quartermaster, Billy Smith and Charley Crooks, both serving under Willson. December 2 was spent bringing the wagons and teams across the stream and in burying the drowned troopers. "I shall never forget how mournful and Sad the strains from the Band sounded in that lonesome, dreary woods," commented Henry Campbell.

The division now began marching through dangerous country, and on November 30 a trooper of the Second Michigan was "bushwhacked." The next day the First East Tennessee and part of the Ninth Pennsylvania rode ahead into Sparta, where they had a savage fight with a band of guerrillas, in which four of the Tennessee troopers were killed, a captain of the Ninth Pennsylvania wounded, and eleven of the bushwhackers killed.[12]

[10] Digby Gordon Seymour, *Divided Loyalties: Fort Sanders and the Civil War in East Tennessee* (Knoxville: Univ. of Tennessee Press, 1963), p. 209; *O.R.* Ser. 1, XXXI, pt. 3, 257.
[11] *O.R.* Ser. 1, XXXI, pt. 3, 320.
[12] *Ibid.*, pt. 1, 436, 591.

On December 3 the remainder of the division marched to Sparta, which Henry Campbell described as "a miserably poor excuse for a town. Shut out from all civilization by the Cumberland uplands and extensive barrens and inhabited by such ignorant beings as live amoung the hills, it could hardly be expected to look like human habitations." The division remained at Sparta until December 7 because it was the last place where they could fill the wagons with forage before starting across the barren Cumberland plateau.

At 3:00 P.M. on December 7 the column left Sparta and began the ascent of Cumberland Mountain. The cavalry and artillery reached the top about 7:00 P.M., but the wagons did not arrive until midnight. "Consequently we had no supper or anything to sleep on," wrote Henry Campbell, "built up a large fire out of cedar rails and slep on horse blankets." Marching only a few miles the next day through hard rains that turned the road into a quagmire, the artillerymen went into a miserable camp in houses that had last been occupied by wild hogs— "No other habitation within 5 miles, the mountain top being so unproductive as to admit of but few settlers."

During the march, the soldiers had to remain alert because a strong band of guerrillas remained on the flanks watching for an opportunity to attack parties who might wander too far from the main column. On December 9, they attacked the sutler wagons that were having difficulty in the mud at the rear of the column, destroying several wagons and killing eight soldiers guarding the train and the Ninth Pennsylvania sutler.[13]

Two more days of marching through the mud brought the column to the eastern edge of the mountain, and during the morning of December 11 the division descended into the valley, marched six miles south, and encamped near an inn that had been converted into a hospital. Because of rain that began to fall that evening and continued for the next two days, the division remained in this camp until December 14 and then marched to the Clinch River, which they crossed on a pontoon bridge that the Confederates had left when they evacuated the area.

By this time, General Longstreet had discontinued the siege of

[13] *Ibid.*

Knoxville and had withdrawn his corps to Morristown and Rogersville. Major General John G. Foster now had replaced General Burnside in command of the Army of the Ohio and ordered Elliott to operate against Longstreet's cavalry in the area between Morristown and Knoxville. The hardest campaigning and fighting would have to be done by the Cumberland troopers because the Army of the Ohio cavalry had become weak from the earlier campaign against Longstreet. Colonel Frank Wolford's division numbered only 800 mounted, on-duty men and Colonel Israel Garrard's division consisted only of an understrength brigade. For artillery, the Ohio troopers had only four mountain howitzers,[14] and so Lilly's six long-range guns were a welcome addition.

On December 15, Elliott's column passed through Kingston, which Henry Campbell described as "a very pretty town, situated in a beautiful valley at the Junction of the Holston and Clinch rivers." The morning of December 16 was spent foraging and filling the wagons with corn because word reached the command that no supplies were available in Knoxville since the siege had been lifted only ten days before. During the afternoon of the sixteenth, the division marched through part of Knoxville and continued along the north bank of the Holston, where the Second Brigade and Lilly's battery went into camp after the First Brigade had forded the river and encamped on the south bank.

General Elliott intended that the remainder of the division would cross the next morning, but the water was too deep for the guns of the battery, and the First Brigade was ordered to recross. The reunited division then marched upstream to Strawberry Plains, where the East Tennessee and Virginia Railroad crossed the Holston River.[15] According to Henry Campbell, the railroad bridge, which had been destroyed a few months earlier, was 1,500 feet long and was supported on twenty stone piers. He said that the Confederates had not repaired this bridge but had "built a small trussel work by the side of it and made a switch and grade up and down to it from each side of it." The Rebels, retreat-

---

[14] Eastham Tarrant, *The Wild Riders of the First Kentucky Cavalry* (Lexington: Henry Clay Press, 1969), pp. 278–79.

[15] *O.R.* Ser. 1, XXXI, pt. 1, 436, 591.

ing from Knoxville, had destroyed this trestle bridge about one week before the First Division arrived.

Campbell attributed the destruction of the original bridge to Federal Brigadier General Samuel P. Carter, who had made a raid into East Tennessee one year earlier. Although Carter did destroy two bridges along the East Tennessee and Virginia Railroad, these were near Kingsport, and his raiders did not get as far west as Strawberry Plains. The original Strawberry Plains bridge had been destroyed by Colonel William P. Sanders's Union cavalry during another raid in June 1863.[16]

Although Union army engineers had begun to repair the trestle bridge, neither bridge was in a usable condition when the First Division reached Strawberry Plains, and so they marched upstream to McKinney's Ford, where the First Brigade crossed to the south bank once again during the afternoon of December 18. That night the river rose four feet, making fording impossible for the rest of the force[17] but fortunately, the Rebels did not choose this time to attack the isolated brigade.

The division remained separated by the flood until December 23, and the men used this period to gather food and forage; "the country is our only chance for rations now and a slim chance at that. Longstreets army lived off this part of the country and it is pretty well cleaned out. don't know how the citizens will live for the Soldiers of both armies take everything in the eating line that they can find," reported Henry Campbell. A squad from the battery found enough potatoes, corn meal, flour, jellies, and other food to feed the battery for a few days, but "the most remarkable attraction was two large turkeys hanging from his [Lt. Martin J. Miller's] saddle for our Christmas dinner."

The division had been ordered to coordinate their operations with the cavalry of the Army of the Ohio, commanded by Brigadier General Samuel D. Sturgis, who was in charge of the combined cavalry operation. After the hard campaigning around Knoxville, the Confederate

16 Rowell, pp. 95–110; Seymour, p. 78.
17 *O.R.* Ser. 1, XXXI, pt. 1, 631–32.

cavalry might have preferred to go into winter quarters, but Sturgis, according to General Longstreet, "seemed to think that the dead of winter was the time for cavalry work; and our General Martin's orders were to have the enemy under his eye at all times."[18] Thus a hard campaign developed that did not benefit either side.

On December 23 a small boat was obtained, and the Second Brigade and battery were ferried across the river, the boat being so small that twenty-six trips were required for the battery alone. Once across the river, the division rode to New Market, and just beyond town, the advance of the column encountered a small force of Confederate cavalry "who immediately skedaddled but the battery was ordered up to the front at a gallop as if we had met the whole of Longstreets army."

At 3:00 A.M. on December 24 two sections of Lilly's battery, commanded by Lieutenant Joseph A. Scott, left New Market with the First Brigade of Cumberland cavalry and Colonel Israel Garrard's division of the Army of the Ohio cavalry for Dandridge. Upon arriving at this town at about 9 A.M., Colonel Campbell, commanding the First Brigade, received word from Garrard that he was engaged with an enemy force east of town on the Bull's Gap road. Campbell immediately marched to Garrard's support.

About four miles from town, the First East Tennessee met enemy skirmishers, and the Ninth Pennsylvania went forward at a trot to support them. Then both regiments charged the skirmishers, killing several and capturing fifteen but the attack was halted when a Rebel battery opened on them "with great precision." To answer the artillery, the Third Section of the Eighteenth Indiana Battery was moved forward and emplaced on a hill near Hay's Ferry, four miles east of Dandridge. These guns opened fire on the Confederates who had counterattacked the Yankee cavalrymen, and according to Colonel Campbell, the shots from the two guns succeeded in "scattering their line and starting them [the Confederates] back."

Just after this attack was underway, Colonel Campbell received a dispatch from Colonel Garrard that advised him to continue advancing, and that his force would move forward on a side road on the left

---

18 Longstreet, p. 531.

and never be more than two miles away. Campbell sent the Ninth Pennsylvania and the First East Tennessee forward again with their flank on the French Broad River, while the Second Michigan was dismounted to support the battery. The advance regiments had pushed forward about one-half mile when an order was received from General Sturgis to return to New Market, and so Campbell began a withdrawal of his advance units. A Rebel brigade attacked the retiring Federal troopers, while a second brigade that had worked its way around the Union position struck the Yankees from the rear.[19]

When the Third Section of Lilly's battery had been positioned on the hill at the start of the fight, the First Section had been parked behind the hill, and to this supposedly safe position, no cavalry support had been assigned. While the men of the section were lying down listening to the battle, a battalion of Rebel cavalry suddenly came charging out of some nearby woods and across an open field directly for the guns. Henry Campbell, who was told of the action the next day by Lieutenant Scott and others reported:

> The Crawfordsville boys rushed to their guns and endeavored to unlimber. The drivers started up the hill with the teams, and would have got the guns in a safe place but just as they reached the top, No. 1 closed with a tree and the lead driver of No. 2 not giving way far enough, hooked limber wheels and broke their pole. this left both guns in a disabled condition. The Boys seeing all was up broke for the trees and the Lt in command started also, the Sergt of No. 1 ditto. Corpl. Gus Newell, the only Officer who seems to have had any presence of mind endevored to unlimber his gun and get in a charge of canister but the rebels were upon them before it could be accomplished. The Rebel major, a fine looking young man with a commission as Col in his pocket (which our boys afterward took possession of) ordered Corpl Newell to surrender and made him hand over his haussa which he mistook for a revolver, turned around to Pat Fitzpatrick, ordered him to pull off his overcoat. Pat told him to "go to hell" as impudently as possible. A half dozen of the other boys were then gathered around the gun. compelled to disgorge their haversacks, overcoats, and revolvers, &c. By this time the Brigade commander was made aware of the capture and the 2d Mich was recalled from the line, formed and charged down the hill emptying their 5 shooting rifles[20] as they came. 18th boys dropped down close to the ground and the storm of lead passed

19 *O.R.* Ser. 1, XXXI, pt. 1, 635–39.

20 The 2d Michigan was armed with Colt five-shot, revolving-magazine carbines. Marshall P. Thacker, *A Hundred Battles in the West: St. Louis to Atlanta, 1861–65* (Detroit: M. P. Thacker, 1884), p. 30.

harmlessly over them. The rebel major was killed about the first shot   fell off his horse near the gun   soon as the rebs seen their leader fall, they broke and scattered in all directions. Newell mounted the lead team of his gun and brought it saftely up the hill out of danger where he met the Leiut. & Sergt of the Sec. returning from their skedaddle. No. 1 limber pole being broke, the limber was abandoned and the Caisson limber substituted in its place, leaving the rear part of the caisson. in this way the gun was gotten off.

Being almost entirely surrounded, with a brigade in front and another in the rear, Colonel Campbell sent to Colonel Garrard for support "which he did not send." Campbell then ordered the artillery, ambulances, and led horses to move toward the New Market road along a path that ran through the woods on the left of the original front, and when these were well along the path, the Tennessee and Pennsylvania regiments followed, leaving the Second Michigan, dismounted, to cover the retreat.

After the Yankees moved one mile along the path, the enemy pressure on the rear and left flank became so heavy that the Ninth was dismounted and formed into line on the flank, and the battery was again emplaced on a hill. Both the Pennsylvanians on the flank and the Michiganders in the rear fell back slowly toward the artillery position, and suddenly the battery opened fire over their heads and into the ranks of the Confederates, then massing for another attack. After cutting up the Rebel line with artillery, Colonel Campbell sent the Tennessee cavalry at them in a mounted saber charge, while the Second Michigan and Ninth Pennsylvania "opened a galling fire," which drove the Confederates back and ended the fight.[21]

The artillery began to hitch up to leave the field, but when hooking Sergeant William E. Starr's gun to the limber, the gun axle broke, leaving the gun in the mud; and with no time to improvise a major repair, Lieutenant Scott ordered the crew to spike and abandon it. They drove a priming wire into the vent and put a shell down the barrel wrong end first. No one knew why the axle broke but the consensus of the men was that it happened because the gun had been fired sixty or seventy times while in deep mud and the inability to recoil properly had weakened the axle.

21 *O.R.* Ser. 1, XXXI, pt. 1, 632, 635–39; Thacker, pp. 161–65.

The brigade marched to New Market without further interference. In the fights 7 men of the brigade were killed, including a man of the Fourth Indiana detailed to the battery; 27 were wounded; and 27 were missing. Colonel Campbell estimated Rebel casualties to be 180.

At 8:00 A.M. of the same day two brigades of Confederate cavalry attacked the Second Brigade's pickets, posted about two and one-half miles west of Mossy Creek on the New Market road. A section of Confederate artillery opened fire on the Second Section of Lilly's battery from one mile away and the two guns replied a few times. Then cavalry skirmishers forced the enemy back, enabling the battery to move ahead one-half mile, where they emplaced the guns in the yard of a frame house that "belonged to an old English Doctor who is very nicely situated here. house finely furnished an elegant piano Shotguns and rifles   fishing tackle and everything a sportsman could wish for. all of which our boys 'borrowed' from him. he must have been of rather an excentric turn of mind as he had his family vault about 20 ft from his front door." The battery remained here while the dismounted cavalrymen slowly drove the Rebels out of some woods, and then the guns were moved forward another half mile, but could not be placed in any position to fire effectively. And so the section, supported by a battalion of cavalry, moved around the right flank, undetected by the Johnnies, and went into position on a hill behind the enemy lines; "opened out on them suddenly and caused considerable stampeding of their exposed line of battle which fell back across Mossy Creek," reported Henry Campbell.

"Up this morning at 4 A.M. harnessed and hitched and waited for the enemy to start the Christmas festivities," Henry Campbell wrote the next day, "but he seemed to be satisfied with yesterdays proceedings and wanted to enjoy a quiet holiday." Upon learning that the remainder of the battery had returned to New Market, Captain Lilly, accompanied by Henry Campbell, rode back to get a report of the previous day's activities. "About half way there met Sergt [William E.] Starr wearing a woebegone countenance who hestitatingly told us the astounding news that they were minus One gun and caisson in yesterdays proceedings *Captured?* Capt. Lilly raved at this information. he allways predicted that the Battery would be captured when we were transferred from Wilders and shure enough the first fight we were into after Joining the 1 Div. away goes a gun and caisson."

When Lilly and Campbell returned to the Second Section at Mossy Creek and told the men of the capture, the news "threw all the boys into the blues and a rather sorry Christmas we had of it. About 4 P.M. the gloomy face of Wallace our cook brightened up the dark aspect of things by complacently uncovering to our rapturous gaze two, Jucy, Brown roasted turkeys to the destruction of which we immediately commenced."

The division was up at four o'clock on December 26 and formed a line of battle in "a slow drizzly penetrating rain that wets you through in a little while." The second section of the battery went about one mile south of town with the First Brigade, while the remaining guns took position with the Second Brigade on the Morristown road, east of Mossy Creek. "Remained in these positions all day inactive except for an occasional shot when a body of Johnies would expose themselves," wrote Henry Campbell. "Cavalry skirmish line kept up a desultory firing to keep one another awake and the main lines built up fires to keep themselves as dry as possible." Late in the afternoon, a Rebel battery began firing at the Second Section, which returned the fire; and then the three guns on the Morristown road joined in, catching the Confederate battery in a cross fire that killed two Confederate gunners and ended the duel.

When the Union lines began to move back at 4:00 P.M., preparatory to going into camp, the Rebels advanced and a battery began to fire on the retiring Yankee skirmishers. Lilly's battery took position on a hill just east of the creek, "opened out with percussion shell, which stoped their advance and the skirmishers came in without further molestation." The battery then moved through the town and encamped in some woods "near the church," and Henry Campbell commented, "rations Scarce   havent drawn any of the latter articles from the govt. since we left Knoxville."

The slow steady rain continued on December 27, and so Campbell slept late in the church "listening to the rain drop off the roof. A sound I am not much accustumed to of late." The Yankees remained in camp until 3:00 P.M. "waiting for the Rebs to dry their powder and attack

us but they not seeming willing we moved out and attacked them."
The entire division, in line from the Morristown to the Chunky Bend
roads, advanced steadily through the rain and mud, and pushed the
Confederates back three miles.

"Had a sorry night of it," reported Henry Campbell, "No corn for
our hungry horses .... No Supper and no place to sleep. Built a rail
house threw a tarpaulin over it started a huge pile of rails on
fire in front of it and complacently lay and watch the steam rise from
the tarpaulin until I fell off to sleep. Waked up by the indefatugable
Wallace who had succeeded in boiling some coffee, the soldiers greate
solace which after drinking a redhot tincup full greatly relieved out-
ward sufferings."

On December 28, Lilly's battery moved forward one mile behind
the cavalry, which reached Talbot's Station, without meeting any resistance. As a result, Colonel McCook reported that he did not believe
that the Confederates planned to fight in that area, and that night
General Sturgis sent all of the Army of the Ohio cavalry to Dandridge,
where a brigade of Rebels was foraging and, to help them, he pulled
the Second Brigade of Cumberland cavalry and the Second Section of
Lilly's battery, commanded by Lieutenant Beck, from the line on the
Morristown road and sent them half way to Dandridge.[22]

Instead of the expected action at Dandridge the next day, three divisions of Confederate cavalry, some 6,000 strong, under Major General
William T. Martin, appeared in a battle line extending across the
Morristown road. When Colonel Campbell saw this force approaching,
he sent the Ninth Pennsylvania to the rear to support the three remaining guns of Lilly's battery and ordered the Michigan and Tennessee
regiments to dismount and to retire slowly to give him time to establish a line at the rear.[23]

Unknown to the Confederates, the One hundred eighteenth Ohio
Infantry regiment was camped in the town of Mossy Creek, and they
were placed into dense woods across the road from Lilly's position.
Also, a section of brass smoothbores of the Fifth Illinois (Elgin) Bat-

[22] *Ibid.*, 632, 648, 652.
[23] *Ibid.*, 656–57. The Confederates were Maj. Gen. William T. Martin's, Brig.
Gen. Frank C. Armstrong's, and Brig. Gen. John T. Morgan's divisions.

tery was emplaced on the Chucky Bend Road with some odd cavalry detachments placed in support. The Union force numbered about 2,500 men. By eleven o'clock, the Confederate line had moved within range of Lilly's guns, and these fired the first round of the Battle of Mossy Creek[24] that John Rippetoe described as "the hottest work we ever had as a battery."

In spite of the shelling by Lilly's battery, the Confederates pressed on, driving the Yankee skirmishers back toward the battery and the infantry hidden in the woods. These soldiers held their fire until the Rebels were nearly to the edge of the woods and then staggered them with a volley; and before the Johnnies recovered from this surprise, Colonel Campbell sent the Tennessee cavalry on a mounted saber charge into the center of the line, adding to the confusion.

While these actions were taking place, the Confederates emplaced a four-gun battery on a hill about 1,000 yards in front of Lilly's position, which began an artillery duel that lasted nearly three hours. After one hour, the Rebel battery was joined by three guns emplaced on another hill just south of the first position, and at the close range both Union and Rebel gunners placed shells consistently into the others' position "doing terrible execution."

"The only thing that saved us," wrote Henry Campbell, "was that we retired the guns down the slope of the hill so nothing but the tops were visible and the rebel guns overshot us nearly every time." Captain Lilly wrote that he refused to answer the Confederate artillery after the second battery went into position except for an occasional shot, "but worked with energy on their lines of dismounted cavalry and infantry which were in good canister range."[25]

When the Rebels recovered from the initial repulse, they extended their line beyond the Union left, forcing the Federal commanders to extend their own line and withdraw all but one battalion of the Ninth Pennsylvania from the battery's support. When the Confederates continued to threaten to come around the flank, the First East Tennessee, mounted, and the Second Michigan, on foot, charged and broke the Rebel line, temporarily drawing the artillery fire away from Lilly's bat-

24 *Ibid.*, 660–61.
25 *Ibid.*

tery. The charge, which captured twenty-five prisoners, ended the Confederate plans to encircle the left.[26]

After the return of the cavalrymen to the line, the Rebel batteries resumed their duel with Lilly, and "their shells burst all around us in a perfect shower we had no time to dodge. The boys stood up in that terrible storm of death without a falter. Hits were made by both sides." Henry Campbell related that Corporal John Corbin was leaning over sighting his gun, and Private Ezra Lloyd was bent over managing the trail when an enemy shell hit the left trunnion of the gun. The shell glanced into Corbin's face and exploded, "scattering his face and brains in every direction, taking all his head and neck away down to his shoulders. After exploding, a piece struck Lloyd in the top of the head and carried his brains and the entire back part of his head and neck away."

The gun crew was stunned by the tragedy; but Lieutenant Joseph A. Scott, directing the firing of this and Sergeant Crouse's gun, ordered Private Albert Allen to take over Corbin's duties. The crew quickly put the gun back into action and continued to work it over the bodies of their fallen comrades.[27]

Confederate shells continued to land among Lilly's artillerymen, with one exploding near James Dodd and a piece of it taking off the calf of one leg. John Runey had his left arm shattered by a shell; and Huey Sprague, a detail from the cavalry, was wounded in the ankle by a piece of a shell. James Wilcoxen, another detail, was stunned by a shell exploding over him and hurt when a horse fell on him. Henry Campbell had a narrow escape when a shell cut off a sapling to which he was tying his horse and the captain's.

Following the failure of the flanking movement on the Union left, the Confederates began to build strength at the opposite end of the line for what General Elliott correctly interpreted would be an attack on the Elgin battery; and to counter this, he withdrew the remainder of the cavalry support from Lilly's battery, sending this battalion of the

[26] *Ibid.*, 656–57; Stanley F. Horn, comp. and ed., *Tennessee's War, 1861–1865, Described by Participants* (Nashville: Tennessee Civil War Centennial Commission, 1965), pp. 246–48; Thacker, pp. 167–73.
[27] Lilly Archives, Joseph A. Scott to William O. Crouse, Aug. 8, 1916.

Ninth Pennsylvania to the right flank, where they succeeded in repulsing an attack with their revolvers.[28]

After this repulse, the Confederates began a frontal assault on the unsupported guns of Lilly's battery after advancing unnoticed through a field of standing corn to within 150 yards. " . . . it looked like they would march right over us," wrote Henry Campbell. "We were obliged to stop firing at the Battries & commence with Canister on the advancing rebel troops on our front and right. We fired nearly 100 rounds of canister among them putting 2 & 3 charges in each gun which tore great gaps in their ranks at each shot   still they continued to advance pouring volleys of musketry into us with dreadful effect on our horses and exhausted men." The intense fire of the battery stopped the attack, however, and sent the Johnnies reeling back to their original line.

"It was the sharpshooters that pegged it to us," wrote John Rippetoe. After the repulse of the frontal assault on the guns, enemy sharpshooters moved into a railroad cut, within fifty yards of the battery, and they began picking off the men and horses of the battery. During this action, Lieutenant Scott concentrated his attention on the action of his guns. He glanced down at his boot and noticed a break in it which he showed to Captain Lilly. Lilly thought it was a wound and suggested that Scott go back to the field hospital. Scott had felt no pain, however, and decided to remain with his guns. He picked up ammunition at the caisson to carry to a cannon, but after taking a few steps, he nearly fell from a sudden pain in his foot. Some men supported him to his horse, which he mounted and rode to the field hospital.[29]

The sharpshooters also wounded Marion Barr and Charles Butcher, both having balls pass through their thighs. Christian Beaver was wounded in the leg, and Captain Lilly was struck by two spent balls and badly bruised. All the while, the enemy batteries continued to shell the position; and when Lilly requested support, Colonel McCook told him "that every available man was engaged and that no troops could be spared from any point on the line and we must take care of ourselves."[30] The battalion of the Ninth Pennsylvania returned from

28 *O.R.* Ser. 1, XXXI, pt. 1, 641, 654, 658.
29 Addison M. Dowling Collection, Joseph A. Scott, "East Tennessee Campaign."
30 *O.R.* Ser. 1, XXXI, pt. 1, 660–61.

the right after their skirmish and forced the sharpshooters to take cover.

After nearly three hours, only three or four men remained with each gun, and they were too exhausted to move the guns back into firing position after recoil. Captain Lilly requested permission to move the guns, which was granted, and General Elliott ordered the infantry in the woods to charge toward the Rebel batteries to draw the fire from Lilly's position while he moved his pieces. The artillerymen succeeded in hitching-up and moving two cannons to a new position on a high hill northeast of Mossy Creek, but the few exhausted men left on John Rippetoe's gun were unable to control their horses, and these ran off before the gun was hitched to the limber.

"I drew my old sabre and rallied some of the men and caught the horses and straightened them up and then turned them for the gun and went in with about 40 cavalry on a charge and retook it," Rippetoe wrote. The forty cavalrymen were General Elliott's entire reserve which Captain Lilly met at the same time that he learned of the loss of the gun. He led the troopers up the hill, recaptured the piece, and saw that it was taken off the field and emplaced with the remainder of the battery.[31]

Shortly before the battery retired to their new position, Henry Campbell went back to a spring at the foot of the hill behind the guns to get a canteen of water for the wounded men. He was on his way back just when the first two guns were retiring, and where the route crossed the road, he found John Runey, his shattered left arm hanging uselessly, holding up the telegraph wire with his right so that the horses, guns, and limbers could pass under. Campbell found a wounded horse, helped Runey mount, and led him to the field hospital, an old church in the town of Mossy Creek. He then went to the battery's new position in time to see them fire some shells into a valley on the left to stop a final encircling maneuver by the Confederates.[32]

The entire Union force now had fallen back to a new line, and Lilly's men had time to transfer ammunition from a wagon to the ammunition chests. The situation remained critical, and Colonel McCook

31 *Ibid.*
32 Indiana State Library, Indiana Division, Henry Campbell, "The Battle of Mossy Creek"; Lilly Archives, William O. Crouse to Joseph A. Scott, Sept. 18, 1919.

reported that the line had a quarter-mile gap in the center.[33] If the more numerous Johnnies came through the gap or around the flanks, they might capture the entire force because there was little possibility for retreat, but Henry Campbell thought "the enemy seemed afraid to follow us to our new line."

At about 3:00 P.M., "a loud, ringing cheer broke from our men" because they saw a column of blueclad cavalrymen of the Second Brigade circling the Rebel left flank. After fording Mossy Creek, Colonel LaGrange had organized his men in the woods at the extreme right of the Union line, and while half the brigade made a mounted sweep around the Confederate left, the remainder, dismounted, attacked obliquely into the left of the Confederate line.[34] The two guns of Lilly's battery that had accompanied the Second Brigade, commenced firing into the Rebel line when the charge began.

Seeing the enemy line breaking with the assault, the First Brigade attacked along their front, completing the rout. Most of the Johnnies ran but some fought for a while from woods and other strong points along their line of retreat. The Yankees pressed on, however, driving the Confederates beyond the position of the morning and camped on "the old ground" that night.

During the battle, the three guns of Lilly's battery fired 512 rounds and ten men of the fifty engaged were killed or wounded,[35] with six of the wounded belonging to John Rippetoe's detachment. In spite of these losses, morale remained high, and Captain Lilly reported, "The old 18th is still on its 'pins' and ready for another muss."[36]

The total Union loss was 17 killed, 87 wounded, and 5 missing. Most Confederate dead and wounded had been carried to the rear in wagons during the battle, but from what civilians told them, Colonel McCook estimated enemy casualties at 250, and General Elliott believed there were 500.[37] Henry Campbell said, "20 dead rebels were found in a hole in the ground where they had been dragged & 35 more

---

33 *O.R.* Ser. 1, XXXI, pt. 1, 654–55.

34 *Ibid.*, 658–59; William M. Winkler, "A Leaf from a Soldier's Diary," Columbus *Republican*, Mar. 16, 1876.

35 Lilly Archives, Eli Lilly report Dec. 30, 1863.

36 Putnam *Republican Banner*, Jan. 21, 1864.

37 *O.R.* Ser. 1, XXXI, pt. 1, 651–55.

in an old barn   both places about 1 mile in the rear of the battle field."

The Yankee artillerymen examined the ground on which the Confederate battery stood to see what damage they had inflicted and found a number of dead horses and part of a limber chest. They also saw some shells that appeared to be too large to fit the Confederate guns and determined that these were some of their own shells that had been lost with the caisson at Dandridge. On December 30, both armies rested in their camps, and the men of the battery buried Corbin and Lloyd in the church cemetery, after their mess mates had made wooden coffins to hold the remains.

The weather changed from wet to extremely cold during the afternoon of December 31, and that night, Henry Campbell and Captain Lilly slept under a gun tarpaulin with a large fire of fence rails at their feet. Other campfires surrounded a house in which Colonel McCook and his staff had their headquarters, and sometime during the night, the house caught on fire. Upon hearing the alarm, Henry Campbell woke the captain, but they concluded that the fire was out of control, rolled over, and went back to sleep. They and the other soldiers slept more comfortably with the warmth of the burning house, but Colonel McCook and his staff had to find new quarters. The next morning, while digging in the ashes of the house, the soldiers found a large quantity of potatoes that had been stored in the cellar which were thoroughly roasted, and "the battery all had roast potatoes for our empty stomachs."[38]

The artillerymen also found the guns frozen solidly into the ground and had to chop them out with axes, and the horses had great balls of frozen mud around their legs. The temperature in the area was reported to be fifteen degrees below zero.[39]

The entire division suffered in this weather because "None of our men had overcoats. Very few were so fortunate as to own good stockings, and none was prepared to meet such weather as this." But Henry Campbell observed philosophically, "The rebels were worse off than

[38] Indiana State Library, Indiana Division, Henry Campbell, "That Cold New Year's Day."
[39] Seymour, p. 217.

we were   for half of them had nothing on their feet at all." Many Johnnies came into the Federal lines with hands, feet, and ears frozen, and the Yankees shared their own scanty rations with them.[40]

On January 2 camp was moved to Mossy Creek because other water sources were frozen solid. Henry Campbell commented that they had received no rations since leaving Strawberry Plains on December 23, and that the men were living on flour made from "sick wheat," which they had ground at a nearby mill, and corn.

James C. Dodd died on January 8 from the wound received at the Battle of Mossy Creek, but Henry Campbell reported that the other wounded men were "doing well." For the first two weeks of January the weather remained abnormally cold, and little military action was initiated. General Longstreet wrote, "Even the cavalry had a little quiet."[41]

40 Henry Campbell, "That Cold New Year's Day."
41 Longstreet, p. 524.

X

Dandridge and Fair Garden

The troops fell into column sullen and silent. After all our marching & fighting all winter, everything was lost in one big blunder.

Henry Campbell told of the reaction of the soldiers when orders came to retreat from their positions at Dandridge during the night of January 17. The men believed that they had drawn Longstreet's corps into the open and that they could win a battle the next day, end the campaign, and go into winter quarters; but Major Generals John G. Parke, Gordon Granger, and Phillip H. Sheridan,[1] finding that their expedition to Dandridge had attracted Longstreet's infantry, as well as his cavalry, to the area and believing that Longstreet had advantages of numbers and position, ordered a retreat instead of fighting a battle.

Henry Campbell's information was that the purpose of the campaign was to get into position to attack Longstreet at Morristown, but the Federal officers' reports indicated that the expedition was made to cross the French Broad River to obtain the forage from the unravaged country south of the river. The Federals did make an attempt to cross, and General Parke reported, "During the day, General Sheridan built a bridge of wagons at the bend below town and crossed

---

[1] General Parke was in active command of the Army of the Ohio because General Foster was suffering from an old wound. Parke remained at Strawberry Plains during the campaign, and Granger was in charge of the expedition to Dandridge with Sheridan commanding until Granger's arrival.

167

Harker's brigade, but to his mortification he found at dark that he was on an island."[2]

General Longstreet agreed with Henry Campbell about the purpose of the expedition since General Grant had ordered General Foster to drive Longstreet beyond Bull's Gap, and also because the march was made in more strength than was necessary for a foraging foray, with the IX and XXIII Corps marching to Dandridge and the IV Corps held in reserve at Strawberry Plains. Also, Longstreet thought that if the Federals wanted the forage south of the river, all they needed to do was cross on the pontoon bridge at Knoxville and march up the road to Sevierville.[3]

The campaign started on January 14 when all of the Yankee cavalry and Colonel Samuel R. Mott's infantry brigade marched to Dandridge, followed by the IX and XXIII Corps the next day, in response to a report that all three Confederate cavalry divisions were in that area. Henry Campbell thought that Dandridge was built on the most unfavorable ground that could possibly be chosen for a town. "The ground is so hilly that each house has one [hill] of its own. The center of the town is in a deep hollow [in which] stands the Court House allmost out of sight from the rest of the town." The scenery appealed to him, however: "A beautiful view of the surrounding country is obtained from a hill above town. Away to the east over a succession of valleys and hills the Smoky Mountains loom up into the clouds in a distinct blue outline presenting a ragged and rough appearance   distant about 30 miles. They are the highest Mtns. we have seen yet."

On January 15, Captain Lilly announced that Sergeant John D. Johnson was promoted to orderly (first) sergeant, Sergeant David W. Rippetoe to quartermaster sergeant, Corporal Marion J. Barr to sergeant, and Privates Sidney Speed and Albert Allen to corporals.

When the infantry plodded into Dandridge, Campbell saw several Crawfordsville acquaintances of the Eighty-sixth Indiana who reported "hard times & nothing to eat. Our boys entertained them with 'Sick wheat' flap Jacks as hard and black as dirt which they seemed to relish exceedingly." He remarked that the infantry was in no condition to

---

2 *O.R.* Ser. 1, XXXII, pt. 1, 78.
3 Longstreet, pp. 525–30.

fight after marching around with little or nothing to eat, but that the soldiers, who belonged to the Army of the Cumberland, were eager for a fight because a victory would mean a return to that army's area of jurisdiction and its superior supply system.

By January 16, the Federal commanders at Dandridge became suspicious that the enemy forces in the area were stronger than cavalry alone; and to find out, Colonel Wolford's Ohio cavalry division marched out the Chucky Bend road, which followed the French Broad River, while Garrard's division, followed by the Army of the Cumberland cavalry, moved eastward on a road variously called Bull's Gap and Morristown. On the march, three guns of Lilly's battery were assigned to the Second Brigade and two pieces to the First Brigade, which was bringing up the rear of the column on the Bull's Gap road. Because Colonel McCook was ill, Colonel Campbell was acting division commander and Colonel Thomas J. Jordan of the Ninth Pennsylvania commanded the First Brigade.

While on the march, Colonel Campbell was ordered to go to Colonel Wolford's support on the Chucky Bend road because Wolford had encountered most of the three Rebel cavalry divisions; and since the fields between the roads were impassable, the First Division was forced to countermarch on the Bull's Gap road to a cross road about two miles east of Dandridge, with the First Brigade becoming the advance on the countermarch.[4]

"We had not proceeded more than half a mile [on the cross road] . . . when I came up with Colonel Wolford's division in full retreat, galloping away from the enemy, leaving my flank entirely exposed," Colonel Jordan wrote of the situation on the Chucky Bend road. He ordered the Second Michigan to dismount, hold a small hill until the remainder of the brigade could be brought up, and told the section of the battery to take position at the rear of the Michigan regiment. The guns were slow getting into action because of broken harness; but the Second Michigan, "though outnumbered five to one, by steady, unflinching bravery held the enemy . . . ." By the time the Ninth Pennsylvania had formed on the left of the Michigan regiment, the battery

---

4 *O.R.* Ser. 1, XXXII, pt. 1, 80, 84–88.

was in position and "opened with such effect as to silence the battery of the enemy."

The Rebel battery moved from their exposed position near the road to one in the woods facing the Ninth Pennsylvania, where according to Henry Campbell, Lilly's guns could not reach them. However, the Pennsylvania troopers, aided by the Second Indiana, which formed on their left flank, advanced into the woods and slowly pushed the Confederate skirmishers back. Within five minutes, the Johnnies were driven from the cover of the woods, and Lilly's guns were able to fire over the heads of the Yankee troopers and strike them. This fire, combined with the small arms fire from the woods, caused the graybacks to retreat "in wild confusion." The Yankees pursued for about one mile, but darkness and the failure of Wolford to come up to cover the right flank caused Jordan to halt the pursuit.[5]

On the morning of January 17, the Union cavalry was in a defensive line on hills east of Dandridge extending from the French Broad River to the Mossy Creek road. The Ohio cavalry divisions were on the right across the Chucky Bend road, the Second Brigade of Cumberland troopers and three guns of the battery were on the Bull's Gap road, and the First Brigade and two of Lilly's guns guarded the left flank.

About noon action exploded on the line when the Rebels attacked so suddenly and furiously along the Bull's Gap road that they drove the First Wisconsin from their camp and captured a number of the cavalrymen. The Wisconsin troopers reformed behind camp; stopped a further advance; and although hard pressed, held the enemy until the remainder of the Second Brigade came to their aid.

Within fifteen minutes of the initial attack, the Second Brigade made a spirited countercharge, released the captured Wisconsin troopers, and captured fifteen Johnnies. To the amusement of the Yankee soldiers, one of the captured men told them, "You'ns had better be making your self scarce, as the whole of 'Jinkins Brigade' was coming up."[6]

Colonel McCook was not amused, however, because the prisoners taken were from three different Confederate infantry regiments and

5 *Ibid.*, 87–88.

6 Brig. Gen. Micah Jenkins' brigade of Hood's division.

they told him that another infantry division was in reserve. The Union line also had a gap between the First and Second brigades, and McCook asked the commander of an infantry regiment posted in his rear to move up into the gap. The officer told McCook, "he was placed there on picket and had no orders" and did not come to the aid of the cavalry then or during the fighting that followed. McCook had to spread the First Brigade to fill the gap.[7]

After beating back some uncoordinated attacks, the Yankee troopers, late in the afternoon, advanced all along the line and slowly drove the Rebels back beyond the position of the morning. Lilly's battery took little part in the conflict for fear of hitting their own men in the close fighting in the woods. After dark the cavalrymen returned to their camps of the previous night.

Both men and officers now believed that General Longstreet planned to bring on a battle the next day, and the soldiers, according to Henry Campbell, were for such a fight because "if the rebels are beaten it will end the campaign for this winter." The officers thought differently and at 9:00 P.M. issued orders for a retreat to New Market. The wounded were placed in ambulances and started back,[8] and then "The troops fell into column sullen and silent. After all our marching & fighting all winter, everything was lost in one big blunder."

Unknown to the Union officers and men, Longstreet had found a narrow road that came out on the New Market road, and when the decision to retreat was made, he was beginning to march infantry and artillery to get between Dandridge and New Market to cut the Federal troops off from their base. His advance reached the road shortly after the Yankee rear guard passed through.[9]

The retreating Federals marched all night, reaching New Market at dawn, where the battery picked up Lieutenant Scott, wounded at Mossy Creek, and brought him with them in an ambulance. At 10:00 A.M. they reached Strawberry Plains, where the wounded were placed on a train and taken to Knoxville.[10] The artillerymen then crossed

7 *O.R.* Ser. 1, XXXII, pt. 1, 85.
8 Indiana Historical Society Library, Andrew Jackson Smith diary.
9 Longstreet, pp. 528–29.
10 Andrew Jackson Smith diary.

the Holston River on the railroad bridge, which had been rebuilt and floored, and on the north side of the river, they delayed long enough to raid a corn crib, feed their horses, and make coffee. They also picked up the battery wagon and transportation teams that had been left when they had crossed the river on December 23.

With sarcasm, Henry Campbell reported, "It began raining at daylight this morning and continued all day which, mixed with nothing to eat, roads allready knee deep in mud, and no sleep during the night added to our comforts amazingly." A thaw, causing the bottom to drop out of the roads, was actually a benefit for the Federals because the mud and the poor condition of the cavalry horses prevented a pursuit by the Confederates.[11]

As soon as the horses had finished eating "their corn and mud," the Yankee column moved on toward Knoxville—"Roads getting worse & worse and the horses and men both exhausted & starved," Henry Campbell wrote. "I was so fatigued that I went to sleep several times on my horse and once got raked off in the mud by my horse going out to the side of the road under a tree to nibble some grass." In the evening, camp was made along the road, eleven miles from Knoxville, with everyone "wet, tired and hungry" and Henry Campbell thought that "a bed in a mud hole was a luxury."

At eleven o'clock the next morning, the battery reached Knoxville, where they had a two hour stopover. They found that three or four stores had been opened by men from the North since their passage through town in December. "But what suited us most," wrote Henry Campbell, "was a *baker shop* where they vended nice *white bread* such as what we used to get up North   all our flour & extry cash was soon expended and our boys enjoyed something they had not seen for some time."

At 1:00 P.M. the battery crossed the Holston River on the pontoon bridge, marched four miles, and encamped. According to Henry Campbell, the horses were so worn out, they could go no farther, and he added, "The roads on this side of the river are the very worst we ever travelled over   hilly, rocky, and very muddy. The Battery Wagon stalled just after it crossed the bridge and is there yet."

11 Longstreet, p. 530.

Colonel McCook in the lead with the Second Brigade told Colonel Campbell that he should push on to Sevierville, where he would have forage gathered. Captain Lilly had advised him that the battery horses were exhausted, and McCook told Colonel Campbell to leave the battery if it impeded his progress and to push on to where he could get forage,[12] but instead of leaving the battery behind, the officers on the spot decided that some of the cavalrymen should be dismounted and their animals used in the artillery teams and, in this way, the battery acquired thirty new horses.

John Rippetoe wrote, "I do not know what these movements mean but I reckon they are right and for the best." The Federal cavalry was marching to Sevierville because reports had reached headquarters that Rebel troopers had crossed the French Broad and were foraging in this area of abundant supplies. The Union cavalry was going into the area to forage for themselves and also to prevent the Confederates from supplying their forces with the food and grain available between the French Broad and the mountains.

The column left camp at 9:00 A.M. the next morning and marched "thro a desolate region & halted near a corn field and fed our horses. the first corn we have found since leaving Dandridge." After feeding the stock, they marched another five miles through a cold rain and made camp in a corn field with headquarters established in a corn crib that was made comfortable by hanging blankets along the walls to keep the rain out and with the enlisted men bivouacked in an old log house. Both officers and men had their most comfortable and restful night for many weeks.

About 10:00 A.M. on January 21, the battery reached Sevierville, "one of the nicest little towns in East Tenn   situated on level ground near Big Pigeon River. It is a union town and when our troops made their appearance the citizens hauled up an old torn flag to the flag staff on the Court House with the 'Union forever' on it."

The column continued through the town and marched toward the French Broad River—"roads fearful   hill after hill. up and down all day. dont see how we ever got over them at all." Camp that night

12 *O.R.* Ser. 1, XXXII, pt. 2, 153–54.

was ten miles from Sevierville "in a very fertil valley near the French Broad."

Lilly's battery remained in camp all day on January 22, but the cavalry scouted widely through the area, and the First East Tennessee Cavalry captured a forage train of twenty-five loaded wagons. For Lilly's battery, Lieutenant Rippetoe made a raid through their valley and captured "three first rate horses." Campbell commented, "Country in very good condition up here. they havent had any war yet." The next day the battery moved three miles upriver camping about five miles south of Dandridge, where they could hear Rebel pickets on the north bank of the river firing at Yankee troopers on the south side.

The situation of the cavalry now was serious since they were thirty miles from Knoxville with only the French Broad River between them and all of Longstreet's corps. The Union infantry had withdrawn to Knoxville, and so they no longer were a threat should Longstreet decide to assault the cavalry. General Elliott had received a communication from General Sturgis that all of Longstreet's forces were near Morristown and to push forward because "every mile gained . . . will be so much less to fight for," but loyal citizens told Elliott that Confederate troops already were south of the river, and so he sent McCook's division to the French Broad, where it drove some small forces from the fords near Dandridge.

On January 22, Elliott received another message from Sturgis advising that General Foster "hardly expected the troops to be as far advanced as they are at present, considering the very bad condition of the roads."[13] Serving under Sturgis and such contradictory orders made Elliott request transfer from duty in the Department of the Ohio, and orders were received sending Elliott back to the Army of the Cumberland. He left Sevierville January 23, but his troopers were not withdrawn from the area and would have more fighting before they also retired.

During the night of January 24, Brigadier Generals John T. Morgan's and Frank C. Armstrong's divisions of Confederate cavalry crossed the French Broad; and the next morning, the battery, accompanying the Second Brigade, was pulled back to a position four miles

13 *Ibid.*, pt. 1, 83.

west of Sevierville. The First Brigade was posted on the Newport Road, four miles east of Sevierville; Wolford's division was at Flat Creek, two miles beyond the First Division; and Garrard's division was near the French Broad River, downstream watching for possible crossings.[14]

Captain Lilly received word that the division quartermaster in Sevierville had received boots from Knoxville and sent some men with a wagon to draw sixty pairs. "These were very much needed," wrote Henry Campbell, "as some of the boys were allmost barefooted."

At 4:00 P.M. on January 26 the battery and the Second Brigade received urgent orders to move through Sevierville toward the First Brigade's camp because John T. Morgan's Confederates had attacked and routed Wolford's division. Henry Campbell wrote, ". . . the whole Div. was disgracefully routed   they came rushing back on to the 1st Brig. of our Div. every man for himself. part of them throwing away their arms   so badly were they scared. The whole Div. is a disgrace to the army anyhow. they never did accomplish anything."

Colonel Campbell allowed Wolford's racing troopers to pass through his lines and then withdrew to the west bank of the Middle Fork of the Little Pigeon River. The Confederates came up to the creek, emplaced artillery on the hills opposite the Union position, and began to shell the First Brigade, but without any effect as darkness came on. When the action ceased, the Second Brigade and Lieutenant Beck's section of the battery were ordered back to a position near Sevierville to protect the rear, while Lieutenant Rippetoe's section and Lieutenant Miller's gun, with Captain Lilly, remained with the First Brigade. Wolford's division was sent west of Sevierville to guard the road to Knoxville. This maneuvering set the stage for the Battle of Fair Garden that Henry Campbell called "the nicest battle we ever fought."

On January 27, Colonel Campbell's brigade alone faced a far superior enemy force, Colonel McCook reporting that his line was necessarily thin and weak "from his paucity of numbers" since it was spread out to reach the flanks of the Confederate line, and Henry Campbell thought they were "strung out to look as large as possible." The Second

14 *Ibid.*, 135.

Michigan, dismounted, was in line on both sides of the road along the fork; the Ninth Pennsylvania, also dismounted, was spread along the creek to the left; the First East Tennessee, mounted, formed a line on the right; and two guns of the battery were on a high hill near the center of the line. This position was only 400 yards from the high ridge between the Middle and East Forks of the Little Pigeon on which the Confederate artillery was emplaced.

The fight began with the Yankee skirmishers moving down to the stream firing at the Johnnies on the opposite side. After skirmishing on this line for an hour, part of the Ninth Pennsylvania succeeded in crossing the fork and capturing a high hill from which they enfiladed the Confederate skirmish line, a movement that caused the Rebels to retreat toward their main line.

As soon as they began to fall back, the Second Michigan crossed the stream and charged across the open fields beyond. Captain Lilly's two guns fired over the heads of the charging men, who continued on up the ridge, driving the Confederates down the opposite slope and across the East Fork. When the Michiganders had secured the ridge, Lieutenant Rippetoe's guns were hurried forward and emplaced where they commanded the fields beyond the fork and Lieutenant Miller's gun was temporarily held in reserve.[15]

The topography here was much the same as the first position, with the Rebels' main line on a high ridge east of the fork, over which the road crossed through a covered bridge. The Confederates had the bridge covered from earthworks on a heavily wooded ridge. Lilly's battery first shelled the open area across the stream, driving the Johnnies up the ridge and into the woods.

Then, while Lilly's guns shelled the woods, the Second Michigan crossed the bridge, charged up the hill, and drove the Rebels from the earthworks and back into the woods; but the Johnnies counterattacked with a strong force, and the Yankees were driven back toward the bridge.

Lieutenant Miller's gun was hurried into position in a field about 150 yards from the bridge, and as soon as the Michigan troopers were clear of the woods, all three guns opened with percussion shell over

15 *Ibid.*, 142, 146; Thacker, pp. 176–78.

their heads. "When the rebels appeared on the hill, above the bridge, close after the 2d Mich   yelling and Cheering like wild cats   we let into them with short range canister as rapidly as we could load," Henry Campbell reported. This checked the enemy until the troopers could get across the bridge and reform their line in the woods behind Miller's gun.

After the retreat of the Michiganders, the Rebels were only 200 yards from Miller's cannon, which was exposed on the brow of a hill, "and for a few moments the rifle balls rained around us like hail." As soon as the Second Michigan had reformed their lines, the gun was "limbered up & pulled back thro the fence into the woods, as fast as horses could go   making a circut around thro the woods and gaining the road in rear of the 2d Mich."

Fortunately, Henry Campbell had had the foresight to take down a section of the fence and find a route through the woods when the gun had been emplaced, but just as the guns started back, Samuel Mills, driver of the swing team, was shot through the head.[16] Campbell "guided the gun thro the woods, at a gallop without hanging on a single tree when I don't think they could go over the same road again at a walk without hanging on the trees half the time."

While this action was taking place at the bridge, the Ninth Pennsylvania on the left crossed the fork and began advancing toward a high hill. Seeing a Rebel column form for the purpose of attacking them, Lieutenant Rippetoe shelled it, ending this threat, and aiding the Pennsylvanians to capture the hill but, since they were the only Yankees across the stream, they were in danger of being surrounded.

The threat to the Ninth ended with the appearance of the Second Brigade, which had marched down a road parallel to the Newport road with the intention of getting behind the Confederates. Their arrival was announced by the firing of Lieutenant Beck's guns "around in the rear and left of the rebels," his first shot killing a man and a horse and his second smashing the wheel of a caisson.

The arrival of the Second Brigade on the flank forced the Confederates to retreat and form a new line two miles farther back. This

---

16 Private Samuel Mills, a detail from the 4th Indiana.

line also was in a heavily wooded area and crossed both roads, with two pieces of artillery emplaced on each road. The Federal troopers moved forward and formed a new line facing open fields, across which the Rebels had established their line but did not attack since Lilly's guns were delayed passing through the woods.

When the artillery arrived the Confederate guns were shelling the Union lines, and Lieutenant Beck soon began dueling with the Rebel guns at his end of the line. Henry Campbell said, "Our skirmish line had been pushed out as far as they could go but the rebels seemed determined to hold their ground at all hazzards and were annoying the right of our line considerably, with their Battery posted on the left of the road behind a log house."

Colonel Campbell asked Lieutenant Miller if he could get his gun in position on the skirmish line to stop the firing of that battery. Miller replied, "Yes, before the enemy can load,"[17] moved to within 400 yards of the Rebel battery, and exploded his second shot in the enemy position, killing three and wounding two. The Confederate battery immediately limbered up and began to retreat on the road.

Lieutenant Rippetoe's pieces, emplaced in the road, began firing at the same time as Miller's gun, and when they heard these shots, the entire Union line raised a shout "and with one impulse moved forward on the double-quick .... their entire line began to fall back slowly at first and in good order, but as our men kept advancing at the double-quick   they kept moving faster & faster   we advanced gun at a time   right along with the line   and poured in a continuous rain of percussion shell without a moments cessation." The Second Indiana, advancing on the left of the line, ran into more stubborn resistance; and when their skirmishers began to be pushed back, a battalion of the Fourth Indiana was dismounted to support them.[18]

Seeing a column of mounted men forming in the woods with the obvious intention of moving around his left flank, Colonel LaGrange ordered Lieutenant Colonel Joseph P. Leslie of the Fourth Indiana to make a saber charge into the column[19] with four companies of his regi-

---

17 *O.R.* Ser. 1, XXXII, pt. 1, 143.
18 Bartholomew County Public Library, William M. Winkler diary.
19 *O.R.* Ser. 1, XXXII, pt. 1, 144.

ment.[20] "The 4th dashed on into the woods, right into the thickest of the rebel forces, cutting them down right and left . . . routing the entire body of them," wrote Henry Campbell. "Our entire line caught the infection and run right into the woods regardless of all danger, or numbers. Our Batt. advanced down the road at a gallop & opened out on every point the rebels attempted to make a stand."

During the charge of the Fourth, Colonel Leslie was killed, and Solomon Glick, following close behind, cut down the Rebel who had fired the fatal shot.[21] The small force of troopers followed the routed Johnnies through the woods, coming out in open fields beyond, and Henry Campbell reported, "just out of the woods on the crest of a hill, was a fresh regiment of rebs drawn up in line, ready to charge the moment our men issued from the woods but the 4th hesitated not a moment, but dashed right at them so impetously that they became panick stricken & fled down the hill with out firing a shot."

Posted on high ground, Campbell watched the most spectacular individual feat of the day—"As the 4th emerged from the woods, a Sargent and 4 men, on the right seen the rebel Artillery hurring down the road as hard as they could go. with only his 4 men he dashed after them, and overtook them in a narrow defile running between two hills,

runing the Officer commanding the section thro the body with his Sabre. he dashed on to the forward gun, cut down the wheel driver as he passed, Killed the lead driver & shot his horse which stoped the gun & so Jambed up the road so that the rest could not get past. the four men coming on behind took all the men prisoners. . . ."

This hero was Sergeant William M. Winkler,[22] who underplayed his accomplishment in his diary:" . . . I with 4 men captured 2 Canones and 10 men after killing myself the Battr. Lt. and 1 man and wounding 4 Cannonires . . . Got congratulated by Col. LaGrange & Division

20 Indiana Historical Society Library, James Henry Harris diary.
21 William M. Winkler, "A Leaf from a Soldier's Diary," Columbus *Republican*, Jan. 27, 1876.
22 *Indiana, A Biographical History of Eminent and Self-made Men of the State of* 2 vols. (Cincinnati: Western Biographical Publishing Co., 1880), I, dist. 5, p. 48; Columbus *Republican*, May 10, 1890. Born in Prussian Poland, Winkler had graduated from the Prussian military academy at Breslau and had been a lieutenant, light artillery, in the Prussian army before emigrating to the U. S. in 1849, and to Columbus, Indiana, in 1855.

Head Quarters." His service also was cited in Colonel LaGrange's report.[23]

Seeing how few Yankees were with the captured guns, the Confederates organized a force to retake them, but before they could reach the artillery, this column was met and routed by an attack of four companies of the Fourth that had not been in the earlier saber charge.[24] Lilly's guns then were emplaced on one of the hills above the defile, and Captain Lilly reported, "The main column on the road presenting a good target, were practiced on it with lively effect till out of range."[25]

The Fourth Indiana, being widely scattered, was recalled, and the First East Tennessee took up the chase; but they pursued only about one mile when darkness made further action unsafe. Henry Campbell wrote, "Had we only one hour more of daylight, we would have bagged all of the rebels."

As it was, Colonel McCook reported, "We captured 2 3-inch rifled guns, with their horses; about 800 small arms, which we destroyed; 112 prisoners (9 of them commissioned officers, 2 of the latter being regimental commanders), General Morgan's battle-flag[26] and his body servant, General Morgan himself narrowly escaping . . . . I estimate their loss in killed and wounded, exclusive of prisoners taken, at upwards of 200." McCook placed his losses at 4 killed, 24 wounded, and 3 missing and remarked that he could account for such small losses only "by the rapidity of our movements and the consternation produced by the saber charges."[27] Although the loss was small, these were more than cold statistics to Colonel LaGrange, and John Rippetoe remarked, "Col. Lagrange . . . as brave a man as any, when he came to where Leslie's body lay cried."

Captain Lilly reported on some of his best shots: "One shot from my left section [Beck's] killed one man, a mule, and 3 horses; a second took off a gun-wheel, and cut in two a sponge-staff in the cannoneer's hand; a third went through a caisson. From my guns on the right one

23 *O.R.* Ser. 1, XXXII, pt. 1, 145.

24 *Ibid.,* 144.

25 *Ibid.,* 147.

26 Indianapolis *Journal,* Sept. 3, 1893. Morgan's battle flag, captured by the 4th Indiana Cavalry, was displayed for many years in the Indiana Capitol.

27 *O.R.* Ser. 1, XXXII, pt. 1, 140–41.

shot killed 1 and wounded 3 at the rebel guns." Lilly's battery fired 150 rounds during the fight and had one man killed.[28]

For a few days, Colonel James P. Brownlow of the First East Tennessee was among the missing, having become separated from his men during the pursuit, and was unable to distinguish friend from foe in the darkness. Henry Campbell wrote that Brownlow captured a Texas Ranger and agreed to give him a fine gold watch and his liberty if he would guide him through the Rebel lines. When safely beyond the Confederate pickets, Brownlow released the prisoner with the watch, as agreed, and Campbell concluded, "He ran a fearful risk   for if the rebels only knew he was in their power, they would never get over it. they would rather have *his head* than a whole regiment of our forces."[29]

On January 28, Wolford's division became engaged with some Rebels near the French Broad and sent back for help. The Second Brigade came up, passed Wolford's lines, and moved to within 200 yards of the Confederate main position, finding Armstrong's Confederate division fortified behind barricades of logs and rails, masked in dense woods. Colonel LaGrange sent forward a reconnaissance party from the Second Indiana that moved to within sixty yards of the fortifications, and John Rippetoe wrote that here," . . . one of my classmates at old Asbury, Lieutenant [William D.] Stover of the 2nd Ind. was killed."

Stover's death incensed Colonel LaGrange. " . . . it is believed [he] was shot accidentally by some of our men in our rear," he wrote, implying that the culprits were of Wolford's division. "Thousands of rounds were fired in this skirmish by men who could not see the enemy. The habit of allowing cowards to fire over the heads of their own party from a safe distance in the rear is one of the most reprehensible [actions], and officers who cannot prevent it ought to be shot themselves."[30]

---

28 *Ibid.*, 147.

29 Brownlow was the son of the famous Parson William G. Brownlow, outspoken Tennessee Union man and critic of the Confederacy. The parson was one of the men most hated in the South.

30 *O.R.* Ser. 1, XXXII, pt. 1, 145.

Shortly after this incident, LaGrange received orders to retire, and his force left the field. He reported losses of only one killed and four wounded in the engagement, but the soldiers did not agree, Henry Campbell calling the losses "severe," William Winkler writing "... got repulsed, lost 75 men in the divisions," and others saying "got whipped" and "got the worst of it."[31] Meanwhile, the First Brigade, posted farther downstream, observed strong infantry columns fording the French Broad River.

On January 29, the Union force began to retreat from the area because "the country has got *too hot for us.*" The Confederate infantry now was across the road to Knoxville, forcing the Yankees to retire into the Smoky Mountains by way of Wear Cove. Along Cove Creek the route passed through a defile "extreamly narrow   the wheels of the guns allmost touching on each side . . . . Twenty men could prevent our entire Div. from going through."

Campbell continued, "still I noticed two or three log huts perched along the side of the Mtn., one side resting against the slope, & the other on poles about 20 feet in the Air with a long line of steps leading from the front door to the ground and generally each step will be occupied with a dirty faced young one of all ages and colors, with one or two old women standing in the door holding their arms full of babies." He observed that each place had a small cornfield at an angle of at least 45 degrees.

The column came out of the defile into Wear Cove about which Campbell wrote, "The place is about 3 miles long and 1 wide and is occupied by 5 or 6 families. No war has ever reached this cozy retreat and consequently 'things' are in the greatest abundance." The force camped in the cove that night, and on January 30, they crossed into Tuckaleechee Cove, following Little River toward Maryville. That night battery headquarters was "in a house owned by an old union man named Allen   who has never been out side the Cove since he first came here. 40 years ago."

The next day the column marched over the "crookedest and nar-

31 James Henry Harris and Andrew Jackson Smith diaries.

rowest" pass they had yet encountered. "the road for about 5 miles lay along the banks of Little river, first on one side & then on the other crossing the stream about 50 times. Reached Millers Cove about 11 oclock, which is the last of the Mtns. the road now lays over a good country—Passed a *School house*!!" The column reached Maryville about 2:00 P.M. "Three Cheers!!" Henry Campbell wrote, "we are back to the limits of the 'Dept. of the Cumberland' once again. Willichs Div. of 14th Corps is camped near town."

Campaigning in the winter rains, mud, snow, and cold had not adversely affected the soldiers' health, and John Rippetoe observed, "Though it was tolerably cold down here we did not suffer any, at least I did not as we made good use of fence rails, and we are much healthier this winter. [Cornelius] Murphy seems to be rather under the weather at present. I think his lungs are easily affected. [Henry] Tiffin has not been able to do anything for a long time and I think that he is rather dropsical, the truth of the matter is he ought to have been discharged four months ago." The battery lost four men, however. Corporal Nelson Corey died of pneumonia in the Knoxville hospital, Privates James M. Johnson and William C. Slupe died in Knoxville, and Henry P. Sunman died in Evansville, Indiana, during December and January.[32]

After marching and fighting almost continuously, the battery now had three months of less active duty while Major General William T. Sherman, now commanding the armies in the west, prepared for his spring campaign. During this time, men who had business at home were given furloughs, and after seeing some of these men, Mary Rippetoe scolded John about his inability to do likewise. John explained, "I think you were tolerably hard on me on this furlough business. I know it would be useless for me to apply at this time as it is determined by the Captain that those only that have urgent business could go home, and two of those that he had approved were sent back disapproved by the commanding General."

With Captain Lilly's assistance, Henry Campbell was more for-

32 National Archives, "Descriptive Book."

tunate. Lilly detailed him to the quartermaster department, and his friend Captain James Willson appointed him a "citizen clerk" and provided him with "a Provost Marshall Citizen's pass."

On February 7, Henry and Willson rode to Knoxville on horseback and slept together that night causing Campbell to comment, "not having had a change of clothes for nearly 6 months I was consequently full of 'Body guards' . . . and he being a well fed, fresh victim, [they] deserted me in large numbers (as he allways afterward avowed)." The next day, they took the train to Loudon, and Campbell wrote that the engine and cars "were old worn out affairs which the rebels did not think worth destroying when they evacuated Knoxville but which our troops fixed up and have run ever since, in fact the Dept. could not have maintained itself here without them. Rations were brought up to Loudon in Steamboats & there transfered to the Cars & soon run into Knoxville."

On February 9, they took a steamboat bound for Chattanooga and found that their fellow passengers included a large number of women and children, "the wives and families of rebel sympathizers who were to be sent to Chattanooga and sent south beyond the lines where they could have a good opportunity of sympathising with their husbands who were in the rebel army. They went much against their will." The boat arrived in Chattanooga that night.

The next day, Willson secured a pass for Campbell, good for ten days. Henry took the train to Nashville, where he caught the first Louisville train. He stayed overnight in Louisville; the next morning he crossed to New Albany and took the train to Crawfordsville. "My feelings on getting across the Ohio into the 'Glorious old North' were indescribable," he wrote. "I could not get used to feeling safe, every thing seemed to go on as if no war had ever been in the country." Henry remained at home for "10 or 12 days long after my pass was out."

On the return trip, he escorted Mrs. Lilly to Nashville, where she expected to meet the captain. This courtesy delayed him two extra days because it took that long for him to procure a pass for Mrs. Lilly in Louisville. The first morning after their arrival in Nashville, Captain Lilly "Arrived to my great Joy, as I had no idea where the Battery had got to. He was glad to see me & got my pass renewed on to Chattanooga."

At Chattanooga he met Samuel Hartman, the former first lieutenant of the battery, then employed selling clothing in a sutler's tent, and stayed overnight with him. The next day, "Being in the disguise of a citizen, I was obliged to present myself at the Enrollment office & get myself Enroled so as to stand my chance in the next Draft. this had to be done before I could get a pass for Cleveland   at which point the Battery was now camped." He reached the battery on March 14—five weeks on a ten day pass—and found the battery now had seven guns, having acquired the two cannons captured at Fair Garden.

John Rippetoe gave details of the organization, naming the commanders of the detachments: "of the first detachment Sergeant [William E.] Star[r] has charge, [William O.] Crouse of the second, I have the third, [William L.] McAninch the fourth, [Marion] Barr, who was wounded at Mossy Creek in my detachment has the fifth but is not in the battery on account of his wound, [George S.] McMullen has the sixth and we have a seventh detachment in charge of Corporal [Frank A.] Greenwood."

While Henry Campbell was away, the battery had moved slowly from Maryville to Cleveland; and by February 28 they were at Madisonville, about which John Rippetoe wrote, "this is a regular secesh place, there is but two union men in town. Sherman's men destroyed the jail here last fall and released the union men that the rebels had placed there for safekeeping." From Madisonville, the battery marched through Athens, which Rippetoe thought was "one of the best looking towns I have seen in East Tenn." and then passed through Calhoun and Charleston, on opposite banks of the Hiwassee River, arriving in Cleveland on March 12.

As the war continued, religious interest increased among the men of both armies, with the first revival occurring during the winter of 1863–64, with more concern being shown thereafter.[33] Lilly's men were among those who participated, and on March 23, John Rippetoe wrote, "I can tell you of our forming a little religious society in the

[33] Bell Irvin Wiley, *The Life of Johnny Reb* (Indianapolis: Bobbs-Merrill, 1943), pp. 180–85; Wiley, *Billy Yank*, p. 274.

battery, heretofore we had no organization. several of us thought we would form a class or society for the purpose of prayer and class meeting and met at sun down. there were more present than we looked for and 9 subscribed their names to a paper to meet twice a week if practicable for the purpose of religious worship."

One month later, Henry Campbell wrote, "Lt. Rippetoe and some of the men built a 'Church' last week out of Hemlock poles covering it with a wagon sheet & stuffing hemlock branches in the cracks between the logs. It was dedicated today most all the boys attending."

He continued, "In the evening we had prayer meeting and 'Old Uncle Jo' (our black Hd. Qr. teamster) 'lead' in prayer and a right good effort the old man made. He is the only man in the Department that can drive a mule team without swearing. Uncle Jo will plant himself by the side of his camp fire, at the end of his wagon   all by himself

he dont 'sociate' with the other 'common niggers.' here of evenings you will hear him 'line out'[34] a line of some old darkie hymn, in a monotonous tone, as if he had a large congregation before him. then he will sing over the line with all the pomp and flourishes of the Country singing teacher."

At the end of March, John Rippetoe was in Nashville as part of a detail to get horses. The enlisted men of the detail stayed in the barracks at the Zollicoffer House "and most of them did not like to stay there" but John stayed with Benson in a hotel, "the first time that I have slept in a bed more than my blankets since I left home." Although the detail had received their horses, they were delayed, waiting until the Eighth Iowa Cavalry, which would escort them through the guerrilla infested neighborhood around Tullahoma, was fully mounted and ready to ride.

The detail started back to Cleveland with the Iowans on April 2. "I had the sorest throat I ever had," John Rippetoe wrote. "I went to the doctor of the 8th Iowa to get something to help my throat but he said that his medicines were all packed away in the wagon and he would not put himself to any trouble to get them so I had to ride all

---

34 "Line-out" was the practice of the minister reciting one or two lines of a hymn, followed by the congregation singing those lines, and then doing the same for the next lines, as done in churches without hymnals.

day Saturday suffering just because of his laziness." That evening in Murfreesboro, John bought a box of "Brown's bronchial Troches" and felt much better the next morning.

The horse detail reached camp April 12, and John learned that his younger brother Leonidus Hamline had enlisted in the battery. He told Mary that he thought Hamline should have stayed home until the next spring "as it would not be very long after that till I could be home if I am spared." He had had some difference of opinion with Benson about Hamline's enlistment—"I do not know whether Benson advised him to enlist or not. if he did, I have told him my opinion about it tolerably plain. I told him that he was needed at home . . . his loss in helping father tend the place is not so much as his sisters want a brother to go with them . . . . I do not know what he [Benson] thought of my plain talk, as he could not or did not answer me."

On April 13 a Confederate cavalry force attacked a Yankee picket post, capturing twenty-five men,[35] and Union cavalry, with John Rippetoe's section of the battery, marched eighteen miles to the post, but since the Rebels had a three-hour start, the Yankee force returned to camp. The easy camp life showed an effect on the men's condition, and John Rippetoe wrote, "it was a tolerably hard trip on our new horses, as we had to go in a sweeping trot a good part of the way, some of them were very stiff the next morning. it also made some of the boys tolerable sore, but it never fazed me as I was use to being in the saddle every day for the last 10 or 12 days."

One week later, John wrote that all the neighborhood boys were in good health except William Art—"They were playing ball when one of the boys let his club slip out of his hand hit Billy on the mouth and knocked him down, his mouth is considerably swelled but he is getting better."

[35] Rowell, pp. 173–74.

XI

The Atlanta Campaign

To the entire batterys great grief and disappointment Capt. Lilly has accepted the position as Major in the 9th Ind. Cav. the boys all feel blue over this, as we have found out that we had no such officer left as Capt. Lilly.

Perhaps Eli Lilly first began to consider the possibility of transfer and promotion when the battery was moved from his good friend John T. Wilder's brigade and into the cavalry. At the time of the move he feared that the battery would be captured; and the campaign in East Tennessee, in which the incompetence of General Sturgis had brought such heavy losses to the battery at Mossy Creek, may have determined the point.

The artillery organization, with individual batteries serving under cavalry and infantry commanders, limited the opportunities for promotion in that arm, and Lilly's only chance for higher rank was to transfer to another branch of the service. Whatever the reasons, he joined the cavalry and rose to be colonel of the Ninth Cavalry before the war ended. Although promoted rapidly, he may have regretted leaving the battery because, in a chance meeting with Henry Campbell in January 1865, he told Henry, "The cavalry is worse than the artillery."

William O. Crouse confirmed Campbell's impression about the feelings of the man, but the opinion was not unanimous, John Rippetoe writing, "I for my part am not sorry that he is gone. He never did me any harm but he is a very vulgar, swearing kind of a man and therefore disagreeable to me. He is not the good religious kind of a fellow that he pretended to be when he was recruiting for the battery."

A few weeks later, Rippetoe expressed another opinion: "Everything seems to go on so smoothly since Lilly left us. He seemed to study for something to keep the men at work. It looked like it was a punishment for him to see us have any leisure time but since we came here . . . we have taken our time to everything and are better fixed than we commonly are in our camp arrangements."

Captain Lilly's resignation and transfer were announced on April 10, and on the same day, Lieutenant Joseph A. Scott[1] returned. He was promoted to captain, William Benson Rippetoe to first lieutenant, and First Sergeant John D. Johnson to second lieutenant. About Scott, John Rippetoe wrote, "I like him very much," but Scott had not recovered from the wound received at Mossy Creek. He still had to use a crutch, and after a few weeks, realized that he was not able enough for active campaigning. He resigned on May 2, and Moses M. Beck[2] was promoted to captain, Martin J. Miller to first lieutenant, and David W. Rippetoe to second lieutenant.

Beck was ill, however, and remained at the rear through most of May. On May 25, he took a leave of absence because, as John Rippetoe wrote, "he has had to go to the rear to recruit his health. The Dr. told him he could do as he pleased, go on and die or go back and try to get well." Consequently, Benson Rippetoe was in command of the battery for the Atlanta campaign since Beck did not return and resume command until September 7.[3]

During April the battery was reequipped in preparation for the upcoming Atlanta campaign, receiving new gun carriages and caissons since "our old ones had seen so much service that they were nearly worn out," and also new harness, "a complete outfit for all the Battery we have needed them for a long time but this was our first chance to get them."

---

[1] Joseph Addison Scott was a partner with his father, William T. Scott, in a general store in Bainbridge when he enlisted in Co. K, 16th Indiana, during the spring of 1861. After discharge as first sergeant in 1862, he assisted in the recruiting of Lilly's battery.

[2] Moses Milton Beck was a clerk in a store in Bainbridge when he enlisted in the Asbury Guards in 1861. He became a corporal in Co. K, 16th Indiana, and aided in recruiting Lilly's battery after the 16th was mustered out in 1862.

[3] *O.R.* Ser. 1, XXXVIII, pt. 1, 101.

Manpower was increased with forty veterans of the Tenth Indiana Battery and sixteen of the Eighth Battery assigned to the Eighteenth, and all cavalry details were returned to their regiments.

This was only a small part of the activity of reequipping Major General William T. Sherman's army for their march into Georgia. Sherman began the campaign with 93,131 infantrymen, 12,455 cavalrymen, and 4,537 artillerymen.[4] Sherman's object was to defeat the Army of the Tennessee, now commanded by General Joseph E. Johnston, which had some 48,000 men on duty on April 30, of whom one-tenth were cavalry.[5] Sherman had less advantage than the numbers indicate because he had to campaign through a mountainous country with many impregnable defensive positions.

General Grant, now commander in chief of all U. S. armies, had directed Sherman to break up Johnston's army, but Johnston adopted a strategy that would preserve his army by retreating when necessary to successive strong positions, hoping for a situation in which his smaller force would have an advantage as the Yankees moved farther from their base at Chattanooga. Sherman developed a strategy of flanking Johnston's strong positions and threatening to cut the railroad from Atlanta, and these movements forced the Confederate army to evacuate one strong position after another until they had reached the vicinity of Atlanta and had run out of maneuvering space.

General Sherman's force consisted of three armies. The Army of the Cumberland, nearly 70,000 strong, commanded by Major General George H. Thomas, was made up of the IV Corps, commanded by Major General O. O. Howard; the XIV Corps, commanded by Major General John M. Palmer; the XX Corps, commanded by Major General Joseph Hooker; and a cavalry corps commanded by Brigadier General Washington L. Elliott. Brigadier General John M. Brannan served as chief of artillery, in overall administrative command, although the batteries were assigned to the various infantry and cavalry divisions.[6]

The Army of the Tennessee, totaling 30,000 men and commanded

4 *Ibid.*, 115.
5 Guernsey and Alden, II, 601.
6 *O.R.* Ser. 1, XXXVIII, pt. 1, 90–102, 115.

by Major General James B. McPherson, consisted of the XV Corps, commanded by Major General John A. Logan; the XVI Corps, commanded by Major General Grenville M. Dodge; and the XVII Corps, commanded by Major General Francis P. Blair, Jr.[7]

Major General John M. Schofield commanded the Army of the Ohio, which was made up of the XXIII Corps with some 10,000 infantry and artillery; and the Army of the Ohio cavalry, now commanded by Major General George Stoneman, had been rebuilt to a force of nearly 3,000 mounted men.[8]

Elliott's Army of the Cumberland Cavalry Corps was made up of three divisions. Brigadier General Edward M. McCook's First Division, in which Lilly's battery served, numbered fewer than 2,500 men; Brigadier General Kenner Garrard's Second Division had some 4,500 men; and Brigadier General Hugh Judson Kilpatrick's Third Division numbered about 1,700 men.[9] A Fourth Division under Brigadier General A. C. Gillem, only partially mounted, was guarding the railroad from Nashville to Bridgeport, Alabama, and serving under the command of Major General Lovell Rousseau, commandant of the Nashville military district.[10]

In addition to Lilly's battery, the First Division had three cavalry brigades. The First Brigade, commanded by Colonel Joseph B. Dorr, was made up of the Eighth Iowa, Second Michigan, and First East Tennessee regiments. The Second Brigade, commanded by Colonel Oscar LaGrange, included the Second and Fourth Indiana and the First Wisconsin cavalry regiments. A third brigade, under Colonel Louis D. Watkins, consisted of the Fourth, Fifth, and Sixth Kentucky, but this brigade was only partly mounted and was used principally for behind-the-lines patrol duty.[11]

The army was to march unencumbered by excess baggage. General Sherman told Thomas, "When we move we will take no tents or baggage, but one change of clothing, on our horses, or to be carried by the men, and on pack animals by company officers. Five days' bacon,

[7] *Ibid.*, 103–10.
[8] *Ibid.*, 111–15.
[9] *Ibid.*, 101–102, 115. McCook was promoted to brigadier general April 27, 1864.
[10] *Ibid.*, pt. 2, 746.
[11] *Ibid.*, pt. 1, 101; pt. 2, 746.

twenty days' bread, and thirty days' salt, sugar, and coffee. Nothing else but arms and ammunition . . . . Look well to our supply of beef cattle on the hoof and salt in large excess of the rations."[12]

The Conferedate army defending Dalton was dug in on Rocky Face, a north and south ridge west of the town. The railroad from Chattanooga to Dalton went through the ridge at Buzzard Roost Pass and the railroad from Cleveland to Dalton passed east of this ridge through a valley between two other ridges. The Army of the Cumberland was to march from Chattanooga and take position opposite Rocky Face; the Army of the Tennessee would take position on their right near the town of Villanow and the western end of Snake Creek Gap; and the Army of the Ohio, moving south from Cleveland, would be the left flank of the Union Army. McCook's cavalry division was to operate on the extreme left, moving generally along the railroad from Cleveland.

On May 3, General Sherman's army began to march, and Henry Campbell reported, "Everything but what was absolutely necessary was turned over this morning. Camp equippage, Wall tents, Officers baggage, Co. desk &c &c. They are to be sent to Chattanooga for storage and Binford was detailed to go with them." The stripping down completed, the battery began their march at 10:00 A.M. They marched south from Cleveland on the Dalton road, followed by the XXIII Corps, and camped that night at Red Clay, Tennessee, on the Cleveland and Dalton railroad, fifteen miles north of Dalton.

At dawn the next morning they resumed marching, leaving the Dalton road and moving west on the Tunnel Hill road, and camped on Tiger Creek near Catoosa Springs, east of Ringgold. Henry Campbell described Catoosa Springs, "It evidently has been a very beautiful place but it is sadly in ruin at present and our soldiers have helped it along considerably. It has one large 3 story hotel, built on the southern style, varrandas entirely around it with numerous out buildings, for games, bathing houses, stables &cc &cc. I counted 25 buildings nearly all of them large   the springs are some 24 in number   all with different names, but the water is nearly all the same the sulphur tasting stronger

12 Guernsey and Alden, II, 601.

in some than in others. The springs are adorned with fancy little houses built over each of them & the ravines & branches are crossed by rustic bridges . . . altogether they make a very nice appearance."

The battery remained near this resort for two days, but Henry Campbell was gone for part of that time on an errand. He and Dennis, "Our cook," rode to the Second Kentucky Infantry camp at Ooltewah, Tennessee, to pick up Lieutenant Benson Rippetoe's valise, which he had left with the Kentucky regiment. They rode into the town the next morning, picked up the valise, and Henry met acquaintances from Crawfordsville. "Seen Geo Hough. He is Sutler of the 1 Ky. Sam Smith is assisting him." On their way back to Catoosa Springs, they "got dinner at the house of a union family. Paid them 10cts. in silver   astonished them beyond measure."

On May 7 the cavalry division marched east to the railroad and the Second Brigade occupied Varnell's Station, while the First Brigade moved into a gap in the hills east of this place with the battery emplaced to cover the gap. The Second Brigade moved south from Varnell's until they encountered resistance from two Rebel infantry brigades, one cavalary brigade, and an artillery battery. The Fourth Indiana, serving as dismounted skirmishers, "killed . . . the first Reb in that Campagne."[13] General McCook told General Schofield that "No country could be worse than this to operate cavalry in," and that his line was five miles long and could not be shortened and cover the roads he had been ordered to guard.[14]

In the afternoon when the Second Brigade was pulled back and the First Brigade occupied Varnell's, they were attacked by infantry and cavalry with two cannons, but the Rebels were repulsed and driven from the field. Henry Campbell remarked, "Our new regiment the 8 Iowa stood well, they lost several men wounded by shells."

On May 8 the battery remained in camp, and Henry Campbell wrote, "Gen [Mahlon D.] Mansons brig of inf. came up & formed in front of us. Called on the Gen. was very glad to see me, he looks as usual and is roughing it as plain as any of his soldiers, has no tent, sleeps out of doors the same as his men. He told me if I got hurt to let him know

13 William M. Winkler diary.
14 *O.R.* Ser. 1, XXXVIII, pt. 2, 750.

of it immediately." Ironically, Manson was the one who was hurt, Campbell learning on May 14, that the general "had been very badly stunned by the bursting of a shell and had gone back to Chattanooga."[15]

On May 8 the cavalry division marched three miles toward Dalton from Varnell's Station, with Henry Campbell describing the terrain: "The face of the country is unusually rough, consisting of several ranges of high hills running north & south with narrow valleys   about 500 yds. wide   between them. These all end in a small valley and against a high range of hills, running East and West which joins Rocky Face at nearly right angles." The cavalry was moving down a valley called Potato Hill Valley "after a high conical shaped hill that stands alone near the center of it."

On May 9 the Second Brigade, about 1,100 strong, moved down Potato Hill Valley in what was supposed to be a feigned attack ordered by General Scofield, but the maneuver "was converted into a battle by an overwhelming force of the enemy consisting of two divisions of Wheeler's cavalry and Stewart's division of infantry."[16] The dismounted Yankee cavalrymen drove Confederate skirmishers back into the fortifications, but instead of retiring when this much was accomplished, the troopers attacked the barricades and earthworks of the Rebel infantry, a daring and unusual action for cavalry. The attack resulted in a fight that lasted four hours, during which the dismounted troopers fought the infantry in fortifications while beating off attacks by cavalry on the flanks, one such attack being repulsed by four companies of the Fourth Indiana.

Fighting on the front and attacked in the flank, the brigade was finally forced to retire because " . . . our men were simply overwhelmed." McCook reported losses of 136 men and 11 officers,[17] but William Winkler wrote, "the Reb. loss was 3 times so big." Among those

---

15 *Montgomery, Parke, and Fountain Counties Indiana, Portrait and Biographical Record of* (Chicago: Chapman Bros., 1893), p. 118. Manson was struck in the shoulder by a piece of shell, making his arm permanently useless.

16 *O.R.* Ser. 1, XXXVIII, pt. 2, 766; John P. Dyer, *"Fighting Joe" Wheeler* (Baton Rouge: Louisiana State Univ. Press, 1941), p. 163. Wheeler's troops were Dibrell's and Allen's brigades and the 8th Confederate and 8th Texas regiments.

17 *O.R.* Ser. 1, XXXVIII, pt. 2, 650.

Map 6.
MARCHES OF LILLY'S BATTERY DURING
THE ATLANTA CAMPAIGN, MAY–NOVEMBER 1864

lost was Colonel LaGrange, who was captured, and Henry Campbell commented, "His loss will be very great to our Div. as he was the best officer we had in the div. by far."

At 4:00 P.M. on the same day the XXIII Corps assaulted the first hill forming a part of Rocky Face Ridge. Henry Campbell wrote that the fighting was unusually heavy and that "our troops fought for two hours along the sides and top of the mountain, drove the Confederates out of the works, and took possession of the hill. The troops remained under arms all night & every few moments a roll of musketry would break out would show both sides ready for a night attack."

On May 10 the cavalry division moved down Potato Hill Valley, and the battery shelled the positions on Potato Hill from two and one-half miles away. Campbell reported, "Shells very bad. none exploded." About 10:00 A.M. a rebel skirmish line was seen advancing up the valley, and "we turned our guns on them and soon put them to flight." The cavalry remained in this position until replaced by an infantry division later in the day.

After a brief skirmish about noon the next day, the division marched on a road through a gap in Rocky Face Ridge to Tunnel Hill, and after dark, continued their movement behind the Union army positions to about the right center of the line "where we relieved [Brigadier General John W.] Geary's Brig. [Division] of the position they occupied in front of 'Dug Gap' Geary's Brig. going further down to the right." On May 12, Henry Campbell reported, "we got word that Gen. McPherson troops had taken Snake Creek Gap . . . . Fourteenth Corps is moving down to reinforce them. If they can hold the place this will compel the enemy to evacuate one of the strongest positions an army could possibly occupy."[18]

The next day, Rocky Face was evacuated, and Lilly's battery marched across. The climb on a bad road was made doubly difficult by boulders "that the rebels pryed loose from the clifts and rolled down on our men when they attacked this place a few days ago" but the hard climb was rewarded by "the most magnificent panorama I ever had the

18 The movement was part of Sherman's first flanking maneuver of the campaign. After marching through the gap, Union infantry attacked Resaca causing Johnston to evacuate Dalton and Rocky Face Ridge.

fortune to gaze upon . . . From Waldrons [Walden] Ridge . . . . on the north to the Alltona [Allatoona] mtns. on the south a disance of more than 100 miles. So abrupt is the mountain at this point that before the guns were fairly on top the lead horses had begun to make the desent." From the foot of the ridge, the division marched six miles on the Rome road; and after a "brisk fight" with Confederate cavalry lasting about one hour, the force went into camp.

On May 14, the division marched to Tilton on the railroad where they could hear "heavy and continuous canonading" from the direction of Resaca. The next day the firing at Resaca "began very early and harder than ever. A Terrible battle raged there all day yesterday."

At 2:00 P.M., the Second Brigade and First Section moved down the railroad and took position on the left of the XX Corps, then the extreme left of the Union line. "We had been in position but a short time," Henry Campbell wrote, "when Hooker's Div. [XX Corps] charged the enemys works and after a fearful struggle carried part of their line. during this charge the musketry was dreadful. one continuous rattle."

The Confederates then took notice of the cavalrymen on the Union flank, formed a line of dismounted troops, and charged across an open field in front of the battery section. "The Sec. was in a position in a garden with a hedge fence in front which completely ambushed them. The guns were double shotted with long range canister and we waited until they were within easy range & then let them have it   they turned at the second shot   scattered in every direction."

That night trains came into Tilton bringing forage for the battery horses, demonstrating the speed with which Sherman's engineers had repaired the railroad from Chattanooga. That same night the Confederate army evacuated their works at Resaca, and the Federal army moved south in pursuit, "leaving details to bury the dead & gather up the wounded rebels." Henry Campbell rode over the part of the field where Hooker's men had charged the previous day and wrote, "I never seen as many dead rebels on any Battle ground as there were here. the ground & hill sides was fairly covered with dead. they were so thick that I could hardly ride thro them."

At 1:00 P.M. the battery marched east, forded the Conasauga River, and then turned south through swamps and thick woods to the Coosawattee River, where they camped with Stoneman's cavalry division and close to Hooker's corps. On May 17 the battery crossed the Coosawattee, which was slow work since only one boat was available and eighteen trips were required to get the guns across. They marched to a place that Campbell called Big Spring (probably Salacoa Spring) and camped with the Second Brigade. Here Henry Campbell met "Lew Ketchum and Josh Hadley of the 70 Ind. Josh had a bullet hole thro his chin   but was still doing duty with his regt."

Henry wrote that Big Spring was the "Bigest thing in the 'Spring' line I ever seen. it runs out from under a large rock in a swift stream 40 ft. wide by 2 deep   clear, cool water." The next morning, the battery marched with the infantry in a southerly direction, halted at a place with a signboard reading "10 miles to Cassville," and after supper, marched on and rejoined the cavalry division.

On May 19, McCook's division marched toward Cassville, and after marching ten miles to a point within four miles of that town, the advance encountered Rebel skirmishers. A line was formed on the left of the road, while the First Section of Lilly's battery took position on the right of the road, with dense woods between the section and the road. The guns faced an open field that sloped to Two Run Creek, about two miles distant.

The Confederate infantry advanced toward the artillery position, but the gunners waited until the Johnnies were within one-half mile before they fired a dozen rounds. At this point, "Gen. McCook rode up and ordered us to get back off the field as quick as possible as a column of rebel Infantry was charging up the woods and would cut us off.[19] Limbered up and pulled off as soon as possible." They retired about one mile to a new position. Here they were told to wait until the Union infantry came up since "We have advanced to rapidly for them which leaves our right flank exposed. We are nearly 10 miles ahead of them."

Henry Campbell continued, "About 1 o'clock we could hear heavy canonading in the direction of Kingston. this gradualy became nearer and nearer." This announced the arrival of Major General David S.

[19] McCook identified the Confederates as Maj. Gen. Carter L. Stevenson's infantry division.

Stanley's[20] infantry division which drove the Confederates nearly to Cassville and protected the cavalry flank.

Part of both cavalry brigades then were dismounted and advanced toward Cassville with the battery following, moving by sections, and "shelling the rebels over the heads of our lines." The Confederates made a stand at the creek "until the 8 Iowa made a gallant Sabre charge on them when they retreated across the creek." The battery then commenced shelling the woods on the other side while the Iowans crossed the stream. After these troops had crossed "the rebels opened out on them from a 4 gun Battery located on the hills ½ mile from the creek," and so Lilly's battery crossed the creek on a log bridge and took position on the edge of woods facing the Confederate battery in the fortifications and the Rebel skirmishers in the open field between.

Henry Campbell reported, "We opened a heavy fire on the rebel battery which soon limbered up & retired behind their 2d line of works from which they occasionally sent us a shot at long range." In this action, McCook reported, "My artillery knocked one of their guns and one of their caissons all to pieces, which they left on the field."[21] Later, Henry Campbell found three dead horses where their first shell landed and was told by prisoners that this first shot "took off the rebel captains leg."

Campbell continued, "We kept up a furious fire of shell along the line of rebel fortifications & drove the rebels back into their works." While this was keeping the Johnnies under cover, the Second Brigade flanked the first line of fortifications, causing the Confederates to retreat to their second line; and "While doing so the 2d Ind. made a brilliant saber charge on them & captured 33 prisoners from the 18 Geo. [Alabama] *Infantry.*"[22]

McCook's cavalrymen and artillerymen continued to push, driving the Rebels from their second line of fortifications. "We continued to drive them until we had gained the town of Cassville, when we met the Infantry of Stanleys Div. coming up on the double quick, very much supprised to find Cavalry fighting *Infantry* .... This days fight is the

---

20 Stanley commanded the 1st Division, IV Corps.
21 *O.R.* Ser. 1, XXXVIII, pt. 2, 751–52.
22 *Ibid.* McCook identified the prisoners as 18th Alabama infantry.

first in the history of the Department of the Cumberland, in which cavalry attackted *Infantry in their works* & drove them out."

Stanley's infantry occupied Cassville,[23] and the cavalry retired to a plantation where they found 1,000 bushels of corn, just enough to feed the division's horses night and morning. Henry Campbell rode back to Cassville after dark and found that the town had been deserted by the citizens and the houses already had been ransacked by the soldiers. He reported that a house near which the Confederate battery had been temporarily placed "was riddled by our shells," and that "The streets were all barricaded & earth works thrown up all around." Henry "picked up a few books and returned to camp."

On May 20 the battery marched to Kingston and "Went into camp on the edge of town near the main road, where we could get a full share of the dust." When they remained in camp the following day, John Rippetoe wrote, "this is the first day we have not been harnessed by daylight and we hardly ever unharnessed til dark or sometimes until 9 or 10 at night but so far it has not hurt us." General McCook did not agree with the last part of Rippetoe's statement, and he reported, "Both men and horses of my division need rest. They have been in the saddle from eighteen to twenty hours each day since the 2d of this month."[24] On May 21, Henry Campbell observed, "The Railroad brigade run the cars thro town & on to Cassville today.[25] It is suprising how they keep up with the army   Building bridges & laying track as they advance."

General Sherman, anticipating that the Confederates would occupy the strong position at Allatoona Pass after their retreat from Cassville, marched west, away from the railroad, in another flanking maneuver that he hoped would cause Johnston to evacuate the pass. Johnston, however, anticipating Sherman's movement, also shifted westward on a line from Marietta to Dallas, leading to the Battle of New Hope Church east of Dallas in which the Union flanking maneuver was repulsed.

23 Guernsey and Alden, II, 606. Johnston evacuated the entrenchments at Cassville during the evening of May 19.

24 *O.R.* Ser. 1, XXXVIII, pt. 2, 751.

25 Cassville was two miles east of the railroad.

On May 24, the division marched south, forded the Etowah River at Island Ford, and continued on to Euharlee, eight miles from Kingston, where they waited until the infantry caught up. "Gen. Thomas made his head Quarters here," Campbell reported.

At 3:00 P.M. the Second Brigade and Second Section led the advance of the division and the Army of the Cumberland to the south, and after marching three miles, they met John T. Morgan's and L. S. Ross's Confederate cavalry brigades at Stilesboro, nine miles from the railroad. The Rebels had a six-gun battery that began firing on the advance from one mile distant. The Second Section replied, beginning an artillery duel that lasted an hour. "The shells fell thick and fast around them but fortunately no one was hurt although some of the men had narrow escapes," Campbell reported. "The Rebel fire was very accurate   but our guns being behind a house that was fired by the bursting of a shell, it caused them to miss the range."

After finding the Johnnies had left their position, the cavalry division pursued on May 25, left the open fertile area, and "entered a hilly, 'Jack Oak' country just like the Cumberland plateau in Tennessee. This rough country is the borders of the Altoona [Allatoona] Mountains." The Second Michigan in the advance skirmished all day with a few companies of Confederate cavalry, and the division camped that night at Burnt Hickory, "a little spot of cleared ground with one log house and barn on it. Woods all around so thick that it is impossible to even see through them."

The next day, the division continued the march, crossing Pumpkin Vine Creek, and the battery went into position on a range of hills while the cavalry skirmished in the valley and "captured about a dozen prisoners who report the entire rebel army are passing down the Marietta and Dallas road, having evacuated their strong positions in the Allatoona Mountains and making forced marches to get in front of our army now concentrating near Dallas." The battery had a prisoner of their own: "One of the battery boys while strolling in the woods in rear of the battery, found a rebel hid in some bushes and brought him into camp."

On May 26, the division moved about five miles southeast "to where the Dallas & Marietta [road] crossed the Burnt Hickory"; and the Second Brigade, with the Third Section, advanced, shelling a column of Confederate infantry that were marching on the Marietta road. There is some disagreement about who was attacked; Campbell said that it was a column of infantry, William Winkler wrote that it was a force guarding a wagon train, and General McCook claimed that it was "Wheeler's whole cavalry force."

While the Third Section was shelling the column, the Second Brigade made a saber charge led by Colonel James W. Stewart of the Second Indiana, then serving as brigade commander. Winkler wrote that the attackers were two battalions of the Fourth Indiana and two companies each of the First Wisconsin and Second Indiana, and upon getting into the Rebel column, they captured fifty-two prisoners at a cost of twenty-five men, including Colonel Stewart, who was captured.

On May 27, Rebels were reported to be advancing on the division's flank, and so they changed front and erected fortifications. Henry Campbell said the position was very important "as we hold the extream left flank of our army and the roads leading to our base of supplies in the rear." General McCook also reported that an enemy breakthrough would give uninterrupted access to the Union trains, hospitals, and the rear of the infantry line.

Colonel Brownlow had asked Brigadier General John H. King for infantry support and was told that he could expect no reinforcements in any emergency. General McCook, with memories of a similar situation in East Tennessee the previous winter, sarcastically commented, "I hope there will be no necessity for asking any. Should there be, I will transmit my request through the proper channels, in order that, as at Dandridge, I may receive it after the need has passed."[26]

The next morning the Rebels made an attack with two divisions in front and a brigade on the flank and rear that McCook called "the most stubborn and persistent one I have seen them make during this campaign."[27] The Confederates made two charges on the First Brigade but were unable to dislodge the cavalrymen from their barricades, and the fight settled down to rifle firing, with both sides remaining in their

26 *O.R.* Ser. 1, XXXVIII, pt. 2, 753-54.
27 *Ibid.*

fortifications. The battery could not assist since "The woods were so thick we did not get a chance to open out."

Campbell reported, "towards evening our lines were advanced and drove the enemy back into the woods   troops found quite a number of guns scattered around on the ground their owners having been killed or wounded." He also told of a feat of marksmanship—"a Capt. in the 8 Iowa killed a Rebel sharpshooter up in a tree, with his revolver."

The First East Tennessee was in an exposed position, named "Brownlow's Hill" by the soldiers, that the Confederates attacked at 11:00 P.M. and then kept up a scattering fire all night. About 2:00 A.M. the firing became so heavy that the entire division was aroused, and "one regt. saddled up in readiness to support Brownlow if needed. The Battery had everything ready to harness if it got too serious." Brownlow maintained his position, however, without aid, and the next day there was no action except firing on the skirmish lines.

At 11:00 P.M. on May 29, heavy Confederate artillery firing began on the extreme right of the army, and according to Henry Campbell, "It gradually rolled up the line toward the left until it became one continual rattle all along the entire line and continued during the entire night without cessation." The battery was harnessed when firing became especially heavy on their front "to be ready for any emergency." At daylight, everything became quiet, and General McCook reported that there were no results "except to keep my command awake all night. I could not see their object."[28]

At ten o'clock the next morning, the First Section traveled by a circuitous route to the top of Brownlow's Hill, a position so exposed that "boys built heavy rail barricades to protect them from Sharp Shooters   a few shells were sent into the rebel skirmish line."

Except for sharp skirmish-firing on Brownlow's Hill, there was little action on May 31. Lieutenant David Rippetoe returned from Chattanooga with fifty-eight fresh artillery horses, and Henry Campbell reported that the other horses had had nothing to eat for three days "but

---

28 *Ibid.*

green wheat, and little of that" and that "Gen Thomas and Gen Elliott were up to see us today." On June 1, Campbell rode toward Dallas to find the wagon train and observed that the battle line extended along the east side of the Dallas road, and that "Hospitals and graves are scattered all along the road."

The next day infantry relieved the cavalry division; and on June 3, Lilly's battery marched to the Acworth road, a movement that Campbell correctly interpreted as a maneuver to the left flank to get to the railroad at Acworth. The next day a foraging party found a large amount of corn, "the first our horses have tasted for seven days been subsisting entirely on green wheat."

For the next few days the battery remained in camp, while the infantry passed to the left toward Acworth,[29] and although the Union army occupied the area, the men could not become careless. "Pat Fitzpatrick and Huey Plymale went outside of the lines last night and have not been heard of since. Supposed the bushwackers captured them." These men were indeed captured and spent the remainder of the war at Andersonville prison.

During this lull in the campaign, the artillerymen found time for nonmilitary activities, and John Rippetoe wrote, "we have put up a little chapel by putting posts in the ground and covering it with wagon sheets and the sides are weatherboarded with green cedar boughs in this little chapel we have our prayer and class meetings and sabbath school and [once] in a while we have a minister to preach for us."

"There is more religious feeling in the company at present than there has been at any time since we left home," he reported. "Those who have been trying to be religious all the time have come out more boldly and those who have never made a profession of religion seem to feel more on the subject . . . . There is not more than half the swearing and card playing there was three weeks ago. . . . I have found it a great help to read those religious books and papers which I can get; the books are not very plenty but the Advocate and the Telescope, the Brethren church paper, come to the Battery regularly . . . ."

29 *Ibid.*, pt. 4, 411–12. After the Battle of New Hope Church, the Union army moved to the railroad at Acworth. Sherman ordered Hooker to send a brigade to cover the crossing of Allatoona Creek and advised him that a section of the 18th Indiana Battery would accompany the brigade.

The soldiers, campaigning without shelter, suffered from the heavy June rains, and for forty-eight hours on June 13 and 14, it rained continuously. On June 14, Henry Campbell wrote, "Had a very sudden & severe attack of rheumatism last night in both my legs   pained me so severely I was obliged to sit up by the fire all night & rub them.   the first attack of the kind I ever experienced   brought on by having to sleep in damp and wet places for the last 8 or 10 days. This morning it suddenly left my legs and went into my arms without any warning whatever."

The flank movement of the Union army to Dallas and then back to the railroad at Acworth forced General Johnston to fall back to Kennesaw and Lost mountains. Kennesaw was an impregnable bastion north of Marietta; and Lost Mountain, eight miles west, "is an isolated mound   conical in form & very steep sides and rises up about 600 ft. above the surrounding country   there is no other hill or Mountain nearer than 8 miles, which gave it the name of 'Lost Mtn.' "

Lost Mountain was the extreme left of the new Confederate line, and when the First Cavalry Division rode forward to its vicinity on June 16, they found that it was defended with a section of artillery in a fort on top. "Stoneman's Cav. made an attempt to take the place yesterday but failed," Campbell wrote.

Upon arriving at a small hill in the vicinity of Lost Mountain, the Second Brigade was dismounted and advanced over the hill; but as soon as they came into the open, they were shelled by the Confederate battery on the mountain. As movement to the foot of the hill would have exposed the troopers to the fire of the battery across a long, clear, level space, they were withdrawn. General McCook reported that the north side of the mountain was inaccessible, but that the Fourth Indiana and First East Tennessee had reached the first line of barricades on the west and could advance no farther.[30]

"The 2d Sec. was run forward in position and opened out a hot fire on the fort," Henry Campbell reported. "We had scarcely fired a dozen rounds when the Rebel Battery limbered up and moved out of the fort and . . . beat a hasty retreat down the mountain and out the road to Atlanta." The Second Section fired about twenty more shells; and when

30 *Ibid.*, pt. 2, 756.

they received no reply, the cavalry advanced to the foot of the mountain, where they skirmished until dark.

While this action was taking place, the Third Section was sent to the extreme right of the Union infantry line, east of Lost Mountain, and "here they got a point from which they could enfilade the rebel line, and sent about 70 shells screaming thro the woods in which the rebel lines ran." John Rippetoe commented, "the firing was said to be by 3 Generals the best they ever saw, nearly every shell went to the right place."

On July 17 the battery and part of the division reached the rear of Lost Mountain, forcing the Confederate cavalry to evacuate the position. Henry Campbell climbed the mountain "and was amply paid for the steep ascent, by the beautiful view of the country it afforded," which included Kennesaw Mountain and Marietta at its foot.

The next day he reported that the fighting at Kennesaw Mountain "was kept up all night without a moments rest . . . . Fighting continued all day harder than ever   the cannonading is incessant, one continuous roll like musketry. whole batteries firing together. Our troops must be worn out   this is the 4 day of the Battle."

On June 19, "Gen. Schofield commanding the right wing of our army, drove the rebel left about 8 miles [between Kennesaw and Lost Mountains]. Our lines is now in the shape of a letter L with Kennesaw Mtn. in the elbow." The Confederates tried to recover the lost ground "and attacked Schofield fiercely and kept up a terrible cannonade until after dark. Rebels opened out their batteries from the sumit of Kennesaw   we could see the smoke of their guns plainly . . . . Our cavalry protects the rear of the right wing from our Station on Lost Mountain."

The soldiers understood the various maneuvers of the armies, and on June 20, Henry Campbell wrote, "Our line keeps stretching farther south every day. We will flank the place after everything gets a good ready." He also commented, "We have a very important signal station on top here. Receives signals from Scofields Hd.Qrs. on the extreme right of our army and sends them to the Hd.Qrs. of Gen. Sherman 8 miles distant."

On June 23, Henry Campbell climbed Lost Mountain, viewed Atlanta through Signal Corps' glasses, and "Could easily distinguish the windows and chimneys on the houses   the distance is 28 miles from here." On June 27, Henry observed, "Everything seems to be quiet along the lines but there is something evidently brewing. Sherman ain't still for nothing."

Campbell must have written this before the Federal batteries began the cannonade that preceded the Union assault on Kennesaw Mountain during the same day. In an attempt to storm the Confederate positions, both the Army of Tennessee and the Army of the Cumberland attacked and were repulsed with heavy loses. The direct assault having failed, Sherman resumed the flanking maneuvers. On July 1, the First Cavalry Division broke camp at Lost Mountain, marched to the right, and camped for the night at Powder Springs, ten miles south of Marietta, where they were joined by Stoneman's cavalry. The next day the combined cavalry force crossed Sweetwater Creek.

Sherman now had pulled the Army of the Tennessee out of line and started them marching toward Mason's and Turner's Ferry on the Chattahoochee River, about four miles below the bridge of the Western and Atlantic Railroad. General Johnston, seeing the purpose of the move, evacuated his position on Kennesaw Mountain during the night of July 2.[31]

On July 2 the battery was divided—the Second Section marching northeast with Stoneman's cavalry; the First Section moving with the Second Brigade on the Atlanta road; and the Third Section, with the First Brigade, remaining in position to guard the crossing of Sweetwater Creek. After a march of three miles, the Second Brigade encountered Confederates in line-of-battle behind barricades. The cavalrymen were dismounted and skirmishers were advanced close to the enemy barricades, while others "built a log pen on a slight hill about 400 yds. from their line for one of our guns."

Henry Campbell continued, "No. 1 was unlimbered down behind the hill and run up into it by hand. It was shure death to expose your self as the enemy were so close that it was an easy matter for their sharpshooters to pick their man off. No. 1 fired 6 rounds of canister and 15 of shell but could not dislodge the enemy. Every shell would tare thro the Barricades with a crash scattering rails and splinters in every

31 Guernsey and Alden, II, 609.

direction. The log breast work in front of the gun was filled with bullets but it proved a good shelter for the men as none of them were hurt in the least."

Before dark the Yankees withdrew to Sweetwater Creek and from a captured Rebel learned that they had been fighting infantry and "that Johnson has fallen back from Kennesaw and is crossing the river all so reported that our troops had possesion of Marietta."

"Awakened this morning by the Brig. Band playing the national airs   learned from that, that it was the 4 of July." In the afternoon, the battery marched back to the vicinity of Lost and Kennesaw mountains and "Passed some 'Palmetto trees' today for the first time, shows we are getting pretty well south."

The next day they marched to Marietta, which Henry Campbell said had much the same appearance as Murfreesboro after the Battle of Stones River because nearly all the inhabitants had left town and the houses were filled with wounded Rebels. Henry Campbell reported 1,600 wounded in one hospital and that "Just South of town are two fine looking buildings called the Georgia State Military Institute, now nursing the very offspring it taught the art of war."

He reported that the streets of Marietta were very broad and well shaded, and that "Business Houses are mostly brick 2 and 3 stories in hight. The R. R. runs through the center of town, with the track beautifully shaded with long rows of shade trees extending the entire length thro town."

On July 6, the division marched in an easterly direction on the left flank of the army to the bank of the Chattahoochee. That evening, Campbell and Lieutenant Benson Rippetoe rode down to the river to look for a position to emplace the battery; "found a good one on top of a high hill overlooking the river for some distance each way. The stream is about 150 yds. in width, running thro a valley 600 yds. wide bordered by abrupt hills on both sides." The battery remained in this position until July 15, and as early as July 7, John Rippetoe reported, "the cars run right up to the rear of our army and it does not look like starving at present."

The cavalry engaged in some unusual skirmishing during this period. On July 9, General McCook reported, "[Colonel] Brownlow performed one of his characteristic feats today. I had ordered a detachment to cross at Cochran's Ford. It was deep, and he took them over naked, nothing but guns, cartridge-boxes and hats. They drove the enemy out of their rifle-pits, captured a non-commissioned officer and 3 men, and the 2 boats on the other side. They would have got more, but the rebels had the advantage in running through the bushes with clothes on. It was certainly one of the funniest sights of the war, and a very successful raid for naked men to make."[32]

At 8:00 A.M. on July 15 the battery marched down the river to within one-quarter mile of Vining's Bridge, where the Western and Atlantic Railroad crossed the Chattahoochee River. The railroad bridge and the wagon bridge upstream had been burned when the Confederates evacuated the north bank of the river, but Henry Campbell wrote, "The R. R. Bridge was a very fine one, over 1000 feet in length and about 120 in height supported on 10 large stone piers with a hundred foot span between them."

Henry also commented, " . . . it was considered quite a valuable place by the rebels as the numerous heavy fortifications around it testify." The war had now reached a period when troops moving into a new position threw up heavy earthworks, adequate to protect against artillery, if time allowed. Batteries were located in forts of heavy earthwork parapets and often roofed with bombproof structures of logs and earth.[33]

At 2:00 A.M. on July 6, after the moon had gone down, "the guns were hitched up and silently moved down the road   across the R.R.

along the brow of the hill and then up into the fort on the right of the R.R. This had to be done very quietly and under the cover of darkness as we had to move for some distance along the bank of the river within 200 yds. of the enemys sharpshooters." Henry Campbell continued, "All six of the guns were got into the fort without any accident or being discovered by the enemy. The ammunition chests were dismounted and the limbers and Horses brought back to camp."

[32] *O.R.* Ser. 1, XXXVIII, pt. 2, 760–61; Connelly, *Autumn of Glory*, pp. 395–96. Cochrane's Ford was one of several points where the Union army forced crossings of the Chattahoochee River.

[33] Henry D. Dwight, "How We Fight at Atlanta," *Harper's New Monthly Magazine*, XXXIX (Oct. 1864), pp. 663–66.

According to Lieutenant Benson Rippetoe, the earthwork, named Fort McCook, was crudely constructed, only partly finished, and unroofed. The men spent July 16 working to improve the condition of the structure.[34]

On July 16, Campbell reported, "Just after daylight this morning we fired two shells at a squad of rebels about ¾ of a mile off who were enjoying a quiet breakfast in fancied security. One shell burst right among them, scattering them in all directions and evidently hurting several as we noticed them carrying them away on stretchers. This was all the firing that was done to day."

The artillerymen determined that "The fort is in a very bad position, as the rebels get a complete cross fire on it from up and down the river. The sharpshooters line the bank of the river and are so troublesome that we are obliged to keep constantly under cover all day long. A covered way had to be constructed from the fort to the railroad bank in order to get in and out of the fort in the daytime." A sharpshooter, firing through an embrasure, wounded Mark Shomber in the leg.

An upstream Rebel fort was only 800 yards distant, with four cannons dug into a hillside, and the Yankee artillerymen could bring only one gun to bear on this fort. A second fort on Peachtree Creek was thought not, and proved not, to be dangerous since it had only two guns that four pieces of Lilly's battery had in range and could force to keep silent.

On July 17, "The Rebels . . . resolved to give us a bombardment," opening with the guns of the upriver fort. Henry Campbell remarked, "They had the range perfectly and nearly every shot burst above and in the fort and as we could only reply one shot to their 4 they had it all their own way." The parapet and embrasure at one gun was caved in by the explosion of a shell, and soon afterward, the same gun was struck over the trunnions by a 12-pound shot, "making a deep dent but otherwise not injuring the gun."

Three shells exploded under the second piece "smashing the spokes of the wheel and cutting the prolonge in to pieces. All three of the shells bursted right among all the cannoneers . . . but strange to say

---

34 *O.R.* Ser. 1, XXXVIII, pt. 2, 801–802.

none were hurt. [William J.] Wolfe was severly stunned but not hurt." Number 3 and 4 guns were not damaged but Number 5 had its embrasure filled up by a shell exploding under the parapet cover. After this the weapon could be aimed and fired only with difficulty.

"Soon after the firing began, a shell entered the port hole of No. 6 Knocked down the slope, filled up the embrasure completely and then exploded right under the muzzle of the gun,   allmost in the faces of the cannoneers who were just in the act of firing the gun. One piece struck Copl. Frank Greenwood in the knee, carrying away the cap entirely.   he was the only one wounded,   how the rest escaped is a miracle,   the wheels and axle were hit in several places   one peice going clear thro a tent & pile of blankets strapped to the limber chest."

After this damage, the bombardment continued for about two hours, and then the Confederates fired only occasional shells until noon, when they ceased firing entirely. The artillerymen felt fortunate at the few casualties, because the only wounded man other than Greenwood was John Crystal, who was shot through the fleshy part of the leg by a sharpshooter.

John Rippetoe had duty away from the fort and wrote, "I was not in the works during the fight as my place was not there. I never go out of my place into danger but if duty calls me into danger I never let it keep me away from my post. I always think it is foolhardiness to be going into danger when you have no business there."

"About an hour before sun down, the rebels were seen to limber up their artillery very hurriedly and start off in the direction of Peachtree Creek in a gallop," wrote Henry Campbell. "Infantry following as fast as possible, all in great confusion." The cause of this retreat was the movement of the Union XIV Corps down the south bank of the river. They had crossed the river upstream and were marching toward Peachtree Creek. The Yankee artillerymen did not yet know the cause, but "As soon as we perceived what they [the Rebels] were doing, we run our guns out on top of the fort and shelled them vigorously."

Since the Union army was south of the Chattahoochee River in front of Atlanta, Johnston's strategy of defensive maneuvering no longer was possible, and the Confederate army would have to fight to save Atlanta. On July 17, Johnston was replaced as commander of the Army of Tennessee by John Bell Hood, known to be a fighter, and on July 20, he attacked the right of the Federal line, already across Peachtree Creek, but was repulsed in the hard-fought Battle of Peachtree Creek. Two days later, he attacked the Union left flank northeast of the city but again was driven back in the Battle of Atlanta, during which Federal Major General James B. McPherson was killed. After these offensive movements, the Confederate army remained in defensive positions around Atlanta.

The artillerymen spent the night of July 17, aided by a detail from the First Brigade, repairing the fort. "During the night a large light was visible across the river, some distance inland," Henry Campbell reported, "supposed to be the burning of Peachtree Creek bridge by the rebels." Henry received a letter from home with five dollars enclosed "which as I was strapped came very handy," but he continued, "The only thing money is any account for here in this benighted country is to pass among the Sutlers of the army. When we want anything from the country   if we think of paying for it at all   any kind of a paper with a picture on it will pass."

On July 19, the Fourth Kentucky Mounted Infantry, Colonel John T. Croxton commanding, "a large well mounted and well armed regiment" joined the First Brigade. As senior officer, Croxton took command of the brigade.

On July 22, the battery marched two miles upriver and "crossed over a trussle bridge (built by the Engineer Corps) then down the south bank to opposite our fort." Later, they marched two miles farther "where everything got mixed up some way or other and after a deal of marching and counter marching we did not get into camp until 11 o'clock."

The next day the division marched on the Carrol Goldmines and Atlanta road, camping at Mason's Church,[35] four miles below Vining's bridge, where "we built rail barricades across the roads and in front of the troops   also threw up light breast works in front of our guns." Except for a clearing around the church in which the guns were emplaced, the area consisted of very thick woods.

[35] *Ibid.* William Benson Rippetoe called the place "Mason's Academy," but other reports refer to it as "Mason's Church."

"Just before dark, after the troops had unsaddled and were getting their supper, the rebels charged in suddenly on the 2d Brig. camped in our front," Henry Campbell reported. "The 2d was considerably confused at first and the rebels came clear up in the edge of their camp just in view from our position. We opened on them with shell and soon put them to flight before they could capture anything."

John Rippetoe verified the confusion of the cavalrymen. "... they were not expecting anything of the kind and were not as well prepared as they should have been." One man of the First Wisconsin was killed, and two were wounded. Other than this, the Rebels "accomplished nothing more than a big scare." The scare seems to have affected the troopers, however, and William Winkler wrote that the night was spent fortifying the position.

XII

A Disastrous Raid

. . . I expended all the canister and nearly all the shells. I reported these facts to Brig. Gen. E. M. McCook who ordered me to abandon the artillery. The guns were spiked and otherwise injured; the carriages and harness were utterly destroyed.[1]

Lieutenant Martin J. Miller reported the sad fate of the First Section of Lilly's battery during the dual campaign south of Atlanta generally known as Stoneman's and McCook's Raid. The opposing Confederate general, Joseph Wheeler, called this raid "the most stupendous cavalry operation of the war."[2]

The purpose of the raid was to destroy the railroads south of Atlanta to stop supplies from reaching Hood's army and to defeat Wheeler's cavalry if he attempted to interfere. Major General George Stoneman, with his own division and the larger division of Brigadier General Kenner Garrard, was to ride down from the east of Atlanta, meet McCook's division, which would move in from the west, at Lovejoy's Station on July 28, and demolish the Macon and Western Railroad. Stoneman's division totaled 1,800 men; Garrard's, 3,700; and McCook's 1,600.[3] In addition, McCook's force included a brigade of Major General Lovell Rousseau's[4] cavalry that had arrived in the area on July 22 after a thirteen-day, 400-mile raid through Alabama

---

[1] *O.R.* Ser. 1, XXXVIII, pt. 2, 802–803.
[2] *Ibid.*, pt. 3, 957.
[3] *Ibid.*, pt. 1, 116.
[4] Rousseau commanded the military district of Nashville.

and Georgia during which Rousseau was wounded, leaving Colonel Thomas J. Harrison in command.[5]

To oppose the raid, Wheeler had eight brigades numbering about 3,800 men comprising the Army of Tennessee Cavalry Corps southeast of Atlanta and three brigades of the cavalry corps of the Army of Mississippi, commanded by Brigadier General William H. Jackson, were southwest of Atlanta, directly opposed to McCook.[6]

General Sherman reviewed the plans for the operation thoroughly with the cavalry officers involved and believed that the objectives of the raid were clear; but he gave Stoneman permission, just before the campaign commenced, to ride on to Macon and Andersonville with his own division to try to rescue prisoners at these places after destroying the railroad. Stoneman, apparently trying for national hero rank, made the rescue of the prisoners his first priority and did not attempt to join the other divisions for the destruction of the railroad. Once the raid began, McCook and Garrard heard nothing from Stoneman advising of a change of plan.

On July 26, McCook's division marched to Mason's Church, south of the Chattahoochee River, on the extreme right of the army; and the guns of the battery were placed in an earthwork, previously constructed, to cover the laying of a pontoon bridge over which Harrison's men planned to cross to join McCook. While this work was progressing, a Confederate cavalry force attacked, driving in the pickets, and charged into an open field in front of the battery. "As soon as they came in sight we opened on them with canister which sent them back into the woods immediately," Henry Campbell reported. McCook had planned to start his raid from Mason's the next day, but since his force had been observed and would likely be harassed on the march, he decided to begin the expedition farther downstream.

At two o'clock the next morning, the entire command crossed to the north bank of the river on the pontoon bridge, and while the men were getting breakfast, the pontoon bridge was taken up. Then the

[5] Indiana Historical Society Library, Thomas J. Harrison to his wife, July 22 and July 25, 1864.
[6] *O.R.* Ser. 1, XXXVIII, pt. 3, 657.

division marched downstream followed by the pontoon train. As far as Campbellton, Confederate pickets were posted at the fords, and although McCook could have forced a crossing, he did not want to give an alarm. At sundown the column went into camp opposite this town and waited for the pontoon train, which arrived at 2:00 A.M. on July 28.

The force then marched to Smith's Ferry, six miles below Campbellton, where the First Brigade crossed to establish a bridgehead, a slow process as only a single batteau was available. The bridge was built by 3:00 P.M., and the men designated for the raid crossed.

These were the First East Tennessee Cavalry, Eighth Iowa Cavalry, and Fourth Kentucky Mounted Infantry forming the First Brigade, commanded by Colonel John T. Croxton; the Second and Fourth Indiana Cavalry of the Second Brigade, commanded by Lieutenant Colonel William H. Torrey; and the Eighth Indiana, Fourth Tennessee, Fifth Iowa, and Second Kentucky Cavalry from the Fourth Division, commanded by Colonel Harrison. The First Section of Lilly's battery, commanded by Lieutenant Miller, was the artillery assigned for the raid.[7]

After these troops had crossed, the First Wisconsin was sent back through Campbellton as a diversion with orders to join the main column at Fayetteville if possible; but after marching seven miles, the First ran into Armstrong's brigade of Jackson's cavalry and was chased back to the river with a loss of ten men, including their commander, Major Nathan Paine.[8] McCook's secrecy and the attention attracted by the First Wisconsin confused the Confederates, and Jackson's cavalry did not interfere with the main column until after they had reached their objective. The next day the bridge was taken up and the remainder of McCook's command—the First Wisconsin, the Tenth Ohio, four guns of the battery, and the dismounted men of the division—marched back to Marietta.

By this time, Garrard's division had marched to the position where they were to meet Stoneman and were opposed by all of Wheeler's corps, but Stoneman did not appear since he was riding farther east through

7 *Ibid,* pt. 2, 747.
8 *Ibid.,* pt. 1, 780–84.

Covington. In the absence of orders covering this contingency, Garrard ultimately pulled back to Decatur.

After crosing the Chattahoochee River, McCook's division, led by the Fourth Indiana, marched southeast to the Atlanta and West Point Railroad at Palmetto. They reached this town just after dark, and in two hours, destroyed three miles of track, the depot, telegraph lines, two trains of cars with provisions, buildings with military stores, and about 100 bales of cotton. The fires at Palmetto lit up the sky, warning the citizens of Newnan, fifteen miles south, that Yankee cavalry was on a raid and the townspeople sent "whiskey and everything else of value elsewhere."[9]

"After cleaning out Palmetto,"[10] the division continued the march toward Fayetteville, twenty-five miles to the east. The column moved quietly and, near Flint River, they surprised over 500 wagons, including "headquarters trains of nearly their whole army, Hardee's [corps] entire transportation and the cavalry command supply train."[11] This wagon train had been marching to Atlanta when they learned of Garrard's movement, and fearing capture, had marched west, running into McCook's expedition. Seventy-two commissioned officers and 350 men were captured, the prisoners being quartermasters, commissary department men, and paymasters.

William O. Crouse wrote, "Our march had been so noiseless, not a shot having been fired throughout the night, that we surrounded the Rebels, and were in their midst before they were aware of it. They could hardly realize that we were Yankees until daylight made apparent our arms and uniforms."[12] Here the battery replaced their worn out horses with fresh animals from the wagon train, and many cavalrymen were remounted on captured horses. Eight hundred horses and mules were captured with the train, and those not taken by the men were sabered. The wagons and supplies were burned, including chests of Confederate money intended to pay the army in Atlanta.

[9] Kate Cumming, *Kate: The Journal of a Confederate Nurse*, ed. by Richard Barksdale Harwell (Baton Rouge: Louisiana State Univ. Press, 1959), p. 214; *O.R.* Ser. 1, XXXVIII, pt. 2, 761–62.

[10] Indiana Historical Society Library, Samuel A. Hall diary.

[11] *O.R.* Ser. 1, XXXVIII, pt. 2, 761–62.

[12] Merrill, II, 734.

After destroying the train, the division marched on toward Fayetteville, and the First East Tennessee in the advance found the covered bridge over the Flint River on fire. Colonel Brownlow, with a detail, galloped through the burning bridge, captured the guard, and extinguished the fire, allowing the division to cross.[13] At about daylight on July 29, the Yankee troopers reached Fayetteville, where they captured some additional prisoners. After resting for two hours, the time usually allowed on a march to feed the horses, they continued on to Lovejoy's Station.

About this time, Wheeler learned that Stoneman's division was riding to the east and toward Macon and also was notified by Brigadier General Francis A. Shoup[14] that McCook's division was coming from the west. Shoup ordered Wheeler to go to General Jackson's assistance because Jackson had only two brigades available to try to stop McCook's force, since Armstrong's brigade was watching a movement by Union infantry on the army's flank.[15] Wheeler still was facing Garrard's division, but he sent Brigadier General Alfred Iverson, with three brigades, to follow Stoneman; and sensing that Garrard would not make an aggressive move, he left only Brigadier General George C. Dibrell's brigade to watch this largest Union division. He ordered another brigade to Jonesboro, north of Lovejoy's on the railroad, and with the remainder of his command, which he stated was fewer than 500 men, Wheeler set out to reinforce Jackson and deal with McCook.[16]

McCook's division rode into Lovejoy's at 7:00 A.M. on July 29, one day later than the date set for the meeting with Stoneman. Finding no evidence that Stoneman had been there, the division spread out along the Macon and Western Railroad destroying two and one-half miles of track, five miles of telegraph line, and supplies. The only known casualty here was Williamson Ward of the Eighth Indiana, who was thrown by a wild mule he had captured and was trying to break. Although he said that he was seriously hurt when his shoulder and back

13 William Randolph Carter, "McCook's Raid," Letter to the Editor, *National Tribune*, n.d., clipping in Henry Campbell Journal, Wabash College Archives.
14 Shoup was chief-of-staff, Army of Tennessee.
15 *O.R.* Ser. 1, XXXVIII, pt. 5, 927.
16 *Ibid.*, pt. 3, 953–54; Dyer, p. 182.

struck the roots of a tree, he remained with his regiment and participated in all of its actions.[17]

At 2:00 P.M., learning that Wheeler was between his force and McDonough, from which direction Stoneman and Garrard should have come, McCook ordered a retreat by way of Newnan to the Chattahoochee River. After marching two miles, most of the column passed a crossroad, but before all were through, Brigadier General L. S. Ross's Texas brigade of Jackson's cavalry attacked along the crossroad, striking the Eighth Iowa, next to last in the column. The rear guard, the Fourth Kentucky came up, relieved the Iowans, and fought the Texans for two hours. The Fourth advanced too far and was cut off from the main column but succeeded in cutting their way back after losing two companies[18] and then continued as rear guard. The Rebels were now on all roads and fighting was necessary on flanks and rear, but William Winkler wrote that the fighting "kept the Reb. cavalry from pressing us to hart; both sides lost heavily."

The rear guard burned the bridge over Flint River about dusk, and although the column was not harassed so much during the night, darkness brought other problems. The men had not slept for two nights and began falling asleep in their saddles, and the weary horses, no longer urged on, stopped. Men and horses not moving in the road caused men in the rear to pull up, thinking the column was halted, while a packtrain of several hundred mules just ahead of the rear guard had halted and men and animals were found to be fast asleep.

Moreover, the Rebels had the principal roads blocked ahead of the column; but fortunately, when the force seemed trapped, they found a Negro guide who led them by back roads to the vicinity of Newman. On the march, they ran into another train of fifty Confederate army wagons which they destroyed, but did not burn, because fires would have betrayed their position.

The guns of the battery became entangled in the woods, and General McCook ordered the artillerymen to leave them, but William Crouse reported, ". . . actuated by the strong affection a soldier has for

[17] Indiana Historical Society Library, Williamson Ward journal.
[18] *O.R.* Ser. 1, XXXVIII, pt. 2, 778–80.

his arms, we refused, and after a half hour's delay we succeeded in getting them through, and on the road again."

Crouse also told of the difficulties of the night march. "The excessive exertion of the two days and nights travel, without rest or food, overcame many. They gave out from sheer exhaustion. Our mules could scarcely be urged along, by coaxing or beating, when we crossed a stream of water, but orders were imperative not to stop for water or any other purpose. If a horse or mule fell dead, the carriage was driven to the roadside and a fresh animal put into the harness. The carriage must regain its place as it could."[19]

The column became spread out in the darkness although ordered to keep closed up, and the hundreds of prisoners marching with the column escaped whenever they saw a chance. Some prisoners misled the Yankees at crossroads and by-paths, and squads of men became lost and were captured.

The Fourth Kentucky built barricades across the road in the rear of the column, and about 3:00 A.M., were attacked but repulsed several charges. After two hours, the Rebels swung through the woods, surrounding most of the Fourth, whose ammunition had nearly all been used, and captured most of the regiment. The fighting at this point had been so severe that the Confederates established a hospital on the spot.[20]

At daylight the Eighth Indiana in the advance of the column approached Newnan, and Lieutenant Colonel Fielder Jones sent two companies ahead into the town, where a train was stopped at the depot because of the break in the railroad at Palmetto. The engineer saw the bluecoats riding into town and blew the whistle, alerting the passengers of the train, who happened to be Brigadier General Phillip D. Roddey and 600 men of his cavalry brigade on their way to join Wheeler at Atlanta.[21] These men disembarked, took position in buildings and along the track, and began firing at the Yankee troopers who retreated out of town "without a scratch"[22] to await reinforcements.

19 Merrill, II, 735.
20 *O.R.* Ser. 1, XXXVIII, pt. 2, 778–80.
21 *Ibid.*, 875–78; Cumming, pp. 214–15.
22 Williamson Ward journal.

Roddey's men formed a battle line at the edge of town and were joined by some "impetuous boys" of the town and by convalescents from the military hospitals in Newnan. Most other citizens stampeded getting out of town at the approach of the Yankees because "McCook, by his unparalleled cruelty, had made his name a horror," and because rumors spread that the town was surrounded and that the Yankees were about to fire on it.[23]

Although hard pressed at Newnan, McCook's men cut the railroad and telegraph line in three places, but he was more anxious to find a way around town than to destroy track. A two-hour search was necessary since his Negro guide now was beyond his area of familiarity, but then an open road two miles south of town was found. The division marched around Newnan and headed for the Chattahoochee River with the Eighth Indiana protecting the rear, and Colonel Jones heard heavy skirmishing ahead at 11:00 A.M.

Wheeler's cavalry rode into Newnan at noon[24] and immediately marched toward the sound of fighting. His force had increased en route, and he now had 700 with him and soon was joined by 400 mounted men from Jonesboro and by Roddey's dismounted 600.[25] A second train with an infantry regiment also arrived in town, and these soldiers joined Wheeler.[26]

About five miles from Newnan, the Second Kentucky Cavalry in the advance ran into a force of Johnnies across the road, and according to William Winkler, the Fourth Indiana went forward to assist the Kentuckians. "We fought them well and the Rebel Cavalry give away, we pursued when at once the Rebel Infantry closed in between us and the Main Colume under General McCook. There was hevy fighting all around and at last about 200 of us with Major [George H.] Purdy rallied and started for the Chattahoachy River 15 miles distant."

According to Major Purdy, the men cut off were 150 men of the Fourth, two companies of the Second Indiana, and four companies of

---

23 Fannie A. Beers, *Memories* (Philadelphia: Lippincott, 1888), 139–41. Newnan was a principal hospital center for the Confederate Army of Tennessee with seven hospitals.
24 Cumming, p. 215.
25 *O.R.* Ser. 1, XXXVIII, pt. 3, 957–62.
26 *Ibid.*, pt. 2, 780–84.

the Second Kentucky. After trying to cut their way back to the division, Major Purdy led 180 men through the Rebel lines. After the break out, he was joined by Lieutenant P. J. Williamson, brigade assistant adjutant general, who had led another 100 men through the encirclement. A Negro guide was found who led the troopers on a zigzag course through thick woods, miry swamps, and steep hills, so that the Confederates in pursuit lost the track.[27] The Yankee troopers reached the Chattahoochee fifteen miles above Franklin, and as William Winkler reported, "Arrived there at mid night. We crossed the Saddles in 3 Canoos and swam the Horses. Got all saft over at Daylight."

The infantry that had separated this part of the Second Brigade from the main body stopped further progress by the main column, beginning a fight called the Battle of Brown's Mill. The First Brigade found a strong position in the edge of dense woods with an impassable ditch in front, and when Wheeler tried to work around to take the position in flank, McCook placed other troops to prevent it. Although surrounded, the Yankees held their position until late afternoon by vigorous counterattacks.

In one of these counterattacks, McCook reported, ". . . the whole right of their line was broken and demoralized. Ross' Texan brigade was destroyed, all his men and horses captured or killed, and General Ross himself a prisoner."[28]

McCook appears to have exaggerated the results of this action, during which the Eighth Iowa rode around the dismounted men of Ross's brigade and captured some 500 of the brigade's horses. An hour-long fight ensued with men of both sides, including General Ross, being captured and recaptured; but the Iowans finally were surrounded, and only three officers and ten men engaged here broke out. The brigade commander, Colonel Thomas J. Harrison, became a prisoner while dismounted, when the man holding his horse failed to bring it up.[29]

The battery had a most difficult time after they took position on a slight eminence facing an open field bordered by thick woods that

27 *Ibid.*, 780–84; 786–88.
28 *Ibid.*
29 *Ibid.*, 776–77; pt. 3, 963–65.

were 150 yards in front and occupied by Union skirmishers. Lieutenant Miller reported, ". . . suddenly a terrible fire of musketry from the enemy drove back and completely routed the skirmishers, some of whom threw away their guns as they passed the battery. The section opened with canister and after rapid firing for nearly half an hour, succeeded in checking the enemy when within eighty yards of our position."

Miller said the advance of the Rebels was supported by three solid lines of infantry, one of which reached the open field and poured volleys among the cannoneers. "No support or assistance of any kind was brought up, except that Lieutenant [Roswell] Hill, of the Second Indiana Cavalry, with twenty or twenty-five men, charged through the open field on the right of the battery and halted when in line with the guns. The enemy quickly observed the confused condition of our officers and men and made a second and third charge on the exposed section but were repeatedly checked and driven back into the woods." The battery's fight lasted two hours, during which all the canister and most of the shells were used, and Miller then was ordered by McCook to abandon the guns. The guns were spiked, the carriages chopped down, the harness cut up, and the artillerymen mounted the battery mules, staying near McCook.[30]

Late in the afternoon, when many of the Yankees were out of ammunition, the Confederates sent in a flag of truce requesting that McCook surrender; but he called a council of his officers, who decided to cut their way out. One soldier reported, "All now excitement and confusion. We are ready for the worst and will make some rebel bite the dust."[31]

The First Brigade, led by Colonel Brownlow and his Tennesseans, formed one column that broke through toward the northwest. After the Tennesseans and those left of the Fourth Kentucky were successful in breaking through the lines, Colonel Croxton went back to hurry up the Eighth Iowa; but the Rebels cut between him and the men already out, capturing the Fourth, except for the men holding the horses of

[30] *Ibid.*, pt. 2, 763; 802–803.
[31] Williamson Ward journal.

the skirmishers. Croxton with two orderlies, all dismounted, hid in the woods.[32]

Brownlow, with 600 men, rode to Moore's Bridge, twenty miles above the point where Purdy's men crossed; but because the Confederates were close on his tail, only 150 of his men succeeded in crossing the river.[33]

Lieutenant Colonel Jones, now commanding Harrison's brigade, was ordered to lead the breakout of the remainder of the force. Returning from the council, he found that a stampede of the mule team and led horses had destroyed all organization; but he extricated the Eighth Indiana, Fifth Iowa, and part of the Fourth Tennessee. The Eighth was said to be the only unit in the division that still retained its organization, an accomplishment that the soldiers attributed to their Spencer repeating rifles.[34] Finding an obscure road leading toward the south, Jones assembled his force at 6:00 P.M., was joined by McCook with parts of the Second and Fourth Indiana and the artillerymen,[35] and assigned sixteen picked men of the Eighth to serve as an advance guard.[36]

The breakout was successfully accomplished "in the midst of a most terrible fire,"[37] through which all the artillerymen went out with no one being hit or hurt. Colonel Jones found a Negro who guided the column to Corinth, where two bridges over New River were destroyed, gaining five hours, advantage over the pursuing Rebels.[38]

Rumors reached the troops in Marietta that the entire division had been captured. Colonel Brownlow with only twenty-eight of his men reached that place during the night of July 31. The following day, Major Purdy and his men came into camp, but their arrival only increased the gloom because these men truthfully reported that the division had been surrounded when they left. On August 2, the four remaining guns of the battery with remnants of the cavalry division

32 *O.R.* Ser. 1, XXXVIII, pt. 2, 769–74.

33 *Ibid.*, 774.

34 Merrill, II, 735; Williamson Ward journal; Indiana Historical Society Library, Jacob Bartness to his wife, Amanda, Aug. 11, 1864.

35 *O.R.* Ser. 1, XXXVIII, pt. 2, 875–78.

36 Williamson Ward journal.

37 *O.R.* Ser. 1, XXXVIII, pt. 2, 763.

38 *Ibid.*, 875–78.

moved to Vining's Bridge again, the artillerymen taking position in the forts.

On August 5, Henry Campbell wrote, "We were startled about noon today by the boys in the western part of the camp   cheering. And on running out to find the cause were astounded to see Lt. Miller and the Boys of his Section all riding in on mules. Of course we were overjoyed, to see all of our boys come in without a scratch." The only personnel losses in the section had been two men, detailed from the Tenth Indiana Battery, whose horses gave out on the north bank of the river. John Rippetoe was confident that the two men would return to camp if bushwhackers did not capture them, but Lieutenant Benson Rippetoe reported that these men still were missing on September 10 and assumed that they had been captured.[39]

Once they had broken out of the encirclement, the artillerymen remained with the main body as it marched southwest during the night of July 31. At about dawn on August 1 they reached the Chattahoochee south of Franklin, where one group of soldiers found the ferryboat partly full of water, which made difficult pulling. Even so, they ferried across. Most soldiers, however, built rafts to float their accoutrements and swam their horses and mules. McCook reported that soldiers of the Eighth and Second Indiana defended the crossing, and that all were captured, but one of the soldiers wrote that all troopers crossed safely except for a few stragglers who had fallen asleep on the bank.[40]

After crossing the river, the column marched to Wedowee, Alabama, where they replaced their worn out horses and obtained animals for the dismounted men at the plantations in the area. Then they marched to Marietta through Buchanan, Draketown, and "a little rebel town named Possum Snout."[41]

The Federal surgeons had remained on the battlefield and were joined by Confederate doctors and nurses from the military hospitals in Newnan. The wounded of both sides, including 200 Union soldiers, were taken into Newnan, while hundreds of unwounded prisoners were marched into town and placed in a large cotton warehouse. Con-

---

39 *Ibid.*, 801–802.
40 Williamson Ward journal.
41 *Ibid.; O.R.* Ser. 1, XXXVIII, pt. 2, 763.

federate soldiers coming into Newnan complained of Wheeler's generalship, saying that Roddey was all ready to make a final charge, but that Wheeler would not issue the necessary orders. A Confederate officer gave an explanation, "Wheeler has no taste for raiding or running after raiders. His forte is in defending the rear of the army in a retreat, and in that capacity he can not be excelled."[42] Southern newspapers also criticized Wheeler for not destroying the entire Yankee division.[43]

About 1,200 men came into Marietta with McCook on August 5 and Henry Campbell reported that 530 had arrived earlier. McCook claimed that his losses did not exceed 500, but Confederate reports indicate as many as 800 prisoners were marched into Newnan.

Men continued to straggle in from the raid at a rate of about ten a day for two weeks according to Henry Campbell. Three men of the Second Indiana appeared with their horses and horse equipments after having ridden all the way around Atlanta, and Colonel Croxton with his orderly came into camp on foot after walking at night, hiding during the day, and living on green corn.

Although a large part of the division reached Marietta, Wheeler was correct in reporting that the campaign "destroyed the flower of General Sherman's vast cavalry organization."[44] General Elliott's returns for August 8 showed that the First Division had only 1,139 officers and men present and that only half of these were mounted and equipped. Since 125 of the mounted men were credited to the Eighteenth Indiana Battery,[45] fewer than 500 cavalrymen were prepared for service.

McCook's division accomplished all that could have been expected in the circumstances, and McCook regarded the raid as a "brilliant success," citing the destruction of wagons, military equipment, and railroads[46]; but when the Confederates had put the railroads back into operation within three days, General Sherman became skeptical of the ability of cavalry raids to damage railroads substantially and afterwards assigned this work to infantry and engineers.

42 Beers, p. 151; Cumming, p. 218.
43 *O.R.* Ser. 1, XXXVIII, pt. 2, 764.
44 *Ibid.*, pt. 3, 957–62.
45 *Ibid.*, pt. 5, 432–33.
46 *Ibid.*, pt. 2, 764.

General Stoneman's part of the raid was an even greater disaster. Near Clinton his division was caught between Iverson's cavalry, coming from the north, and infantry and militia from Macon. Only one brigade got away and returned to the Federal lines, and Stoneman surrendered the remainder of the force.[47]

Lilly's battery remained in the forts at Vining's Bridge when the cavalry regiments were moved back to Kingston to be reoutfitted. On August 15, General Elliott heard that 500 Confederate cavalry were moving toward Vining's Station and warned Lieutenant Rippetoe, "Have your men well in hand to guard against any surprise,"[48] but nothing came of this threat.

General Sherman now was moving his army to the right with a plan to march toward the railroads south of Atlanta. Although he had been disappointed at the small damage done to the railroads on the McCook raid, he sent the Third Division of cavalry under Brigadier General Hugh Judson Kilpatrick to try to cut the railroads more effectively, and on August 19, Lilly's battery began to march to Sandtown, eight miles below Vining's Bridge, but were delayed until twelve day's rations were obtained.

On August 25, the battery reported to General Kilpatrick at Sandtown and were ordered to guard the pontoon bridge when Kilpatrick moved out on his raid the next morning. This was a key location in Sherman's tactics, and Henry Campbell reported, "This point will be the base of supplies for our army, in the contemplated flank movement to the Macon R.R. The wagons loading at Vinings Bridge and moving down the north bank of the river to this place and then crossing in perfect safety   this arrangement will save about 15 miles of lines from being strongly guarded."

The men had no action while at Sandtown but began to live more comfortably, because Lieutenant Miller returned from Chattanooga with all the company and personal baggage that had been stored there during the campaign. On August 27, Wilder's brigade passed through Sandtown, and the artillerymen "seen all the old boys that were detailed in the battery."

[47] Tarrant, pp. 360–68.
[48] *O.R.* Ser. 1, XXXVIII, pt. 5, 510.

Sherman's flank movement toward the south was successful, causing the Confederate army to evacuate Atlanta and its fortifications, and on September 4 the XX Corps marched from Vining's Bridge and occupied the city. Men were curious to see the place, and Lieutenant Miller with a squad of artillerymen, armed with carbines borrowed from the dismounted cavalry, "went down to view the sights of the city."

The following day, a foraging party from the battery captured two Confederate soldiers who had become separated from their commands and were trying to get back to Atlanta, not knowing that it had been captured. On September 7, Captain Beck returned to the battery, Campbell reporting that he was entirely well.

On September 11 orders came for the battery to march to Atlanta, load their equipment on trains, and rejoin their division at Cartersville. Since cars were not immediately available when the battery reached Atlanta, Henry Campbell rode through the city "and took a good stare at the 'Gate City' of the South." He observed that Atlanta was about the size of Lafayette, Indiana, "with the streets running in all directions totally regardless of one another."

He wrote, "Three or four tolerably fine residences is all the place can bost of and they are nothing to brag on. Colonel Lanes house[49] at home is equal to any of them. I rode thro every street in the place and did not see a single place that would begin to compare with some of the fine houses in Indianapolis, everything looks old and worn out."

Henry was more impressed with the transportation and industrial developments, observing that the three railroads made a wide passage through the center of the city and that a Union passenger depot that "resembles the one at Indianapolis, on a smaller scale," was built between the railroads.

"The round house for the Georgia R.R. is the largest I ever seen holds 42 engines   besides the repair shops," he wrote. "The Macon road has a Stone round house, used by the Rebels as an arsnel. In the S.E. part of the city near the R.R. was a large rolling mill,   cost 400,000   destroyed by the rebels. They made their cannon here. 5

49 Henry S. Lane, then U. S. senator. His home is a historic site operated by the Montgomery County Historical Society.

engines and 80 cars loaded with ordinance stores guns   cannon, shot and shell were burnt near this place." Campbell remarked on the damage the Federal artillery had done, especially in the northwest section, reporting "The yards of all the houses had 'gopher holes' dug in them where the citizens took refuge during the firing."

At 3:00 P.M., a train with eight flat cars backed into the depot, and "by 7 o'clock we had them loaded getting the guns and caissons, Battery and forge wagons on. As no more flats could be procured, the remaining 4 wagons had to be taken apart and loaded on Box Cars. Horses and mules were placed in cattle cars. At 8 o'clock started with two trains . . . rode all night on top of the box cars. Arrived at Cartersville at daylight" and went into camp on the bank of the Etowah River.

Just because Atlanta was in Union control and the Confederate army had moved south did not mean that danger to the soldiers along the line of the railroad had ended. On September 13, a forage train was attacked by forty or fifty Confederate cavalry scouts within four miles of the camp.

John Rippetoe was with the battery wagons at the rear of the column, and the artillerymen had turned their wagons and started back toward camp before any of the enemy troopers got to that part of the column. No more than four did come toward the rear, and one of these had his horse killed within ten steps of Rippetoe.

John was unarmed until he borrowed a pistol from a Negro during the skirmish—"The darky did not like to let me have it. He said he had borrowed it to defend himself with but I saw that he depended on the running qualities of his mule to save him and took the shooting iron from him. . . ."

When mounted men came up, John joined them in the pursuit of the Rebels, riding to Stilesboro, some six miles from where the train was attacked. Here 200 men of the Fourth Indiana Cavalry joined them and chased the graybacks for another seven miles, but Rippetoe did not join in this because his horse was "pretty well tired down and I had nothing but a pistol to fight with." He said that he had accomplished nothing "only that I showed a willing spirit." The Fourth Indiana cavalrymen caught up with the Rebels, however, and William Winkler reported, "We killed 1, wounded several, captured 2 Lieuts and 1 Reb. Pris. and recaptured the most of our mules and teamsters."

On October 16, John Rippetoe "Came nearer to being captured by guerrilas than is agreeable" while he was in charge of some forage wagons being loaded in a corn field.

"A party of them dashed upon us while we were loading the wagons and got within 50 yards of us before we saw them," he wrote; "the cavalry guards that were with us were on the wrong side of us, but there happened to be a fence in front of us which was so high that the rebels could not get there horses over without throwing it down and by that time we had got to where the cavalry picket was stationed and the whole guard heard the firing and came charging and the rebs retreated as fast as they came."

The guerrillas captured Rippetoe's horse and that of the wagon master. ". . . mine was hitched behind one of the wagons and I was before the wagon gathering corn . . . I did not have time to get him which was fortunate for me for if I had been mounted I could not have got my horse over the fence before they would have caught me." William Black of the battery was not so fortunate. He was shot in the back by a large ball and three buckshots and died that night.

The next day, General McCook sent his scouts to burn all the houses in the area where the attack occurred, and the battery men could see smoke from a number of fires. John Rippetoe said that three or four plantations were burned "and I think he [McCook] intends to do that way in every neighborhood which is troublesome to his foraging parties. It looks hard to put the people out of doors but we intend to put this rebellion down if the whole south has to be burnt off without leaving a single building standing."

The soldiers took a straw vote on the upcoming elections while at Cartersville, and John Rippetoe wrote that "among the old eighteenth boys" the result was Abraham Lincoln and Andrew Johnson seventy-seven votes; George B. McClellan and George Pendleton, two; Governor Morton, eighty-one, and his opponent, Joseph E. McDonald, none. The results in the detail from the Tenth Battery were not so lopsided, and those of the Eighth Battery even less so because "There are seven or eight of the Eighth Battery who are regular butternuts in principal . . . but one thing is certain if the soldiers get to vote Lincoln, Johnson, Morton and [Conrad] Baker[50] will be elected at the coming elections this fall."

The draft also seemed to be bringing "butternuts" into the army and John Rippetoe asked Mary "to let me know who were drafted in Sugar Creek twp. I have heard of some, which if true is a very good joke."

With Atlanta in Union hands, Confederate General John B. Hood had to determine the best way to use his army. In early October he circled to the rear of Sherman's army and attacked the Yankee garrison at Allatoona Pass, which was a major supply depot, said to contain one million rations.[51] Lilly's artillerymen, only six miles away, heard heavy cannonading beginning at 8:00 A.M. on October 5 and later heard heavy musketry in what Henry Campbell described as the most stubborn fight of the war. Heavy Union reinforcements coming up from the south forced the Confederates to break off the attack, and Hood's army headed toward West Point and the Alabama line.

Hood's strategy now was to march for Middle Tennessee, believing that a threat to that region would draw Sherman's army out of Georgia to defend Nashville. Sherman pursued Hood to the Alabama line, but there he stopped, sent General Thomas to Nashville to build up a new army, and made his own plans for the March to the Sea.

On October 17 the battery and the Second Brigade began a march to Kingston, and the next afternoon when three miles from Adairsville, came up to a large herd of convalescent horses being escorted to Chattanooga by a small guard. They had been attacked by guerrillas and the guard driven off, but the timely arrival of the cavalry column drove the bushwhackers away and recaptured about 700 of the horses.[52]

On October 31, Campbell reported, "The 9 Penn Cav. passed here today on their way to join Kilpatricks Div. they . . . have been filled up, now numbering 1,000 men." Kilpatrick's division had been designated as the cavalry force for the march to Savannah.

At home, events proceeded normally. Henry Campbell "Recd a card to Mary Barbours Wedding."

---

[50] Union party candidates for president, vice-president, governor, and lieutenant-governor.

[51] Guernsey and Alden, II, 671.

[52] William M. Winkler diary.

XIII

A Lyon Hunt
in Kentucky

*Yesterday evening we began loading
our guns & caissons on the cars
this A.M. we turned over all our
horses to Kilpatrick. Wagons and
mules go through by land in charge
of Lt. D. W. Rippetoe.*

Henry Campbell's journal entry of November 3 reflected General Sherman's new strategy. General Hood now was marching through Alabama to threaten Middle Tennessee, hoping to draw Sherman's army away from Georgia to defend Nashville, but Sherman had decided to make his now famous March to the Sea with 60,000 men, including Kilpatrick's cavalry division, which was equipped by stripping the other divisions. General Thomas went back to Nashville to assemble a new army from units already in the field and recruits from the North.

Rail accommodations for the artillerymen returning to Nashville were far from luxurious because the battery could not procure any box cars and had flat cars only to carry men and equipment. Upon his arrival at Nashville, John Rippetoe wrote to Mary, "... if you had seen us during the five days that we were on those flat cars, coming from Calhoun, to this place through the cold rain you would have been sorry for me." It rained all the time of their trip.

Although loaded early on November 3, the two trains with the battery did not start until 2:00 A.M. the next day. When within three miles of Dalton, the car on which John Rippetoe was riding jumped the track, but since the train was traveling very slowly, no one was hurt. The engines and the cars ahead of the derailment were uncoupled and driven into Dalton "to get another car to load the guns on so the conductor stated, but the truth was they were afraid of the bushwackers and wanted to get out of the way." That part of the train did not return from Dalton before the second train came up in the rear of the derailment.

Then, according to Henry Campbell, "all the men with the assistance of the engine pulled the car back on the track   the rear train was then coupled on & the engine took both into Dalton." Henry remarked that the Confederates had torn up the track from Resaca to Dalton and noticed, "Scattered all along the track were great quantities of chewd bits of sugar cane. The only thing they [the Confederate soldiers] have to live on." The Union engineers had, of course, rebuilt the railroad.

The artillery trains reached Chattanooga at dusk on November 5 and left at 1:30 P.M. the next day. The soldiers crawled under shelters they had fashioned by spreading tarpaulins across the cars. During the night Henry Campbell and Lieutenant John Johnson slept directly under the center of one of these shelters and the jarring of the train caused one of the props to fall, allowing the canvas to sag and collect a large volume of water, which began trickling through onto Henry Campbell. This awoke him, and on raising up he bumped his head on the canvas, knocking it loose from one of the stakes and "let all the water down on us in a torrent soaking everything on that side of the car. Our bedding was as wet as if it had been dipped in the creek." Campbell and Johnson received no sympathy: "The Capt.   Gains Rippetoe & Allen, who was sleeping on the other side of the car escaped   and enjoyed the laugh at our expense."

"The rain was so severe that it rushed down the mountain sides and poured over into the cuts in perfect waterfalls coming down on the train in regular torrents. . . . Just as the train emerged from the first tunnel a stream of water as large as a water tank spout gushed out sideways from a fissure with tremendous force. It happened to be about on a level with the flat cars and as the train slowly passed by it completely drenched everything on it . . . The Captains party had all got to sleep again. It rolled them clear across the car and soaked them from head to foot."

The train pulled into Nashville at nightfall on November 7 and here the division came under the command of Major General James

Wilson, commanding the Cavalry Corps, Department of the Mississippi. General Wilson was the most respected of the so-called "boy generals" of the Union cavalry. An 1860 graduate of West Point, he had quickly impressed the top generals with his intelligence and ability; and after some service with General Grant, he was made head of the Cavalry Bureau in Washington early in 1864, cleaning up a mess by prosecuting fraudulent contractors, an unheard of practice until that time.

Wilson worked hard at impressing the high-ranking generals and those on the way up but was inflexible so far as nonmilitary, political people were concerned. When Andrew Johnson, then military governor of Tennessee, wanted some newly recruited, poorly trained regiments mustered into Federal cavalry service, Wilson refused, earning Johnson's enmity.[1]

Arriving in Middle Tennessee in November 1864, Wilson saw that his first task was to remount his troopers, and he scoured Tennessee and Kentucky for horses. His troopers had orders to take all animals fit for cavalry service, and they seized Johnson's fine team of bays. When Johnson, then vice-president elect, asked Wilson to return his horses, Wilson refused, further angering Johnson.[2]

A proven administrator, Wilson now wanted military glory and hoped to achieve it in some independent campaign with his cavalry. He immediately began to reequip, remount, and recruit to make his force the strongest in the entire army and tried to arm his whole corps with Spencer repeating carbines. He eventually built the largest cavalry force ever seen in North America, and he would need the best because he ultimately would be opposed by Nathan Bedford Forrest, who had not yet been defeated while serving as an independent cavalry commander.

The battery drew their horses on November 19 and also were paid for the first time in ten months. John Rippetoe received $201 of which he sent $190 to Mary by the allotment rolls. On the same day, Henry

1 Edward G. Longacre, *From Union Stars to Top Hat: a Biography of the Extraordinary General James Harrison Wilson* (Harrisburg: Stackpole Books, 1972), pp. 95–104.
2 *Ibid.*, pp. 179–81.

Campbell bid good-by to his battery mates, accepting an appointment as second lieutenant in the One hundred first U.S. Colored Infantry and remarked, "Was very sorry to leave the old companions in the battery and all seemed sorry to have me go but ever since Capt. Lilly went away it did not seem like the same command."

During November, the battery was·strengthened through recruiting in Indiana and with the consolidation of the sixty-five men remaining in the Eleventh Indiana Battery after that unit was mustered out at the completion of its three-year term.[3] Although the men detailed from the Eighth and Tenth batteries were returned to their commands, the Eighteenth Battery numbered 197 enlisted men at the end of the year. The officers were: Moses M. Beck, captain; William Benson Rippetoe and Martin J. Miller, first lieutenants; John D. Johnson and David W. Rippetoe, second lieutenants; William E. Starr, first sergeant; Samuel H. Scott, quartermaster sergeant; William O. Crouse, John H. Rippetoe, William L. McAninch, George S. McMullen, Marion Barr, and David H. Heizer, sergeants; and Augustus E. Newell, Albert Allen, John Johns, LaFayette Payne, Thomas G. Evinger, James Emory Rippetoe, Sidney Speed, Nathaniel McClure, Mark Schomber, Hosier Durbin, Robert Madden, and William Glenn, the last from the Eleventh Battery, corporals.[4]

A crisis now was developing in Middle Tennessee because the Confederate Army of Tennessee was advancing toward Nashville. Major General John M. Schofield with the Union IV and XXIII corps retreated slowly ahead of the Confederates through Columbia and Franklin, and on November 30 at the latter place, stopped behind strong fortifications upon which General Hood made a frontal assault, losing over 6,000 men from his army that numbered fewer than 40,000.

In early January when the battery passed through Franklin and over the battlefield, John Rippetoe wrote, " . . . in front of our breastworks there was a line of rebel graves as far as we could see on either

[3] Indiana State Library, Archives Division, "Muster and Descriptive Roll, Detachment of 11th Indiana Battery attached to 18th Indiana Battery, Nov. 13, 1864"; Department of the Cumberland, General Field Order 319, Nov. 21, 1864.
[4] Addison M. Dowling Collection, "Muster Roll, Captain Moses M. Beck 18th Ind. Batt. Horse Arty., Dec. 31, 1864."

side of the road. I have passed over several battlefields, but I never saw anything to equal this one."

Schofield then withdrew to join Thomas at Nashville, and Hood followed to within a few miles of that city and halted. He faced a quandary since he did not dare attack the city's fortifications or dare to march around the city and thus leave the much stronger Union army in his rear. Consequently, he sat in front of Nashville until General Thomas had his army completely ready to attack him.

Thomas's delay in attacking caused consternation in Washington, and even General Grant became worried. Perhaps they should have consulted the soldiers, who seemed to understand the situation. On December 4, John Rippetote wrote, " . . . there is some probability there will be one of the severest battles of the war fought here in a few hours but then we have no fears of the result, expecting if it is God's will to literally annihilate the rebel army . . . . I believe the rebels have got into a trap and will find it out when it is too late to get out. I think it was the intention of our commander to try to get them to do just what they have done . . . ."

One week later, John wrote, "the rebels seem to be afraid to make an assault on this place and well they may be for when they attack this place it will be the last fighting for many of them." He did not expect that the battery would be engaged in the actual battle but would be involved in the pursuit afterward.

General Thomas had everything ready to attack by December 9, but a sleet storm struck the area that day covering the ground with an inch of ice and causing cancellation of the plans. About the same time, word reached Nashville that Confederate Brigadier General Hylan B. Lyon with his cavalry brigade had crossed the Cumberland River below Nashville and was headed for Bowling Green and the Louisville and Nashville Railroad.

Lyon was commander of the Confederate Department of Western Kentucky, but since the Rebels did not occupy any territory in Kentucky at the time, his current assignment was the organization of a brigade of cavalry at Paris, Tennessee. Here he received orders from General Hood to take his force across the Tennessee and Cumberland

Map 7.
MARCHES OF LILLY'S BATTERY DURING
LYON'S AND WILSON'S CAMPAIGNS, NOVEMBER 1864–JUNE 1865

rivers; capture Clarksville, Tennessee; and then move into Kentucky to try to damage the Louisville and Nashville Railroad.

He started the campaign with 800 men, mostly recruits, and two 12-pounder brass howitzers. Lyon reported, "My command was poorly equipped, except in arms, 100 of my men were dismounted, but few had blankets or overcoats, and many were destitute of shoes or clothing sufficient to make a respectable appearance."[5]

Upon reaching the Cumberland River, Lyon's artillery forced a steamboat to surrender, and it was converted into a ferry on which his men crossed the river. Then, finding Clarksville too well defended, Lyon headed for Hopkinsville, Kentucky, but by this time many of his poorly dressed soldiers were frostbitten "and it was with the greatest difficulty that they could be made to move from the fires built along the road."[6]

At 6:00 P.M. on December 11, the Eighteenth Battery with the Third Brigade of McCook's division went "off on a Lyon hunt," as John Rippetoe described the campaign, instead of remaining at Nashville for the impending battle. Because of the ice, the soldiers had to walk and lead their horses most of the way to Gallatin, and John Rippetoe reported, "my mare fell flat before we got out of camp" and remarked that many of the other horses had hard falls.

In an all-night march, the battery covered only seven miles, stopping near "the venerable Bishop Soule's residence,"[7] and did not reach Gallatin until 9:00 P.M. on December 12. The next morning the march was resumed, accompanied by rain "making the roads more slippery"; but after a few miles the ice was melted, and the soldiers had to contend with their old enemy, mud, on their march to Franklin, Kentucky, which was reached at 2:00 A.M. on December 14.

The force marched slowly the next day to Russellville, where they left their wagons and baggage. After a four hour lay-over, they moved

5 *O.R.* Ser. 1, XLV, pt. 1, 803–806.
6 *Ibid.*
7 Joshua Soule, head of the Southern M. E. Church following the schism of the national church in 1845, had presided over the organizing conference of the Indiana Conference in 1832 and in 1840. Johnson and Malone, IX, 404–405. Donald J. Olson, Archives of DePauw University and Indiana Methodism, letter to author, Nov. 28, 1973.

on, reached Elkton at 4:00 P.M., where they learned that Lyon's raiders were at Hopkinsville; and so they continued marching, stopping about midnight at a place named Fairview,[8] about ten miles east of Hopkinsville. Lyon had left half his force at Hopkinsville and with the remainder had gone to Cadiz, Princeton, and Eddyville, chasing the Negro garrison troops from these towns toward Fort Donelson and burning the courthouses of the towns.

The Union force now had been reinforced by the Second Brigade that had been procuring horses in Louisville. At Fairview, McCook divided the force, sending Colonel Louis D. Watkins and the Third Brigade on by-roads to attack Hopkinsville from the north, while the battery and the Second Brigade advanced on the main road from the east. William Crouse wrote, "We reached the town at daylight, our advance made a dash into the outskirts, but were driven back by the rebel force supported by two pieces of artillery"; and William Winkler reported that the Confederates "had position on the hills about the large Collage building."

After the repulse of the initial attack, the battery was unlimbered and fired seventeen shells into the Confederate position, probably to keep the Rebels' attention focused on the force coming in from the east because after an hour of artillery firing, Watkins's brigade came in from the north, surprising the Johnnies. Winkler wrote, "the Reb. were drove in every direction, we captured 1 canon, 48 Prisoners, Killed 1 Col. & som 30 Reb. lost 3 men."

McCook was disappointed with the result since he had hoped to bag the entire Confederate force, but Colonel Watkins had failed to block one of the roads leading north, and most of the Johnnies escaped along this road or through the woods.[9] The arrival of the Yankee cavalry was timely because, as John Rippetoe wrote, "they [the Confederates] were making it pay by conscripting the men into their army and pressing all kinds of property for their own use and they had levied a tax on the citizens of Hopkinsville which is a nice county town and tolerably strong union. The rebels said if they did not pay $4000 in

[8] The birthplace of Jefferson Davis, a fact remarked by John Rippetoe.
[9] *O.R.* Ser. 1, XLV, pt. 1, 792.

Greenbacks that they would burn the town but we got there a little too soon."[10]

The entire Yankee force followed the fleeing enemy for twenty miles toward Princeton and encamped for the night; but on December 17, the battery and the Third Brigade returned to Hopkinsville, while the Second Brigade continued to chase the Rebels.[11] The artillery remained at Hopkinsville until December 23, when they marched to Trenton, twenty miles southeast, about which John Rippetoe observed, "this is a rebel town and a kind of headquarters for the guerrillas, most of the citizens being of that class and the meanest looking set of men I nearly ever saw. They look like a gang of robbers. There are only two union men in the town and they have to be very quiet." After a few days, the battery marched on, reaching Nashville again on December 29.

On December 15, while the battery was away, the Battle of Nashville had been fought. Henry Campbell, whose regiment was in reserve, received permission to ride out on the battlefield along the Granny White Pike. Just as he reached the lines "the charge was made on the key point of the rebel lines   this was a high conical pointed hill with a flat place about half way down each side of it."[12] After Union batteries shelled the earthworks on the hill, the order to charge was given, and the men attacked "in the midst of a terrible range of Bulletts & grape   down the hollow they were out of range but the ascent of the hill was steep & difficult. Here was the great trial, but our men new no faltering. On the brow of the hill, as our men came over

the rebels poured one terrible rain of death but with one wild long shout, our men sprang over the works and fought with their bayonets & butt end of their guns. All the enemy along this front were captured. They were too close to run."

After this success "our line toward the left began charging   one

---

10 *Ibid.*, 805. Lyon reported that he conscripted 400 men in the area before McCook arrived and also took money from the bank.

11 *Ibid.*, 792. The move to Hopkinsville was made to prevent Lyon from doubling back through that town and to the Cumberland River.

12 Connelly, *Autumn of Glory*, pp. 509–12. Campbell reported the action at Shy's Hill.

regt at a time   in one great tidal wave of victory   across the cornfields as far as I could see." Climbing the hill, Henry watched the retreating Confederates and the attacking Federals. At the Battle of
Nashville, General Thomas's army shattered the Confederate Army of
Tennessee so that it no longer was an important factor in the war.

Although McCook's Second Brigade pursued General Lyon's force
until they left Kentucky, the news of the Battle of Nashville did more
damage. Lyon reported, " . . . within two days after it was ascertained
that the Confederate army had left Tennessee 500 of my men deserted
and returned to their homes."[13]

During early December, Lieutenant David Rippetoe was on leave
in Indiana and signed up a number of new recruits for the battery.
He also attended to personal business and married Louisa Virginia
Malcom, John Rippetoe's sister-in-law, on December 14, causing John
to write, "Now I feel it is my duty to treat him as my brother."

On January 9, when Henry Campbell was writing a letter to James
Binford, "who should step in but Lt. Rippetoe of the Battery   was
taken completely by surprise . . . . I went back with Lt. R. to see the old
18th once more . . . . Battery was camped over in Edgefield." Henry
was homesick for the battery and had written on Christmas, "had a
better time even, way down in east Tenn. fighting Longstreet, last
year, without tents or overcoats."

On January 10, the First Cavalry Division marched south, but were
delayed at Columbia two days later. "After we had crossed the bridge
here over Duck river which is, or was very high, while the first Wisconsin regiment was crossing, the bridge gave way letting some of them
in the river," John Rippetoe wrote, "but there was not more than one
man lost, and I am not certain that there was any[14] . . . it left our wagon train on the other side and we will have to wait till it can cross
before we can start. The pontoons had to be brought from Nashville
and are not put down yet."

The soldiers had an unusual excitement while in Columbia, the

---

13 *O.R.* Ser. 1, XLV, pt. 1, 805.

14 William M. Winkler diary reported that 30 men were dropped into the
river but none were drowned.

shocks of an earthquake; ". . . the first and heaviest shook things considerably and it was funny to see the boys run out of their tents to see what was the matter, and could not see anything."

John also wrote that he would not be surprised if the war ended soon because "the rebels show more signs of giving up than at any time since the war commenced . . . . I believe that the Southern people are about ready to lay down arms and return to father Abraham's bosom." John also mentioned, "Benson was ordered to take command of another battery, but as we were scarce of officers the order was countermanded and he is still with us."

By January 29, the division was camped at Waterloo, Alabama, and were busy fixing winter quarters. In the cavalry camps there and at Gravelly Springs on the Tennessee River, where General Wilson was assembling the cavalry corps, many troopers complained of short rations. The horses seemed to have plenty of corn and the men began to believe that Wilson cared more for the horses than for the men. William Winkler appeared to recognize the real problem: "We are on not mohr than 1/4 Rations for the reason that the steamboats dont arrive mor regularily. But now the fleets are comencing to com in an Rations are getting plenty."

John Rippetoe was pleased with their camp "because we [have] better provisions for religious meetings than we ever had in any other camp." The men had constructed a chapel upon reaching the place, and John wrote, "our little chapel has payed well, we have meetings about three times a week. The other nights are taken by the boys either in their club meetings or spelling school."

Of course, the men did not know how long they would enjoy their camp and chapel before orders for the next campaign would arrive, and on March 3, John Rippetoe wrote, "The Chaplain of the first Wisconsin preached for us today . . . if we stay here two weeks he will preach for us again so you see we have a two weeks circuit, but we do not know when the conference year will be out."

William J. Rinewalt used part of his time in this camp to compose the following poetical summary of the battery's history:[15]

15 Lilly Archives, William J. Rinewalt, "Lilly's Light Battery."

LILLY'S LIGHT BATTERY
Air. (Root Hog or Die)

It was down at Murfreesboro,
In eighteen and sixty-three,
That old Rosey told Wilder
To take a little spree,
He went to Hoover's Gap,
I will tell you the reason why,
To make old General Bates sing,
    Root Hog or die.

The second time we met them,
Was on top of Stringer's ridge,
Lilly, with his battery,
Spoiled their pontoon bridge;
He sunk the steamer Dunbar,
And whipped Cameron hill so high,
And made the Jonnie's sing, boys,
    Root hog or die.

The third time we met them,
Was in Georgia, at Ringold,
The Georgia State militia,
Tried to look very bold;
But Wilder, could not see it,
And that was the reason why,
That he made the State militia sing
    Root hog or die.

The fourth time we met them
It was not quite so nice,
We had to gain the field,
With a little higher price,
But Wilder played his cards so fine,
It made them open their eyes,
And Pegram told his boys, it is
    Root hog or die.

The fifth time we met them,
Was at Chickamauga creek,
They thought they would take us in,
And do it up so quick,
But old Rosey fell back
And done it up so sly,
They had not time to make us sing,
    Root hog or die.

The sixth time we met them,
Was on the raid that Wheeler took,

At the foot of the mountain
He fell in with General Crook;
With Wilder in the front,
Old Wheeler he did cry,
Follow me my bully boys, or,
    Root hog or die.

The seventh time we met them,
Was at McMinville, Tennessee,
Old Wheeler stopped there
For to take a little tea,
But Wilder, Crook and Lilly,
They did not like the fry,
Therefore, they made him sing,
    Root hog or die.

The eighth time we met them,
It was at Farmington,
The boys worked hard,
Before they made them run;
But when they got them started,
Old Wheeler he did cry,
We are bound for Muscle Shoals, boys,
    Root hog or die.

It was on the sixteenth of November,
That we all remember well,
We had to leave our old Brigade,
Which we did not like so well,
We joined old Ed. McCook,
And you could tell by the wink of his eye,
He was the man to make the Jonnies sing,
    Root hog or die.

The ninth time we met them,
It was at New Market, Tennesseee,
The way old Ed. played his hand,
I would like for you too see,
He charged them on the flank,
And he made the Jonnies fly,
It was back to Mossey Creek, boys, or
    Root hog or die.

The tenth time we met them,
It was at Mossey Creek,
Old Longstreet came on us,
Just like a thousand bricks;
But old Ed. had the mortar,
And he built his name so high,

That he is still remembered with,
    Root hog or die.

Then we marched around too Dandridge.
To meet the eleventh time,
And that is the way we will bring,
Gen. Foster in our ryhme,
I do not like his style,
I will tell you the reason why,
He does not like the song called,
    Root hog or die.

The twelfth time we met them,
It was at Fair Garden,
And that is the place,
That they tried to ask pardon,
But old Ed. could not hear them,
And that was the reason why,
That he took their artillery with,
    Root hog or die.

The thirteenth time we met them,
Was down at Tater Hill,
When it come to fighting,
I guess they got their fill,
They could not whip Jim Brownlow,
I will tell you the reason why,
Jim is altogether on,
    Root hog or die.

Then we marched to Burnt Church,
To meet the fourteenth time,
Beck's little battery,
Made the Jonnies climb,
Ed's eagles left his shoulders
And flew up to the sky,
And left him with a star we call,
    Root hog or die,

The fifteenth time we met them,
Was in Georgia, at Cassville,
The Rebels opened on us
From the top of Miller's Hill,
But their howitzers could not reach us,
And that was the reason why,
We made the Cassville Jonnies sing,
    Root hog or die.

The sixteenth time we met them,
Was down at Fort McCook,

We had to fight hard,
Too hold the fort we took,
But Rippetoe done his best,
And that is the reason why
We did not have to sing, boys,
    Root hog or die.

The seventeenth time we met them,
Was down at Mason's Chapel,
They thought they would take us in,
Just like you would an apple,
They charged into our camp,
And Major Briggs[16] raisd the cry,
Fall in my bulley Second boys, or,
    Root hog or die.

The eighteenth time we met them,
Was on the Georgia Raid,
They sent old Ed. McCook,
Because they knew that he was not afraid,
He burned their wagon train,
And threw the railroad up so high,
That the Johnnies had to sing boys, it is,
    Root hog or die.

The nineteenth time we met them,
Was at Hopkinsville, Kentuck.,
Old Ed. followed Lyon,
It was just to try his pluck,
He met him at the town,
Before the sun was in the sky,
But his pluck could not stand the song
    called,
    Root hog or die.

Now I have sung about our battles,
And I hope we will have no more,
We have fought four years,
And I think it is time to end the war,
But if the Jonnies will not submit,
Old Abe will surely try,
To make the Rebels sing, Abe, it is,
    Root hog or die.

16 David A. Briggs, 2d Indiana Cavalry.

XIV

Wilson's Alabama Raid

...we received orders to move just after dark and that right away; this time the boys were having a very interesting spelling match when the orders came .... We went to the river and were ferried over by steam boats and transports.

Although the soldiers had expected to receive orders to start the next march at any moment, their actual arrival on March 10 surprised them, as related by John Rippetoe. The immediate movement was made to position Wilson's cavalry force on the south side of the Tennessee River preparatory to their next and what would be the final campaign of the war with the battery and First Division going into camp at Chickasaw Landing, near Eastport, Mississippi.

General Wilson had aggressively built, equipped, and trained the Cavalry Corps, Military Division of the Mississippi, so that it was the largest, best armed, and best organized mounted force ever assembled on the continent—nearly 25,000 men, of whom 13,000 were armed with Spencer repeating carbines. The full force was not yet mounted, but Wilson expected to receive enough horses in a few weeks to provide for his remaining dismounted troopers.[1]

For a while, Wilson hoped to be able to use this mighty force as an independent command for a campaign that would play a significant role in closing the war, demonstrate the effectiveness of cavalry when used properly and when operated independently, and establish Wilson's reputation as a great military leader. He was frustrated in this plan because, on February 3, he was ordered to send one of his six divisions south to join Major General E. R. S. Canby for that general's

[1] *O.R.* Ser. 1, XLIX, pt. 1, 355, 465.

campaign to capture Mobile, and to complete the mounting of this division, he had to take horses from a second. About the same time, he was ordered to send another division to Middle Tennessee to protect citizens from guerrillas.[2]

On February 23, orders from General Grant instructed General Thomas to send Wilson with about 5,000 men on a raid with the limited objective of diverting some Confederate forces from the Mobile area, but Wilson objected to such an insignificant operation and also to marching with such a small force into an area defended by Forrest. He suggested instead that he be allowed to take his full command, with which he said he could whip Forrest and capture Selma, Tuscaloosa, Montgomery, and Columbus (Georgia). He convinced General Thomas of the wisdom of such a campaign and General Grant approved the plan, giving Wilson "the amplest discretion as an independent commander."[3]

After assembling his command south of the Tennessee, Wilson learned that he would not receive the horses promised by the War Department, and as a result, he was unable to remount the division that had been stripped to supply the force sent to join Canby's expedition. So this division had to be left behind, and they turned over their Spencer carbines to other troopers who would make the march, including the Fourth Indiana. William Winkler wrote, "Went to Eastport, Miss. to exchange our Sharps Carbines for Spencers with the 5 Division, which was to stay there."

More recruits arrived for the battery, among them Jason Rippetoe. John wrote, "He looks tolerably slim. It may be for the good of his health to campaign this summer, but from his looks I should judge that it would have been [better] for him to have stayed at home and assisted in the recruiting business . . . . I have no idea that Jason will be put on duty in this battery as Benson does not consider him able for it, and at present he is assigned to my detachment, my orders are not to detail him for anything . . . ."

Jason had been a summer soldier during 1862, when he had joined

2 Canby commanded the Department of the Gulf. Brig. Gen. Joseph Knipe's 7th Division was sent to Canby, taking horses from Brig. Gen. Edward Hatch's 5th Division, and Brig. Gen. Richard W. Johnson's 6th Division returned to Tennessee.

3 *O.R.* Ser. 1, XLIX, pt. 1, 354–55; Longacre, pp. 195–97.

the Seventy-eighth Indiana, that was enlisted for a term of sixty days and was employed in hunting guerrillas in Kentucky. Jason was not judged strong enough to go looking for bushwhackers, being left to guard the camp and supplies when the other men went foraging or searching for the outlaws.[4]

For the campaign about to begin, the Eighteenth Battery, now called "Beck's Battery," remained a part of Brigadier General Edward M. McCook's First Division, which consisted of two large brigades, the regiments formerly assigned to the Third Brigade having been assigned to the First and Second. The First Brigade, commanded by Brigadier General John T. Croxton, included the Fourth Kentucky Mounted Infantry and the Eighth Iowa, Sixth Kentucky, and Second Michigan Cavalry regiments. The Second Brigade, commanded by Colonel Oscar LaGrange, who had been exchanged after the Atlanta campaign, consisted of the Fourth Indiana, Fourth Kentucky, Seventh Kentucky, and the First Wisconsin Cavalry regiments and a battalion of the Second Indiana Cavalry.

Brigadier General Eli Long's Second Division was made up of Wilder's brigade, commanded by Colonel Abram O. Miller, Colonel Robert H. G. Minty's brigade that had distinguished themselves at Reed's Bridge preceding the Battle of Chickamauga, and the Chicago Board of Trade Battery.

The Fourth Division, commanded by Brigadier General Emory Upton, which had been mounted and equipped in St. Louis, completed Wilson's force for the campaign. Their artillery was Battery I, Fourth United States.[5]

These divisions added up to 12,500 mounted men and approximately 1,500 dismounted men who would march as guards for the wagon train until enough horses could be captured to mount them.[6] Before the march began, Wilson directed his division commanders to see that every trooper carried five days' rations in their haversacks, twenty-four pounds of grain, one hundred rounds of ammunition, and

[4] Terrell, III, 21–22; VI, 268–76; Ernest R. Davidson Collection, Jason Lee Rippetoe to Mary J. Rippetoe, Aug. 15, 1862.

[5] *O.R.* Ser. 1, XLIX, pt. 1, 402–03.

[6] James Harrison Wilson, *Under the Old Flag*, 2 vols. (New York: D. Appleton, 1912), II, 190.

an extra pair of horseshoes. Pack animals were to be loaded with five days' rations of hard bread; ten of sugar, coffee, and salt; and the train of 250 wagons was to carry forty-five days supply of coffee, twenty of sugar, fifteen of salt, and eighty rounds of ammunition. In addition, a pontoon train of thirty light canvas boats and fixtures required fifty wagons.[7]

The first part of the march was through a barren, desolate area that had been devastated by two years of war, and during this part of the march, the men lived on their rations and the horses on the grain carried by the troopers. William Crouse reported, "much difficulty to find subsistence for our stock."

At this stage each division marched on a different road partly to enable them to forage over a larger area but also to conceal the objective of the march from the Rebels. Observers would believe that McCook was headed for Tuscaloosa; Upton, for Columbus; and Long, for Selma, which was the real target.[8]

The Union Corps was opposed by Nathan Bedford Forrest, commanding the Confederate cavalry in Alabama and Mississippi, who had recently been promoted to lieutenant general in recognition of his abilities and his contributions to the Confederate cause. Lieutenant General Richard Taylor, commanding the military district of Alabama, Mississippi, and eastern Louisiana, was Forrest's superior; but Taylor was principally concerned with the defense of Mobile and left Forrest to deal with Wilson.

Wilson estimated that Forrest had 12,500 men, widely scattered through Alabama and Mississippi, organized into divisions commanded by veteran cavalry officers William H. Jackson, James R. Chalmers, Phillip D. Roddey, and Abraham Buford.[9] Although they knew of the force that Wilson had assembled, Taylor and Forrest misjudged the strength and nature of the expedition equating it with the hit-and-run tactics of earlier cavalry raids. Learning of Wilson's march, Taylor ordered Jackson to take his division and "meet, whip, and get rid of that column," believing that Jackson should be able to complete

[7] *O.R.* Ser. 1, XLIX, pt. 1, 356.
[8] *Ibid.*
[9] James Harrison Wilson, II, 196.

this assignment in three or four days and then come to the aid of Mobile.[10]

McCook's division and Beck's battery followed the most westerly route, marching through Cherokee Station, Frankfort, and Russellville. From the last place, they marched on the direct road to Tuscaloosa until they reached Eldridge, where they turned east to rejoin the other divisions at Jasper, which they reached on March 27.[11]

At Jasper, General Wilson learned that Jackson's and Chalmers's Confederate divisions were marching toward Tuscaloosa from the west, and the campaign became a race. If the Yankees moved fast they could reach Selma before these divisions and limit Forrest to Roddey's and Buford's divisions and militia troops for the defense of the city. Consequently, after crossing the west fork of the Black Warrior River, Wilson left the wagon train and dismounted men, taking along only those wagons with artillery ammunition.[12]

The crossing of the two forks of the Black Warrior proved difficult, and William Crouse wrote that several men were drowned at the fords. General Wilson, however, reported a few horses were lost but no men.[13]

On March 29, the column marched forty miles and arrived in "a fine country   plenty of forage." That night they camped near Elyton (now Birmingham), where the Yankees, according to William Winkler, "found the first evacuated fortifications which Rowdy [Roddey] had built two weeks ago." Upton's division, in the lead, also encountered a few of Roddey's cavalrymen and chased the Johnnies across the Cahaba River.

The next morning, Wilson ordered McCook to send Croxton's First Brigade to Tuscaloosa with orders to burn the public stores, military school, bridges, foundries, and factories and then to return to the Selma road by way of Centreville to rejoin the column.[14]

While Croxton marched southwest, the main force moved south

---

10 Robert Selph Henry, *"First with the Most" Forrest* (Indianapolis: Bobbs-Merrill, 1944), p. 428.
11 *O.R.* Ser. 1, XLIX, pt. 1, 357.
12 *Ibid.*, 350, 357.
13 *Ibid.*, 357.
14 *Ibid.*

and destroyed four iron foundries, one rolling mill, five collieries, and much valuable public property. The advance reached Montevallo at 1:00 P.M. on March 31, where they encountered Roddey's division but drove this force out of town and toward Selma.

April 1 was a lucky day for General Wilson because Confederate couriers were captured who carried dispatches containing information on the position of all of Forrest's troops. From them, Wilson learned that Jackson's division had reached Scottsville on the Tuscaloosa to Centreville road, that Croxton had run into Jackson's rear guard the previous evening, and that Croxton was interposed between Jackson's force and the Confederate wagon train, which carried the principal supplies for all of Forrest's cavalry. Jackson, according to the dispatches, planned to turn back that morning and drive Croxton off.

Wilson also learned that Chalmers's Confederate division still was west of the Cahaba River, south of Jackson's position, and had been ordered to cross the river and get between Wilson's force and Selma. This made the bridge over the Cahaba at Centreville a key point because possession of the bridge by the Federals would prevent both Jackson and Chalmers from joining Forrest before the Yankee column reached Selma. Wilson ordered McCook to take LaGrange's brigade and the battery, seize the bridge, try to make a junction with Croxton, and then attempt to break up Jackson's division.[15]

Riding the fifteen miles to Centreville in two hours, a battalion of the First Wisconsin surprised the 150 Rebels guarding the bridge, captured some of the guards, and drove the others away before they had a chance to burn the bridge. The Wisconsin men held the bridge until the remainder of the Second Brigade came up, crossed, and moved five miles north, reaching Scottsville at 5 P.M.[16]

From prisoners, McCook learned that the First Brigade had had a skirmish with Jackson's division that morning and had retreated toward the north, removing the possibility of a junction with the Second Brigade. Information from the prisoners led McCook to believe

15 *Ibid.*, 350, 358, 416.
16 *Ibid.*, 416–17, 427–28.

that Jackson's force numbered 3,500 to 4,000 men, three times his own force.

The next morning, the Second and Fourth Indiana regiments made a demonstration that "caused the enemy to display his numbers, which could not have been less than 3,000, while the brigade, having nine companies detached, only numbered 1,200 men." In the skirmish resulting from the reconnaisance, the Yankees had one killed and eight wounded, including Captain Roswell Hill of the Second Indiana.[17]

William Crouse wrote that a Confederate force was observed on the left, attempting to move around the Union brigade to try to capture the Centreville bridge. Since McCook had already determined that a fight against superior numbers was not necessary to prevent Jackson from joining Forrest, he had his men destroy a factory, a cotton mill and a niterworks in Scottsville, the bridge over a creek, and then retreat to Centreville.[18]

After the main body had crossed the bridge, the rear guard began to destroy it, but the Rebels made a dash and drove the guards off. William Crouse wrote, "A terrible fight raged for the possession, and at last with the aid of our guns, the rebels were driven off and the bridge burned," but William Winkler described the fight as "a little brush with the Reb. across River." Then the bridge was burned; all boats up and down the river were destroyed, and as a result, Jackson's large Confederate division was delayed on the west side of the Cahaba River, unable to join Forrest for the defense of Selma, or to harass the flank or rear of the Union column while the Federal Second and Fourth Divisions marched to Selma. Wilson had beaten Forrest with the latter's famous strategy of "getting there first with the most."

The main column continued to drive the Confederate skirmishers south until they reached Forrest's main force of perhaps 5,000 men at Ebenezer Church, six miles north of Plantersville, a position partially covered by a slashing of pine trees and rail barricades. Here a battalion of the Seventeenth Indiana that had been armed with sabers made a charge that broke through the Confederate line, throwing the Rebels

17 *Ibid.* Driven north, Croxton lost communication with Wilson.
18 *Ibid.* James Henry Harris diary.

into confusion, and before they recovered, General Upton's division came up on their flank. After an hour's fight, the Confederates retreated and the Yankees camped at Plantersville.

Again Wilson had a stroke of good fortune because his men captured the English civil engineer who had supervised the construction of Selma's defenses, and having become disenchanted with the Confederate cause, he gave Wilson a sketch and description of Selma's defensive works.

Reaching Selma several days later, William Crouse described the fortifications: "The city was protected by two lines of entrenchments, the outer or main line consisting of a high parapet of earth faced by a deep ditch, and at the inner edge of this ditch was a row of pine stakes sharpened .... The inner works were built for artillery and did not differ from the generality of rebel works."

The Yankees reached Selma on April 2 and attacked at 4:00 P.M. with Wilder's brigade assaulting the works held by Forrest's best soldiers. At the same time, Upton's division, coming through swamps that were considered impassable, drove defending militia from another portion of the fortifications. The attacks successfully stormed the fortifications, routed the defenders, and drove into the city. The victory was complete, and Wilson reported the capture of 31 field guns, a 30-pounder Parrott gun, and 2,700 prisoners, including 150 officers; but Generals Forrest, Armstrong, Roddey, Daniel Adams, and Buford escaped under cover of darkness.[19]

About the assault by Wilder's brigade, General Wilson wrote, "I doubt if the history of this or any other war will show another instance in which a line of works as strongly constructed and as well defended as this by musketry and artillery has been stormed and carried by a single line of men without support."[20]

The men of McCook's division, of course, did not participate in the capture of Selma, and on April 3, they marched from the Centreville vicinity to the Selma road. William Winkler wrote, "crossed the Battleground [Ebenezer Church] where Wilson 2 days before had

---

19 *O.R.* Ser. 1, XLIX, pt. 1, 351, 357–61. Adams commanded the Alabama militia.
20 *Ibid.*, 316.

whipped so awful General Forrest." The next day the force marched to within twelve miles of Selma, but received orders to return north to escort the wagon train to Selma. They met the train at Randolf, east of Centreville.[21] This move was necessary because Forrest, with some of his men, had swung north after leaving Selma; and the next day, William Winkler reported, "Forrest is scouting about us but dare not attack our small brigade."

On April 6, Winkler wrote, "Passed the place where our Division scouts, Lt. Miller . . . got murdert 2 nights before." This was Lieutenant Martin J. Miller of the Eighteenth Battery, on detached duty serving as McCook's aide-de-camp and chief of the division scouts.[22] After the capture of Selma, Miller, with twenty-five men, was riding to reestablish contact with the Second Brigade; and that night, the small force encamped near Plantersville. Forrest with his escort of 100 men discovered the camp. William Crouse wrote that Miller had left only one picket on the road; and after the picket was captured, the camp was surrounded, and the Yankees shot after they had surrendered, with only two escaping. He reported that Lieutenant Miller lived for twelve hours after the fight.

Crouse's account generally agrees with the report of Surgeon Francis Salter, U. S. Army medical director, who wrote that Forrest "Charged on them in their sleep, and refusing to listen to their cries of surrender, killed or wounded the entire party . . . ."[23]

The Confederates did not agree with this account, reporting that there was a fight after the Yankees fired the first shot. Lieutenant George Cowan, commanding Forrest's escort, reported "not a single man was killed after he surrendered," and that several prisoners were taken.[24]

Forrest apparently was not seeking revenge for his recent defeat because, according to Crouse, he moved on to Ebenezer Church after the action against the scouts, captured the wounded Union soldiers that had been left there, and "These were paroled and treated kindly."

21 Samuel A. Hall diary.
22 Addison M. Dowling Collection, "Muster Roll . . . Dec. 31, 1864." Miller had served as McCook's aide-de-camp from Sept. 17, 1864.
23 *O.R.* Ser. 1, XLIX, pt. 1, 406.
24 Henry, p. 432.

After this, Forrest joined Jackson's and a part of Chalmer's division but refrained from attacking Wilson during the remainder of the campaign.[25]

At 3:00 P.M. on April 6, the battery and the Second Brigade, with the wagon train, reached Selma, which William Winkler described as "the greatest military Depot of Western Confederacy." The destruction of this arsenal had already begun, and Winkler wrote, "Large conflagrations everywhere, Shells exploden and gunpowder blowing up. The beautiful city is in ruins. A fortifyed city Sherman dare[d] not attake 1 year ago is captured and sacked by Cavalry without using one spade or trowing up a single breastwork by only one grand rush on theyr works."[26]

Among the spoils was the printing plant of the Chattanooga *Rebel*, which had been moved from its home town when Lilly's battery began to shell that place in August 1863. For a time, the paper was published in Marietta and then in Griffin, Georgia, and after Atlanta was captured, the plant was shipped to Selma. During the occupation, the equipment was used to print a new paper *The Yankee Cavalier*, but when Wilson's men moved on, they broke up the press, melted the type, and burned the files of the *Rebel*.[27]

In Selma, William Crouse observed, "The Rebel prisoners were confined in the stockade where our captured were confined heretofore. The chivalric gentlemen of the south   captured officers   were highly indignant at this outrage, but cooled considerably when General Wilson ordered all such to be ironed."

On April 8, after all property of military value in Selma had been destroyed, the pontoon bridge, 870 feet long, was constructed across the Alabama River, and the Second and Fourth divisions crossed "but it is tedious work for 3 times the pontoon bridge broke." At 10:00 P.M. on April 9, McCook's division crossed, and William Crouse wrote, "It was raining and intensely dark. We set fire to the business buildings

---

25 *Ibid.*, p. 433.

26 Winkler had reference to Sherman's Feb. 1864 campaign from Vicksburg to Meridian, Miss., where he turned back instead of marching to Selma because the cavalry corps that was to join him at Meridian had been defeated and driven back to Memphis by Forrest. (Guernsey and Alden, II, 569–76.)

27 Livingood, "Chattanooga *Rebel*" pp. 51–54.

on the wharf to light up the river and to guard against driftwood." After the crossing, the bridge was taken up, and the pontoons and all spare wagons were burned.

Wilson had ordered the bridge and wagons destroyed to enable his command to move "as rapidly as possible to the theater of operations in North Carolina and Virginia." Enough horses had been captured in Selma to mount all dismounted men, and Wilson also "directed the column to be cleared of all contraband negroes, and such of the able-bodied ones as were able to enlist to be organized into regiments, one to each division. Efficient officers were assigned to these commands, and great pains were taken to prevent their becoming burdensome. How well they succeeded can be understood from the fact that, in addition to subsisting themselves upon the country, they marched (upon one occasion) forty-five miles and frequently as much as thirty-five in one day."[28]

An April 10, William Winkler reported, "Take up our March against Montgomery Our Brigade in advance. Near Benton found the Reb. Advance, which we after several charges dislodged . . . We follow the retreating Enemy across the big Swamp." The battery camped at the border of the swamp, thirty miles from Selma, and the next morning followed the cavalry through the swamp, a difficult march during which six horses were lost.

On April 11, the brigade pushed rapidly ahead until they met a Rebel force at Hayneville that they drove to Potomac Creek, six miles from Montgomery. Here they found a strong Confederate force of cavalry and militia on the opposite bank with whom "we had a severe skirmish"[29] until dark. The Johnnies had cut down the bridge and barricaded the road, and so McCook did not try to cross the stream, desiring artillery support, and delaying action until the battery could catch up, which they did at 3:00 A.M. on April 12.

The guns were not needed. William Winkler reported, "In the morning when our advance come up on the creek bank the Reb. were gon and soon our Brig were in hot pursuit towards Montgomery. Arrived within 5 miles of the city. the city authority came with a white

28 *O.R.* Ser. 1, XLIX, pt. 1, 362.
29 Samuel A. Hall diary.

flage surrendering Montgomery to Brig. Genl. E. McCook. for Reb. Genl. Adams did not as he promist defend the city to his last ditsh and with the last drop of his blood; but had scedadled the night before; leaving their proud capitol to our mercy.   Our 2d Brig. 1st Cav. Division had the honor of raising the Stars & Stripes on Montgomery Capitol."

The citizens, having heard of the destruction in Selma, were relieved when they found that "General McCook permitted no straggling nor pillaging." They had already suffered enough because, according to William Crouse, "The rebel General Burford [Buford] had been in command of the city, and during the night of the 12 [11th] had given it up to pillage. The rebel troops had broken open the stores and carried away everything of value . . . ." The destruction included the burning of 90,000 bales of cotton.[30]

The Seventh Kentucky had continued through the city, marched east on the Columbus road, and when two miles from town, they met seven hundred Confederate cavalry commanded by General Buford. The Seventh drove this force eight miles, capturing three stands of colors and thirty prisoners. On April 14, the brigade had a running fight for thirty-eight miles with a brigade of Confederate cavalry during which twelve Rebels were killed and one hundred prisoners taken, with a loss of one killed and eleven wounded.[31]

On April 14, William Winkler reported, "Marched through Tuskegee a small, but very beautiful town in a fine country. this aristocratic town surrendert without fight." On April 15, he continued, "After building a bridge over Potomack [Ufoikee] Creek which the Reb. had burned the day before we head the advance to within 12 miles of Columbus, when all at once our Brig. turned north & hurried on to Auburn where we found a large Confedr. Hospital & capt. som dozen officers."[32]

Wilson had ordered the Second Brigade to capture West Point, and when he heard General Wilson issue the orders, Major Roswell Hill of the Second Indiana left the ambulance in which he was riding,

30 *O.R.* Ser. 1, XLIX, pt. 1, 363.

31 *Ibid.*, 428

32 *Ibid.*, 428. Wilson ordered LaGrange's brigade to march to West Point while Upton's and Long's divisions continued on to Columbus, Ga.

mounted a horse, rejoined, and resumed command of his battalion, although he still was suffering from the wound received at Centreville.[33]

At 2:00 A.M. on April 16 the troopers broke camp at Auburn and resumed the march, with the Second and Fourth Indiana and one gun of the Eighteenth Battery forming a flying advance column. After passing through Opelika, this force approached West Point at 10:00 A.M., and William Winkler reported, "Soon we seen the Reb. flag proudly flying over the fort and a 32 shell exploded close to us."

This was Fort Tyler, which Colonel LaGrange described as "a remarkably strong earthwork, thirty-five yards square, surrounded by a ditch twelve feet wide and ten deep, situated on a commanding eminence and protected by an imperfect abatis." The fort was defended by "265 desperate men," two field guns, and a 32-pounder siege gun. The Second and Fourth Indiana were placed in sheltered positions while the battery "amused the fort by a steady, well-directed fire until 1:30 P.M. when the remainder of the brigade arrived."[34]

Detachments of the First Wisconsin, Second Indiana, and Seventh Kentucky were dismounted and advanced on the fort from three sides; and while the guns in the fort were busy with these troopers, the Fourth Indiana dashed into the town, captured the railroad and highway bridges across the Chattahoochee River, and scattered a large force of Rebel cavalry that was coming to reinforce the garrison in the fort. The shots from the 32-pounder in the fort, which had been emplaced to protect the bridges, fell short, possibly because the gunners were nervous and demoralized since fourteen shots from the Eighteenth's Rodman guns hit the 32-pounder during the artillery duel.[35]

While these actions were taking place, the men of the First Wisconsin, Second Indiana, and Seventh Kentucky built portable bridges with lumber from nearby houses, and when the bugler sounded the charge, the three regiments rushed forward, "under a scathing fire," threw their makeshift bridges across the ditch, and raced to see who would be first into the fort. The race was won by Sergeant Edward Farel of the Wisconsin regiment.[36]

33 James Harrison Wilson, II, 273.
34 *O.R.* Ser. 1, XLIX, pt. 1, 428–29.
35 *Ibid.*
36 *Ibid.*

William Winkler wrote, "The fort was after the capture a awful look 31 dead or dying stretched on the parapets." LaGrange reported 18 Confederates killed, 28 seriously wounded, mostly shot through the head, and 218 captured. The Federal losses were 7 killed and 29 wounded.[37]

Among the Yankee wounded was Major Roswell Hill, hit in the leg within one inch of the wound received at Centreville. This ball shattered the bone, making amputation necessary. After the operation, he was left at West Point, and while there, lost about one-fourth of his weight; but in twenty days he reported for duty, requesting that he be permitted to resume command of his battalion.[38]

The Yankees blew up the fort and destroyed captured property, including 19 locomotives, 340 railroad cars, quartermasters stores, public buildings, and machinery from factories. Captured sugar, corn, bacon, and other food were left in charge of the mayor to provide a hospital fund to care for the wounded of both sides with instructions to distribute any surplus among the poor. On April 17, after destroying the bridges, the command left for Macon, Georgia, marching by way of Griffin and Forsyth.[39]

Also on April 16, Wilson's main column captured Columbus and also started for Macon. The roads converged, and on the night of April 19, LaGrange's camp was eight miles north of the Second Division and the men could see the campfires in the distance.

At daylight on April 21, the Fourth Indiana took the lead and advanced cautiously. William Winkler wrote, "We marched within 2 miles of town inside the outer works and no rebels in site. Still on, on we cautiously pressed. When in site of the inner defenses we found all the works manned with Jonny's but their arms stackt in their rear. Genl. Cob [Howell Cobb][40] had his whole force uncondishanelly surrendert."

[37] *Ibid.*

[38] James Harrison Wilson, II, 272–73. Henry Campbell met Hill in Nashville on July 29, 1865, when Hill was on his way home after mustering out. Campbell commented that Hill had been promoted to lieutenant colonel of the 2d Indiana, and that he "looks fine."

[39] *O.R.* Ser. 1, XLIX, pt. 1, 429.

[40] Maj. Gen. Howell Cobb, commanding the Confederate Military District of Georgia was a former U. S. secretary of the treasury.

When thirteen miles from the city on the preceding day, the Seventeenth Indiana had met a Rebel party with a flag of truce that advised that Generals Johnston and Sherman had agreed to an armistice in North Carolina. Colonel Minty ordered the Seventeenth to continue the advance while the message was sent back to Wilson, and this regiment soon entered Macon.

William Crouse reported that rumors of peace were heard by the soldiers, but they did not give the reports credence, and William Winkler wrote, "Great talk about peace and an armistice is talked of," and that "The Yankees & Jonnys mingel freely & hardly any distinction is made . . . . The Reb are getting accustomed to our blue present and treat us as theyr friends not looking on theyr guards with mistrusty eyes."

On April 29, General Croxton and the First Brigade rode into Macon. From the time he had left the command at Elyton, all communication with the main column had been cut off. He had been able to burn Tuscaloosa, but meeting strong enemy forces, was forced to move in a northeasterly direction and was chased through Jasper, Talladega, and Newnan.

The soldiers in Macon had no contact with the outside world, and as late as April 30, William Winkler reported, ". . . we can heare the most estravagent rumors about the procidings of our Government. The President is reported to be killed, Lee captured & Johnston rady to surrender. We are cut-of[f] from any communication with the North. Thousands of paroled Reb. Prisoners arrived here from the East on their way home."

Mail neither was received nor sent until May 15, and then John Rippetoe received three letters from Mary. He had put off writing until he could be certain that mail would go out, but on May 16 he wrote, "The death of our good President caused universal regret and sorrow throughout this army, and even the rebels seem to think they have lost their best friend and detest the cowardly manner of his death." At this time, William Winkler reported, "Get plenty of grub, but scarce in clothing," while John Rippetoe wrote that his health was tolerably good "though cornbread and fat meat does not agree with me very well."

The great excitement of early May was the arrival of the fugitive Jefferson Davis in Georgia. A battalion of the First Wisconsin, commanded by Lieutenant Colonel Henry Harnden, and one of the Fourth Michigan, commanded by Lieutenant Colonel Benjamin D. Pritchard, were sent to look for him on May 7. On May 9, the Wisconsin troopers picked up the trail and followed it toward Irwinville, nearly 100 miles south of Macon, where Davis and party camped that night. The Michigan battalion also learned of the location of Davis's camp, reached Irwinville early on the morning of the tenth, and captured the Confederate president.

Soon afterward, the Wisconsin men came charging into the camp, and mistaking the Michigan soldiers for a Rebel guard, began to fire at them. The Michigan troopers shot back, and in this last skirmish of the war, two men were killed and four wounded before both groups realized their mistake.[41]

News of the capture reached Macon on May 14, and William Winkler wrote, "We got news from the two squads wish went out to see about the renown President of the played out Southern Confederacy. It is reported that Lt. Col. Pitchart with the 4th Mishigan captured the archtraitor." The next day he continued, "About 4 A.M. Jeff Davis was brought to town."

General McCook was appointed military governor of Florida in early May and was ordered to march with 500 men from Macon to Tallahassee. There was speculation in camp about which men the general would pick for his escort, and William Winkler hoped it would be the Fourth Indiana but was disappointed because McCook took the battalion of the Second Indiana and a battalion of the Seventh Kentucky.

The soldiers now began to concern themselves with plans for their future. John Rippetoe apparently gave some thought to the ministry but rejected it: "I do not like the idea of travelling a circuit, I like farming the best." About David Rippetoe he wrote, "I am pretty certain that he will never be a farmer, and I expect that he will have good reason for not being one, as his leg, that was broken several years ago

41 *O.R.* Ser. 1, XLIX, pt. 1, 376–79; Guernsey and Alden, II, 778.

hurts him sometimes very much." A few weeks later, John continued the subject, ". . . I believe that he intends to be a merchant, lame leg or no lame leg." James Emory Rippetoe had made his decision earlier to "enter upon the pleasant duties of the house of God."[42]

On May 24, the battery left Macon for home, marching through Forsyth, Griffin, and McDonough and reaching Atlanta on May 27. John Rippetoe observed that the country south of Atlanta had not suffered very much from the war, but "Atlanta is but little more than the heaps of crumbled walls with some few of them standing, smoked by the fires which destroyed the city."

As they continued the march toward Chattanooga, John observed that Marietta and Cartersville were in about the same condition as Atlanta, and that "Cassville is now called Chimneyville, hardly anything left standing but the chimneys. This last place was burnt on account of its being a kind of headquarters for Guerrillas last summer."[43] He also reported that the railroad from the Chattahoochee River to Cartersville, a distance of forty miles, was entirely destroyed, "the ties being burnt, and the rails bent and twisted so as to be worthless. It will be sometime before this country will attain its former prosperity, but it will not be long till they will be able to live again." Beyond Cassville, he observed that "there is not much destroyed only the fencing."

The battery reached Chattanooga on June 3, and John Rippetoe wrote, "we may seem to come very slowly, but we will be sure." He believed that they would be sent home, or at least to Indianapolis, as soon as they turned in their quartermasters and ordnance stores but this did not take place in Chattanooga. On June 7, they loaded guns, equipment, and horses onto railroad cars and rode to Nashville, arriving there June 9.

Here they turned in their equipment and horses and left Nashville June 23, arrived at Indianapolis two days later, and were payed-off and discharged on June 30. According to William Crouse, the battery

---

[42] Ernest R. Davidson Collection, James Emory Rippetoe to Mary J. Rippetoe, Aug. 14, 1863.

[43] Cassville was burned by the 5th Ohio Cavalry Nov. 5, 1864. (Historical marker at site.)

had marched 6,070 miles and had traveled an additional 900 miles by rail[44] during their three-year term of service. Only 77 of the 156 men who had originally enlisted in Lilly's battery were present for muster out, attesting to the severity and hardship of the battery's service.

44 Terrell, III, 431–32, reported that the battery marched over 5,000 miles and traveled over 1,000 miles by rail.

The Veterans

*Indianapolis in Gala Dress . . . . The
business streets from end to end are
resplendent in red, white, and
blue . . . . Monument Place looks
like a section of old Athens clothed
with the gay colors of the Persians.*[1]

By Friday, September 1, 1893, Indianapolis was prepared to receive
and entertain the tens of thousands of Union army veterans who would
begin to arrive during the week end to attend the twenty-seventh
National Encampment of the Grand Army of the Republic on September 4, 5, and 6. All business buildings and most houses had some
patriotic decoration, the most common being a fan formed of red,
white, and blue bunting but Eureka shields surmounted by groups of
small flags, sometimes held by a golden eagle, also were used frequently.
Streamers and draperies were everywhere, with the red, white, and
blue motif relieved somewhat by decorations of yellow bunting
brought down from the Columbian Exposition in Chicago. Store
buildings and many houses had been decorated by professional deco-
rators, a new line of business resulting from the annual reunions of
the G. A. R.

The Soldiers' and Sailors' Monument was one of the principal attractions; and pillars made of canvas to look like marble, one for each
corps of the Union army, were placed around Monument Circle. But
the main attraction was the more than 5,000 electric lights that were
arranged to provide a lighting display on the monument that some
people said was more spectacular than any single display at the Colum-

[1] All description of the G. A. R. encampment and events are from the Indianapolis *Journal*, Sept. 1–10, 1893.

bian Exposition. Many citizens had their own ideas for decorations. The owner of the gas company, for one, had carefully started flowers of different colors so they would be in full bloom and planted twenty-two beds with various G. A. R. and patriotic designs.

The bare walls of the Capitol were a relief from the highly decorated buildings since there was no place to fasten bunting on the structure but a full size replica of the U.S.S. *Kearsage*, the famous ship that had sunk the Confederate raider, the *Alabama*, was displayed on the Capitol grounds. The entrances to the Capitol were guarded by cannon and Gatling guns, which gave amusement to the small boys of the city who played around them all day, and at night, a natural gas display on the Capitol grounds made "the whole place for a block around lighter than in the glare of the sun."

Some other noteworthy displays were Charles Mayer's store with a flag 29 feet high and 31 feet wide, the largest in the State; the When Clothing Store which had its own electric plant with cut-offs arranged to show different lighting designs; and English's Hotel on the Circle that featured Union army corps badges.

Organization of a city for an event as large as a Grand Army encampment required an aggressive and respected man to obtain the cooperation of business, government, and the citizens. For the Indianapolis encampment, this leader was Colonel Eli Lilly, president of the Citizens Executive Board of the Commercial Club, about whom a contemporary wrote, "Col. Lilly during his active career in Indianapolis did not have a superior among his contemporaries either in the practical achievements of business or in the civic pride and energy that made Indianapolis a great city. . . ."[2]

Immediately after the war, Lilly had entered a partnership in a cotton plantation near Port Gibson, Mississippi, that became a disaster: Mrs. Lilly died of the complications of a pregnancy, two years of drought used up the capital of the venture, and the partner skipped, leaving Lilly with the debts. As a result, Lilly filed a petition in bankruptcy that was granted on September 20, 1869.[3]

2 Dunn, II, 689–93.
3 Logan Esarey, *History of Indiana from Its Exploration to 1922*, 4 vols. (Dayton: Dayton Historical Publishing Co., 1924), IV, 743–45; Lilly Archives, court order, District Court of the United States, District of Indiana, Sept. 20, 1869.

One month before the court declared him bankrupt, Colonel Lilly formed a partnership with James W. Binford, ex-sergeant and company clerk of the Eighteenth Battery, to enter the drug store business in Paris, Illinois, with Binford furnishing the money and Lilly the knowledge. In addition to drugs, the firm sold "chemicals, paints, oils, varnishes, dye-stuffs, window glass, &c."[4] This firm was dissolved four years later when Dr. James F. Johnson offered Lilly a partnership in a company to manufacture pharmaceuticals and chemical preparations in Indianapolis, an enterprise for which Johnson put up $10,000 and and Lilly $2,000. This partnership was dissolved March 27, 1876, with Lilly receiving $1,000 in cash and $400 in marketable stock.[5]

With this capital, Eli Lilly started his own pharmaceutical company in a rented building that "was not big enough to swing a cat in" and with a staff consisting of his son, fourteen year old Josiah K., and two employees. Ten years later the company was called "A Great Laboratory" having produced 23 million pills the previous year. By this time, the Colonel had delegated the operation of the company to Josiah, assisted by James E. Lilly, Eli's brother, and Evan F. Lilly, a cousin.[6]

Colonel Lilly's civic activities began during the early years of the company. In 1879, he was one of the sponsors of the Charity Organization Society that was formed to coordinate the charity agencies of the city to more effectively implement social reform and help the needy—a forerunner of the United Fund and Community Chest concept now common in most American communities. In 1884, Lilly was named chairman of the Relief Committee of the Indianapolis Board of Trade, and that same year he organized an exceptional effort for the relief of victims of a disastrous Ohio River flood in Ohio, Indiana, and Illinois. In 1889, the first money and clothing to reach the victims of the Johnstown flood came from the Indianapolis Relief Committee, and the next year, Lilly had a relief train in Louisville the day following a devastating tornado in that city.

4 Lilly Archives, James W. Binford to "Ma," Aug. 16, 1872.
5 Lilly Archives, James F. Johnson and Eli Lilly, partnership agreement, July 3, 1873, and dissolution of partnership, Mar. 27, 1876.
6 Esarey, IV, 743–45; Indianapolis *Journal*, June 7–10, 1898.

Seeing a need for an improved water system for Indianapolis, Lilly was instrumental in the formation of the Indianapolis Water Company in 1881. Six years later he organized the Consumers Gas Trust Company, raising $500,000 in stock subscriptions from small investors, believing that ownership of public service companies should be broadly held. He then supervised the work in the gas fields near Noblesville and the installation of a pipe line to Indianapolis, a project completed nine months after the formation of the company.

With the organization of the Commercial Club in 1890, Lilly was able to give full expression to his vision for an improved city. Elected president at its organization, he insisted that he also be chairman of the Finance Committee so he would have complete control of the Club's projects. Some noteworthy achievements while he held these offices were the initiation of a street-paving program, obtaining a new city charter from the state legislature, construction of a new county jail, and blocking the construction of railroad grade crossings in favor of elevated track. During the depression of 1893, the Commercial Club organized a relief program whereby the unemployed worked on city projects and were paid with food and clothing. Over 28,000 rations were dispensed weekly and between 4,000 and 5,000 individuals were aided. One prominent political scientist said that the relief program developed by Colonel Lilly and his committee was the best welfare assistance plan devised in the United States.[7] Lilly resigned as president of the Commercial Club in 1895 but remained active in its affairs and was engaged in several of its projects until the onset of his fatal illness eleven months before his death on June 6, 1898.

During this same period, Eli Lilly continued his military interests, serving for a time as colonel of the First Regiment Light Artillery of the Indiana Legion and for one year, as colonel and chief-of-artillery of the State of Indiana.[8] He also was a member of the George H. Thomas Post of the G.A.R. and a companion of the Military Order of the Loyal Legion,[9] the veteran officers' organization, and a member of

[7] Lilly Archives, Gene E. McCormick to J. S. Thomas, Sept. 28, 1966.
[8] Lilly Archives, Albert G. Porter, Governor, discharge Oct. 10, 1884 and commission Oct. 13, 1884.
[9] Lilly Archives, Winfield Scott Hancock, membership certificate issued to Eli Lilly, Aug. 4, 1883.

the Council of the group's Indiana Commandery. Colonel Lilly's continued interest in veterans' affairs, combined with his position as president of the Commercial Club, led to the invitation to hold the 1893 National Encampment of the Grand Army in Indianapolis and its acceptance.

On December 12, 1892, Lilly told the citizens of the city about the plans and the work necessary to prepare for the encampment. An organization equal to an army brigade, thirty committees with nearly 3,000 members, would be required to prepare for the reception of between 50,000 and 80,000 veterans, with a daily arrival and departure of from 40,000 to 50,000 people. In addition to temporary buildings to house no fewer than 50,000 men, "every private and public roof in Indianapolis will have a duty to perform."

The plans called for electric lights on the principal streets with the greatest concentration at the Circle and displays of natural gas on all public squares. The traction company would install electric lines and "every mule car should disappear from Indianapolis before the encampment." As to the money required, Lilly told the citizens that the Washington encampment in 1892 had cost that city $150,000.[10]

Camp Wallace, on East Washington Street, consisted of temporary barracks to house 16,000 men, and smaller camps were built in other locations and cots installed in all schoolhouses. The committee signed a contract that would provide 48,000 meals a day to the veterans at Camp Wallace at prices of twenty-five cents for breakfast and supper and thirty-five cents for dinner and made arrangements to serve meals at the same prices at other camps, schools, and sleeping quarters. During the encampment the Citizens Committee assigned over 100,000 lodgings, and the Standard Oil Company furnished oil free of charge for lighting barracks and schools.

Railroads counted 217,000 passengers coming into Indianapolis during the encampment. In addition to the veterans and their families, the arrivals included "a small army of Chicago fakirs and card sharks," pickpockets, peddlers of jewelry and souvenirs, and other types who profited from the encampments.

W. P. Bane, a veteran from Washington, Pennsylvania, attracted

10 Lilly Archives, Eli Lilly, address to citizens of Indianapolis, Dec. 12, 1892.

the attention of veterans and citizens alike because he was seven feet tall, stood head and shoulders above everyone else, and seemed to enjoy the crowds of little people that gathered wherever he went. Major William McKinley, governor of Ohio, also attracted attention.[11] He said he did not want to talk politics because this was a patriotic occasion, but when called upon by the veterans, gave what some listeners described as the best speech of his life. Of course, former president Benjamin Harrison,[12] an Indianapolis resident, was a popular attraction for the veterans and addressed them on September 4. After Harrison finished his address, "There was a general call for Colonel Lilly, chairman of the Citizens Committee and he responded in his hearty way, bringing applause at every period almost."

Each day had a major spectacle—on Monday there was a Labor Day parade by the local labor organizations; on Tuesday, an estimated 22,000 veterans paraded; and on Wednesday, a pageantry parade was held with floats depicting the *Merrimac*, the burning of Fort McHenry, the Civil War, and other historic events.

Brigade and regimental reunions were regularly scheduled events during the days and especially during the evenings. Colonel Lilly held a reception and campfire for the Eighteenth Battery and Ninth Cavalry in a large tent in the yard of his home; and Lilly, General Wilder, and Major Moses Beck[13] were featured speakers, while a letter from Lieutenant William Benson Rippetoe, regretting his inability to attend, was read. The next day, the business meeting of the Eighteenth Battery Association was held with William J. Wolfe presiding. During his talk at the Wilder Brigade reunion, General Wilder told the veterans that the brigade's monument at Chickamauga Battlefield should be completed by the next Decoration day and advised that $3,500 had been expended on the structure, of which $1,200 was "from the boys."

The Wilder monument became a sore point with William O. Crouse. As secretary of the Eighteenth Battery Association, he had written 500 letters and had raised $125, which was matched by a donation from Colonel Lilly, for the monument, but when the booklet on

11 Elected president of the United States in 1896.

12 President of the United States, 1889–1893.

13 Beck was referred to as "Major" after the war, but I did not find confirmation of promotion.

the monument dedication was published, Captain Lawson Kilborn was credited with the collection from the battery veterans. In addition, Crouse was not listed as a visitor at the dedication, although he had been present. Consequently, he refused to deliver the books to the Battery Association members and claimed that this was another example of officers taking the credit for enlisted men's work.

For some years after the war Crouse and a brother operated a bookstore in Lafayette, but in 1893, he began selling farm and livestock insurance. In 1920, at eighty years of age, he wrote that he had to drive "50 to 100 miles, climb 20 to 30 wire fences, chase a lot of farmers over ploughed ground ... so I seem to be good for some time yet." William was pretty much alone in the world then since his wife and only daughter had died during the influenza epidemic of 1918; and a few years later, nearly blind and deaf, he entered the Soldiers' Home at Danville, Illinois. Eli Lilly, the Colonel's grandson, visited him at the home and received a warm thank you from Crouse's niece for giving the "poor old man" one pleasant day. Crouse died at the home July 6, 1926.[14]

The dedication of Chickamauga and Chattanooga National Military Park, the first and largest national military park, on September 18-20, 1895, was a high point for the veterans of the Union Army of the Cumberland and the Confederate Army of Tennessee. An estimated forty to fifty thousand visitors attended the ceremonies, and as in Indianapolis, special arrangements were necessary to house the veterans and their families. In addition to large camps on Chickamauga Battlefield and in the environs of Chattanooga, quarters were provided in private houses and in Pullman cars. Unlike Indianapolis, where the attractions and sleeping quarters were within walking distance, transportation was necessary for the park dedication; and carriages and other conveyances were shipped in from all the surrounding area and from as far away as Nashville, Knoxville, and Birmingham.[15]

14 Lilly Archives, William O. Crouse correspondence; Lafayette *Journal and Courier*, July 8, 1926.
15 H. V. Boynton, *Dedication of Chickamauga and Chattanooga Military Park, September 18-20, 1895* (Washington, D.C.: Government Printing Office, 1896), pp. 11-17, 281-82; James W. Livingood, "Chickamauga and Chattanooga National Military Park," *Landmarks of Tennessee History* (1965), p. 105.

On September 18, the various state monuments were dedicated, and in the evening, the Society of the Army of the Cumberland met with over 10,000 veterans in attendance. On September 19, the Chickamauga part of the park was dedicated, and the next day ceremonies were conducted on the Chattanooga portion.

The monument to the Eighteenth Battery had not been erected in time for the park dedication but was in place about a year later. Appropriately, Sidney Speed, then in the monument business in Crawfordsville and the battery's hero of the battle, was the person chosen to erect the monument. He had some problems with the officials because he was told to change his design to suit a large tablet and then was given a small one that would not fit. Also, the tablet was made of copper and covered with green corrosion and he asked for Lilly's help to get a new tablet from the Indiana commissioners made of bronze. Speed also thought that the positions of guns and markers should be corrected, telling Lilly, " . . . what we want is that the two rodman guns, now marking a position for the 18th Battery on the Poe field, [be replaced] with howitzers and take the two rodman guns out and mark our position at Alexanders house." He also remarked that the guns meant to mark the position of the section that enfiladed the ravine at the Viniard field were not in the right place, and that a sign at the Alexander house pointed toward Jay's Mill and read, "to beginning of the battle at Jay's Mill 2 miles. . . . *Someone ought to make them take it down*. My recollection is that our battery fired the first shot that was fired by union troops and fired it in answer to a rebel battery in our immediate front."[16]

Speed continued in the monument business until 1911 when he had a stroke of paralysis, but his later correspondence indicates that this did not affect his good nature and sense of humor. He lived until July 12, 1923.[17]

Henry Campbell also remained in Crawfordsville, becoming active in the Grand Army of the Republic, first as a charter member of Post No. 1 in Crawfordsville, organized in 1866, but which apparently became defunct for lack of interest in 1869. In 1879, Campbell be-

16 Lilly Archives, Sidney A. Speed to Eli Lilly Oct. 15 and 19, 1896.
17 Crawfordsville *Journal*, July 13, 1923.

came a charter member of the large and active McPherson Post No. 7, which continued to function until 1930.[18] He also was a member of the Military Order of the Loyal Legion.

Henry was in the hardware business for a number of years after the war; but when his father was killed in a train accident in 1879, he and his brother, Stephen, took over the dry goods business and operated it for eighteen years. Henry then became vice-president of the First National Bank and served in this position for the rest of his life. He become well acquainted with Eli Lilly, the Colonel's grandson, who was made an honorary member of the Eighteenth Battery Association. Lilly accompanied Henry Campbell to some of the veterans' reunions, and thought so highly of Henry's Journal that he had the entire document photographed. Henry Campbell died on July 22, 1915, following a prolonged illness from a complication of diseases.[19]

In 1899, Wilder's brigade met at Chattanooga for their monument dedications, and twelve of the battery veterans attended. They were Major Moses M. Beck, Captain Joseph A. Scott, Lieutenant William Benson Rippetoe, Samuel H. Scott, William E. Starr, Henry Campbell, Robert Madden, Basil Tilson, Hosier Durbin, William J. Wolfe, William O. Crouse, and Albert Allen.[20] The Eighteenth Battery Association also held annual reunions, and as late as 1915, sixteen men met at Collett Park in Terre Haute.[21] The last meeting of the association was two years later at Greencastle.[22]

The Wilder brigade reunions, beginning in 1882 and continuing at least until 1919, were much larger events, with 1,500 veterans of the brigade attending the 1887 meeting at Greencastle.[23] Usually the men gathered in different towns in Indiana and Illinois but occasionally held their reunions on Southern battlefields. During most of the period General John T. Wilder was the motivating influence; and even when a

---

[18] Montgomery County Public Library, Rosters, Minute Books, Treasurers' Books, G.A.R. Posts 1 & 7, Crawfordsville.

[19] Crawfordsville *Journal*, July 22, 1915.

[20] Beck, "Second Visit."

[21] Addison M. Dowling Collection, photo of 18th Battery reunion, June 14, 1915.

[22] Lilly Archives, William O. Crouse correspondence.

[23] Greencastle *Banner*, Sept. 8, 1887; Mrs. M. G. Rippeteau Collection, invitation to Wilder's brigade reunion, May 1919.

frail eighty-six year old, he traveled from his home in Jacksonville, Florida, to attend the brigade's 1916 reunion in Frankfort, Indiana.[24]

Seeing an opportunity for industrial development of the Chattanooga area because of the iron and coal deposits that he had observed during the war, Wilder moved there and became a successful industrialist, attracting Northern capital and resources to the region. He became a leading citizen and promoter of Chattanooga, was elected mayor in 1871, and was one of the original trustees of Chattanooga University.[25] Wilder was one of the men most interested in promoting the establishment of the Chickamauga and Chattanooga National Military Park and was elected president of the Chickamauga Memorial Association when it was organized September 19, 1889, while the former opponent of the brigade and battery, General Joseph Wheeler, was named vice president,[26] reflecting the cooperative efforts of old enemies to establish the battlefield park. Wilder turned much of his great energy to veterans' affairs during the 1890's after he lost much of his wealth during the depression early in the decade and the failure of the iron and steel industry in Chattanooga resulting from competitive advantages of the Birmingham region.[27]

Moses M. Beck, Joseph A. Scott, and Samuel H. Scott frequently took the long train ride from their homes in Kansas to attend the brigade and battery reunions. In 1865, Beck and Joseph Scott formed a partnership, buying the general store in Bainbridge owned by Scott's father, William T., and a more personal relationship developed when Beck married the Scott's sister, Mary. Because the value of their stock fell during the deflation that followed the war, the store failed; and the Becks, accompanied by Joseph, Samuel, and William T. Scott and by David Beck, who had been an 1864 recruit of the battery, moved west to Holton, Kansas.[28] Moses Beck first became a druggist, but in 1875 founded the Holton *Journal* and the *Recorder*. He remained editor and publisher of the papers until 1897, when he assigned finan-

---

24 Indianapolis *Journal*, Oct. 22, 1917.
25 Govan and Livingood, pp. 286, 295–96. Chattanooga University is now the University of Tennessee at Chattanooga.
26 *Ibid.*, p. 368.
27 *Ibid.*, pp. 354–55; Beck, "Second Visit."
28 Moses M. Beck, "The End of the War," Holton *Recorder, ca.* Feb. 1962.

cial control to a son and daughter but remained active in the editorial function until three days before his death February 3, 1931, at the age of ninety-two.[29]

Joseph A. Scott, with his father, opened the first hardware store in Holton upon their arrival. Later he was twice elected county treasurer and, for many years, served as agent to the Pottawatomie Indians. He was an active elder in the Presbyterian church and served as superintendent of the Sunday school. In his later years he corresponded with other old soldiers and with Eli Lilly, the Colonel's grandson, sending him the recruiting poster that is displayed now in Lilly Center. Scott was nearly eighty-seven years old when he died on June 7, 1924.[30]

John Rippetoe returned to his farm and developed it into one of the best in the area. His son, Peter, and a daughter died while children, but two daughters grew up and John had eight grandchildren when he died March 7, 1911.[31]

James Emory Rippetoe entered Indiana Asbury University following his discharge and became a Methodist minister, serving churches in southern Illinois and Nebraska before transfer in 1886 to establish churches in the frontier state of Colorado. He returned to Nebraska in 1893 where he served several churches; and after his retirement in 1913, he lived in Clay Center, Nebraska, where he died January 8, 1928.[32]

Cousin David Rippetoe became a druggist in Sandford, later moving to Terre Haute, and then to Indianapolis. He was divorced from Louisa Virginia in the early 1870s, remarried in 1878, and lived until 1920.[33]

William Benson Rippetoe returned to Indiana Asbury University after the war, and while there, Bishop Matthew Simpson persuaded him that the church was his true calling. From 1867 until 1869, he traveled circuits in Indiana, and in 1869, he accepted assignment to a circuit at Shelbyville, Tennessee. During the next twenty years he was

[29] Holton *Journal*, Feb. 5, 1931.
[30] Holton *Recorder*, June 12, 1924; Lilly Archives, Joseph A. Scott to Eli Lilly, the Colonel's grandson, June 11, 1915.
[31] Terre Haute *Tribune*, Mar. 8, 1911.
[32] Mrs. M. G. Rippeteau to author, May 16, 1973.
[33] National Archives, David W. Rippetoe service and pension records.

minister to churches in Middle Tennessee, and in 1893, went to the eastern part of the state, serving churches in Sevier, Blount, and Knox counties.[34] In 1901, he returned to the Indiana conference, serving churches near Terre Haute until he was superannuated in 1907. William Benson continued to preach for many years thereafter, retaining his vitality and keenness until shortly before his death January 25, 1932, at the age of ninety-one.[35]

He was the last of the principal characters of this history to go and very likely the last old soldier of the Eighteenth Indiana Light Artillery Battery to fade away. They had been one small group of a great generation of Americans that had gone forth when their country called, all giving their bit to the preservation of the nation, and afterwards, going their individual ways, contributing to the country's growth and its welfare. Some, like Lilly and Wilder, were successful in business and industry; and others, like the Rippetoes, aided the nation's welfare through religion and education. The Becks and Scotts moved west helping to eliminate the frontier, while most of the men contributed simply by performing their daily tasks.

34 Arthur G. Marshall to author, May 27 and June 28, 1973.
35 Terre Haute *Tribune*, Jan. 26, 1932.

Commissioned Officers

EIGHTEENTH INDIANA
LIGHT ARTILLERY
BATTERY[1]

Captain

LILLY, ELI, Greencastle, Ind., Commissioned August 6, 1862; resigned April 3, 1864, to accept commission as major in Ninth Indiana Cavalry.

SCOTT, JOSEPH ADDISON, Bainbridge, Ind. Promoted from first lieutenant April 5, 1864; resigned April 24, 1865, because of wound.

BECK, MOSES MILTON, Bainbridge, Ind. Promoted from first lieutenant April 24, 1864; mustered out with battery June 30, 1865.

First Lieutenant

HARTMAN, SAMUEL L., Crawfordsville, Ind. Commissioned August 6, 1862; dismissed from U. S. service August 9, 1863, by general field order 218, Army of the Cumberland.

SCOTT, JOSEPH ADDISON, Bainbridge, Ind. Commissioned August 6, 1862; promoted to captain.

BECK, MOSES MILTON, Bainbridge, Ind. Promoted from second lieutenant August 10, 1863; promoted to captain.

RIPPETOE, WILLIAM BENSON, Sandford, Ind. Promoted from second

---

1 Compiled from Indiana State Library, Archives Division, muster-in and muster-out rolls of the 18th Indiana Battery, Adjutant General's files; and from National Archives, "Descriptive Book of the 18th Battery, Indiana Light Artillery."

lieutenant March 5, 1864; mustered out with battery June 30, 1865.
MILLER, MARTIN J., Crawfordsville, Ind.[2] Promoted from second lieutenant April 25, 1864; killed near Selma, Alabama, April 2, 1865.

Second Lieutenant

BECK, MOSES MILTON, Bainbridge, Ind. Commissioned August 6, 1862; promoted to first lieutenant.

RIPPETOE, WILLIAM BENSON, Sandford, Ind. Commissioned August 6, 1862; promoted to first lieutenant.

MILLER, MARTIN J., Crawfordsville, Ind. Promoted from first sergeant October 18, 1863; promoted to first lieutenant.

JOHNSON, JOHN D., Pendleton, Ind. Promoted from quartermaster sergeant April 25, 1864; mustered out with battery June 30, 1865.

RIPPETOE, DAVID W., Sandford, Ind. Promoted from first sergeant April 25, 1864; mustered out with battery June 30, 1865.

2 Records in Wabash College Archives show Miller's residence as being Cologne, Prussia.

Roster of 1862 Volunteer Enlisted Men

EIGHTEENTH INDIANA
LIGHT ARTILLERY BATTERY
WITH RANK AT MUSTER-IN
AUGUST 6, 1862*

First Sergeant

LANE , ROBERT W., 27, mechanic, born Rush County, Ind. Enlisted at Bainbridge July 26. Died April 11, 1863, at Big Spring, Tenn.

Quartermaster Sergeant

WATSON, CHARLES D., 23, physician, born Spencer, N. Y. Enlisted at Hillsboro July 28. Discharged Dec. 20, 1862, to accept appointment as assistant surgeon, 54th Indiana Regiment.

Sergeant

MILLER, MARTIN J., 22, student, born Cologne, Prussia. Enlisted at Crawfordsville July 12. Promoted to first sergeant and second lieutenant.

BINFORD, JAMES W., 18, student, born Crawfordsville, Ind. Enlisted at Crawfordsville July 28. Mustered out with battery June 30, 1865 as private.

JOHNSON, JOHN D., 28, shoemaker, born Holmes County, Ohio. En-

* Compiled from Indiana State Library, Archives Division, muster-in and muster-out rolls of the 18th Indiana Battery, Adjutant General's files; and from National Archives, "Descriptive Book of the 18th Battery, Indiana Light Artillery." All enlistments were for three years.

listed at Pendleton August 5. Promoted to quartermaster sergeant and second lieutenant.

CROSBY, DANIEL W., 21, teacher, birthplace unknown. Enlisted at Greencastle July 11. Deserted August 20, 1862, with $600 belonging to men of the battery.

MILLER, JOHN W., 23, farmer, born Kentucky. Enlisted at Alamo July 16. Mustered out with battery June 30, 1865, as private.

JOHNS, JOHN, 23, clerk, born Preble County, Ohio. Enlisted at Greencastle July 20. Mustered out with battery June 30, 1865, as corporal.

Corporal

RUNEY, JOHN, 23, occupation and birthplace unknown. Enlisted at Crawfordsville July 19. Died of chronic diarrhea at Indianapolis July 27, 1864.

SPERRY, FREDERIC, 19, miller born Ogdensburg, N. Y. Enlisted at Crawfordsville July 19. Mustered out with battery June 30, 1865, as private.

McCORKLE, ABRAM S., 27, farmer, born Putnam County, Ind. Enlisted at Greencastle July 14. Died of wounds at Poe's Tavern, Tenn., Aug. 25, 1863.

SCOTT, SAMUEL H., 19, clerk, born Bainbridge, Ind. Enlisted at Bainbridge July 29. Mustered out with battery June 30, 1865, as quartermaster sergeant.

McMAKEN, BENJAMIN M., 22, farmer, born Montgomery County, Ind. Enlisted at Crawfordsville July 19. Died at Alamo, Ind., January 19, 1863.

CASSITY, OLIVER A., 21, born Barren County, Ky. Enlisted at Bainbridge July 16. Mustered out with battery June 30, 1865, as private.

RIPPETOE, JOHN H., 25, farmer, born Vigo County, Ind. Enlisted at Sandford July 14. Mustered out with battery June 30, 1865, as sergeant.

McMULLEN, GEORGE S., 26, engineer, born Philadelphia County, Pa. Enlisted at Indianapolis August 7. Mustered out with battery June 30, 1865, as sergeant.

McANINCH, WILLIAM L., 27, farmer, born Putnam County, Ind. Enlisted at Crawfordsville August 1. Mustered out with battery June 30, 1865, as sergeant.

NEWELL, AUGUSTUS E., 21, shoemaker, born Crawfordsville, Ind. Enlisted at Crawfordsville July 12. Mustered out with battery June 30, 1865.

McBROOM, MARTIN V., 26, farmer, born Fountain County, Ind. Enlisted at Hillsboro July 28. Mustered out with battery June 30, 1865, as private.

LYON, THEODORE S., 23, harness maker, born Ohio. Enlisted at Indianapolis August 7. Mustered out with battery June 30, 1865, as private.

Bugler

ANDERSON, WILLIAM H., 19, student, born Putnam County, Ind. Enlisted at Greencastle July 18. Died of erysipelas at Gallatin, Tenn., Dec. 28, 1862.

CAMPBELL, HENRY, 18, clerk, born Vermillion County, Ind. Enlisted at Crawfordsville July 12. Discharged Nov. 24, 1864, to accept commission as second lieutenant of 101st U. S. Colored Infantry Regiment.

Wagoner

SMITH, JOHN M., 19, clerk, born Indiana. Enlisted at Bainbridge July 21. Deserted October 18, 1862.

Artificer

ELLIS, JOHN H., 28, blacksmith, born Pendleton County, Ky. Enlisted at Waynetown July 9. Mustered out with battery June 30, 1865.

GRANT, JOHN, 36, blacksmith, born Posey County, Ind. Enlisted at Portland Mills July 10. Mustered out with battery June 30, 1865.

HENDRIX, JACOB J., 30, wagonmaker, born Parke County, Ind. Enlisted at Mansfield July 21. Mustered out with battery June 30, 1865.

KRUG, WILLIAM J., 45, saddler, born Pendleton County, Ky. Enlisted at Pleasant Hill July 19. Discharged December 24, 1862.

WAMPLER, GEORGE W., 23, wagonmaker, born Lawrence County, Ind. Enlisted at Bainbridge July 18. Mustered out with battery June 30, 1865.

WINTERMOTE, PETER K., 33, harness maker, born Darke County, Ohio. Enlisted at Greencastle July 23. Died at Bowling Green Ky., January 9, 1863.

Private

AGNEW, SAMUEL B., 38, farmer, born Hamilton County, Ohio. Enlisted at Crawfordsville July 14. Discharged January 4, 1863.

ALDRIDGE, WILLIAM, 18, farmer, born Putnam County, Ind. Enlisted at Bainbridge July 18. Mustered out with battery June 30, 1865.

ALLEN, ALBERT, 22, farmer, born Putnam County, Ind. Enlisted at Greencastle August 6. Mustered out with battery June 30, 1865, as corporal.

ART, WILLIAM, 18, farmer, born Edgar County, Ill. Enlisted at Sandford July 16. Mustered out with battery June 30, 1865.

AUSTIN, ARCHELAUS C., 18, farmer, born Crawfordsville, Ind. Enlisted at Crawfordsville August 4. Mustered out with battery June 30, 1865.

BARR, MARION J., 21, bricklayer, born Crawfordsville, Ind. Enlisted at Crawfordsville July 12. Mustered out with battery June 30, 1865, as sergeant.

BAYNE, JOHN, 28, shoemaker, born Northampton County, Pa. Enlisted at Bainbridge July 18. Discharged February 8, 1863, as corporal.

BEAVER, CHRISTIAN C., 20, farmer, born Fountain County, Ind. Enlisted at Hillsboro July 28. Mustered out with battery June 30, 1865.

BIRCHFIELD, THOMAS F., 18, painter, born Hendricks County, Ind. Enlisted at Crawfordsville July 18. Mustered out with battery June 30, 1865.

BIRCHFIELD, WILLIAM V., 25, butcher, born Morgan County, Ky. Enlisted at Crawfordsville July 21. Transferred to Mississippi Marine Brigade January 4, 1863.

BISHOP, JOHN B., 23, farmer, born Henry County, Ky. Enlisted at Bainbridge July 19. Discharged March 18, 1863.

BLACK, WILLIAM, 24, farmer, born Montgomery County, Ind. Enlisted at Crawfordsville August 6. Died of wounds at Cartersville, Ga., October 17, 1864.

BUTCHER, CHARLES W., 19, farmer, born Hamilton County, Ohio. Enlisted at Crawfordsville July 18. Mustered out with battery June 30, 1865.

CARTER, JAMES V., 20, farmer, born Bainbridge, Ind. Enlisted at Bainbridge July 18. Mustered out with battery June 30, 1865.

CARTER, JOHN E., 24, silversmith, born Bainbridge, Ind. Enlisted at Bainbridge July 26. Mustered out with battery June 30, 1865.

CLICK, SOLOMAN, 23, farmer, born Franklin County, Ohio. Enlisted at Indianapolis July 25. Died at Gallatin, Tenn., January 2, 1863.

CLINGER, CHARLES F., 20, bricklayer, born Shelbyville, Ind. Enlisted at Shelbyville August 3. Mustered out with battery June 30, 1865.

COMBS, RICHARD S., 24, occupation and birthplace unknown. Enlisted at Brunerstown July 23. Prisoner of war. Discharged May 15, 1865.

COMBS, WILLIAM B., 26, farmer, born Ohio. Enlisted at Mansfield July 21. Discharged April 25, 1864.

COOPER, MARION, 20, farmer, birthplace unknown. Enlisted at Hillsboro July 28. Died April 9, 1863.

CORBIN, SAMUEL W., 27, cooper, birthplace unknown. Enlisted at Indianapolis August 4. Promoted to corporal. Killed in action at Mossy Creek, Tenn., December 29, 1863.

COREY, NELSON H., 24, carriage maker, born Steuben County, N. Y. Enlisted at Crawfordsville July 20. Promoted to corporal. Died of pneumonia December 12, 1864.

CRAWFORD, JOHN A., 18, no occupation, born Crawfordsville, Ind. Enlisted at Crawfordsville July 14. Mustered out with battery June 30, 1865.

CROUSE, WILLIAM O., 21, farmer, born Point Pleasant, Ind. Enlisted at Indianapolis August 4. Mustered out with battery June 30, 1865, as sergeant.

CRYSTAL, JOHN, 24, nurseryman, born County Sligo, Ireland. Enlisted at Indianapolis August 6. Mustered out with battery June 30, 1865.

CULVER, CHARLES O., 23, occupation and birthplace unknown. Enlisted at Indianapolis August 6. Died at Murfreesboro, Tenn., January 9, 1863.

Cummins, Francis M., 24, farmer, born Edgar County, Ill. Enlisted at Terre Haute August 7. Mustered out with battery June 30, 1865.

Davis, Charles E., 18, farmer, born Fountain County, Ind. Enlisted at Hillsboro August 6. Mustered out with battery June 30, 1865.

Davis, John C., 23, farmer, born Vigo County, Ind. Enlisted at Sandford August 6. Died at Gallatin, Tenn., December 13, 1862.

Day, Alexander, 18, tanner, born Waterford, Ireland. Enlisted at Sandford July 28. Listed as deserter April 9, 1863, but believed to have been killed by guerrillas.

Dodd, James C., 19, farmer, born Putnam County, Ind. Enlisted at Carpentersville July 14. Died of wounds at New Market, Tenn., January 6, 1864.

Durbin, Hosier, 18, tanner, born Dearborn County, Ind. Enlisted at North Salem July 22. Mustered out with battery June 30, 1865, as corporal.

Edmiston, Tilghman G., 20, farmer, born Owen County, Ind. Enlisted at Sandford August 6. Mustered out with battery June 30, 1865.

Ellsworth, William, 22, farmer, birthplace unknown. Enlisted at Pendleton August 5. Died of typhoid fever at Frankfort, Ky., November 9, 1862.

Ervin, Patrick, 26, carpenter, born Richmond, Ind. Enlisted at Bainbridge July 23. Died at New Albany, Ind., November 15, 1862.

Eslinger, Absalom, 22, carpenter, born Sullivan County, Ind. Enlisted at Crawfordsville August 1. Mustered out with battery June 30, 1865.

Evans, Francis M., 24, engineer, born Tippecanoe County, Ind. Enlisted at Indianapolis July 29. Discharged at Nashville, Tenn., February 15, 1865.

Evinger, Thomas G., 25, farmer, born Hamilton County, Ohio. Enlisted at Sandford July 24. Mustered out with battery June 30, 1865, as corporal.

Fitzpatrick, Patrick, 21, watchmaker, born Ireland. Enlisted at Crawfordsville July 21. Prisoner of war. Mustered out June 30, 1865.

Flint, George W., 26, occupation and birthplace unknown. Enlisted at Greencastle July 19. Discharged at Louisville, Ky., February 28, 1863.

FULTON, MELVILLE W., 21, farmer, born Wayne County, Ind. Enlisted at Bainbridge July 15. Mustered out with battery June 30, 1865.

GILKEY, DANIEL, 23, occupation and birthplace unknown. Enlisted at Alamo July 15. Mustered out at Indianapolis May 8, 1865.

GILMORE, BENJAMIN H., 18, farmer, born Putnam County, Ind. Enlisted at Greencastle July 19. Discharged at Gallatin, Tenn., January 18, 1863.

GILMORE, JAMES J., 31, farmer, born Putnam County, Ind. Enlisted at Indianapolis August 8. Mustered out with battery June 30, 1865.

GOODWIN, WILLIAM W., 19, occupation and birthplace unknown. Enlisted at Greencastle July 27. Died at Bardstown, Ky., 1862 (date not recorded).

GORHAM, OLIVER B., 19, occupation and birthplace unknown. Enlisted at Indianapolis July 30. Deserted September 1, 1862. Later sentenced to military prison at Nashville, Tenn.

GRAY, GEORGE W., 20, farmer, born Putnam County, Ind. Enlisted at Greencastle July 20. Died at Murfreesboro, Tenn., February 6, 1863.

GREENWOOD, FRANK A., 25, merchant, birthplace unknown. Enlisted at Hillsboro August 6. Promoted to corporal. Died of wounds at Chattanooga, Tenn., October 16, 1864.

HAIR, STEPHENSON, 20, farmer, born Hamilton County, Ind. Enlisted at Pendleton August 6. Mustered out with battery June 30, 1865.

HAMMEL, GEORGE W., 23, farmer, born Butler County, Ohio. Enlisted at Crawfordsville July 15. Mustered out with battery June 30, 1865.

HARDEE, JOHN, 45, occupation and birthplace unknown. Enlisted at Crawfordsville July 17. Discharged at Indianapolis April 12, 1863.

HARTMAN, MARION, 19, occupation and birthplace unknown. Enlisted at Carpentersville July 14. Died at Frankfort, Ky., November 10, 1862.

HAYS, ELISHA, 37, farmer, birthplace unknown. Enlisted at Pleasant Hill July 27. Deserted at LaVergne, Tenn., February 15, 1863.

HEANEY, JAMES M., 19, miller, born Blakesburg, Ind. Enlisted at Bainbridge July 10. Died of smallpox at Knoxville, Tenn., March 10, 1864.

HEIZER, DAVID H., 28, clerk, born Augusta County, Va. Enlisted at Indianapolis August 7. Mustered out with battery June 30, 1865, as sergeant.

HOWARD, SIMPSON, 18, occupation and birthplace unknown. Enlisted at Bainbridge July 16. Died of typhoid fever at Indianapolis September 2, 1862.

HOYT, BYRON, 33, cooper, born Vernon, Ind. Enlisted at Indianapolis August 11. Mustered out with battery June 30, 1865.

HUBBARD, HARVEY W., 23, farmer, born Putnam County, Ind. Enlisted at Putnamville August 6. Mustered out with battery June 30, 1865.

JANES, SAMUEL, JR., 18, farmer, born Brighton, England. Enlisted at Ladoga August 4. Mustered out with battery June 30, 1865.

JOHNSON, ANDREW, 23, occupation and birthplace unknown. Enlisted at Crawfordsville August 1. Killed in action at Chickamauga, Ga., September 19, 1863.

JOHNSON, JAMES M., 21, engineer, born Butler County, Ohio. Enlisted at Crawfordsville July 14. Died at Knoxville, Tenn., February 10, 1864.

JOHNSON, JOHN B., 23, occupation and birthplace unknown. Enlisted at Greencastle July 16. Promoted to bugler. Discharged March 3, 1863.

JOHNSON, SIMON A., 19, farmer, born Indiana. Enlisted at Bainbridge July 14. Discharged at Murfreesboro, Tenn., April 12, 1863.

JOYNER, WILLIAM H., 18, farmer, birthplace unknown. Enlisted at Mansfield August 4. Mustered out with battery June 30, 1865.

KESTER, JESSE P., 20, shoemaker, birthplace unknown. Enlisted at Bainbridge July 15. Mustered out with battery June 30, 1865.

KILCH, MICHAEL, 34, farmer, birthplace unknown. Enlisted at Crawfordsville July 22. Mustered out with battery June 30, 1865.

KNOX, BENJAMIN F., 19, druggist, born Crawfordsville, Ind. Enlisted at Crawfordsville August 1. Discharged at Murfreesboro, Tenn., April 12, 1863.

LANE, DAVID F., 18, farmer, born Putnam County, Ind. Enlisted at Bainbridge July 16. Mustered out with battery June 30, 1865.

LINDBURGH, SPENCER A., 19, occupation and birthplace unknown. Enlisted at Crawfordsville July 21. Died at Louisville, Ky., January 9, 1863.

LOGSTON, SAMPSON, 23, farmer, born Holmes County, Ohio. Enlisted at Hillsboro August 1. Died of consumption at Jeffersonville, Ind., December, 1864.

LLOYD, EZRA, 21, student, birthplace unknown. Enlisted at Greencastle July 18. Killed in action at Mossy Creek, Tenn., December 29, 1863.

McBROOM, EDWARD, 26, farmer, born Fountain County, Ind. Enlisted at Hillsboro July 28. Discharged at Indianapolis February 4, 1865.

McCLURE, NATHANIEL, 18, farmer, born Pleasant Hill, Ind. Enlisted at Pleasant Hill July 19. Mustered out with battery June 30, 1865, as corporal.

McCOY, ISAAC, 33, farmer, born Clinton County, Ohio. Enlisted at Sandford August 7. Discharged at Gallatin, Tenn., February 20, 1863.

MADDEN, ROBERT, 22, horticulturist, born County Meath, Ireland. Enlisted at Indianapolis August 6. Mustered out with battery June 30, 1865, as corporal.

MALCOM, JOHN R., 28, farmer, born Ohio. Enlisted at Sandford July 16. Discharged at Murfreesboro, Tenn., March 7, 1863.

MASON, CHARLES M., 18, farmer, born Montgomery County, Ind. Enlisted at Crawfordsville August 3. Mustered out with battery June 30, 1865.

MURPHY, CORNELIUS, 35, farmer, born Ireland. Enlisted at Sandford August 6. Mustered out May 27, 1865.

NEWHALL, SAMUEL R., 25, miller, born Bristol County, Mass. Enlisted at Bainbridge July 15. Mustered out with battery June 30, 1865.

PAIR, ALBERT F., 18, woolen factor, born Terre Haute, Ind. Enlisted at Crawfordsville July 20. Mustered out with battery June 30, 1865.

PAYNE, LAFAYETTE, 21, farmer, born Adams County, Ill. Enlisted at Carpentersville July 15. Mustered out with battery June 30, 1865, as corporal.

PERKINS, IRA, 21, farmer, born Putnam County, Ind. Enlisted at Greencastle July 18. Mustered out with battery June 30, 1865.

PLYMALE, GABRIEL, 18, farmer, born Wayne County, Ind. Enlisted at

Sandford August 1. Discharged at Murfreesboro, Tenn., March 18, 1863.

PLYMALE, HUEY A., 27, farmer, birthplace unknown. Enlisted at Sandford July 16. Mustered out June 30, 1865, as prisoner of war.

POPE, HENRY T., 18, farmer, born Indianapolis, Ind. Enlisted at Greencastle July 20. Mustered out with battery June 30, 1865.

PYLE, JOHN W., 45, shoemaker, born New Castle County, Del. Enlisted at Crawfordsville July 19. Died at Bowling Green Ky., November 13, 1862.

REDMAN, JEFFERSON B., 20, farmer, born Knox County, Ky. Enlisted at Mansfield July 27. Died at Murfreesboro, Tenn., March 30, 1863.

REESE, JAMES H., 21, farmer, born Vigo County, Ind. Enlisted at Sandford July 17. Died at Murfreesboro, Tenn., March 19, 1863.

RICE, CALVIN S., 25, farmer, born Franklin County, Pa. Enlisted at Bainbridge July 20. Mustered out with battery June 30, 1865.

RINEWALT, WILLIAM, 17, farmer, born Pendleton, Ind. Enlisted at Pendleton August 6. Mustered out with battery June 30, 1865.

RIPPETOE, JAMES E., 19, farmer, born Vigo County, Ind. Enlisted at Sandford July 14. Mustered out with battery June 30, 1865, as corporal.

RIPPETOE, DAVID W., 20, farmer, born Vigo County, Ind. Enlisted at Sandford July 17. Promoted to corporal, sergeant, first sergeant, and second lieutenant.

ROSE, EDWARD S., 35, occupation and birthplace unknown. Enlisted at Crawfordsville July 16. Died at New Albany, Ind., December 12, 1862.

SCHOMBER, MARK, 20, farmer, born Franklin, Ind. Enlisted at Indianapolis July 24. Mustered out with battery June 30, 1865, as corporal.

SCOTT, ALBERT C., 24, farmer, born Vigo County, Ind. Enlisted at Sandford August 6. Died at Gallatin, Tenn., December 29, 1862.

SCOTT, WILLIAM W., 21, cooper, born Crawfordsville, Ind. Enlisted at Crawfordsville July 12. Discharged at Indianapolis April 1, 1863.

SHANKS, TRUMAN, 19, farmer, born Kentucky. Enlisted at Sandford July 14. Mustered out with battery June 30, 1865.

SHEPHERD, JOHN P., 18, shoemaker, born Crawfordsville, Ind. Enlisted at Crawfordsville August 7. Discharged at Indianapolis February 28, 1863.

SLUPE, WILLIAM C., 18, farmer, birthplace unknown. Enlisted at Crawfordsville July 21. Died at Knoxville, Tenn., January 31, 1864.

SMITH, ERASTUS H., 22, farmer, born Hendricks County, Ind. Enlisted at Bainbridge July 14. Mustered out with battery June 30, 1865.

SMITH, FRANCIS M., 20, farmer, born Montgomery County, Ind. Enlisted at Crawfordsville July 19. Mustered out with battery June 30, 1865.

SMITH, GEORGE A., 31, blacksmith, born Vigo County, Ind. Enlisted at Sandford August 6. Discharged at Bowling Green, Ky., January 18, 1863.

SMITH, GEORGE C., 21, carpenter, born Pleasant Hill, Ind. Enlisted at Pleasant Hill August 4. Mustered out with battery June 30, 1865.

SMITH, JOHN A., 18, farmer, born Pleasant Hill, Ind. Enlisted at Crawfordsville July 21. Deserted October 20, 1862. Discharged November 16, 1863.

SNYDER, JOHN I., 18, clerk, born Cumberland, Md. Enlisted at Crawfordsville July 12. Deserted October 20, 1862. Sentenced to military prison at Louisville, Ky.

SOMERVILLE, JAMES, 19, farmer, born Vermillion County, Ind. Enlisted at Greencastle July 29. Mustered out with battery June 30, 1865.

SPEED, SIDNEY A., 18, clerk, born Montgomery County, Ind. Enlisted at Crawfordsville July 15. Mustered out with battery June 30, 1865, as corporal.

STARR, WILLIAM E., 18, student, born Putnam County, Ind. Enlisted at Bainbridge July 12. Mustered out with battery June 30, 1865, as first sergeant.

SUNMAN, HENRY P., 19, farmer, born Franklin County, Ind. Enlisted at Indianapolis July 22. Died at Evansville, Ind., January 6, 1864.

THOMAS, EDWARD S., 22, drover, born Woodford County, Ky. Enlisted at Bainbridge July 16. Mustered out with battery June 30, 1865.

TIFFIN, HENRY, 38, farmer, born Meade County, Ky. Enlisted at Sandford August 4. Mustered out with battery June 30, 1865.

TILSON, BASIL, 19, farmer, born Huntsville, Ind. Enlisted at Huntsville August 5. Mustered out with battery June 30, 1865.

TORR, JOHN, 22, farmer, born Bartholomew County, Ind. Enlisted at Indianapolis August 6. Died at Murfreesboro, Tenn., May 24, 1863.

TRUETT, GEORGE M., 20, farmer, born Monroe County, Ind. Enlisted at Greencastle July 27. Mustered out with battery June 30, 1863.

TURNER, LEWIS C., 18, farmer, birthplace unknown. Enlisted at Greencastle July 27. Discharged February 8, 1863.

TYLER, JOHN C., 20, farmer, born Highland County, Ohio. Enlisted at Greencastle July 19. Discharged April 10, 1863.

WASSON, MAHLON L., 34, blacksmith, born Richmond, Ind. Enlisted at Mansfield July 21. Mustered out with battery June 30, 1865.

WELLS, JOHN W., 18, farmer, born Marion County, Ind. Enlisted at Indianapolis August 7. Mustered out with battery June 30, 1865.

WELKER, THEODORE, 21, teacher, born Putnamville, Ind. Enlisted at Putnamville August 7. Mustered out with battery June 30, 1865.

WOLFE, WILLIAM J., 18, student, born Romney, Ind. Enlisted at Crawfordsville July 12. Mustered out with battery June 30, 1865.

WOOD, JOEL H., 20, farmer, born Guilford County, N. C. Enlisted at Huntsville August 6. Mustered out with battery June 30, 1865.

YATES, JAME: M., 20, farmer, born Putnam County, Ind. Enlisted at Greencastle July 19. Mustered out with battery June 30, 1865.

Roster of 1864 Recruits

EIGHTEENTH INDIANA
LIGHT ARTILLERY
BATTERY[1]

ADAMS, JAMES B., 25, farmer, born Putnam County, Ind. Enlisted at Indianapolis September 12. Mustered out with battery June 30, 1865.

BALLARD, WILLIAM E., 24, farmer, born Orange County, Ind. Enlisted at Terre Haute October 13. Mustered out with battery June 30, 1865.

BECK, DAVID D., 18, farmer, born Wayne County, Ind. Substitute;[2] enlisted at Terre Haute August 18. Mustered out with battery June 30, 1865.

BOLTON, ISAAC J., 18, carpenter, born Vigo County, Ind. Enlisted at Terre Haute October 7. Mustered out with battery June 30, 1865.

BULLOCK, THOMAS G., 18, farmer, born Indiana. Substitute; enlisted at Terre Haute August 18. Mustered out with battery June 30, 1865.

BULLOCK, WILLIAM A., 31, farmer, born Putnam County, Ind. Enlisted at Indianapolis April 1. Mustered out with battery June 30, 1865.

CALLICOTT, JESSE, 18, farmer, born Johnson County, Ind. Enlisted at Indianapolis October 25. Mustered out with battery June 30, 1865.

COFFMAN, WILLIAM, 18, farmer, born Indiana. Substitute; enlisted at Terre Haute August 22. Mustered out with battery June 30, 1865.

---

1 Compiled from Indiana State Library, Archives Division, muster-in and muster-out rolls of the 18th Indiana Battery, Adjutant General's files; and from National Archives, "Descriptive Book of the 18th Battery, Indiana Light Artillery." All enlistments were for one year unless otherwise noted.

2 Served in place of a draftee.

DAVIS, ALBERT C., 28, laborer, born Stark County, Ohio. Enlisted at Lafayette October 9. Mustered out with battery June 30, 1865.

DAVIS, GEORGE, 35, farmer, born Indiana. Enlisted at Terre Haute October 10. Mustered out with battery June 30, 1865.

GARVER, WILLIAM L., 18, butcher, born Ohio. Substitute; enlisted at Terre Haute August 22. Mustered out with battery June 30, 1865.

GOODWILL, JEREMIAH, 18, farmer, born Ohio. Enlisted at Kendallville December 7. Mustered out July 1, 1865.

GRAVES, GEORGE, 35, farmer, born Indiana. Enlisted at Terre Haute October 10. Mustered out with battery June 30, 1865.

GRAY, JOHN F., 18, farmer, born Indianapolis, Ind. Enlisted for 3 years at Prairieton March 31. Not on muster-out roll.

GRAY, JOSEPH C., 19, farmer, born Madison County, Ind. Enlisted for 3 years at Prairieton March 30. Mustered out with battery June 30, 1865.

GREGORY, THOMAS R., 18, farmer, born Putnam County, Ind. Enlisted at Indianapolis September 29. Mustered out with battery June 30, 1865.

HARLAN, LEWIS, 31, farmer, born Lancaster, Pa. Enlisted at Terre Haute October 7. Mustered out with battery June 30, 1865.

HARMAN, WESLEY H., 30, cooper, born Kentucky. Enlisted at Terre Haute October 7. Mustered out with battery June 30, 1865.

HANSELL, ELIJAH C., 21, farmer, born Putnam County, Ind. Enlisted at Indianapolis August 29. Mustered out with battery June 30, 1865.

HOOPS, LEWIS G., 18, farmer, born Indiana. Enlisted at Terre Haute October 14. Mustered out with battery June 30, 1865.

HUNNELL, JOHN W., 25, farmer, born Kentucky. Enlisted at Terre Haute October 12. Mustered out with battery June 30, 1865.

HUSSING, ALBERT N., 18, farmer, born Vigo County, Ind. Enlisted at Terre Haute October 12. Not on muster-out roll.

JOSEPH, WILLIAM A., 19, farmer, born Virginia. Enlisted at Terre Haute October 14. Mustered out with battery June 30, 1865.

LACKEY, ALEXANDER, 22, laborer, born Vigo County, Ind. Enlisted for

3 years at Terre Haute March 26. Mustered out with battery June 30, 1865.

LACKEY, CALEB, 26, farmer, born Vigo County, Ind. Enlisted for 3 years at Terre Haute March 26. Mustered out with battery June 30, 1865.

LAFOLLETTE, JACOB G., 18, farmer, born Indiana. Enlisted at Terre Haute October 14. Mustered out with battery June 30, 1865.

LAFOLLETTE, LOUIS G., 38, farmer, born Hardin County, Ky. Enlisted at Lafayette November 21. Mustered out with battery June 30, 1865.

LAGERS, AUGUSTINE, 25, farmer, born Preble County, Ohio. Enlisted at Lafayette December 28. Not on muster-out roll.

LAYMAN, JOHN H., 25, farmer, born Butler, Va. Enlisted at Terre Haute October 8. Mustered out with battery June 30, 1865.

MILLER, JACOB F., 27, wagonmaster, born Germany. Enlisted at Kendallville December 7. Mustered out with battery June 30, 1865.

NETHERCUTT, ISAAC M., 18, farmer, born Indiana. Enlisted at Terre Haute August 17. Mustered out with battery June 30, 1865.

RHODES, ANDREW, 18, farmer, born Indiana. Enlisted at Terre Haute October 14. Mustered out with battery June 30, 1865.

RICE, FRANK, 37, cooper, born Vigo County, Ind. Enlisted at Terre Haute October 8. Mustered out with battery June 30, 1865.

RIPPETOE, JASON L., 25, teacher, born Vigo County, Ind. Enlisted at Indianapolis November 18. Mustered out with battery June 30, 1865.

RIPPETOE, LEONIDUS L. H., 19, farmer, born Vigo County, Ind. Enlisted for 3 years at Indianapolis March 21. Mustered out with battery June 30, 1865.

ROBINSON, WILLIAM H., 26, teacher, born Vigo County, Ind. Enlisted at Terre Haute October 7. Mustered out May 13, 1865.

RYAN, JOHN A., 36, farmer, born Virginia. Enlisted at Terre Haute October 8. Mustered out with battery June 30, 1865.

SCOTT, JOHN T., 18, tanner, born Indiana. Enlisted at Terre Haute August 17. Mustered out with battery June 30, 1865.

SHANKS, DANIEL, 32, farmer, born Virginia. Enlisted at Terre Haute October 8. Mustered out with battery June 30, 1865.

SHEETS, FRANCIS M., 21, farmer, born Vigo County, Ind. Enlisted at Terre Haute October 7. Mustered out with battery June 30, 1865.

SHEETS, JOHN B., 28, carpenter, born Vigo County, Ind. Enlisted at Terre Haute October 7. Mustered out with battery June 30, 1865.

SHORES, HENRY M., 20, farmer, born Vigo County, Ind. Enlisted at Terre Haute October 18. Mustered out with battery June 30, 1865.

SHORES, WILLIAM A., 22, farmer, born Vigo County, Ind. Enlisted at Terre Haute October 8. Mustered out with battery June 30, 1865.

SMITH, GEORGE A., 33, blacksmith, born Vigo County, Ind. Enlisted at Terre Haute October 8. Mustered out with battery June 30, 1865.

SMITH, JACOB H., 20, farmer, born Vigo County, Ind. Enlisted at Terre Haute October 8. Mustered out with battery June 30, 1865.

SMITH, JOHN A., 29, farmer, born Vigo County, Ind. Enlisted at Terre Haute October 10. Mustered out with battery June 30, 1865.

STARR, GEORGE W., 18, tanner, born Indiana. Enlisted at Terre Haute August 17. Mustered out with battery June 30, 1865.

STEFFEY, ERASMUS, 24, farmer, born Vigo County, Ind. Enlisted at Terre Haute October 7. Mustered out with battery June 30, 1865.

STERLING, REUBEN, 19, farmer, born Edgar County, Ill. Enlisted at Terre Haute October 15. Mustered out with battery June 30, 1865.

STERN, JOHN F., 23, farmer, born Wurttemberg, Germany. Enlisted at Indianapolis December 16. Not on muster-out roll.

TABLER, ADDISON, 36, farmer, born Marion County, Ky. Enlisted at Terre Haute October 8. Mustered out at Jeffersonville hospital June 26, 1865.

TAYLOR, NOAH, 22, farmer, born Virginia. Enlisted at Terre Haute October 8. Mustered out with battery June 30, 1865.

TIFFIN, HARRISON, 26, farmer, born Illinois. Enlisted at Terre Haute October 7. Mustered out with battery June 30, 1865.

WARD, JONATHAN, 20, farmer, born Vigo County, Ind. Enlisted at Terre Haute October 16. Mustered out with battery June 30, 1865.

WOODWARD, JOSEPH J., 18, farmer, born Putnam County, Ind. Enlisted for 3 years at Bainbridge March 20. Mustered out with battery June 30, 1865.

Roster of Detachment

OF THE ELEVENTH INDIANA
BATTERY TRANSFERRED
TO THE EIGHTEENTH
INDIANA BATTERY,
NOVEMBER 13, 1864[1]

Quartermaster Sergeant

SAWTELL, WILSEY H., 21, merchant, born Fort Wayne, Ind. Enlisted at Fort Wayne August 14, 1862. Mustered out with battery June 30, 1865.

Corporals

GLENN, WILLIAM, 20, fireman, born Morgan County, Ohio. Enlisted at Fort Wayne August 8, 1862. Mustered out with battery June 30, 1865.

DREWS HENRY F., 31, farmer, born Rheine, Prussia. Enlisted at Fort Wayne August 12, 1862. Mustered out with battery June 30, 1865.

MEYER, FREDERICK, 22, clerk, born Minden, Prussia. Enlisted at Fort Wayne August 12, 1862. Mustered out with battery June 30, 1865.

PASTOR, ADAM, 19, baker, born Europe. Enlisted at Fort Wayne August 13, 1862. Mustered out with battery June 30, 1865.

Privates

ANNEN, CHRISTIAN, 28, laborer, born Switzerland. Enlisted at Columbia City February 25, 1864. Mustered out with battery June 30, 1865.

---

[1] Compiled from Indiana State Library, Archives Division, roll of detachment of the 11th Indiana Battery transferred to the 18th Indiana Battery; and from the muster-out roll of the 18th Indiana Battery, Adjustant General's files. All enlistments were for three years.

BALLOU, FERDINAND, 18, farmer, born DeKalb County, Ind. Enlisted at Fort Wayne March 22, 1864. Mustered out with battery June 30, 1865.

BALMER, JOHN, 28, farmer, born Switzerland. Enlisted at Fort Wayne March 22, 1864. Mustered out with battery June 30, 1865.

BEAMER, EDWARD, 33, teamster, born Fort Wayne, Ind. Enlisted at Fort Wayne August 5, 1862. Mustered out with battery June 30, 1865.

BEARSS, EDWARD, 18, laborer, born Indiana. Enlisted at Fort Wayne January 25, 1864. Mustered out with battery June 30, 1865.

BODEN, JAMES, 23, railroader, born Lewisburg, Pa. Enlisted at Fort Wayne August 8, 1862. Mustered out with battery June 30, 1865.

CALDWELL, HENRY F., 20, clerk, born New Castle, Del. Veteran;[2] reenlisted at Chattanooga, Tenn., March 5, 1864. Mustered out with battery June 30, 1865.

CHAPMAN, WILLIAM M., 29, laborer, born Wayne County, Ind. Veteran; reenlisted at Chattanooga, Tenn., February 25, 1864. Mustered out with battery June 30, 1865.

COTHERELL, ANDREW J., 20, clerk, born Providence, Ohio. Enlisted at Fort Wayne August 13, 1862. Mustered out with battery June 30, 1865.

CUTSHALL, WILLIAM A., 25, farmer, born Dayton, Ohio. Enlisted at Fort Wayne March 29, 1864. Mustered out with battery June 30, 1865.

DOLLOFF, ELIJAH, 23, farmer, born Crittenden, Vt. Veteran; reenlisted at Fort Wayne March 29, 1864. Mustered out with battery June 30, 1865.

EHLE, RICHARD, 18, occupation unknown, born Rudolstadt, Germany. Enlisted at Fort Wayne March 29, 1864. Mustered out with battery June 30, 1865.

ENGLERT, GEORGE G., 24, railroader, born Germany. Enlisted at Fort Wayne August 23, 1862. Mustered out with battery June 30, 1865.

FERRIS, CHARLES E., 18, farmer, born Allen County, Ind. Enlisted at Fort Wayne August 22, 1864. Mustered out with battery June 30, 1865.

FERRIS, ORVILLE B., 22, farmer, born Saratoga County, N.Y. Enlisted

---

2 A veteran was a soldier who reenlisted after completing his original three-year term.

at Fort Wayne December 12, 1863. Mustered out with battery June 30, 1865.

GARWOOD, JOSEPH, 22, railroader, born Columbiana, Ohio. Enlisted at Fort Wayne August 8, 1862. Mustered out with battery June 30, 1865.

GOOD, JACOB, 22, fireman, born Richland County, Ohio. Enlisted at Fort Wayne August 8, 1862. Mustered out with battery June 30, 1865.

GOODWILL, EPHRAIM, 24, farmer, born Trumbull County, Ohio, Veteran; reenlisted at Chattanooga, Tenn., February 28, 1864. Died of wounds received in an affray January 14, 1865.

GRIBE, GOTTLEIB, 23, laborer, born Switzerland. Enlisted at Fort Wayne March 22, 1864. Mustered out with battery June 30, 1865.

GROTHEN, WILLIAM, 19, file cutter, born Bremen, Germany. Enlisted at Fort Wayne February 10, 1864. Mustered out with battery June 30, 1865.

HARNES, JOHN, 22, farmer, born DeKalb County, Ind. Enlisted at Fort Wayne August 11, 1862. Mustered out with battery June 30, 1865.

HOCUSTINE, JOHN, 21, machinist, born Fort Wayne, Ind. Enlisted at Fort Wayne February 6, 1864. Mustered out with battery June 30, 1865.

HOHL, JOHN, 23, cooper, born Switzerland. Enlisted at Fort Wayne March 22, 1864. Mustered out with battery June 30, 1865.

HOUGH, GEORGE D., 22, farmer, born Delaware County, Ohio. Veteran; reenlisted at Chattanooga, Tenn., February 28, 1864. Mustered out with battery June 30, 1865.

ISELI, RUDOLPH, 39, baker, born Berne, Switzerland. Enlisted at Fort Wayne February 22, 1864. Mustered out with battery June 30, 1865.

ISMER, CHARLES, 18, clerk, born Erfurt, Prussia. Enlisted at Fort Wayne January 28, 1864. Mustered out with battery June 30, 1865.

JEROT, JOSEPH P., 18, laborer, born France. Enlisted at Fort Wayne February 29, 1864. Mustered out with battery June 30, 1865.

JOHNSON, ISAAC, 31, farmer, born Columbiana County, Ohio. Enlisted at Fort Wayne February 26, 1864. Mustered out with battery June 30, 1865.

JONES, JOHN P., 21, fireman, born Carrollton, Ohio. Enlisted at Fort Wayne, August 15, 1862. Mustered out with battery June 30, 1865.

KELKER, SAMUEL, 21, fireman, born Butler, Pa. Enlisted at Fort Wayne August 8, 1862. Mustered out with battery June 30, 1865.

KIMBALL, WILLIAM P., 19, carpenter, born Boston, Mass. Enlisted at Fort Wayne February 8, 1864. Mustered out with battery June 30, 1865.

LAMPMAN, GEORGE, 19, farmer, born Batavia, N. Y. Enlisted at Fort Wayne February 15, 1864. Mustered out with battery June 30, 1865.

LIEBNITZ, CHARLES, 16, farmer, born Baden, Germany. Enlisted at Fort Wayne January 20, 1863. Mustered out with battery June 30, 1865.

LUDWICK, JASPER, 20, teamster, born DeKalb County, Ind. Enlisted at Fort Wayne February 1, 1864. Mustered out with battery June 30, 1865.

McBOATNEY, HUGH, 23, farmer, born Ireland. Enlisted at Fort Wayne August 12, 1862. Mustered out with battery June 30, 1865.

McGUIRE, ADDISON, 23, farmer, born Allen County, Ind. Veteran; re-enlisted at Chattanooga, Tenn., February 28, 1864. Mustered out with battery June 30, 1865.

MASON, JOHN, 18, farmer, born Ohio. Substitute;[3] enlisted at Kendall-ville July 27, 1864. Mustered out with battery June 30, 1865.

MICHAELIS, HERMAN, 39, occupation unknown, born Baden, Germany. Enlisted April 13, 1864, place unrecorded; does not appear on muster-ed out with battery June 30, 1865.

MILLARD, WILLIAM, 25, carpenter, born Bergen, N. Y. Enlisted at Fort Wayne August 14, 1862. Mustered out with battery June 30, 1865.

MONASHIETH, MARTIN, 18, farmer, born Mahoning County, Ohio. En-listed at Fort Wayne March 14, 1864. Mustered out with battery June 30, 1865.

OTTO, HERMAN, 19, boilermaker, born Erfurt, Prussia. Enlisted at Fort Wayne February 1, 1864. Mustered out with battery June 30, 1865.

---

3 Served in place of a draftee.

RANK, GEORGE, 27, farmer, born England. Enlisted at Fort Wayne August 12, 1862. Crippled in camp. Discharged December 31, 1864.

RINDLE, MARTIN E., 19, fireman, born Sandusky County, Ohio. Enlisted at Fort Wayne August 8, 1862. Mustered out with battery June 30, 1865.

RODGERS, CHARLES E., 18, printer, born Allen County, Ind. Enlisted at Fort Wayne February 8, 1864. Mustered out with battery June 30, 1865.

SHELL, EDWARD, 22, blacksmith, born Tippecanoe County, Ind. Enlisted at Fort Wayne August 9, 1864. Mustered out with battery June 30, 1865.

SHERRER, JOHN, 18, laborer, born Berne, Switzerland. Enlisted at Fort Wayne February 26, 1864. Mustered out with battery June 30, 1865.

SMITH, JACOB, 18, shoemaker, born Switzerland. Enlisted at Fort Wayne March 4, 1864. Mustered out with battery June 30, 1865.

SMITLEY, JACOB, 21, cooper, born Westmoreland, Pa. Veteran; reenlisted at Chattanooga, Tenn., February 28, 1864. Mustered out with battery June 30, 1865.

SNYDER, JAMES A., 27, carpenter, born Montgomery County, N. Y. Enlisted at Fort Wayne August 16, 1862. Mustered out with battery June 16, 1862. Mustered out with battery June 30, 1865.

STOKES, PATRICK, 22, fireman, born Ireland. Enlisted at Fort Wayne August 6, 1862. Died of disease November 23, 1864.

STRATTAN, JOHN, 18, stonemason, born Fort Wayne, Ind. Enlisted at Fort Wayne February 9, 1864. Mustered out with battery June 30, 1865.

TALLY, JOHN, 21, fireman, born Ohio. Enlisted at Fort Wayne August 6, 1862. Mustered out with battery June 30, 1865.

TYNER, WILLIAM B., 18, blacksmith, born Logansport, Ind. Enlisted at Fort Wayne February 8, 1864. Mustered out with battery June 30, 1865.

VILTSHIE, GOTTLIEB, 28, clerk, born Berne, Switzerland. Enlisted at Fort Wayne February 22, 1864. Mustered out with battery June 30, 1865.

VORDERMARK, JOHN W., 19, bookkeeper, born Fort Wayne, Ind. Enlisted at Fort Wayne August 11, 1862. Taken prisoner at Chickamauga September 20, 1863.

Vose, Lewis, 25, mason, born Buffalo, N. Y. Enlisted at Fort Wayne August 25, 1862. Mustered out with battery June 30, 1865.

Walters, David, 18, clerk, born Fort Wayne, Ind. Enlisted at Fort Wayne December 12, 1863. Mustered out with battery June 30, 1865.

Webber, Henry, 25, boatman, born Hanover, Germany. Enlisted at Fort Wayne August 12, 1862. Mustered out with battery June 30, 1865.

Yeaky, Andrew J., 17, farmer, born Seneca County, Ohio. Veteran; reenlisted at Chattanooga, Tenn., February 28, 1864. Mustered out with battery June 30, 1865.

Young, Julius, 30, farmer, born Hanover, Germany. Enlisted at Fort Wayne August 2, 1862. Mustered out with battery June 30, 1865.

Zollinger, Henry, 21, farmer, born Germany. Enlisted at Fort Wayne August 2, 1862. Mustered out with battery June 30, 1865.

Bibliography

Manuscripts

Bartholomew County Public Library, Columbus, Ind. "Bartholomew County Civil War Soldiers' Manuscripts."

Library of Congress, Manuscript Division, Washington, D. C. "Records of the Frontier Guard."

Ernest R. Davidson Collection, Lynnwood, Wash. Rippetoe family Civil War letters.

Archives of DePauw University and Indiana Methodism, Greencastle, Ind. William H. Anderson Journal. "Putnam County in the Civil War—Local History of a Critical Period" [by Carl A. Zenor].

Addison M. Dowling Collection, Indianapolis, Ind. Papers and mementoes of Joseph Addison Scott, including "Muster Roll, Captain Moses M. Beck 18th Ind. Batt. Horse Arty., Dec. 31, 1864."

Indiana Historical Society Library, Indianapolis, Ind. Indiana Civil War soldiers' letters, diaries, and journals, including "Journal of W. O. Crouse."

Indiana State Library, Archives Division, Indianapolis, Ind. Civil War Files of the Adjutant General of Indiana and especially Eighteenth Battery correspondence, muster-in and muster-out rolls, and "Clothing Book."

Indiana State Library, Indiana Division, Indianapolis, Ind. Four postwar papers by Henry Campbell: "A Spirited Raid," "Hoover's Gap," "The Battle of Mossy Creek," and "That Cold New Year's Day."

Archives of Eli Lilly and Company, Indianapolis, Ind. Eli Lilly papers covering service in 21st Indiana Infantry, 18th Indiana Light Artillery, and 9th Indiana Cavalry. Civil War letters of James C. Dodd. Eli Lilly postwar papers pertaining to personal, veterans', and civic activities, including correspondence with 18th Battery veterans. William O. Crouse papers and correspondence as secretary of 18th Battery Association. Eli Lilly, the Colonel's grandson, correspondence with 18th Battery veterans. Photographs.

Montgomery County Public Library, Crawfordsville, Ind. Minute Books, Treasurers' Books and Rosters of G.A.R. Posts 1 & 7, Crawfordsville.

Mrs. M. G. Rippeteau Collection, Evanston, Ill. Papers and mementoes of James Emory Rippetoe.

U. S. National Archives, Washington, D. C. Service and pension records of Civil War soldiers. 1860 Census of Montgomery, Putnam, and Vigo counties, Ind. "Descriptive Book of the 18th Battery Indiana Light Artillery." U. S. Signal Corps Civil War photograph collection.

The University of Tennessee at Chattanooga, Chattanooga, Tenn. John T. Wilder Collection.

Vigo County Historical Society, Terre Haute, Ind. John H. Rippetoe, typewritten copies of 96 letters written to his wife, Mary, 1862-65, trans. and ed. by Ernest R. Davidson.

Wabash College Archives, Crawfordsville, Ind. Henry Campbell Journal, "Four Years in the Saddle," and "Scrapbook."

Government Publications

Boynton, H. V. *Dedication of Chickamauga and Chattanooga National Military Park, September 18-20, 1895.* Report of Joint Committee of Congress. Washington, D. C.: Government Printing Office, 1896.

Illinois, Report of the Adjutant General of the State of. 7 vols. Springfield: Baker, Bailhache & Co., Printers, 1867.

Indiana Commissioners. *Indiana at Chickamauga: Report of Indiana Commissioners Chickamauga National Park.* Indianapolis: Sentinel Printing, 1901.

Manucy, Albert. *Artillery Through the Ages.* Washington, D.C.: Government Printing Office, 1962.

Mugridge, Donald H. *The Civil War in Pictures: A Chronological List of Selected Pictorial Works.* Library of Congress. Washington, D. C.: Government Printing Office, 1962.

Munden, K. W., and H. P. Beers. *Guide to Federal Archives Relating to the Civil War.* National Archives pub. no. 63-1. Washington, D. C.: Government Printing Office, 1862.

Stephenson, Richard W., comp. *Civil War Maps: An Annotated List.* Library of Congress. Washington, D. C.: Government Printing Office, 1861.

Terrell, W. H. H. *Indiana in the War of the Rebellion: Official Report of W. H. H. Terrell, Adjutant General.* 8 vols. Indianapolis: Douglass & Conner, 1869.

U. S. House of Representatives. *Atlas of Chickamauga, Chattanooga, and Vicinity. House Docs.*, Vol. 101, No. 515, 56 Cong., 2 sess., 1900–1901. Washington, D. C.: Government Printing Office, 1901.

_____. Library of Congress. *Military Map Showing the March of the United States Forces Under Command of Maj. Gen. W. T. Sherman, U.S.A. during the Years 1863, 1864, 1865.* Capt Wm. Kossak and John B. Muller: St. Louis, 1865.

_____. Library of Congress. *Map of Northwestern Georgia (with portions of adjoining States of Tennessee and Alabama) being part of the Department of the Cumberland.* Engineer Bureau of the War Department, Jan., 1863.

_____. Library of Congress. *Military Map Showing the Theater of Operations in the Tullahoma, Chickamauga and Chattanooga Campaigns.* Chickamauga and Chattanooga Park Commission, 1896–1901.

_____. National Park Service. *Chickamauga and Chattanooga Battlefields,* Historical Handbook No. 25. Washington, D. C.: Government Printing Office, 1956 (rpt. 1961).

_____. War Department. *The War of the Rebellion: A Compilation of the Official Records of the Union and Confederate Armies.* 128 vols. Washington, D.C.: Government Printing Office, 1880–1901.

Books and Articles

Amann, William Frayne, ed. *Personnel of the Civil War.* New York: Thomas Yoseloff, 1961.

Andrews, J. Cutler. *The South Reports the Civil War.* Princeton: Princeton Univ. Press, 1970.

Avery, Isaac W. "Wheeler's Raid—Unwritten History of the War of the Rebellion," Cincinnati *Enquirer,* n.d. (clipping in Henry Campbell Scrapbook, Wabash College Archives).

Barnhart, John D. *The Impact of the Civil War on Indiana.* Indianapolis: Indiana Civil War Centennial Commission, 1962.

Batchelor, John, and Ian Hogg. *Artillery.* New York: Scribners, 1972.

Beck, Moses M. "A Second Visit to Chattanooga," Holton (Kan.) *Journal, ca.* 1899.

———. "Volunteers in Boxcars," Chicago *Tribune,* Jan. 27, 1962.

———. "The End of the War," Holton *Recorder, ca,* Feb. 1962.

Beckwith, H. W. *History of Vigo & Parke Counties.* Chicago: H. H. Hill and N. Iddings, 1880.

———. *History of Montgomery County.* Chicago: H. H. Hill and N. Iddings, 1881.

Beers, Fannie A. *Memories.* Philadelphia: Lippincott, 1888.

Benefiel, W. H. H. *History of Wilder's Lightning Brigade.* Pendleton, Ind.: The Times Print, *ca.* 1913.

———. *The Seventeenth Indiana Regiment: A History from its Organization to the End of the War.* N. p., *ca.* 1910.

Bruce, Robert V. *Lincoln and the Tools of War.* Indianapolis: Bobbs-Merrill, 1956.

Carnahan, James R. "Indiana at Chickamauga," *The Indianian* IV, No. 4 (Apr. 1900).

———. "Camp Morton," Indiana Commandery, Military Order of the Loyal Legion, *War Paper,* Feb. 22, 1892.

———. "Indiana at Chickamauga: Address at Dedication of Chicka-

mauga National Park, September 19, 1893," Indiana Commandery Military Order of the Loyal Legion, *War Paper*, 1898.

————. "Personal Recollections of Chickamauga," Ohio Commandery, Military Order of the Loyal Legion, *War Paper*, Jan. 6, 1886.

Carter, William Randolph. "McCook's Raid," letter to the editor,
National Tribune, n.d. (clipping in Henry Campbell journal, Wabash College Archives) .

Catton, Bruce. *Never Call Retreat*. New York. Doubleday, 1965.

Cist, Henry M. *"The Army of the Cumberland*. New York: Scribners,
1898.

Coggins, Jack. *Arms and Equipment of the Civil War*. New York:
Doubleday, 1962.

Commager, Henry Steele, ed. *The Blue and the Gray*. Indianapolis:
Bobbs-Merrill, 1950.

Connelly, Thomas Lawrence. *Army of the Heartland: The Army of
Tennessee, 1861–1862*. Baton Rouge: Louisiana State Univ. Press,
1967.

————. *Autumn of Glory: The Army of Tennessee 1862–1865*. Baton
Rouge: Louisiana State Univ. Press, 1971.

Connolly, James Austin. "Major Connolly's Letters to His Wife,"
Transactions of the Illinois State Historical Society No. 35.

Cox, Jacob D. *Atlanta*. New York: Scribners, 1882.

Cumming, Kate. *Kate: The Journal of a Confederate Nurse*. Ed. by
Richard Barksdale Harwell. Baton Rouge: Louisiana State Univ.
Press, 1959.

Downey, Fairfax. *Storming of the Gateway: Chattanooga 1863*. New
York: David McKay Co., Inc., 1960.

Duke, Basil W. *A History of Morgan's Cavalry*. Bloomington: Indiana Univ. Press, 1960.

Dunn, Jacob Piatt, ed. *History of Greater Indianapolis*. 2 vols. Chicago: The Lewis Publishing Company, 1910.

Dwight, Henry D. "How We Fight at Atlanta," *Harper's New
Monthly Magazine* XXXIV (Oct. 1864) .

Dyer, John P. *"Fighting Joe" Wheeler*. Baton Rouge: Louisiana State
Univ. Press, 1941.

Esarey, Logan. *History of Indiana from Its Exploration to 1922*. 4 vols. Dayton: Dayton Historical Publishing Co., 1924.

Fitch, John. *Annals of the Army of the Cumberland*. Philadelphia: Lippincott, 1864.

Govan, Gilbert E., and James W. Livingood. *The Chattanooga Country 1540–1962*. Chapel Hill: Univ. of North Carolina Press, 1963.

Gracie, Archibald. *The Truth About Chickamauga*. Boston: Houghton, 1911.

Guernsey, A. H., and H. M. Alden. *Harper's Pictorial History of the Civil War*. 2 vols. Chicago: The Puritan Press, 1894.

Hazlett, James C. "The 3-Inch Ordnance Rifle," *Civil War Times Illustrated* VII, No. 8 (Dec. 1968).

Henry, Robert Selph. *"First with the Most" Forrest*. Indianapolis: Bobbs-Merrill, 1944.

Hoehling, A. A. *Last Train from Atlanta*. New York: Thomas Yoseloff, 1958.

Horn, Stanley F. *The Army of Tennessee*. Indianapolis: Bobbs-Merrill, 1941.

————. "The Seesaw Battle of Stones River," *Civil War Times Illustrated* II, No. 1 (Feb. 1964).

————, comp. and ed. *Tennessee's War, 1861–1865, Described by Participants*. Nashville: Tennessee Civil War Centennial Commission, 1965.

Huebner, Henry Richard. *Civil War Artillery Manual*. Indianapolis: Indiana Civil War Centennial Commission and Indiana Historical Society, 1962.

Indiana Asbury University, *Catalogue of Indiana Asbury University 1853–65*.

Indiana, A Biographical History of Eminent and Self-Made Men of the State of. 2 vols. Cincinnati: Western Biographical Publishing Company, 1880.

Indiana Commandery, Military Order of the Loyal Legion. *War Papers*. Indianapolis: The Commandery, 1898.

Indiana in the Civil War, 1861–1865, A Chronology of. Indianapolis: Indiana Civil War Centennial Commission, 1965.

Johnson, Allen, and Dumas Malone. *Dictionary of American Biography.* 11 vols. New York: Scribners, 1933.

Johnson, R. J., and C. C. Buel. *Battles and Leaders of the Civil War.* 4 vols. New York: Century Co., 1887–88.

Johnston, Joseph Eggleston. *Narrative of Military Operations Directed During the Late War Between the States.* New York: Appleton, 1874.

Julian, Allen Phelps. "From Dalton to Atlanta," *Civil War Times Illustrated* III, No. 2 (July 1964).

Keenan, Jerry. "Wilson's Selma Raid," *Civil War Times Illustrated* I, No. 9 (Jan. 1963).

Kurtz, Wilber G. "The Fighting at Atlanta," *Civil War Times Illustrated* III, No. 2 (July 1964).

Lilly, Josiah K., Sr. "The Name Lilly," *The Lilly Review,* Nos. 4–8 (Apr.–Aug. 1942).

Livingood, James W. "The Chattanooga *Rebel." Publication No. 39.* East Tennessee Historical Society (1967).

_____. "Chickamauga and Chattanooga National Military Park," *Landmarks of Tennessee History* (1965).

Longacre, Edward G. *From Union Stars To Top Hat: a Biography of the Extraordinary General James Harrison Wilson.* Harrisburg: Stackpole Books, 1972.

Longstreet, James. *From Manassas to Appomattox: Memoirs of the Civil War in America.* Philadelphia: Lippincott, 1896 (Republished, Bloomington: Indiana Univ. Press, 1960).

Lord, Francis A. *They Fought for the Union.* New York: Bonanza Books, 1960.

_____. *Civil War Collector's Encyclopedia.* New York: Castle Books, 1963.

Lytle, Andrew Nelson. *Bedford Forrest and His Critter Company.* New York: Minton, Balch and Co., 1931.

McDowell, Robert Emmett. *City of Conflict: Louisville in the Civil War 1861–1865.* Louisville: Louisville Civil War Round Table, 1962.

McGee, Benjamin F. *History of the 72d Indiana Volunteer Infantry of the Mounted Lightning Brigade.* Lafayette: S. Vater & Co., 1882.

McWhiney, Grady. *Braxton Bragg and the Confederate Defeat: Field Command.* New York: Columbia Univ. Press, 1969.

Manhart, George B. *DePauw Through the Years.* 2 vols. Greencastle: DePauw University, 1962.

Merrill, Catherine. *The Soldier of Indiana in the War for the Union.* 2 vols. Indianapolis: Merrill and Company, 1866–69.

Montgomery County, Indiana, History of. Indianapolis: A. W. Bowen & Company, 1913.

Montgomery, Parke, and Fountain Counties Indiana, Portrait and Biographical Record of. Chicago: Chapman Bros., 1893.

Nevins, Allan; James I. Robertson, Jr., and Bell I. Wiley; eds. *Civil War Books: A Critical Bibliography.* 2 vols. Baton Rouge: Louisiana State Univ. Press. 1967.

Nye, Wilbur S. "Cavalry Operations Around Atlanta," *Civil War Times Illustrated* III, No. 4 (July 1964).

Rowell, John W. *Yankee Cavalrymen: Through the Civil War with the Ninth Pennsylvania Cavalry.* Knoxville: Univ. of Tennessee Press, 1971.

Sandburg, Carl. *Abraham Lincoln: The War Years.* 4 vols. New York: Harcourt, 1939.

Seymour, Digby Gordon. *Divided Loyalties: Fort Sanders and the Civil War in East Tennessee.* Knoxville: Univ. of Tennessee Press, 1963.

Strong, Robert Hale. *A Yankee Private's Civil War.* Ed. by Ashley Halsey. Chicago: Henry Regnery Co., 1961.

Sunderland, Glenn W. *Lightning at Hoover's Gap: Wilder's Brigade in the Civil War.* New York: Thomas Yoseloff, 1969.

Tarrant, Eastham. *The Wild Riders of the First Kentucky Cavalry.* Lexington: Henry Clay Press, 1969.

Thacker, Marshall P. *A Hundred Battles in the West: St. Louis to Atlanta, 1861–65.* Detroit: M. P. Thacker, 1884.

Thornbrough, Emma Lou. *Indiana in the Civil War Era 1850–1880.* Indianapolis: Indiana Historical Bureau and Indiana Historical Society, 1965.

Tippecanoe County, Indiana, Past and Present of. 2 vols. Indianapolis: B. F. Bowen & Co., 1909.

Tucker, Glenn. *Chickamauga: Bloody Battle of the West.* Indianapolis: Bobbs-Merrill, 1961.

————. "The Battle of Chickamauga!" *Civil War Times Illustrated* VIII, No. 2 (May 1969).

————. "The Battles for Chattanooga," *Civil War Times Illustrated* X, No. 5 (Aug. 1971).

Turner, Ann. *Guide to Indiana Civil War Manuscripts.* Indianapolis: Indiana Civil War Centennial Commission, 1965.

VanHorne, Thomas Budd. *History of the Army of the Cumberland.* 2 vols. Cincinnati: R. Clarke & Co., 1875.

Wabash College. *Catalogue of Wabash College, 1856–62.*

Watterson, Henry. *"Marse Henry": An Autobiography.* 2 vols. New York: George H. Doran Co., 1919.

Weigley, Russell F. *History of the United States Army.* New York: Macmillan, 1967.

Weik, Jesse W. *History of Putnam County, Indiana.* Indianapolis: B. F. Bowen & Co., 1910.

Williams, Samuel C. *General John T. Wilder.* Bloomington: Indiana Univ. Press, 1936.

Wiley, Bell Irvin. *The Life of Billy Yank.* Indianapolis: Bobbs-Merrill, 1952.

————. *The Life of Johnny Reb.* Indianapolis: Bobbs-Merrill, 1943.

Wilson, George S. "Wilder's Brigade of Mounted Infantry in the Tullahoma-Chickamauga Campaigns," Kansas Commandery, Military Order of the Loyal Legion, *War Paper,* Nov. 4, 1891.

Wilson, James Harrison. *Under the Old Flag.* 2 vols. New York: D. Appleton, 1912.

Wilson, Spencer. "How Soldiers Rated Carbines," *Civil War Times Illustrated* V, No. 2 (May 1966).

Winkler, William M. "A Leaf from a Soldier's Diary," Columbus *Republican,* Jan. 20–Apr. 13, 1876.

Winslow, Hattie Lou, and Joseph R. H. Moore. *Camp Morton 1861–65: Indianapolis Prison Camp.* Indianapolis: Indiana Historical Society, 1940.

Wyeth, John Allen. *That Devil Forrest: The Life of General Nathan Bedford Forrest.* New York: Harpers, 1959.

Contemporary Newspapers and Periodicals

Cincinnati *Gazette*
Crawfordsville *Journal*
Crawfordsville *Weekly Review*
Harper's New Monthly Magazine
Indianapolis *Journal*
Indianapolis *State Sentinel*
Lafayette *Daily Journal*
Putnam *Republican Banner*
Terre Haute *Wabash Express Daily*

Obituaries

Beck, Moses M. Holton *Journal*, Feb. 5, 1931.
Campbell, Henry. Crawfordsville *Journal*, July 22, 1915.
Crouse, William O. Lafayette *Journal and Courier*, July 8, 1926.
Lilly, Eli. Indianapolis *Journal*, June 7–10, 1898.
Lilly, Gustavus. Putnam *Republican Banner*, Aug. 11, 1870.
Rippetoe, John Henry. Terre Haute *Tribune*, Mar. 8, 1911.
Rippetoe, William Benson. Terre Haute *Tribune*, Jan. 25, 1932.
Scott, Joseph Addison. Holton *Recorder*, June 12, 1924.
Speed, Sidney A. Crawfordsville *Journal*, July 13, 1923.
Wilder, John T. Indianapolis *Journal*, Oct. 22, 1917.
Winkler, William M. Columbus *Republican*, May 10, 1890.

Index

Index

Spencer, Christopher M., 65–66
Spencer repeating rifle: description of,
65–67, 73; effectiveness of, 80, 82–83,
114, 118, 121, 129
Sperry, Fred, 20
Sprague, Hugh, 161
Stanley, David S., 145, 198–200
Stanton, Edwin M., 122
Starr, William E., 22, 156–57, 185, 235,
273
Stewart, A. P., 72; Stewart's division,
see Tennessee, Army of (Confederate),
Hardee's corps
Stilesboro, Ga., skirmishes at, 201, 229
Stokes, James H., 135
Stokes, William B., 69
Stones River, Battle of, 56–58
Stoneman, George, 191, 214–16, 227
Stoneman's and McCook's Raid, 214–27
Stover, William D., 181
Strahl, O. F., 108; Strahl's infantry bri-
gade, 108–109
Strawberry Plains, Tenn., railroad
bridge, description of, 152–53
Sturgis, Samuel D., 153–55, 159, 174,
188
Sunman, Henry P., 183
Sweetwater Creek, Ga., skirmishes at,
207

Taylor, Richard, 250
Tennessee, Army of (Confederate), 31,
38, 40, 75, 91, 103–104, 197, 213, 231,
235–36, 240–41: Buckner's corps, 104,
112: Hardee's corps, 72–83, 217; Stewart's division, 72–83, 119, 194–96: Polk's
corps, 104, 109: Forrest's cavalry corps,
85–86, 105–109, 112, 125: Wheeler's
cavalry corps, 57, 64–65, 70, 73–74,
86, 119, 125–36, 152, 159–64, 194, 202,
218–25; Armstrong's division, 174, 181;
Martin's division, 125–26, 133–35,
159n; Morgan's division, 159n, 174–80,
201; Wharton's division, 125–26, 130,
133–35
Tennessee, Army of the (Union), 142,
191–92, 196, 207: XV Corps, 191; XVI
Corps, 191; XVII Corps, 191
Tennessee units (Union): cavalry regiments, First, 144, 150, 154–56, 159–60,
174, 176, 180, 191, 203, 205, 216, 218,

223; Fourth, 216, 224: infantry regi-
ment, Fourth, 130
Terrill, William R., 38–39
Thomas, George H., 30, 66, 76, 83, 120–
24; commands the Army of the Cum-
berland, 141, 190–91, 201, 204; com-
mands the Military Division of the
Mississippi, 231–32, 236, 248
Thomas, William, 39
3-inch Ordnance Rifle: accuracy, 27, 96,
99, 206, 259; description of, 25–27; de-
velopment and manufacture, 25–26;
range, 26
Thruston, Gates, 121
Tiffin, Henry, 183
Tilson, Basil, 273
Torrey, William H., 216
Tullahoma campaign, 75–89
Tullahoma, Tenn., Union occupation
of, 86–87

Upton, Emory, 249–50; Upton's division, see Mississippi, Military Division
of the, Cavalry Corps, Fourth Division
Uniforms, 30–31, 61, 165
United States units: artillery battery,
I, Fourth Field Artillery, 249; cavalry
regiment, Fourth, 70–71

Vance, John, 68
Van Cleve, H. P., 105; Van Cleve's divi-
sion, see Cumberland, Army of the,
XXI Corps
Varnell's Station, Ga., skirmishes at,
193–96
Vaught's Hill, Tenn., Battle of, 64–65
Vining's Bridge, Ga., artillery duel at,
210–11; fortifications at, 209–10
Virginia, Army of Northern: Long-
street's corps, 104, 147, 151, 167

Wagner, George D., 93, 100
Walker, William H. T., 104, 114; Walk-
er's corps, see Mississippi, Army of
(Confederate)
Wallace, Lewis, 4
Ward, William T., 52, 72
Ward, Williamson, 218
Watkins, Louis D., 191, 239
Watson, Charles D., 17–18, 43, 48
Watson, John, 113
Watterson, Henry, 90, 96

319